GW00640706

Sunset of the Raj

John de Chazal

WINCANTON PRESS
NATIONAL SCHOOL, NORTH STREET
WINCANTON, SOMERSET BA9 8AT

To the memory
of
BROTHER LOUIS
and
ADRIAN CARROLL

Publishing details. First published 1987.
Copyright John de Chazal © 1987.
Restrictions upon copying. All rights
reserved. No part of this publication may be
reproduced, stored in a retrieval system, or
transmitted in any form or by any means,
electronic, computerised, mechanical,
photocopying, recording or otherwise, without
prior permission in writing from the publishers.
Printed in Great Britain by Wincanton Litho, at
the Old National School, North Street,
Wincanton, Somerset, telephone (0963) 33643.
Typeset by Irene Howard at SOS, 1 Bell Street,
Shaftesbury, Dorset.
International standard book number
[ISBN] 0 948699 03 5

Contents

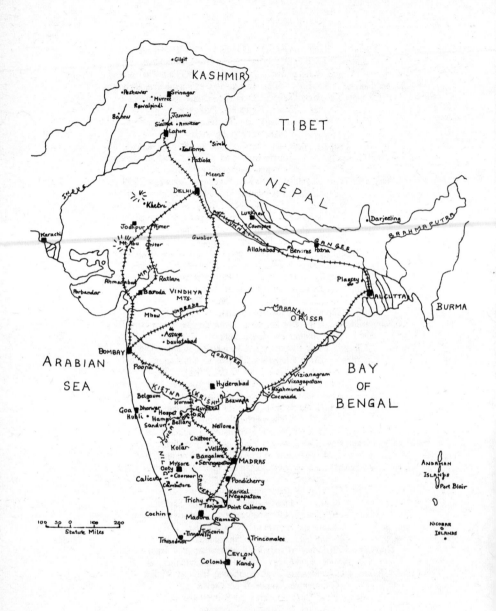

INDIA AND CEYLON

Prologue

ONCE UPON a time there was a smart young Hindu of high caste who graduated at Madras University with a degree in Engineering. He wished for a career on the Railways and was successful in getting a covenanted post in Central India. There he met a beautiful young Rajput girl, still virgin and fell in love with her. So he went home on leave, showed his parents her photograph and said he wished to marry her. But they wouldn't hear of it. Surely he knew that he must marry a girl of the same sub-caste? His parents would select such a girl, discuss the match with her parents, then both sets of parents would consult the astrologers. If the astrologers decided the couple were compatible, his father could then draw up a marriage contract with his lawyer and finally, in consultation with astrologers, fix the wedding with the priests.

Regretfully, the young man gave way and within a year his parents chose a short, fair-skinned and rather dumpy virgin* with a handsome dowry (the plainer the bride, the bigger the dowry). He still dreamt of the ravishing young Rajput beauty, but submitted to his parents' choice.

This little tale I hope serves to illustrate the all-importance in India of religion, of caste, tradition and dharma, which I believe includes, piety, morality and a deep respect for custom and tradition.

> 'Do thy duty, even if it be humble
> Rather than another's, even if it be great.'
> (from the Aryan Gita)

In Western Europe religion has been declining off and on (I exclude Ireland and Poland) but in India the separation of sacred and secular is foreign to the vast majority of people.

To begin to understand India one must realize that Hindu civilisation is much older than ours and when the Druids ruled the British tribesmen India was an enlightened country, enlightened by the teachings of Buddha and his great disciple, the Emperor Asoka and his successors.

Between Asoka and the seventh century A.D. there flourished powerful and cultured emperors such as the Guptas and Harsha. It was during Harsha's reign that sizeable Indian ships carried emigrants who founded colonies in Java and Sumatra. The largest Buddhist temple in the world is situated in Java and has been extensively repaired by UNESCO. It is of interest that this region is now called Indo-nesia. Other Hindu colonies were founded in the land formerly called Indo-

---

* No self-respecting Indian will marry a girl who is not a virgin

China, while Buddhism was extended by missionaries to China, whence it spread to Japan and Korea.

Indian literature, we are told, is vast, but the enquirer should know something of the Vedas and the well-known sagas called Ramayana and Mahabharata which nourish the Indian soul.

I write with hindsight, but I wish more Britishers had tried to penetrate to the essence of Hinduism, to their mutual benefit.

This book was written partly for my satisfaction, partly it is a labour of love, partly because I believe it fills a gap in recent books about India. For many learned books and novels have been written but recent works of biography by a civilian are few, especially ones whose backcloth is the greater part of that vast country.

My aim is to try and convey something of the life, not of one who moved with the great, but of one of junior, then of middle rank in the closing decade of the British Raj and the beginning of Swaraj, or home rule.

When my career ended I was only thirty-four and life had to begin again from scratch, so this patchwork had to be put off till I was semi-retired, many years later.

To make the journal intelligible to those who have not lived in the East it was necessary to include a modicum of history and background material. That so many people are mentioned by name is partly because I remember innumerable acts of kindness, partly because I hope many will find themselves or that their children will find their parents. And, as the reader will discover they, like the Canterbury Pilgrims, were a very varied company.

Introduction

IF THE Imperial sun reached its zenith by the outbreak of the Great War, the war itself produced new tensions and a livelier nationalism. In 1916 the Indian National Congress, influenced by developments in Ireland, passed a resolution that the time had come for Britain to announce that a self-governing India was the goal of her policy.

To his great credit the Viceroy, Lord Chelmsford, accepted the resolution and moved the Secretary of State. So, in 1917, came the solemn declaration from the British Government that Indians should increasingly be involved in the Administration and that Dominion Status was indeed the goal.

Two years later the first stage of the promise resulted in the beginning of dyarchy, or shared government. But this Reform met with a mixed reception: "Too little" said some, others mistrusted the British Government's sincerity. Further, the war had brought higher prices and there was a failure of monsoon. The centre of unrest was the Punjab with its three important communities: Muslim, Hindu and Sikh, and the epicentre was the holy Sikh city of Amritsar.

When the Civil power failed to keep order, martial law was declared and the redoubtable Brigadier-General Dyer was put in charge. Dyer was an unusual officer in that he was an Englishman born, bred and educated in the country. He quelled the unrest with an iron will, not only by imposing humiliating conditions on citizens of Amritsar but also by sustained firing into a peaceful crowd which had assembled against his orders.

As the enquiry clearly established, he exceeded his mandate. The whole of upper India was in a state of shock and Sir Rabindra Nath Tagore, a Nobel Prize winner, led the reaction by returning the insignia of his knighthood in disgust. The Rowlatt (Public Order) Act, as applied by Dyer and the massacre, proved to be a turning point in Indo–British relations.

In 1921 a very serious rebellion by Muslims erupted in Malabar: the Moplah Rebellion, but though worse than the disturbances in the Punjab two years before, it was not made much of by the Indian National Congress. In the Great War, Mr. Gandhi actively supported the Allies, but now he began to turn against the British. He was joined by Motilal Nehru, his son Jawaharlal others who set a magnificent example of leadership.

In an attempt to placate the mounting Congress pressure the British Government sent out a brilliant lawyer, Sir John Simon, Mr Clement Attlee and others with an olive branch, but the mission proved a total failure.

The Cawnpore riots of 1931 turned into communal violence, 300 people were killed and many temples, mosques and houses were burnt down. It was the worst rioting for ten years.

But the hour produced the man: the Viceroy. Lord Irwin was big enough to bridge the gulf and made friends with Mahatma Gandhi. Lord Irwin conceived the Round Table Conference, which all parties attended including the Princes. [1] Though fought at every stage by Winston Churchill and his followers, a new Government of India Bill received the Royal assent in 1935.

This monumental Act provided for a Federal Government in New Delhi in which the Princes could take part. It also provided for Provincial Ministries with considerable powers. The map was changed by the creation of new provinces: Sind and Orissa, while Burma was separated off. (This is of interest in that it created a precedent for the formation of new linguistic Provinces after Independence). The Viceroy, Lord Willingdon, laid down his office and so ended a remarkable Imperial career. He was succeeded by a formidable but shy man, the Marquess of Linlithgow and the burden that awaited him was probably the heaviest borne by any Viceroy.

So, 1936 was a quiet year, a time of transition before the new Constitution and in October a draft of young Civil and Military personnel (I among them) sailed for Bombay, together with several hundred seasoned officers, businessmen and wives returning to India from long leave.

It was a well-ordered ship, we juniors conformed to the conventions of our seniors, but that we accepted without question. We were light-hearted and once the stormy Bay of Biscay was behind us, the days flew by. We were certainly not worrying about the future but some realised that changes were in the air. For one thing my father, with nearly thirty years of Indian service behind him, maintained that the promise of Dominion Status made in 1917 had to be honoured, while two post- graduate Indian students I had met a few months earlier assured me that Independence would come within fifteen years. The older of the two impressed me greatly as a future leader.

But after I arrived in South India the British men and women I met seemed complacent: "Madras is a stable and well-ordered Province" – and they expected little change; "India changes but slowly and the villages hardly at all" and "If we give up, the Hindus and Muslims will fight it out – there will be civil war". They were right up to a point but the fifteen-year prophecy turned out to be a realistic one.

---

[1] i.e. Rulers:- Maharajahs and Rajahs; the Nizam and Nawabs.

Note: To help him picture the country, the Reader is recommended: Francis Watson's "Concise History of India", with its superb collection of nearly 200 illustrations.

1

Recruitment and Passage to Bombay

SOME BOYS are fortunate to feel a vocation; but I had none. My uncle, a doctor, wished me to follow in his steps, but I soon discovered that I had no stomach for medicine. My elder brother, Louis, who was well established in business, said I had a business head and when I matriculated at Bristol University in 1934, he told me to opt for a course in Economics, which I did. I continued my rowing and gained a place in the first VIII. I continued in the Officers Training Corps, joined the debating society, and also became an assistant scout master in the Bristol slums. I was enjoying life, but when my brother discovered I was only working for a Pass degree, he assured me this was not good enough at the time of severe depression and unemployment. Though I had not worried I knew that many of my contemporaries were very worried.

It was after meeting a cadet at the Hendon Police College that I first entertained the idea of a police career. So I consulted the secretary of the University Appointments Board. He informed me that there were only six vacancies at Hendon compared with sixteen in the Indian Police and said: "You had better go for the Indian Police, my boy". My father, who was much older and retired, agreed. So, reluctantly, I gave up university and spent the next five months studying at home with the help of tutors.

The entrance examination was conducted by the Civil Service Commissioners and was held locally at Clifton College, my old school. The other candidates were sitting for the Army, Royal Marines and the Royal Indian Navy.

We were interviewed in London by two senior retired gentlemen, Sir Charles Chitham, formerly Inspector-General of Police, Central Provinces and Sir John Ewart, former Direct of the Intelligence Bureau, New Delhi. They were, of course, very experienced and soon put me at my ease.

There followed two months of waiting, which seemed like eternity. Some cousins took me to a fortune-teller in Hampshire who was considered very gifted. At once she saw the load on my mind and said: "Everything will be alright, soon you'll be crossing the waters".

One morning in late summer my father opened the Times. The results of the examination were published and, much to his surprise and mine, my name appeared high on the list. He shouted for my mother to come at once.

We had to pass a riding test and medical examination. I had never ridden a horse but the Commanding Officer at the Artillery Barracks, a few miles from our home, kindly arranged riding lessons under a bombardier. After only six weeks I met the others at Woolwich Arsenal, managed two jumps without falling off and passed. We had fittings of uniforms at military tailors and of riding boots made to measure. A week later we were summoned to the India Office, sixteen of us. We all passed the medical and then met the Secretary of State. The Marquess of Zetland was of medium height; he had a moustache, spectacles, his hair was parted in the middle and he was very dapper. He made a speech, ending with an exhortation to uphold the fine traditions of the Service. He seemed well pleased with us and ended with a big smile.

Proudly, we stepped out of the building. P.M. Treasure and I felt we should celebrate, which we did with half a pint of beer. That evening we all met for supper at a restaurant.

We had been asked to state our choice of a Province. A family friend, who had been Chief Engineer of the Punjab, pressed me to apply for that Province. But my father, an aunt and cousins, as it happened, had served in Madras and I felt it my duty to follow them.

Finally, my travelling instructions arrived. All arrangements went without a hitch, the India Office was clearly very efficient. My parents accompanied me to London and took me to a play at Leicester Square with Yvonne Arnaud in the leading role. She had a sparkling personality but I did not much care for the comedy which was full of divorce.

In the morning we took a train to Harwich where we saw the pride of the P & O Fleet, the white-painted S.S. Viceroy of India, 20,000 tons. I kissed my parents goodbye, climbed up the gangway and leant over the rail. The vessel got under way, my father watching me till he could see me no longer. It was October 1936. I never saw my father again as he died a few years later at the age of seventy-three.

To sail aboard that famous liner was a great experience. I had a small cabin to myself amidships and without a porthole. The dining saloon seemed huge. We could wear anything for breakfast and lunch but everyone dressed for dinner – dinner-jacket and long dresses. It consisted of seven courses, rather more than one was used to.

The passengers in the first-class were a good cross-section of the Indian establishment. First, His Highness the Maharajah Gaekwar of Baroda, a leading Maratha State. He was short, elderly and square-built. The Maharani had long eye-lashes and rather a sinister expression. There were two wives of Lieutenant-Governors. One grand personage occupying a stateroom[2] was General Evangeline Booth, Chief of the Salvation Army. In accordance with Anglo-Indian custom she, as a religious leader, was treated with great respect and was clearly accustomed to it. There were a number of officers of the Indian Army, Indian Civil Service (I.C.S.), well-to-do businessmen and some twelve Police Probationers, who ranked with the second-lieutenants. Among the latter was a slim, good-looking young man, who did not join in the games and who every evening could be seen sitting by himself sipping a drink and stroking his moustache. If invited by one of us to join in, he always made the same reply: "I'm in the 13th Lancers."

---

[2] A stateroom is like a bedroom on the upper deck with a proper window.

He was clearly a keen soldier but otherwise substandard. A few such officers were perhaps accepted for special family reasons but others only passed the competitive exam. after intensive coaching by a highly competent 'crammer'.

The great ship, with her British Captain, officers and engineers; her numerous Goanese stewards and Lascar (i.e. Indian) crewmen, sailed on with the utmost efficiency. We ran into a severe storm in Biscay, after which the first man I spoke to was a portly Bengali, A.K. Chanda, I.C.S. – who was puffing away at his pipe, quite unaffected by the rolling of the ship. He was most friendly.

In the Eastern Mediterranean I saw a whale for the first time, spouting as he swam.

"There go the ships and there is that Leviathan
Whom Thou hast made to take his past-time therein." Psalm 104.

The long, straight and narrow waterway that is the Suez Canal is one of the wonders of the world, but so many thousands have steamed through it that I refrain from describing it. Beyond the canal, the Red Sea waters are much warmer and one gazes at the sight of flying fish by day and of phosphorescent waves by night.

The senior, grey-haired passengers took little notice of us Probationers. They seemed to be a boring lot who spent much of the day playing bridge. One exception was a Major Shaw, I.C.S. of Assam, who was both friendly and charming. There were no older Police Officers, who preferred to travel on a Line such as Lloyd Triestino, which was a very good one and appreciably cheaper, being Government-subsidised.

On Sundays the Captain took Mattins in the main saloon which was attended by both first and second-class passengers. One of them invited me to their saloon for a game of pontoon, but it lacked the style and luxury of the first class.

I was proud of my steward, Francisco, a Roman Catholic from Goa. he called me in the morning, waited at table and put out my clothes. I wanted to talk to him, but he was very reserved and professional. I took a photograph of him but he did not unbend. At the end of the voyage we tipped our steward a few pounds.

There were unattached young ladies going out to stay with their parents but I had no interest in them. There were deck games and competitions and a fine enclosed swimming pool. There were dances, but the only incident I can remember was when an enormous Army officer got stuck one night in the window of one of the staterooms. Though his wife was on board he was trying to visit an attractive young lady. It took four Lascars to extract him; two pushing and two pulling.

If, early before breakfast, I paced the deck, I would meet a grey-haired Scottish seaman and soon discovered that he could recite stanza after stanza from his favourite poet, Robbie Burns.

After eighteen days' sailing we reached Bombay, drew alongside near the Gateway of India and a great number of coolies and painters crowded the quay. To my surprise, our old Nanny, Mrs Wade, met me; no doubt my mother had written to her. She had left us to marry a soldier in the Suffolk Regiment and had come specially from Mhow in Central India. This was the first of innumerable kindnesses I experienced in India. She gave me my first tin of fifty cigarettes –

Players (made in Bangalore).

After the necessary formalities a party of us went to the Taj Mahal Hotel. The visitor should certainly go to the 'Taj'. It is the most marvellous hotel with a superb view of the city. Afterwards I hired a horse-carriage and went for a drive. The sheer variety of the people struck me forcibly – I had never seen so many different types. Coolies – men and women carrying loads, clerks, white-clad students walking or waiting at a 'bus stop, beggars and loafers. A guide offered his services and tried to get me to buy cottons, silks, brass ornaments, trinkets, white mice, birds, parrots, but I didn't want any of them. I noticed that in the great crowds I was the only European and felt a little apprehensive.

But I had an appointment with an Agent, a smart Indian of about thirty-five and he wanted to see me off. With my steel uniform trunk, steel helmet case and cabin trunk he took me to the Victoria Terminus, which must surely be the grandest station in the Commonwealth. It has been described as a blend of Gothic, Hindu and Venetian styles, of light red stone, like a vast cathedral only bigger. I was impressed by the numerous railway porters who wore khaki shorts, scarlet shirts and turbans. Though they didn't look strong, they knew what they were about and handled heavy luggage efficiently.

During the war, the magnificent S.S. Viceroy of India was torpedoed off North Africa.

2

Life in Vellore – in at the Deep End

I HAD a small, two-berth compartment to myself. The express trains run on five-foot gauge and have no corridors. All I can remember of the journey is that I felt thirsty. I had no drinking water and drank some unboiled tap water from the little toilet room before going to sleep. The journey to Madras took some 32 hours.

I did not stay in Madras, but was soon put on a train for Katpadi near Vellore. Though it was early November it felt warm, like a summer's day and everything was strange – nothing was familiar. Soon I was in a dream. At a dinner party given by the Principal of the College I could not follow the conversation, though with two Indian officials and a missionary doctor present it was quite lively. The Principal could not wait till I was adjusted and for the next few weeks I spent most of the time between the Mess and the Fort, with club nights twice a week at the Vellore Club.

It was my first experience of a Mess: a large, low building in six acres of ground and set well back from the main road – not so much to be quiet as on account of the dust raised by buses, cars and bullock carts. It had a long front verandah and four large double bedrooms. The dining hall had a table which could be extended to hold up to forty persons. The furniture was of polished rosewood from the West Coast and the dining hall had a polished floor, tiled for coolness. All the rooms had overhead ceiling fans.

The most interesting feature to me was the trophies - numerous horns of bison and wild buffalo, antlers of samhbar – the big deer and lesser deer; gazelles, black buck, a panther skin and a bear. All had been shot by former members of the Mess, prominent among whom was the name of Scott-Coward, hero of a rebellion (1922) in the Agency tracts, who was obviously a very fine rifle shot. Besides these were collections of Indian muskets and flintlocks, maces, halberds, battle-axes, swords and lances. They showed how an army of men with cold steel could cause lacerating wounds and terrible casualties. On a hot afternoon one used to lie back in a long cane chair and muse over the trophies, which developed in me a taste for horns and antlers as decoration.

There were only two others in residence, both a little senior to me, R.R.B. Truscott an A.E. Spitteler, for hitherto officers were recruited in pairs and so kept each other company. Truscott was the most mature of us three. He was comfortably off and had a Vauxhall car. He pulled his weight in the running of the Mess but I did not much care for his attitude towards the servants. Spitteler was not well off and had an old motor-bike; he was considerate to servants and humorous, for Tamils appreciate humour. Two Probationers of the Provincial Service, who were paid less, lived in the town.

Vellore Fort[3] is a fine example of military engineering. Built on a mediaeval plan it is protected by a moat, which in former centuries was stocked with alligators. The massive gateway has front and rear doors, the stone walls being at least twelve feet thick. Inside were a number of buildings: barracks for several hundred constable- recruits, quarters for seventy or more sub-inspector cadets, messes; armoury and magazine; classrooms. Also the Sessions Court, District Police office and other offices; a temple, a military-style church and a cemetery. In the latter were the graves of those killed, 129 of all ranks, in the Mutiny of 1806 and many others – young matrons, young men and children. The largest grave held the remains of nearly forty officers, N.C.O's and Privates killed by the mutineers.

The former military horse-lines housed the Police horses of 15.2 hands and over, sixteen in number. Also in the Fort is quite a large Temple with tower covered with carved figures. About the year 1650 a beautiful Temple dancing-girl was pursued and murdered in the precincts, since when the Temple has been disused. The Temple treasures were reputed to have been buried in an underground chamber and have never been found.

Another house was known as the Shorthand Bureau, the headquarters of the Shorthand Sub-Inspectors. For the provincial government wanted accurate and unbiased reports of important political speeches and could not always depend on the Press. These sub-inspectors, who always wore mufti, would therefore travel to political meetings, as directed, and take down the speeches, which was done openly.

Full accounts of the system of training may be found in other books. Suffice to say that we were called at 5.30 a.m. with a tray of tea and a raw egg seasoned with Worcester sauce. By 6.25 a.m. we had to be on parade, two miles away in the Fort. Parade lasted till 8 a.m. ending with slow-marching to the Band. The Probationers drilled in the ranks with the sub-inspectors, smart young Indians of the same age or a little older. The majority were caste Hindus, with a minority of Muslims, Anglo-Indians and some 'Harijans' – to avoid the unpleasant term 'Untouchable' – for a proportion of the places was reserved for the above three categories.

We learnt Infantry drill; I was somewhat indignant at this, having done several years in Officers' Training Corps; but I soon discovered that the drill taught was of a higher, professional standard. We learnt military equitation in the riding school; *lathi* i.e. single-stick drill and bayonet-fighting with hanging dummies. This developed the muscles but served no other purpose. The senior instructors were ex-Army Sergeants and Subedars, a senior Indian Army rank. All the squads were supervised by Mr Hipwood, the senior Sergeant-Major and by the Principal from his horse.

By a quarter to eight we were sweating and dismissal a quarter of an hour later was a relief. We officers returned to the Mess for breakfast, which was always a cooked one. As I had no vehicle I travelled back to the Fort in

[3] Built by one of the Kings, Vijayanagar, Narsingh Raja.

Truscott's car for the classes.

The main subjects taught were Law, Medical Jurisprudence, Police Standing Orders, investigation; finger-prints and foot-prints; the maintenance of buildings and language. My language was to be Telugu. There was an Instructor for each subject, either an Inspector or a civilian, but Law was divided into three subjects. My *munshi* or language teacher was a tall man, always spotlessly dressed in white, with turban and sandals. As I was the only beginner in Telugu he taught me at the Mess in the afternoons, which wasn't the best time as it was warm or hot and one had been awake since 5.30 a.m.

After four, tea and cake made on the premises was brought; the instructors always enjoyed English cake.

After tea there was games or riding; the principal games were hockey and cricket. Indians are superb hockey players; the standard of cricket was also high, one of the staff was a Presidency player and some of the sub-inspectors had played for their College in Madras.

The curricula were laid down and all went smoothly. The officers and sub-inspectors had to pass their exams, none of us wanted to stay at Vellore for a week longer than necessary, so we all worked.

The Principal was a man in his forties, very energetic, keen on drill and riding; but was not competent enough to be the head of a college with at least half of the students university graduates. He never attempted to take a class himself, but spoke Tamil fluently.

We had a fine Mess which was in charge of a very dignified steward, an elderly Moplah, bearded, religious and scrupulously honest. His name – Kasim.

For some reason known to himself, the Principal rarely organised a Mess night though there were sufficient local officers and their wives. A couple of years later there was a change of principal, an intelligent, progressive man was appointed and the academic standard rose.

Twice a week, Wednesday and Saturday, was club night at the Vellore Club. This was a typical district club. Twenty years before it might have had thirty members. When I joined it had half that number, but first I had to call on the members in the afternoon and leave cards. It was housed in a 'bungalow'. Now bungalow is a Hindustani word and means an officer's or foreigner's residence. Many had large rooms, high ceilings and verandahs and were on one floor. But the larger bungalows usually had bedrooms and bathrooms on a first floor. In front there was often a pillared portico where carriages (later cars) could draw up and be sheltered from the heat of the sun.

After Truscott and Spitteler completed their training at the College and departed to a district, I was the only resident in the Mess, which was lonely. But there is always an escape and, living close by, was a charming Irish couple, Major Gerard Kelly of the Indian Medical Service and his wife, May. I could visit them at any time and talk freely, knowing they would never repeat anything. Major Kelly looked after me when I fell ill and I owe them both a big debt of gratitude.

A certain Mrs X was married to a man a good few years older and I rather thought she made eyes at me. But, as she was nearly double my age, I wasn't interested and thought she looked very funny on the tennis court with her massive bust and thin legs. When she realised I wasn't interested she spread some remarks to the effect that I said she was a snob. As, actually, I thought no such thing, it surprised me very much. Some months later her family and I became friends.

At this time, the end of 1936, the crisis known as the Abdication of King Edward VIII was developing. Of course it wasn't totally unexpected, but it was a shocking business after the twenty-five year reign of the happily-married George V and Queen Mary. We thought the Duke would make a steady King, especially in view of the lovely lady, the Duchess of York.

To most Indians, the Abdication was incomprehensible. To their way of thinking a bride must be a virgin and if they had heard that the Duke of York strongly objected to the woman the King wished to marry and, with the help of the Duke of York's Own Cavalry, had arrested the King, confined him in Windsor Castle and proclaimed himself King George VI - the great majority of Indians would have understood and nodded their heads in agreement.

But that King Edward was giving up his imperial throne in order to marry a woman no longer young, who was a foreigner and had already been married to two husbands – this was beyond their comprehension. After King Edward became Duke of Windsor and good King George was safely on the throne, I hardly ever heard an Indian mention the Duke of Windsor again, though British people sometimes did.

After two months in the country my attitude towards servants was changing. I was becoming less familiar and thought they found it embarrassing if treated with familiarity. I had a good servant temporarily, a Christian, his master (E.L. Cox) being on home leave. He knew his place and had no desire to be anything else.

A regular visitor to the Mess was an elderly gentleman called Bertie Ffoulkes. He was an interesting character being one of the fast-dwindling breed of Anglo-Indian zamindars or landowners. A corpulent man of soldierly bearing he had a swarthy complexion, strong features, iron-grey hair and moustache. He was descended from a chaplain of the Madras establishment and a Muslim lady. His estate was in the Madura District and he was respected by all communities. Predictably, he was a strong Tory and nervous of the Indian National Congress. He must have found me an advanced Liberal, but he was no Colonel Blimp and never got heated.

However hot it was he always dressed formally for dinner and as he never mentioned a wife I took him to be single. In effect he was a relict of the East India Company as, after the Mutiny and the opening of the Suez Canal (which changed British society in the country) Englishmen did not marry Indian ladies or purchase or acquire Indian estates. I think it was he who told me there were still two Madras pensioners left, dating from the winding up of John Company in 1858: twin girls, born about two years before to a Factor in Madras, did not marry, so qualified for a pension and in 1937 were living in retirement somewhere in England.

When the members began to arrive at the Club about 7 p.m. the Police Band of some twenty-two men mostly Christians, was waiting to play from the bandstand. There were English magazines to be read and a small library mostly of novels. The old club waiter would ask you for your drink. The older ones mostly had a long whisky and soda, but I was young enough to prefer beer. The men wore black jacket, dinner shirt, black bow-tie and white drill trousers. The ladies wore long dresses to protect them from mosquitoes. Soon a bridge four would be formed, with four men playing billiards in the billiard room. On the walls of country clubs, the pictures were always the same: framed and coloured prints of Leicestershire and Derbyshire Hunts. As I was always the youngest, I played bridge or billiards as required. Usually, there were two or three people left over who took their turn later. No food was served as about 9.30 p.m., the band played its closing march and the members went home for their dinner.

On other days tennis was played after tea. There was only one hard court and the club Writer would always make up a fourth. The Writer was a clerk who kept the accounts and supervised the club servants – the waiter, four ball boys, a gardener and a part-time cook. All the sodas were made on the premises and cost less than 1d each. Behind the court was a small stone structure with massive walls – the old ice-house.

Much has been written about the exclusiveness of British clubs in the East; but Burma was not exclusive. India had been and there were still some exclusive clubs like the Bengal, Madras, Allahabad and the Royal Yacht Club in Bombay. But up-country, half the members were Indians. Our President was a Brahmin, Oxford-educated and highly intelligent – the Collector[4] and District Magistrate. Another was a Sikh, Major Gill Singh, Indian Medical Service, who was Superintendent of the Central Jail – his wife was Scottish. Major Kelly was District Medical Officer. Another was B.K. Roy, the Forest Officer; he and his beautiful wife were Bengalis. Four others were (British) Police Officers, another was the British Inspector of Excise. So it was not exclusive except that only Indian gentlemen were admitted.

As we made our way to parade first thing in the morning, we never failed to see beside the road a white-haired old woman, old and bent; she was dressed in only half a sari which showed her thin brown shins. She was a Harijan or 'Untouchable' from a cluster of huts on a piece of waste land and was walking slowly out of the town.

Returning to the Fort after breakfast we would see her again, this time walking the other way, her morning work done. For she was still a useful member of her family and her task was to search under trees and gather up an armful of dry sticks for cooking the daily meal. She was one of the very poor but, I believe, happier than some of our old people, sitting in a residential home, with nothing to do and waited on by a devoted staff.

[4] Collector of Revenue, chiefly from land and supplemented by duties on paraffin, sugar, salt and Excise.

SOUTH INDIA

3

Madras Interlude, New Year, 1937, at Vellore

AS CHRISTMAS approached I was looking forward to a change. Then an invitation arrived for me to spend a few days with old friends of my parents in Madras. He was a very senior official in the Indian Civil Service.

The Indian Railways had four classes. As I had been buying light-weight uniform and leisure clothes, I could not afford the 1st class and travelled 2nd.

A well-educated Brahmin official was in the compartment, we discussed the world situation, then moved on to philosophy and discussed fate and chance, ending with speculation on the mystery of life. It was the first serious discussion I had had for weeks and left me much refreshed.

My hosts lived in a great, white-painted mansion at Adyar which is a few miles inland. They were very hospitable. The had excellent servants and spoke to them kindly. My hostess had a personal maid or *ayah*. I was allowed the use of the car and driver, which I much appreciated. I think they expected me to visit Fort St George, the Secretariat, the High Court and so on. But I wanted to see the real India and so toured the bazaars and Indian residential districts.

Our Christmas dinner was taken at the residence of a tall, lean High Court Judge, the Hon'ble Mr Cornish, I.C.S. It was a splendid mansion full of art treasures: pictures, plate and china. I talked to a retired Judge, who was most affable and a German artist.

On Boxing Day I watched a soccer match at the Gymkhana Club. The Club side, heavy and slow, played a light Indian team from the Cotton Mills. It was amusing: two kinds of football, but the Indian side, playing with ankle bands in place of boots, were too fast and won.

I met an Indian missionary doctor, with an F.R.C.S. degree and he invited me to tea at the Madras Medical College. Afterwards, we sat on the beach and watched the long white rollers crashing on the sands. As the light failed, the blue of the sea grew darker. The moon rose and cast her brilliance on the waves. Darkness falls quickly in the East.

Next day we met for lunch, one of the guests being a young German with a philosophical-religious turn of mind – Madras attracts such people. Four of us sat down to an Indian meal and were served by the Doctor's niece. It was a delicious meal, tasty but not 'hot'. Afterwards, we washed our mouths out with water, which I thought very hygienic. At first I thought the young Indian woman should have sat with us, but it became clear that she was in no way demeaning herself by serving – she regarded it as an honour. It was interesting to learn that Christians followed Hindu customs and etiquette. They were known as Indian Christians, but 'Christian Indians' would be more appropriate.

At the small house of the German, I met a charming old Brahmin philosopher; he despised wealth, had little to do with caste and believed passionately in the unity of the human race. He thought it vital to educate men of character and to develop character, which very few Indians, he said, possessed. We had a long talk, at the end of which he paid me the compliment of saying that I should study for an external degree in philosophy. Though he had never travelled, he had a perfect mastery of the English language, besides his knowledge of Tamil and Sanskrit.

But my hosts did not like the way I was spending my days and before the week was up I was recalled by telegram. Later, I was made to realise how very discourteous I had been to my hosts, using their house as an hotel.

I realised my fault but had an enquiring mind and was in a fascinating new country. The finest police officers were men who spoke the language well and were able to mix with people; some even could use a disguise. When I tried to mix and enquire I was told not to. Perhaps they were afraid I would lose my footing

I just had time to purchase a second-hand motor cycle, which I needed in Vellore.

On new Year's Day, 1937, E.S. (Bill) Treasure, the Assistant Superintendent, called and suggested a walk. It was dull and cool and we had a long walk through the countryside. His younger brother, P.M., was my contemporary and was posted to Bihar. Before joining the Police, Bill had taught in a preparatory school. Asked why he did not go to a university for a degree, he told me that his father was a tobacco planter in the Telugu country. He had lived in India as a boy and to such, India often calls.

Next day the probationers were sent on a change of routine, visiting town and rural police stations, also the District Police Office and Stores.

Everyone seemed to be very set in their ways and I wondered why. In fact I was realising for the first time the strength of Indian tradition. If something was always done in such and such a way, that was the way to do it. Indians wisely have no use for change for the sake of change.

An Indian Deputy Superintendent[5] and the Inspector took me to a village where a *panchayat* or meeting had been arranged. Five of them, men of standing in their villages, were waiting in the shade of a tree to hear words of encouragement and exhortation. It reminded me of the greybeards meeting in Mowgli's village in the Central Provinces. I was impressed by their air of wisdom and goodness. This was the real, unchanging India, also an expression of good relations between the local police and village officers. One of the features of Indian villages is the council of five elders – the *panchayat*. It is an excellent institution.

Not long afterwards, I was talking with the same Deputy Superintendent during the break in morning parade. He was a Muslim, large, rather corpulent and perfectly content with his position. He said he admired the way the British kept order and had no interest in Swaraj (or Home rule).

[5] Kalimulla Chida

"So I tell the Indians, why bother about home rule? Now you can sleep in safety. Without the English there will be civil war.

Look at the wars before there was British rule."

Though I couldn't be expected to realise it at the time, his prophecy was justified by the terrible events of 1947-8, just eleven years ahead.

The strength of the police in India was much less comparatively than in Britain. For one thing India was a poor country. For many years, part of a district force was called the Armed Police. They paraded every day; they were armed with rifles, also with bamboo *lathis* for crowd control. They had lorries, signalling equipment and, later, Bren-guns and gas grenades. So small numbers of police could control the huge crowds which gather during festivals or times of unrest.

Part of their regular training was the route-march. It was a popular duty as it took them away from the Lines and parade- ground. I too enjoyed the experience of my first route-march with a well-trained force. The pace is a fast one, five miles per hour to five and a half. The men carry only rifles, bayonets, water-bottles and maybe twenty rounds of ammunition. This company had a very good singer – he had composed songs in three or four Indian languages. He would sing a line from some epic, or lyric, the men joining in chorus after each line. I was surprised to find such a gifted man – in the ranks.

Among the varied duties was attending Court. In the 1st and 2nd class Magistrates' Courts, a Prosecuting Inspector presents the case, the investigating sub-inspector gives evidence. Officers such as myself did not usually attend these trials, but were required to sit in at the Sessions Court once a month. For this we dressed formally, out of respect for the Judge and the Court, but did not take part, we merely sat and listened.

My first court case was a murder trial. There was, of course, no eye-witness, there hardly ever is. I thought the circumstantial evidence established the guilt of the accused beyond all reasonably doubt. But the Judge did not agree and acquitted the accused. The verdict was accepted by the prosecution and of course the defence lawyer was delighted.

One day, I had to retire to bed with a severe headache. It turned out to be jaundice, and Major Kelly, the Medical Officer, sent me to his hospital for treatment. I joked with the nurse, a young Anglo-Indian and was horrified to find how strongly the Indian doctor was prejudiced against Anglo-Indians. It was a wonder she put up with his sarcasm. A male nurse washed me every day and an Indian sweeper- woman took the place of the modern flush lavatory and also swept the verandah. She was an 'untouchable'. She was plump and well-favoured and her hips waggled as she walked which gave me ideas. The hospital was near the main bazaar and at night I had plenty of opportunity to listen to Indian music, much of which reminded me of the bagpipes. On the whole, the small district hospital was very noisy, but that wouldn't worry the patients. The Principal, A.E. Spitteler and three young Sub-Inspectors came to see me – that none of the ladies came to see me showed that I was not a popular young man.

I had plenty of time to read the papers and it was plain that the year 1937 began with a lot of political activity. Pandit Nehru, Vallabhai Patel and the Congress stalwarts were addressing big meetings and election crowds, by which I mean 10,000 or more people. Nehru was beginning to travel up and down the country by light aircraft. But the chief event was the fruition of Gandhi's campaign to abolish untouchability. He would not use the term 'untouchable', but coined the term Harijan, or child of God. That month, His Highness the Maharajah of Travancore ordered the opening of all State Temples to Harijans. Gandhi himself toured the State and pronounced it a success, but such a big step could not succeed overnight – the Harijans for the most part were afraid of exercising their newfound right.

Educated Indians seemed to be leading the country inexorably towards Home Rule and the British Government was committed to conceding it.

While the triumph of Communism seemed out of the question, the Communists were also stepping up their campaigns and the numbers of organised labour and of strikes were increasing. But a third kind of activity and much more important than Communism was the Muslim League.

Most of the Indian Muslims were converts, first by invaders, then by zealous Indian Muslims. Originally, the Congress Party was intended to be catholic and to embrace all religions. So Mahomed Ali Jinnah, a leading Muslim lawyer, became a Congress leader, but slowly he grew disillusioned and from about 1937 favoured a separation of the Muslims into two main areas: the North-West and East Bengal, where they were in the majority. This became the objective of the Muslim League. Later I found myself ridiculing such a country of two wings, separated from each other by 800 miles of India.

After treatment I was discharged but was put on light duties. My language teacher was a very respectable man, but on his resuming his teaching I noticed a change in him. He used to conceal his nationalism, but now it was apparent. And why should he not be a nationalist?

So the time came round for the annual inspection of the College which was by the Acting Inspector-General, Mr F. Sayers. Naturally he stayed at the Mess, where he brought his camp-clerk, his bearer, driver and personal orderly. He was an Irishman of about 48 years of age and seemed old enough to be my father. Though his hair was receding he was still very handsome and had kept his figure, for he was a keen horseman and had been a regular rider to hounds. I feel sure he found me rather 'advanced' but he was naturally kind and I liked him, for he was himself, not like some, acting a part. Two of his small habits I noticed favourably – he rolled his own cigarettes, never dropped any ash and, after each meal, carefully folded his napkin and pushed in his chair.

While he was out inspecting, I enjoyed a long walk, climbing one of the steep, craggy hills behind the town, where I had a superb view of the reservoir, the town nestling at the foot of a hill; the *maidan* (a large open space) and beyond, the Fort; palm groves and the river in the distance, which, after the monsoon was almost dry.

4

Hindu Society – The Caste System and the British

"THE CHILD is the father of the Man
And I would wish my days to be
Bound each to each by natural piety"

A small community such as a desert or hill tribe can almost dispense with divisions, but a large society must be structured in some way and the Hindus have devised their own system, which is unique and which gives every individual a place and, originally, a function.

The original inhabitants were probably the Dravidians, dark in colour and adapted to the climate. Then about 1500 B.C. the first Aryan invasions began from the North West. The origins of caste are lost in time, but the ancient Indian word for it is *varna* which means colour. The Aryans (who were light in colour) defeated the Dravidians and tended to push them South. Evidently inter-marriage was discouraged and a five-fold caste system was devised:-

1.   the Brahmins; the twice-born, priests, astrologers, teachers, lawyers, but not rulers.
2.   the Kshatriya or warrior caste, who are also rulers. This caste is strongly represented in Rajputana.
3.   the Vaisyas - merchants, shopkeepers, money lenders.
4   .the Sudras – the largest division; the cultivators, artisans, craftsmen.
5.   the Pariahs, or out-castes.

Moreover caste, first developed by the Aryans became sanctified, as a Vedic hymn declares:-

"The Brahman sprang from the mouth of the Creator,
the Kshatriya sprang from the arms..
the Vaisya sprang from the thighs ..
and the Sudra from the Creator's feet.."

which confirms the primacy of the Brahmin and the humility of the Sudra. These main Castes remain, but have become extensively sub-divided e.g. the Brahmins divide mainly into followers of Vishnu (Preserver) or Shiva (the Destroyer).

One comes across many castes e.g. accountants, goldsmiths, the Naidus, the Reddis (important Telugu castes), weavers, potters, tappers (of palm trees). Two of the lowest castes are shepherds and various Criminal tribes. So even the hereditary criminal has a status.

The Pariahs, or untouchables, must live apart from the caste Hindus and have their own well. They do rough cooly work such as carrying loads, road repairs, leather work and scavenging. And as the flush lavatory is a foreign invention, the Pariahs are essential.

Every caste has its own rules, caste-marks and customs about food and dress; initiation ceremonies, marriage and death ceremonies. Caste is assumed at birth so there is no way that an Englishman or foreigner could become a caste Hindu. The European has no caste.

Some low-caste men became chiefs (as, sometimes Muslim slaves became kings), thus Shivaji, the great Maratha Chief, was of low caste, but appointed a Brahmin as his Chief Minister. The Vijayanagar kings were also of low caste and the wisest of them honoured the Brahmins.

The rules of feeding are strict and each man should eat within his own caste, but all may eat meals prepared by a Brahmin, so the cooks in hotels and cafés are often Brahmins. So Europeans must be careful about inviting a Hindu to a meal for European food would normally defile him.

In North India, both Hindu and Muslim water was sold at Railway stations: it all came from the same tap but was drawn by different men! (The Englishmen didn't favour either, for they needed to drink boiled water.) And as with water so with milk!

The great majority of the British who served in India were middle class, apart from the troops who came for a few years only. Living was cheaper than in England and salaries were sufficient to pay a set of servants a living wage. Of course most of us younger ones were not used to house servants, only to daily helps. Suddenly, we found ourselves with lots of servants, who were not hard-worked and were willing to perform menial tasks such as tying up shoelaces and helping a man out of his clothes. For instance, my personal servant always pulled off my riding boots. Our womenfolk had less to talk about and they spent quite a lot of time discussing their domestic problems.

The population was a teeming one, families were as ours were last century: five to eight children was usual, two children unusual. The result was high unemployment and the sharing of modest incomes between families.

The caste system laid down a division of labour. Christians and Muslims were not bound by caste but, by gentleman's agreement, they would not do two jobs.

In District Headquarters we had electric light and fans but no plumbing. Nearly everything was done by hand such as the making of ice cream. So those who lived up-country, whether Army, Civilian or businessmen needed a set of servants each with his own job to do:-

– a butler-valet, or bearer, the head servant (Hindustani: khitmagar)
– a cook – in larger establishments he had a mate or 'matey'
– an ayah or nanny
– a waterman to draw and carry water, heat it for the daily bath, to clean basins, assist the cook with vegetables and help wash up. He needed to be clean and was a respectable Hindu or Muslim.

– a gardener or *mali* – plants need daily water all through the long, dry season. A gardener could also obtain gifts of plants from his fellow gardeners, a great help when one was newly posted.

– a sweeper/scavenger

– a groom if a horse or horses were kept.

A high-ranking official had one or more extra ones such as an under-butler or footman. And if there were three or more dogs, a dog-boy was often kept, who de-loused, brushed and exercised as necessary – one could not travel very far with several dogs.

But no description of bungalow servants would be complete without mentioning the dhobi or washer-man. In a hot climate one needs daily changes of clothes but the washing is not done at home. Once a week the dhobi, a white-clad figure, arrives with a donkey. The laundry is counted and noted in a little book then bundled into a sheet and laid on the donkey's back. He, the dhobi, often helped by a wife or daughter, takes it to the river or a tap. Some slap the clothes too vigorously on a smooth stone, but a good dhobi is careful. Nature does the drying and within two days it all comes back clean, ironed and neatly folded. Every dhobi has his own way of marking clothes with dots and crosses. In an emergency he will launder a garment in a day. His service is quick, reliable and cheap.

But while the clothes were taken away, the barber came once a month to trim the officer's hair for about nine (old) pence and his wife's cotton frocks and dresses were made by the tailor sitting on the verandah at a sewing machine, with the children looking on. All the sewing-machines, treadle and portable, were by Singer who provided an efficient maintenance service.

All were paid monthly, but besides them the Army or Government provided orderlies or chaprassis, (also called peons) who helped in the office, took messages and dusted all the furniture, a daily necessity. Chaprassis were in two grades, wore broad, coloured sashes over the shoulder with brass plates such as: 'District Judge', 'District Magistrate', 'District Forest Officer', and so on with the name of the district town.

Insensitivity by the General to the feelings and conservatism of the sepoys was the chief cause of the Vellore mutiny in 1806 and one of the causes of the far more serious Mutiny of the Bengal Army fifty years later.

The following anecdote illustrates caste-feelings among the British. While holidaying in Kashmir I met a cheerful Calcutta businessman, whom I will call Harris. He was not the marrying sort, loved horses and was the owner of two racehorses. His business was engineering stores; he supplied the Army and regularly visited the forts along the North-West Frontier. The Army Scouts holding these forts were so lonely that he always received a welcome. One day, while drinking gin with some of them, a subaltern suddenly asked "By the way, what do you do for a living?" "Oh", replied Harris with a twinkle in his eye, "I'm just a box-wallah."[6] "A box-wallah? But you're quite a decent chap."

[6] Derogatory term for a businessman.

Even Mahatma Gandhi was not very successful in his reforms - he introduced Prohibition which, as in America, caused much bribery and corruption and his laudable efforts to remove the stigma of untouchability met with limited success.

One method was the missionary way of turning Untouchables into Christians but, as formerly in an English village, the 'caste Christians' often would not sit with those of inferior origin. There are indeed similarities between Indian caste and British class; perhaps one reason for the mutual understanding and affection between us?

One of the results of the new Indian Constitution was a speeding up of the Indianisation of the All-India Services; so Mr R., another Probationer, arrived a couple of months after me. He had a Madras degree in Botany and Biology.

One evening my language-teacher's son called. He was a good- looking and healthy young man, tall like his father. He was very disappointed at failing to be selected as the new Probationer. So I asked him, "What are your qualifications?" He replied: "A degree in Economics, History and Politics." I thought this degree not very acceptable to the Commissioners. He had done well in the competitive exam, but I still thought that they had preferred the Biology degree. In due course I learnt the truth; there had been a serious irregularity in the competitive exam, a leakage not known to the Examiners. I was shocked, but as the years went by, it transpired that such irregularities increased.

That night a procession passed the front of the Mess compound on its way to a village. It was headed by a twelve-foot high idol, seated on a wooden cow also twice life-sized. They were on a wooden platform fitted with long poles. Fifteen or more men shouldered the poles. The god was preceded by drummers; two big gas lamps gave a brilliant light and a queue of marchers brought up the rear. The new probationer said they had borrowed the idol from the temple in order to scare away a disease - he knew it from the identity of the god.

Mr R. stayed for some time in the Mess. He was from Malabar and so spotlessly clean. He ate European food, but had no car or motor-bike and after a while he obtained permission to rent a small house in town, where he could eat the food to which he was accustomed and would be within easy bicycling distance of the Fort. But before the year was out his probation was ceased – he just wasn't strong and tough enough for the hard training.

5

Police Week, Madras and the Nilgiris

THIS WAS a gathering at Vellore of the senior officers and nearly all the Superintendents, who were mostly British. Assistants were left behind in temporary charge of the districts. In those days it was the fashion for senior officers to wear monocles on formal occasions; a custom soon ended by the war.

The weather in late January was perfect - no danger of rain and cool, even in the afternoons. The Acting Inspector-General was F. Sayers, C.I.E., who was treated throughout like a lord. The senior Indian officer was a highly intelligent Brahmin: Dewan Bahadur Ramanuja Iyengar, who was at home in both orthodox Hindu and British society. He had spent a long leave in England and was prepared to both eat beef and drink whisky. I much appreciated his company at the Mess, his open and liberal mind. He was a Deputy Inspector-General over five districts.

A lunch party for about forty people in the Mess was to be given in honour of the Governor, Lord Erskine and Lady Erskine. Tremendous preparations were made, but unfortunately, His Excellency was indisposed on the day and unable to travel from Madras. All the roads had been re-surfaced, no rubbish was to be seen and the beggars and stray dogs had been driven away.

Morning and afternoon were given over to drill displays, athletics, tent-pegging, horse jumping, cricket, hockey and tennis, but unlike several other Provinces there was no polo. It ended with a fancy-dress dance.

There is no doubt that the Week was good for morale, it was also a tribute to the good order kept in the districts, when most of the officers could absent themselves for nearly ten days.

Next day I was asked to a lunch given for the Indian officers at the Indian Club and was the only European. They were all in Indian dress, sat on the floor on mats and I was struck by the relaxed atmosphere of the meal compared with the elaborate and formal seven-course lunch arranged for the Governor.

When all the visitors had gone, the station seemed dead. It was the only Police Week I was able to attend as the War was soon to put an end to them. I was sorry, because Madras was such a long, straggling Province that without such a Week one could never get to know all one's brother officers.

Early in February I had to report sick. Major Kelly sent me to the General Hospital in Madras as I had a swollen appendix. A fine surgeon, Major F.M. Collins, operated. Unfortunately, the Indian catgut was not sterile and the wound refused to heal. It was lonely in the small four-bed ward, but then a subaltern of the Gloucester Regiment arrived. We played cards and other games which made the hours pass faster.

At home we were proud of the Gloucesters, our County Regiment, they had also supervised my military training, so I asked him: "And why did you choose the Gloucesters? His reply took me by surprise; with a smile he confessed: "Because I liked the Mess kit." It was a young man's reply but not to be despised for all that.

I had three visitors in all. Mr Sayers, the Inspector-General, called and asked me if there was anything I would like. Then two cheerful young sisters called Westerdale, who cheered me up a lot. Mr Sayers called again bringing two quarter-pound tins of my tobacco, which I thought most generous of him.

Being allowed out, I met a Scottish lecturer at the Madras Christian College and we visited the Theosophical Centre at Adyar, famed for Dr Annie Besant and her friend, Krishnamurthi. [7] I had no interest in the subject but wanted to see the place, which was near the sea and cooled by the afternoon sea-breeze. As we sat under a huge banyan tree having tea, a long procession of Indian Wolf-Cubs passed by with their Cub-Masters. We talked to them and they were most friendly. As they marched off we had to stand to attention while they all saluted with white-toothed grins.

On my discharge, Mr Sayers arranged for me to stay at the Officers' Rest Home at Ootacamund. A main line train took me to the foot of the Nilgiri Hills which tower up to nearly 9,000 feet. One then changed into the little mountain railway, which climbed so steeply in places tht the engine and rails were fitted with ratchet and pinion. It was like an ascent to Paradise.

It was late February; the hill-station at 7,500 feet had hundreds of houses and bungalows on the grassy hillsides, all surrounded by gardens of English flowers. In the evening we had a fire of eucalyptus logs, for large numbers of these huge Australian trees had been planted round about; oil was distilled from the leaves but the wood was only fit for fuel.

The Rest Home was in the charge of a kindly man retired from the Indian Medical Service (Lieut. Colonel Stanger-Lees). There were several Army officers and three or four civilians in need of a rest. The Home was endowed, for it had been founded by Lady Willingdon, when her husband was Governor of Madras, for officers wounded in the Great War. And though I was on half-pay, the lowest in the scale, I could afford it and had a little left over for a young servant.

Within days the cool, dry air had healed my wound. There was a light frost on the racecourse one morning but by March it was like an English summer. Showers of rain kept the grass green on the downs and the air pure.

The modern reader will be surprised to hear that we never listened to the wireless. One of the civilians at the Home had a set in his bedroom but no one was invited to listen so we depended on the local paper – the Madras Mail – for news.

One day in March a dish of strange- looking green fruit was placed on the table. "What are they?" I asked. "Mangoes" was the reply. They then showed me how to cut and eat one. As soon as I tasted the soft, pink flesh I knew I had

[7] He left the Theosophist movement, settled in America and, in 1984, was still lecturing.

eaten them before: it must have been before I was five years old. There are many varieties of mango and nearly all are delicious.

A retired Vice-Chancellor of Madras University arrived, R. Littlehailes, who was interesting to talk to and a Major Lloyd who had a fund of Russian stories. Another, Major Fletcher, was a potential staff officer and improved his mind with solid reading; nevertheless, I was still homesick.

But separation from one's family was part of our life in the East, so the importance of letter-writing and the Postal service was inestimable. There was no airmail and of course no long distance telephone; all our letters travelled by mail steamer, and until 1940 letters from home were unloaded in Bombay on Tuesday and delivered at Ooty about lunchtime on Thursday, without fail. So, lunch parties were avoided on Mail Day: which was quiet, but bitter could be the disappointment if a letter, such as from a sweetheart, failed to arrive. I experienced this after Dunkirk when several of my father's weekly letters were lost.

Two or three times I was asked out to lunch, once with L.B. Gasson, the local Deputy Inspector-General; Mrs Gasson was Master of the Ooty Foxhounds, said to be the finest pack in India.

One day we had a pleasant picnic near the Pykara hydro-electric dam, where work was still in progress and saw hundreds of coolies, men and women, their clothes full of dust, carrying the earth away in baskets, the same as the ancient Egyptians. They looked very thin and poor, but the cause was partly malaria.

I was pretty fit and after a hearty picnic lunch, had a row on the lake in a pleasure boat. On the way back we stopped at a tea garden and I saw for the first time, the low, waist-high bushes that mean so much to us Britishers.

A visitor to the Home was an upstanding Indian, Captain K.M. Kariappa. Sandhurst-trained and very professional, he was one of the seniormost Indians in the Army, there being at the time very few above the rank of Captain. I was impressed by him and suggested that we should have a talk. One of the officers, a Lieutenant, was surprised and said: "And what have you got to talk to K. about?" Major Fletcher was also surprised and added: "He's only here for ten days, you know."

By the beginning of the war Kariappa commanded a battalion of the Rajputana Rifles and would have had British officers under him, while not long after Independence he was a full General and Commander-in-Chief of the Indian Army.

I had a very enjoyable tea with him and Mrs Kariappa at the Club and we talked on a whole range of subjects. Incidentally, he thought that the Dutch treated their colonial subjects better than we did. I could not comment but thought British people in India often gave offence without meaning to. When a young Indian Civilian came in with a girl, who looked to me fifteen or sixteen years of age, Mrs Kariappa said to her: "And how are the children?"

* * * * *

> "Away, away, from men and towns,
> To the wild wood and the downs –
> To the silent wilderness."

At the Duke of York's camp at Southwold, which I had attended, one of the public school boys was a lean and athletic Anglo-Indian called Harry Collett. He came back to the Nilgiris to work on a tea estate, but on his arrival found the vacancy closed. So he was hanging on, but did not care for India much except for the shooting, which he loved.

He was keen to bag a tiger and had sat in *machans*[8] for from five to nine hours, tense and motionless, which showed his patience and self-control. Once he said he heard a roar, not a very loud one and he thought it might be a panther but it turned out to be a cow.

One Sunday morning we went for a trek with food and beer in knapsacks. The people in the bazaar thought we were a peculiar kind of sahib in boots, stockings, sweater and knapsacks. After we had covered seven or eight miles, a storm hit us. Once lightning struck less than thirty yards away; the flash was brilliant and the crash simultaneous. The rain soaked all our clothes and knapsacks, we tried to light a fire to cook our sausages but it wouldn't burn, so we ate our food as best we could. It was fun.

We returned to Collett's house to dry clothes, tea and supper; the house was on the tea estate which his father managed. One week-end, which included a Hindu holiday, I obtained three days' leave and Harry and I trekked to a fishing-hut close to a well-stocked trout stream. It is called Hodgson's Hut. It was marvellous to get away from social etiquette and genteel society. We walked over the mountains and climbed the highest one, close on 9,000 feet high. There were no trees, only bushes and coarse grass and on the way we counted thirty-four head of *sambhar*, which is bigger than the red deer of Exmoor.

[8] Small platform hidden in a tree

6

Training in the Nilgiris

AS I became fit I was ordered to have practical training under the Superintendent of Police, who happened to be E.R. Ward Close, having just moved up from Vellore. There was very little crime in the Nilgiris, for with only one main road and the railway it was too risky for professional criminals. Excellent tea was grown in the tea gardens, mostly between 7,000 and 5,000 feet, with coffee lower down below the frost belt. But these gardens were very peaceful and there was no Armed Police, so no formal parades. I was told to report to the Town Inspector, a very smart and capable Brahmin, who, I thought later, was quite capable of managing a District. I began in his office and was intrigued to notice that he pushed all the OUT files and diaries off his desk and onto the floor, where his constable-clerk picked them up. This apparently was normal in the case of a high-caste Brahmin, so I took no notice. I then sat in the town police station to learn the routine. After two or three weeks of observing case-work, the Inspector sent me to the second-class or Sub-Magistrate's Court.

This was equivalent to a Bench court in England, except that it was presided over not by Justices of the Peace, but by a stipendiary magistrate. He could verify serious crimes and, if found to be *prima facie,* would commit them to a higher court. In the case of simple thefts, simple hurt and affrays he could sentence up to two months' imprisonment. Young I.C.S. officers could also sit as Sub-Magistrates and in this case it was such a young (Indian) I.C.S. officer. I listened for hours, but became so disgusted with the lack of order and discipline in the Court that I left.

One day when I had no afternoon work I attended a lunch party with the hostess, her daughter, a handsome young subaltern and myself. We began to talk on dogs, horses, shooting and parrots and continued through lunch to 3.50 p.m. without a change of subject. One young guest and I got dreadfully bored. I longed to leave, but it was raining hard and I had no raincoat. When I did get back to the Home my nerves were on edge. But the house I had been to was quite typical: many elderly British people lived quietly at Ooty, with servants, horses and dogs.

Until the early years of the nineteenth century no one ventured up into the Nilgiris. But, to the white men, they were irresistible and before long tea gardens were planted and established. Then aborigines were found living in small settlements – the Todas. I was curious to see them and got someone to take me to one of their villages. They have neat huts of basket work without a window and with a low entrance, which can be closed against wild animals. They were a good-looking lot, very clean, with lustrous, long wavy hair and beards; but as they were inbred they didn't have much energy. One old man played a pleasing melody on his flute. Their numbers, however, were declining despite Government protection. They keep herds of buffaloes and live on the milk and curds. Later, the Inspector told me that a certain journalist, Paul Brunton, was visiting the Toda villages with an interpreter in order to learn their folk-lore. He wrote down their conversations and then gave them money, which pleased them, so they prolonged the exercise and multiplied the reward by making up long yarns. We met him in 1940 in Trivandrum, he was a most interesting and travelled man.

In April 1937, the elections over, the Congress gained absolute majorities in six Provinces with majorities in two more. Madras was keen to take up office but the All-India Committee wanted the Governors to renounce their residuary powers. This they refused to do and were backed by the Secretary of State, the Marquess of Zetland. In Madras, the Congress felt they could not accept office, so the Governor invited a Liberal, Sir K.V. Reddy, to form a minority government.

Elsewhere, heavy fighting broke out in Waziristan on the North West Frontier with eleven officers killed. Twenty thousand railwaymen of the Bengal-Nagpur Railway and 200,000 jute and cotton-mill workers went on strike in Bengal, which showed the growing power of the Communist Party of India. But the Nilgiri Hills were above all this and no repercussions were noticeable.

By then, the permanent Inspector-General, Sir Charles Cunningham, had returned from leave. In the hot weather many heads of departments moved up to Ooty, among them the head of my department and I was bidden to call on him. This I did in full uniform – booted, spurred and armed with my sword.

Everyone knew that Sir Charles was a very distinguished officer but I had no idea what he looked like. So I called at the house, was admitted by a servant and waited in the hall. Soon, a short, elderly man came with large ears and dressed in a well-worn brown suit. I looked down at him, but didn't know who he was. So I waited. Then I was conscious of a pair of blue eyes boring into mine and realised who he was, clicked my spurs smartly together and saluted. He did not have much to say however.

I returned to the House to change. Captain P.N.R. Hallward was there and said, "How did you get on?" I appreciated his interest and was grateful, for after making friends with him I was able to get on with other officers. We had several long walks together.

One morning, to my great surprise, I heard a field gun firing slowly and was told that it was a salute of 21 guns in honour of the Maharajah of Mysore, who was arriving.

Another morning the Inspector sent for me early, as a human skeleton had been found not far away. He took careful measurements and was of the opinion, partly from the stick which was nearby, that it was the remains of a male Pathan. The flesh had been eaten but not by a tiger or panther. Pathan moneylenders travel all over the country and he may have been one.

Meanwhile I found a delightful friend, an elderly man, Professor E.E. Speight, who had taught for fifteen years in Japan and fourteen at the Osmania, a Muslim University in Hyderabad, after taking degrees at Oxford and London. His wife was a gracious hostess.

Such men carry much prestige with Indians. Another visitor at his house was a short and burly Padre, who talked mostly of Shikar.[9] To my surprise I was told that he was acting for the Bishop of Madras while he was on leave.

One evening when I called, his visitor was a most dignified Muslim gentleman, a scholar. He was tall and straight, with a white beard and spectacles. He had brought a cold *palau*[10] with him and also his hookah, which was black and inlaid with silver. He let me smoke it after dinner and it tasted delicious.

Dr Speight was also a collector and his main collection consisted of Japanese sword hilts, which were made regardless of labour. Even a plain iron one was made to look natural with tiny holes like pin pricks to give the appearance of weathering. Others were inlaid with copper, silver or gold.

After an excellent tea he led me on a walk through forest roads while talking on literary subjects, till I realised what a voracious reader he was. It was a great privilege to listen to such a cultured man and he indicated that he found me a ready pupil. But that is only part of the truth – I was immature, unconventional and opinionated.

My parents never failed to worship on Sunday morning and my early training wasn't altogether wasted. St Stephen's was the local church and I attended Evensong perhaps once a month. The Chaplain was a fine upstanding New Zealander who rejoiced in the name and title: Colonel the Revd. C.E. Wheeler, M.A. He put a good deal of power into his sermon. Afterwards he would join his friends at the Club bar. "How did you get on, Padre? Put the fear of God into them, I hope."

It was at Ooty that I attended a race-meeting for the first time. I entered the five-rupee enclosure and marvelled how the excitement of horse-racing brought together such a variety of people. The Governor was there with A.D.C.'s; there were Princes and Princesses of Hyderabad with their attendants; fashionably dressed Indian ladies in beautiful saris; British and Indian Civil Servants; North-Indian gentlemen looking very horsey; Brahmin priests naked above the waist and numerous clerks dressed in *dhoti* and jackets. As in Madras and Bombay, there were two classes of horses: English or Australian and the even more beautiful Arab stallions, mostly dapple-grey.

But it was not only at race meetings and expensive hotels that one was aware of Hyderabad. As the largest Princely State, dominating the Deccan plateau, it exercised much influence, mainly cultural, across its borders: the Central Provinces to the north, Bombay to the west, Madras to the south and east.

---

[9] Shooting
[10] Rice cooked with mutton and savoury meats

Four fifths of its population were Hindus; the government was firm, well-developed, but on the whole wise and the State enjoyed a greater stability than much of British India. The capital city, with a population of three quarters of a million, is well laid out and contains fine buildings, including the great Palace complex; beautiful mosques, Osmania University, libraries, Government offices, the workshops of the Nizam's State Railway; a great cotton market and a number of factories.

Hyderabad was the first independent State to accept British protection late in the 18th century and to ensure this a treaty provided for a garrison from the Indian Army to be stationed in the cantonment of Secunderabad, five miles outside the city.[11]

Descended from the Mogul Viceroy of the Deccan in 1713, His Exalted Highness the Nizam was the most powerful of all the Princes, ruling over fourteen and a half million people. By tradition every petition addressed to him had to be accompanied by a small gold coin or nugget, the *mohur*. These accumulated and the last Nizam was acknowledged to be the richest man in the world.

Osman Ali Pasha was a most unusual man, of middle height and spare of flesh, with a clipped moustache. As a practising Muslim of the Sunni sect, he invariably went to Friday prayers. He was a model of tolerance towards both Hindus and Christians. He smoked local cigarettes but did not drink. Probably the most striking thing about him was his total lack of vanity. The official uniform was the long-coat buttoned up to the collar. Courtiers and officials wore this, usually beautifully tailored, with tight trousers and fez, (the nobles wore a sort of mitre). But the Nizam never looked smart and sometimes quite shabby – in the Palace he liked to wear English carpet slippers for comfort.

He took little notice of the Viceroy and played no part in the Chamber of Princes, but he accepted British protection and, early in the war, paid for a complete squadron of Spitfires – the Hyderabad Squadron.

While his was the ultimate power in the State, he had very able men under him such as Sir Akbar Hydari, the Prime Minister; Sir Theodore Tasker, I.C.S., the Finance Minister; the Commander of the State Army and the Director-General of Police who were Englishmen from the Indian Services.

Though the Police were very well informed and no subversive organisation was working for a coup d'état, the Nizam, I was told, was not unprepared – he kept cars and lorries loaded with bullion, coinage and jewelry, just in case.

The Nizam had one great luxury – his harem – the largest in the declining years of the Raj. It housed up to eighty courtesans. The babies born had, of course, no royal status and births were not announced, but when a baby was born a special light was lit in the harem, which light was seen two or more times a month.

He also had one vice, which was kept secret for many years – he was an opium addict.

[11] Comprising 4 regiments of cavalry, 4 field batteries and 6 battalions of infantry.

As will be seen later, before Independence, the Nizam was faced with a crucial decision. Landlocked as the State was, should he join the Republic of India or keep aloof? In the event, he chose the latter course; he defied the might of the Indian Army and had to capitulate in a matter of days. The decision, for which the Nizam must be held responsible, proved a disaster and the great State, larger than the British Isles and Northern Ireland, was carved up like a carcass into three parts. Behind this lay the iron will of Sardar Patel in New Delhi.

But the Nizam lived on, comforted by opium and died at the ripe old age of eighty, which in a hot climate is a pretty good age.

★ ★ ★ ★ ★

If Government House, Ooty, was grander than any other hill residence except the Viceroy's House, Simla, it is partly due to the Willingdons. Soon after the Great War, Lady Willingdon arrived to inspect. It was no surprise that she had all the rooms redecorated in her favourite pastel shade – mauve – but afterwards she inspected the servants' quarters in the grounds. On completing her inspection she said: "These won't do. They must be pulled down and rebuilt." Which to my mind is much to her credit.

Another story comes from the Lawley Institute, a club for Indian gentlemen. Lady Willingdon was raising funds for Tuberculosis Hospitals. While attending a dinner given in her honour she stood up and said, "I have much pleasure in announcing a generous donation of Rs. 50,000 by the Rajah Saheb of Kollengode", who was sitting at the table. It was the first he had heard of it and he had no alternative but to comply.

In the 1930's Lady Willingdon, as Vicereine, was at Government House, Calcutta, during the Viceroy's annual visit. The House had been built by Marquis Wellesley early in the 19th century and the State Ballroom could accommodate 1,600 guests. All the gentlemen were in full dress, but Lady Willingdon spotted a young Indian officer in (khaki) service dress. She ordered the Military Secretary to ask for his explanation. The Military Secretary returned saying: "It is quite in order, Ma'am. he has just arrived back from Sandhurst and is attached temporarily to a British Regiment. As he has not yet got a regiment he has no full dress." But Lady Willingdon was not satisfied. Whereupon the Military Secretary said, "These are the King's Regulations, Ma'am." "In that case," her Ladyship replied, "They must be changed." And changed they were.

There were two high-days during my four months in those beautiful hills. The first was the Coronation of King George VI. Doubtless there was a parade at the Wellington Barracks some miles away but somehow I did not attend it. However, the officers at the Home were invited to a Ball at Government House.

After dressing in Mess kit, Hallward, a subaltern and I drove there in a taxi. I recognised the manager of the Imperial Bank, a Mr Rae and Mrs Rae and, thanks to them and their party, had several partners. About midnight, in accordance with tradition, Lord and Lady Erskine retired and the dancing continued with a little more verve till 2.30 a.m.; I much enjoyed the playing of the Governor's Band. This was the only time in my service that I received a formal invitation to a Government House and I remember it, as it marked a complete recovery from my illness.

The second event was the King's Birthday Parade at the Wellington Barracks, which was attended by most of the British community and by Indian officers and officials. A battalion of the King's Own Royal Regiment staged the ceremonial parade. But it was not impressive; the men looked beery and one or two of the officers seemed to be under the influence. It ended with what was supposed to be a *feu de joie,* but actually was lke a ragged volley. Later, I discovered that the discipline was bad on account of a weak Commanding Officer who was unable to control his officers. The C.O. became so distressed that he shot himself.

It was an interesting experience for me to be invited to a dance at the Sergeants' Mess. It was well conducted, the Sergeants and Sergeant-Majors looked very smart in their dark blue patrols. We began with beer at the bar, then joined the ladies in the ballroom. To me they were older women, that is in their thirties mostly, but were well turned out. A plump, dark-haired woman, who danced with me, knew from my badges I was a Probationer, newly out from home. She asked my name and invited me to call, giving me her name and the number of her quarters. But I did not take up her invitation.

Not far away is Lovedale School, one of the several Lawrence Memorial Schools founded and endowed last century for Army sons and daughters. Later it was opened to Anglo-Indian and other British children of Railway, Police, Posts & Telegraphs, Customs and similar officials, who wanted an education geared to English Examinations. The Lawrence Schools with their traditions of discipline, learning and sport fulfilled all the high hopes of their founders.

The Madras battalions, the King's Own and Wiltshires, rested by turns at Wellington and, largely on their account, there was a brewery. This was managed by an Englishman but the staff were all Tamils who, of course, were given beer. I found a visit to the brewery most interesting, as the Tamils were fatter and more placid than most of the Tamil plainsmen. Perhaps a German would say: "Man ist wass er trinkt."

So my stay in a superb hill-station was drawing to its close. I was back on full pay and could afford to live as did others of my junior rank. Sir Charles, the Inspector-General, seemed afraid I would enjoy myself too much. He scrutinized my weekly report and made comments; I got a bit tired of these comments and consulted Ward Close, the Superintendent of Police. I said: "I don't think he will be satisfied unless I show work from 7 a.m. to 11 p.m., six days a week. Wardie was sympathetic and showed me a better way of writing them. He then called for drinks and gave me a lesson on Persian rugs (which were being sold by North country traders).

One of my duties was to check the police guard over the District Treasury. It had to be done regularly and at different times up to 11 p.m. But Captain

Collett was most hospitable and always lent me his car when checking the guard after 10 p.m.

The Ooty Hunt was a prosperous one with a large pack. Many of the riders kept two hunters and some three. I did not want to miss seeing them and by getting up at 5 o'clock was able to go to the Meet and report at the Inspector's office at 9 o'clock. But the country round Ooty is open, resembling the Sussex Downs. As soon as the Master blew her horn they were away and those on foot had little chance of seeing them again.

The Ooty climate is perfect, except during the monsoon. I arrived weak and run-down and within three months was fully restored. It was a valuable experience staying in a house with Army officers, of whom I hitherto knew very little. Once I had made friends with Captain Hallward I was able to mix easily with others. Hallward was a loveable man. I should have liked to have kept up with him but in Service life it is impossible. The Indian guest I saw most of was a proud Sikh, Lieutenant Agya Singh. He loved talking about his home and about the Punjab. He was keen on exercise and would always join in our walks. I feel sure he later rose high in the Indian Army.

I also got to know a couple of I.C.S. officers in the Secretariat, one of them, E.W. Bouchier, a confirmed bachelor, befriended me for years and it was interesting to hear about the Interim Ministry of Madras. Evidently, the Ministers knew they were only a stop-gap and so left decisions to the professional Civil Servants – quite unlike the future Congress Ministers who loved exercising their powers to the full.

When the time came for me to leave, the Inspector, the Office Manager and two clerks saw me off. I had formed a very high opinion of the Brahmin Inspector and his integrity. He understood Europeans pretty well but couldn't understand how we could eat mushrooms - he thought it a disgusting habit!

So, from the little narrow-gauge carriage I admired the mountain scenery, the magnificent rugged heights covered with thick green, virgin jungle, so much thicker than on the plains. I was reminded of the Cheddar Gorge in Somerset, but this was on a much grander scale, and after Coonoor, there was hardly a house to be seen.

As we descended, the vegetation changed and the trees got bigger and bigger. Banana trees, tall clumps of bamboo and tree fern appeared, with monkeys and green parrots. Finally the gradient levelled out and the train stopped. Two railway constables met me and saluted: "Tea," they said, "is ready in the Refreshment Room." Doubtless the Ooty Inspector had sent word to them.

After an overnight journey I arrived at Katpadi station near Vellore. Again, Railway policemen met me and saluted. One helped the porter carry my luggage, engaged a taxi and drove me to the Police Mess. For the first time I felt I was someone of importance.

But there is always a snag to returning fom the hills to the plains in the hot weather. It felt so hot in the Mess that I lay awake into the early hours.

7

Return to College, Riding and Sport

BEFORE LEAVING for the hills I had left my motor-cycle at a garage for a thorough overhaul, but when I went to collect it I found it untouched and covered with dust. The mechanic had put it off and off and I was disgusted with him. But I did not yet know India, I should have written to the local Sub-Inspector a month before my return for him to remind the mechanic; in which case the job would have been done thoroughly.

Returning to parade felt quite different. Previously, I had not been fit and found a long parade tiring. Now I could take it in my stride. The second half of our outdoor training proved quite different – I was in the Riding School every day. The Riding Master had been an N.C.O. in the Madras Sappers and Miners, he was a Tamil and a fine horseman. We had one horse who was a good jumper – he could clear a five-foot fence comfortably when ridden by the Riding Master.

Most of us fell off. I fell only once, against the wall of the riding school. The Assistant Medical Officer was a thin old Brahmin, he wore a grey suit and a white turban, trimmed with gold. He knew Major Kelly and I were friends and as he bound up my arm he asked:

"Why does Major Kelly spend all his time on Government work?"

"I don't understand," I replied. "I suppose because he is a Government Doctor."

"He doesn't have a single private patient," continued the old Doctor.

"Some men don't make money in a gold mine!"

I only remember one nasty fall, it was by one of the best sub-inspectors riding a mettlesome horse who bolted and eventually threw his rider on hard ground. The young man was found unconscious, was taken to hospital and soon recovered. Some of the high-caste sub-inspectors hated riding.

Once a week the Riding Master took us out. He led fourteen of us in file and we would ride out seven or eight miles and then return. The village men loved the spectacle and would turn out with big smiles and little boys would clap their hands, for the district had been fought over during the French and Mysore Wars in the eighteenth century and before and had a military tradition.

In the evenings, when it was less hot, games were played in the Fort. I wasn't good enough to play cricket in the first two teams but did play at weekends at nearby Ranipet, where the players were chosen from Parry's factory and the Borstal School. One Saturday I actually managed to score 17 runs.

The other game played on the main sports ground, which was gravelled and rolled, was hockey, a game at which the Indians are outstanding. Mostly they play barefoot and are very fast. I could not keep up with the forwards and so played outside half or full back.

Polo unfortunately was no longer played in the South.

We were, however, taught tent-pegging. The Cavalry and Mounted Police usually use lances, but we used swords. The aim is to pick up a tent-peg stuck in the ground with a sword at full gallop. As the tent peg is less than three inches wide, it is not easy, especially as the horse, seeing the peg, is apt to swerve so as to avoid hitting it with his hoofs. The best tent-pegger I saw at Vellore was F. Sayers, the acting Inspector-General.

An optional sport was boxing. It was noticeable that the Christian sub-inspectors took to it much more than Hindus and Muslims, to whom it was foreign. I boxed the biggest sub-inspector who was Anglo- Indian and heavier, but he was too good for me.

During that hot weather, R.R.B. Truscott came back for a course. He took me to the old racquets court in the Fort where there was also a 16 lb shot and a pit. So we competed, he was very strong and had a better technique so he used to beat me. The court was near the horse- lines so I asked him, "How much do you know about horse-management?" He answered "Very little." For it was no longer in the curriculum. All officers kept a car and so a horse, though useful, was no longer essential.

I did not take to Roger Truscott when I arrived, but when I got to know him, found he had a kind heart which he concealed under a rather gruff manner. I missed him when he left.

It was from him that I learnt to call to the servants sitting on the back verandah" "Boy."[12] (commanding tone); "Sah." (a shout in reply); "Tiffin."[13] (short and sharp); "Very good, Sah". So the clear soup would be taken out of the hot cupboard (warmed by charcoal) poured into the plates and set on the dining-table in half a jiffy.

The ladies were always particular that the soup should be clear. One day a memsahib complained about the soup; "Thambi, do you strain the soup through a sieve?" "No, Memsahib, I strain it through a sock - one of Sahib's socks." When a look of horror crossed her face, he added, "Not a *clean* sock, Memsahib."

E.L. Cox, a Senior Assistant Superintendent, also came to the Mess to fetch his servant who had been lent to me for the duration of his long leave. He knew India well and he and Truscott talked about a number of men I didn't know. But this was not surprising, for Truscott's father was Chief Engineer, Public Works Department, Travancore State; Cox's father (A.R. Cox) had recently retired from the Board of Revenue in Madras, his grandfather also served in the I.C.S., his great-uncle in the Indian Police in Madras Province, while his great-grandfather retired as a Major in the East India Company's Army.

[12] From 'bhai' meaning younger brother
[13] Hindustani for lunch

Borrowing

It would take a bachelor a good three years to furnish his quarters, but in the East, this does not prevent him from doing his share of entertaining. His bearer had only to borrow from other bearers saucepans, crockery and cutlery. And in a village if a small landowner asked me to tea but did not have an English tea set, he had only to ask my bearer and I would arrive and find my tea things neatly set out on a table.

My next job, therefore, was to find a servant; there were several applicants but I didn't know how to pick a good one. Each of them had testimonials but one had to read between the lines and of course the best servants got jobs with more senior people.

One afternoon the Principal's driver brought a petition to the effect that his niece had been raped by Truscott's servant, Muthu, who ws about 21 years old and seemed a smart and well-behaved young man. Truscott doubted the charge and I was rather out of my depth. So we consulted Kasim, the experienced old Mess Butler. Kasim replied: "Muthu only a young boy" and turned away with a broad grin on his face. I don't know what action Truscott took, there seemed little doubt that intercourse had taken place and this with a 15-year-old, unmarried girl, was a very serious matter. But we thought Kasim's reply was priceless.

Punjabi wrestlers would tour the provinces and give exhibition bouts which were very popular. We heard of one to take place in the Fort, so Roger Truscott and I went to watch. An Indian gentleman and we were given chairs in the front. There were a number of Muslims present, including some slant-eyed ones from Indo-China and several rather blousy Anglo-Indian women. One of the wrestlers had terrific neck and shoulder muscles, however the lighter man eventually landed him on his back and was declared the winner. A strong man carried him on his shoulders and the victor was delighted with his win. He then knelt down and lightly touched the knees of the three sahibs – a mark of respect.

Though Vellore was a town of at least 60,000 there was no car dealer – few had cars in those days. My heavy Ariel motorbike was a very bad starter and needed two men to push it when in gear, so I decided to ride it to Madras, where I was to sit for exams. The machine gave me endless trouble and after taking it to the garage where I bought it, I arrived twenty minutes late for the first exam.

As the result of advice to take the machine to the Madras Flying Club for repair I got to know the Flying Instructor, a quiet man who was a clergyman's son and both looked and spoke like a clergyman. His name was Hugh Le B. Tyndale-Biscoe. We got on very well and I subsequently stayed with him and had flying lessons.

My host was H.D. Latham, who was Deputy Commissioner for Law and Order. He had a large American Oldsmobile which he had bought new. What a contrast with my pig of a motor-bike. He took me to see the film 'The Good Earth' featuring Paul Muni and Luise Rainer – it was one of the finest films I ever saw.

The journey back to Vellore of only ninety miles was a ghastly one. The roads were full of potholes, the dynamo became almost useless so that I was dazzled by headlights. I nearly rode over a bank and into a reservoir. Finally I crashed into a small bullock cart, the bullock's nose hitting my chest. A passing lorry driver then insisted on taking my machine and me on board. He was most obliging and I gave him a good tip.

The Principal was sympathetic and wrote to the Deputy Commissioner of Police, Traffic, to find me a second-hand car.

One day a short, trim officer turned up for a short stay at the Mess. He was an actiong Superintendent from a lonely district about a hundred miles away, his name O.L. Burrell. I mention him because he was a good professional officer with the added gift of getting on with Indians. He understood them and never seemed to upset them – his humour, tact and freedom from pomposity were, I am sure, the reason for his success. He stayed on after Independence till he was ready to retire – in 1960 – so he was probably the last British Imperial Officer in the whole country.

Though the Principal had some of the white man's vices - he was a heavy smoker and drank midday as well as evening – he attended Church now and again. He wanted me to come but I declined once, then attended on Remembrance Sunday, in uniform. Somehow I could not adjust to cantonment-type worship, but I did occasionally attend Evening Service at the Medical College. (At this time both the Principal and Mr Wright, the Superintendent of Police prophesied that in twenty years time I would be a churchwarden.)

It was a lovely chapel with thick stone walls, deep windows and a polished marble floor. While the staff sat on chairs at the back, the Christian students, all young women, sat on the floor in their snow-white saris, their jet black hair dressed with jasmine flowers. As the light failed they took tapers to light up their hymn books. It was beautiful but I, immature as I was, thought it rather pretty-pretty.

It was my great privilege to meet the Principal of the Medical College, Dr. Ida Scudder. This remarkable lady was old when I knew her with white hair, plump pink cheeks and gold-rimmed glasses. She looked a benign grandmother.

She had trained in America to be a doctor and gynaecologist with the express object of going to South India. Her church was the (American) Dutch Reformed. So some forty years before, she arrived and began to deliver babies with the help of an Indian midwife. She was attractive and received offers of marriage but refused them. Gradually she built up her maternity work. While on furlough in the States she would appeal widely for funds, and by the time I came to Vellore her ambition was fulfilled: a splendid Medical College of stone, built round quadrangles with gardens and fountains; a chapel, a hospital and several bungalows. She had no difficulty in meeting the Government's requirements and it was accepted as a degree college of Madras University.

I used to have the honour of partnering her at tennis and, a few years later, of holding her arm when she went up or down steps. She was succeeded by another Dr. Ida Scudder, her neice, almost as high- powered and charming.

8

Frustrating Months

"We cannot kindle when we will
The fire that in the heart resides
The spirit bloweth and is still
In mystery our soul abides."

I WAS twenty-one years old, had grown up with other boys, relations and friends and I found the solitude at the Mess trying. Every month two or three guests came to stay, but they were mostly much older and a man of over fifty seemed ancient. My good friends, the Kelly's, had left. I would go to Vellore Medical College where there were two young lady missionaries only a few years older.

I would call on Mr Taylor, the Bandmaster and sing songs and drink lime juice. I had tea more than once with Briggs, the second Sergeant-Major and Mrs Briggs. I liked to talk to the sub-inspectors, many of whom were of good family and educated, but I had no friend my own age – the nearest was Jack Leah, a young Lancashireman who worked for Parry and Company at Ranipet. This was a short journey, but I could not ride there on my machine without reporting to the Principal and asking for his permission, which was not a formality because Jack Leah was in trade – he managed the pottery. And when I invited him to the Vellore Club it was difficult as he might not be considered eligible. I mention this, partly to show that caste in India was not simple and an Englishman engaged in trade ranked well below an Indian officer or Civilian.

One morning, the Principal, dressed as usual in jodhpurs and carrying a riding-crop, with his pipe in his mouth, entered our class-room and said: "Plague has broken out in a village a few miles away." I blinked, surprised that there was still plague in the twentieth century. "Everyone must be injected." And so it turned out. The whole of Vellore, 60,000 people, grown-ups, children and babies, by a team of vaccinators. Next day we were given the day off. I felt a reaction but not much.

As it happened, that evening S. W. W. Wright, our Superintendent of Police, gave a dinner party. The Brahmin District Magistrate and the Forest Officer, a Bengali, were present with their wives. It was a jolly party, and we followed it with games. Finally, we played a kind of wrestling game on the floor (dressed as we were in dinner jackets). We managed to persuade the Bengali to join in, but the Magistrate declined. Such games were often played by officers on Mess nights, but were not really suitable for Indian gentlemen.

It was just a year after my arrival that a new Probationer turned up at the Mess. He was P.F.S. Murray, twenty years old and had not long left King's School, Canterbury. He had a quick brain, abundant energy and could run like a hare on the hockey and cricket fields. He was pleased with my welcome as someone in Madras had said to him: "What the hell made you decide to come out here?"

One evening I had to call for a signature on the Collector and District Magistrate – S.A. Venkataraman, a Brahmin educated in Madras and at Oxford. His English was perfect and he talked brilliantly. I said I was bored in Vellore. He wasn't surprised and said: "I pity you poor Europeans, staring at each other's faces." He was stimulating company but at the same time I felt a little unsettled and could now see that my Principal was an anachronism. About then I learned that he had sent an adverse report on me; it was returned to be read out to me. I could not accept it and he could not be specific. My respect for him dropped further.

The Happy Waterman

Working at the Mess was something like working at a big house in Britain – the servants formed a small community, were never overworked and were happy to be employed there. One of them impressed himself in my memory – the waterman, whose name was Thangavelu or some such name. He was short, about 5 ft 3 ins; dark, with a long face and pleasing Hindu features. There was a well in the compound, walled round, with a pulley, bucket and rope. It was Thangavelu's job to draw all the water needed at the Mess, he also watered the plants in the few flower beds and borders, a daily duty for nine or ten months in the year. He would draw the bucket up, fill two 4 gallon tins and carry them from a yoke. In the evening he heated water over a fire for baths. Making frequent trips carrying 80 lbs of water, he had a muscular body and his carriage was erect. But the remarkable thing about him was his happiness; he sang all the time as he drew the water and as he walked back to the well. His step was light and springy. He had a young wife and small child whom he adored, sometimes we saw each other and they gave me big smiles.

His pay (before the war) was Rupees 10/- the month, less than £1.00. He was provided with second-hand khaki shorts and white vests from the police stores, his white turban and his leisure clothes he bought himself. He was one of the happiest and healthiest men I have ever known.

In September the clear, brazen skies began to change, first came a haze, which lasted for weeks and I suffered from the common skin complaint called 'prickly heat'. Then clouds began to form. If in Europe it feels close before a thunderstorm, in South India it feels several times worse. For weeks one waited for rain, feeling only half alive. But when the monsoon broke – it broke. Over thirteen inches of warm rain fell in five days, with eight inches in twenty four hours. Everything changed. It felt much cooler and the frogs! They were delighted and could be heard in chorus even during a heavy downpour. All the nearby paddy fields were under water.

After several weeks of rain, the clouds cleared and water lay everywhere. The reservoirs were full and overflowing into stream beds, which in the hot weather were bone dry.

Then at last I heard that a car had been found for me by a Police Sergeant in Madras. So I went to Madras to meet him and to try the car which was his. It was a 1928 Hillman 14 tourer. Its maximum speed was just over 40 m.p.h., beyond that it soon overheated. Such was my first car. It could hold a lot of luggage and lasted a year.

When I drove proudly back to the Mess I found the new Deputy Inspector-General, whose seat was at Bellary. J. Beckett was a southern Irishman, a Protestant, as nearly all the Irish were in Indian Government service. And how different from a Catholic. He was very quiet and abstemious, patient, hardworking and methodical. A very worthy man but dull company for a youngster of twenty-one.

As Sir Charles Cunningham had retired, Mr Frederick Sayers succeeded him as Inspector-General. he too arrived at the Mess and for days I listened to their conversations.

The main object of the inspection was the Sub-Inspectors and Constables under training, for a third of the latter were trained at Vellore. The Sub-Inspectors were due to pass out and Mr Sayers addressed them. He knew three temptations to which they would all be subjected. He was very solemn and sincere, it was a sermon and the young men listened with perfect attention. I knew that a certain number would become corrupt, but they were a very good lot, who, I believed, wished to serve their country.

As the year progressed, strikes became more commonplace and there were anti-Government demonstrations. The Principal was dismayed and said to me: "No one wants us now. I give you another five years." But I thought him pessimistic. He did not seem to love his men, and one felt that he took more interest in the horses and horse-lines than in the sub-inspectors' Mess and living quarters.

At the end of the sub-inspectors' year and after their exams, they put on a concert. The Principal told me to sing a song and I chose the Toreador – it sounded jolly. I practised it hard but found the pitch just a tone too high. I invited some guests; when they had gone I felt like a drink and went to the fine big house of Lt Col Gill Singh, the Jail Superintendent. He gave me a drink and put on his gramophone. I must have been tired and he must have been liberal with the whisky, to which I was not accustomed. For I fell asleep and woke up in his house in the morning, he reported me to the principal for being drunk and I was duly put on a charge for this and for missing morning classes. Despite my loneliness it was the only time I drank too much; a stiff warning would have been appropriate. The papers were sent on to the Inspector-General, whose reply was very strongly worded, which hurt me badly.

In those days I did not know how to defend myself – I just took my punishment. Later, I learnt how to defend myself from sometimes hasty criticisms, and these consequently occurred infrequently.

During the monsoon in October, the week for our drill exams approached. I was in charge of a squad of twenty constable-recruits. The Principal said we officers were below standard and gave us extra drill in the evenings in place of games; three hours of drill a day were monotonous.

I would return to the Mess. Dining alone had little attraction and not infrequently I dined off scrambled eggs followed by dessert. I feel sure the Mess Butler found this very sad. Once when Mrs Furness, the Principal's wife, came to inspect the kitchen he must have told her, for she said to me: "You must eat properly."

But I found, if not a friend of my own age, a youngish man who was very friendly. Wright, the new Superintendent of Police, was a man in his mid thirties. I confided to him that I was not in the Principal's good books. He expressed surprise and said he had heard nothing against me.

One day he invited me to dinner. Afterwards he played his guitar and we had a sing-song. I was greatly cheered and wished he was the Principal.

One of the features of Indian Army training in peacetime was long flag marches. Every year Madras battalions marched to Bangalore and in the cold weather of 1937-38 it was the 9th Frontier Force Rifles in the van: fine upstanding North Indians, followed by the 5th Battalion, the King's Own Royal Regiment. The Indian battalion, which was able to pick and choose the recruits, were definitely the finer-looking men, but all admired the (British) barrel-chested R.S.M. marching proudly at the head of the column. Behind, was a column of mule transport carrying automatic weapons and equipment. They all paraded on the flat ground or *maidan* in front of the fort with thousands of interested spectators looking on.

Passing the marketplace one morning I saw a sad sight - a massive wild animal on display. It was a bull bison, nearly full-grown, i.e. sixteen hands, who must have strayed out of the Mysore jungle. He was tied with rope by the legs and horns to a rough cage. Curly white wool grew between his horns. He was beaten and knew it for his grey- blue eyes looked deeply sad. He was being fed but died after a few days.

The Sub-Inspectors' written exminations were naturally held at the College, but the officers were examined by the Public Service Commission in Madras. My host was (to me) an elderly gentleman of fifty-two or fifty-three, A.F. Bulkley, a bachelor. He was head of the Railway Police and C.I.D., one of the old school and still wore a monocle every day. He was a perfect host and even took me to the cinema, something he never did on his own.

I was not ready for my Telugu exam – Telugu was not spoken in Vellore – but sat for the other five subjects. In due course the results were announced – I passed the three Law subjects and Medical Jurisprudence, but failed dismally in Police Standing Orders. I did not know police work yet and found it hard to remember hundreds and hundreds of orders, but I received an adverse report for my failure.

But thanks to the help of Deputy Commissioner H.D. Latham, I managed to escape for Christmas and revelled in the freedom. Social life was easy, I saw Roger Truscott, my friends at the Boat Club and did some flying. Latham, who was a strict disciplinarian, did not think I had been well treated at Vellore.

It was a short break of five or six days, but it was amazing how refreshing such a holiday could be. Somewhat reluctantly I drove back, but comforted partly by Latham's sympathy, partly by the thought that in another six weeks I should be away, though where – I did not yet know. My luck was about to change – from bad to very good.

On New Year's Eve, the Jail Superintendent, Lt Col Gill Singh, gave a formal dinner party. He was a westernised Sikh who had shaved his beard, had an Edinburgh degree and a pleasant Scottish wife. Their official house was a large one and having served in Malabar they had beautiful rosewood furniture, including a dining table made from a single plank more than four feet six inches wide. The ladies, of course, were in elegant long dresses, the men in dinner-jackets. The polished rosewood table set off the English silver, the lights were shaded and their servants served, the white of their clothing contrasting with their broad waist-belts and turban ribbons of the Medical Service. By the time the port and madeira were passed round, the ladies having withdrawn, I felt relaxed and mellow. It was the first time I had this feeling.

During my last week at the Mess, the Inspector-General and Mrs Sayers were staying. He had upset me very much a couple of months before, but there was no rancour in him, he was perfectly friendly. A snipe shoot was arranged and I accompanied Mrs Sayers as I had not yet bought a gun. The snipe are found in paddy fields or beside reservoirs and are very difficult to hit – a real sport.

After tea one afternoon, Mr Sayers sent for the Police Tailor whose contract was due for renewal. Vittal Rao was a short, plump man of Maratha descent and less than forty years old. Dressed simply in a white dhoti and grey coat, he had a pleasant round face the colour of café-au-lait. He was a quiet man and salaamed, but not deeply as he arrived at the Mess.

Mr Sayers faced him smiling. Vittal Rao inclined his head a little to one side and smiled back, for they understood each other. No other tailor in the town could cut uniforms for officers, instructors and sub-inspectors as he could and no other workshop in town could finish more than 2,000 half-made-up sets of uniforms a year for the recruits. And had not Mr Sayers ordered a pair of jodhpurs from him on his last visit?

So Vittal Rao wasn't worried and after Mr Sayers' smile came his reply: "It's alright you old rascal, your contract is renewed."

It may seem ironic that the half-made uniforms and much of the constables' equipment, such as belts and footwear, was made in Central Jails by longer-term convicts, but as the system had been going on for many years it was accepted by all concerned. Only the City Police had other arrangements, such as uniform cloth woven in Binny's Mills in Madras.

February 14th, 1938, St Valentine's Day, was my red-letter day – the day of my release. My posting was for six months' practical training and language study in the District of East Godaveri, in the heart of Telugu country. My officer would be J.F.B. Kaye, a name which, years later, I found was a famous one in British-Indian history.

9

Happy Release: to Cocanada, E. Godaveri

MY SERVANT and I loaded up my old Hillman tourer for a 400 mile journey and soon we were climbing up the Eastern Ghats.[14] The car was fully loaded, which stopped all the rattles, but climbing uphill, got heated and needed careful handling. The granite hills were clothed with green jungle, in the sky great piles of cumulus floated majestically. When the radiator was near to boiling we stopped by a pool in the shade of a tree, where, with the bonnet open, it soon cooled down. I washed and changed into cool clothes while a cart-load of villagers stared at the unusual sight of a European sitting on the ground – just like an Indian!

My servant cranked the car (for the starter didn't work) and we drove on. Before long and near a village a man vigorously waved a piece of white cloth. I took no notice; then the road was blocked by a tree- trunk. A man spoke; "Must not go on. This is cholera village." "Cholera?" I exclaimed. "Yes, cholera. Must not pass; go that way round, Yes, sah." Soon a crowd of forty men and youths surrounded the car. One boy jumped onto the running board, others placed their elbows on the gunwales. My servant looked apprehensive – he didn't like these chaps from the cholera village.

Soon they were cleared and the sentinel pointed the way: "That way round. Very good way, Sah – to Gudur." I waved and engaged the clutch. I do not remember much more of the journey except the long causeway across the Kistna River which was very low.

Thoughtfully, John Kaye, the Superintendent of Police, arranged for me to spend my first week at the Bank House, for he could be called out at any time and didn't want me to be alone. Mr Buckley, manager of the Imperial Bank was still in his thirties, his wife at least seven years younger. They were very English, that is little influenced by Anglo-Indian manners. he was a quiet man, she more lively and very warm hearted. She was so kind and it seemed so long since a woman had made a fuss of me that I felt very touched and went to bed feeling just a little in love with her.

After breakfast I had a thrill: two smart Reserve constables clicked heels and saluted. They were my first orderlies – one was a driver, the other would do anything required of him except cook.

Reporting to John Kaye I found him a straight, upright man of about forty-five with a clipped moustache. He was an ex-Infantry Captain from the Great War and still spoke like a soldier, straight from the shoulder. I was very pleased to find that he was not excitable – a relief after the Principal at Vellore. He had

[14] A range of hills or mountains.

been wounded in the foot and had a slight limp but it in no way impaired his activity.

He carefully explained my list of duties, took me to the stable to show me his horse and then drove me to the Office. A cooly woman crossed in front of the car and panicked. It was a near miss and he shouted to her in fluent Telugu. He was married but his wife did not like the Indian climate and spent most of the time in England.

That afternoon a plump young Brahmin called at Bank House. He had been engaged to teach me the language. Evidently he hadn't been in a large house before for he gazed around in wonderment.

That evening at the Club I met the Forest officer and his wife, Mr and Mrs Cornwell. They had young, healthy-looking children with them, who were a sight for sore eyes, for there were no such happy children at Vellore.

After a few very happy days I left the Buckley's and moved into Cocanada Club, which had three or four bedrooms, a larger club than Vellore.

The Telugu people and language

India has many languages and for administrative convenience the Mogul power devised a *lingua franca* called Hindustani. This has two forms – Urdu written in Arabic script, and Hindi written in Nagari script, but they are variations of the same language, which is understood over most of India.

The natural boundary between North and South is the Vindhya mountains with the deep valley of the Narbada river, just as the natural boundary to the North-West is the mighty Indus River. Further south, Hindustani is not generally spoken and there are four 'Dravidian' languages.

Tamil is spoken at Madras and Southwards
Telugu from north of Madras as far as Orissa and also inland towards Hyderabad
Kanarese is spoken in Mysore and a few districts, of which Bellary is one
Malayalam is the language of Malabar

But these four languages of the South have become differentiated, so that a Tamil cannot follow Telugu and vice versa. The *lingua franca* is English, though the popular Indian film industry has spread the use of Hindi southwards, just as Hollywood has spread English.

The Telugus speak a melodious language full of vowels and well suited for singing; it also contains a number of Sanskrit words. The script is flowing and I found it easier to learn than Arabic writing.

The people are mostly a rich brown colour, but appreciably bigger than most of the Tamils.

For the next six months John Kaye arranged for me to do all the duties from Constable to Inspector, which was the training laid down. So I drilled in the ranks, did twenty-four hours' guard duty at the Treasury; served summons, directed the traffic and escorted prisoners. In the Office were some thirty-five clerks, head clerks and accountants. I spent one day in each seat, finishing as Manager for a day, while the Sergeant-Major had me for some days to learn the routine of the Stores.

One morning, I arrived on parade shortly after Mr Kaye. I marched up and saluted, he returned my salute but said nothing. Halfway through the parade was a break for a smoke and he said to me, "Why were you late?" I replied: "My car was slow to start and I was held up for two or three minutes at the level crossing." "Very well," he said, "but don't be late again." He then took out his cigarette case, offered me a cigarette and asked me how I was getting on in my other duties. He knew how to handle a young man and my respect for him increased.

One of the sergeants, a Londoner, was quite a character; smart, quick-witted and a disciplinarian. He was a bachelor and I was told he could drink a bottle of whisky in a night and parade at six-thirty in the morning, smart and alert. Unlike most British sergeants and inspectors in the Police he planned to return to England on his retirement. "And I keep in touch," he said, "with my M.P."

The Godaveri delta was one of the areas where opium-eating was endemic and he knew which of the Reserve policemen took opium; I myself could not spot them. With opium being a Government monopoly, registered addicts could buy one small square of the dark brown substance each day from the licensed shop and it cost only two annas (twopence). Normally it was taken in the evening and set him, or her, up for the next day.

My most interesting camp was with John Kaye, who drove some fifty five miles into the Agency tracts.

The Godaveri Agency

The Indians living in these jungle or Agency tracts are quite distinct from the plainsmen. They are aboriginals, have no written language and no schooling. They are simple and have not yet learnt how to tell a lie. They practice little cultivation and during the hot season do some hunting and a lot of steady drinking. Crime is almost nil but we saw a whole wooded hillside burning one night – doubtless set on fire by revellers. It would not be possible to collect Excise duty on their liquor, so the Government wisely exempted them.

It was not difficult to understand how in previous decades some officers loved the Agency. It is beautiful country, full of hills, virgin forest and streams. Nature rules and the aborigines are part of her. We visited a couple of small villages and the men were friendly and smiling, well primed with liquor. They showed us their bows, arrows and spears. Accustomed to the shade of the jungle they blinked in the strong sunlight. Further down, coolies – men and women – were building a forest road; but they had to be imported from miles away as Agency men do not like to labour. There were plenty of tales about the Agency tracts, some funny, some not. I will quote one which concerns a distinguished officer, Khan Bahadur Amu Sahib, who won the King's Police Medal in the Moplah Rebellion. He himself was a Moplah of Malabar.

The monsoon had been heavy in part of the Agency and the ballast from a mile or two of railway line had been washed away. Hundreds of coolies were needed to repair the line. The District Magistrate, the Superintendent of Police and Railway officers went to the area to recruit labour. The standard rate was, say, 8 annas a day; but the assembled crowd of men disdained 8 annas. So the Railway Superintendent telegraphed to the General Manager, who sanctioned 10 annas per day. This offer too was rejected out of hand. The Englishmen pleaded but the men said it was not the season for work, so the officers reported their failure to Madras and Calcutta. The Inspector-General of Police proposed trying Khan Bahadur Amu Sahib, which was agreed. He was sent for urgently and arrived within twenty four hours.

First, he went to a liquor contractor and bought his whole stock of arrack, which was in earthenware jugs, then he proceeded to the area with the liquor and ordered a tom-tom to summon all available men. They arrived and were perfectly willing to talk. Amu Sahib then spoke (in Telugu): "As you all know God has caused much heavy rain to fall in these parts, so that the steam trains to Calcutta and Madras have had to stop. The Government is very worried. Even the Great White Chief in England is disturbed that no trains run between Calcutta and Madras. I know that you are all gentlemen and it is not your custom to work during this season, but there is something I wish to show you." He then led the crowd to his big pile of jars, opened one and said: "As you see this is arrack, taste it and see if it is good arrack." So the elders tasted it and said: "Sahib, it is good arrack." "Well," said Amu Sahib, "if you would like to repair the Railway, this arrack is all yours."

The men went to work with a will and before long the trains were running and the Bengal-Nagpur Railway had much pleasure in paying for the arrack, which came to much less than the wages of 250 men.

Another situation which developed deep in the Telugu country, inhabited by simple people – a political agitator had persuaded the men of quite a few villages not to pay their taxes. It was something like a bitter strike in the United Kingdom where the Government has lost the initiative. 'Amu Sahib' was therefore sent for to see what he could do. He went to the main village with a lorry-load of Reserve Police armed with *lathis*. Having concealed them in a grove of trees, he ordered a tom-tom to summon all the leaders. When they arrived they were addressed as follows:-

"I am Amu Sahib, a Moplah from Malabar. I have no connection with this district or with this dispute but the Circar[15] has sent me to see if I can bring the dispute to an end. My message is this – if you agree to call off your no-tax campaign, I will let you off with light punishment."

He then left them to talk it over. After some time their spokesman returned and made a speech, the upshot of which was: "We agree to your terms." So Amu Sahib thanked and dismissed them and as they began to leave the village, he signalled to the policemen, who emerged from cover, brandishing their *lathis* and gave the village leaders a severe beating.

"If that," they said ruefully, "is what he means by a light punishment, we must take great care not to provoke him."

During my stay in Cocanada I got to know an Anglo-Indian family – two ladies of a certain age and a young woman of my age. They were hospitable, but after tea the ladies left the house, leaving the girl to entertain me at the piano while I sang, or to take a walk along the beach. She made no overtures but I soon realised that the ladies were trying to marry us off. I had no plans for marriage and so decided to keep away.

The fact that Mrs Kaye was in England meant that I got no training in housekeeping. And when I left the Club to reside in travellers' bungalows I picked up a germ which troubled me for several years.

I engaged a young cook, who seemed a pleasant young man, but after some weeks I was warned by Mrs Buckley, the Club Secretary's wife, that he had V.D. This was my first experience of such a disease, I accosted him in his kitchen and saw that he had a rash on both arms. Whether or not it was true, I took fright and dismissed him. The proper course was to have sent him to the hospital for a report.

At this time, after having two or three butlers in succession one of whom drank, I engaged Yelliah, a clean, smart-looking Telugu Christian. He had been a servant to Europeans since he was eight. He had spent six months in London and had lived in Rangoon. We became firm friends and I kept him for ten years, but after my marriage my wife was not satisfied with him; he had been a bachelor's bearer for too long, I found him a job, but he didn't seem to get on with memsahibs. I lost his address and bitterly regretted not having given him a small pension. He could speak four languages after a fashion and didn't mind whether he was in South or North India. He was a teetotaller and never permitted a quarrel among servants.

He only made one special request in those ten years. After I had shot a large crocodile and the coolies found the remains of two women in its stomach (one had glass bangles, one had solid gold ones), he asked if he could have the gold ones for his wife, a discreet woman who remained in her village. He was a good servant and of course I agreed.

During the peace and quiet of a Sunday afternoon, I was woken from my doze by shouts from the back of the travellers' bungalow. So I got up to see what it was all about. The ground between the house and the kitchen quarters was overgrown with weeds about a foot high and the servants were running about shouting and brandishing sticks. Then I saw a movement in the vegetation and the men cracked down with their sticks. I soon found a piece of firewood and joined the chase. It was a large snake, which we soon managed to kill – a ten foot python. The skin had good markings and was sent to Madras. Years later it was turned into a pair of shoes, a jewel box and a roomy handbag for my wife.

It was near the sea and, while walking one evening along the firm sandy beach, I saw the carcass of a village dog which I had shot has he raided my larder. In the tropics the first predators on a dead animal are not the insects but the vultures. They seem to know when an animal dies and circle round, high up, waiting. Then they descend and walk or hop clumsily towards the carcass. But on this occasion they were opposed by a bitch who ran up barking and chased the ugly birds away. Again and again they descended but each time the bitch returned and drove them away. Eventually, the horrid birds retired. It was a touching exhibition of canine loyalty.

10

Regatta in Calcutta and end of Practical Training

WITH LEAVE granted by Mr Kaye, I left for Madras to train for the All-India Regatta. There was no need to book at an hotel as a rowing couple had kindly offered to put me up. A few days later, a local regatta was held on the Adyar river. It looks a fair-sized river, but actually is shallow for fast rowing. It was a jolly, good-humoured regatta, much beer was drunk and a couple of chaps got thrown into the river. For the serious Regatta, we trained before breakfast and again in the cool of the evening. The rest of the day passed slowly: we were not allowed to smoke or to drink beer before lunch.

I left a day before the others for reasons of duty and joined them at a station about half-way to Calcutta. It was a boring journey by second class and at every stop in the day-time we got out, hopped, skipped and jumped on the platform to exercise our muscles, much to the amusement of the Indians. Punjabis might not have approved, but southern Indians are less formal and laugh more easily.

The City of the Goddess Kali

The eight days in Calcutta from 10 April were a memorable experience. Two members of the Calcutta Rowing Club put me up in their comfortable flat. Both were businessmen and had rowed for their College at Cambridge, one being the captain.

The 'chummery' had rooms for four but, at the time, there were only two besides myself and we were very well looked after by smart Punjabi bearers in flowing turbans. At tea time each had his own tray though we had it together, while at 5.45 a.m. a bearer not only brought each of us a tray, as we slept on the verandah under a fan, but also a copy of the Statesman newspaper. At home the Englishman likes to have his breakfast behind his newspaper, but in the tropics we liked to read it with our morning tea.

It was both hot and very humid, the sun shining through a haze. Even before breakfast we perspired freely after a hard three-mile row. Then a big breakfast, a swim at the Saturday Club before lunch with a glass of beer. The evenings were very warm: all the crews, British and Indian, practised hard and watched each other, Calcutta Rowing Club being the favourites, their stroke was a 'Leander' and another had won the Wyfolds.

The afternoon temperature was 105 degrees, so we did our sightseeing after breakfast. Chowringee is a wide and imposing street, served by double-decker buses. The banking and insurance centre is Clive Street. All the principal streets, which run straight for many miles with traffic lights, were kept clean, being swept and watered first thing in the morning. The population was very mixed and the traffic moved fast; all the buses, taxis, cars and trams being driven by Sikhs and North Indians while Gurkha ex-soldiers guarded every office and factory. Most of the policemen and the servant class were from Bihar and the United Provinces. The city, with its tall buildings and commerce reminded me very much of London, but the harbour, situated 120 miles up the Hugli River, is much smaller than Bombay harbour. The principal park is Eden Gardens near Fort William which is like Hyde Park without the Serpentine. St Paul's Cathedral (smaller than its namesake in London) is a splendid Gothic building beautifully sited by a lake. It was the seat of the Metropolitan or Archbishop.

The visitor cannot fail to be impressed by the sheer size of Fort William (named after King William III). It was built on the flat Maidan, or open space, which gave a clear field of fire. In effect it is a town enclosed by massive ramparts and was rebuilt from 1757 after the Battle of Plassey. It could comfortably hold the entire European population of Calcutta: 12,000 to 15,000 people. It also shows that in the early period of the Indian Empire, the British did not feel secure and liked to live behind strong walls.

As I photographed part of the ramparts and a watch tower, a loud voice shouted "Hey!" and a smart British Police Inspector doubled up saying "What the hell do you mean by taking photos?" he formally arrested and took me before the Fort Magistrate (the Adjutant) who tried and discharged me. I then introduced myself to the Inspector, who apologised, took me on an interesting tour of the Fort and finally posed for his photograph.

One evening we went to the Metro Cinema in Chowringee, a big air-conditioned one, grander and cooler than any in Madras and also attended by many more elegant Indian ladies than one would see down south.

There was a number of entries for the Regatta and the heats began on the Thursday evening. To my disappointment (I was stroke) the Madras Four was beaten by a length by Calcutta Lake Club, an Indian club. When the times were taken it was found that both crews had broken the record for the course and the Bengalis deserved their win.

The Lake Club won the final (the Willingdon Trophy) after a thrilling race, beating Rangoon University by only three feet. I also stroked the Coxless Pairs and we managed to win the Venables Bowl, beating Rangoon University by two lengths.

The Rowing Association Committee generously gave a dinner party at an hotel for the competitors, some sixty in number and their coaches. Afterwards many of us went to an air-conditioned cabaret, drank more beer and made a lot of noise to encourage, as we thought, the band and the artistes.

When the cabaret finally closed we went into a side street and rugger-scrummed until we were tired. Later that morning I noticed that after our exertions my silk shirt and light-weight dinner jacket were wet through.

This behaviour was quite normal when fit young bachelors got together on a gala night, but after the searing heat of perhaps four hot weathers, rich young blood thinned down.

* * * * *

I was almost half-way through practical training and was put in charge of a small police station, Samalkot, staying at the rest house of the Experimental Farm for three weeks. The daytime temperature reached a moist 103 degrees and as the bungalow had no electricity, youths from a Criminal tribe were engaged to pull the punkah[16] until dawn.

There was a very interesting land dispute; I went to it several times with an armed guard to keep the factions apart for they carried long sticks. The Magistrate with jurisdiction over the area and with whom I worked headed his letters with his full name and title: 'Khan Sahib Sayed Mahomed Azmatullah Khan Sahib Bahadur B.A.', and signed it clearly with his name right across the page. He was a dignified man who did not hurry.

I also investigated the murder of a girl of twelve, who, after the murder, was buried. We discovered the facts and I obtained an exhumation order from the Magistrate. The girl had been dead for about three days and I never felt so sorry for anyone as I did for her father, who squatted a few yards away while she was being exhumed. The Eastern peasant has a tremendous capacity for suffering in silence.

As it happened, in three of my earliest murder cases I felt sympathy with the accused. In the first one a working woman, after the loss of her husband, took to receiving men in her one-room cottage at night. Her sixteen-year old son loved his mother and couldn't bear it. One night he took a big knife and plunged it into his mother's bosom after which he gave himself up. The second was the common murder of an attractive young woman by her jealous husband after she had taken a lover. In the third a small, inoffensive man murdered his wife who had nagged and bullied him for many years.

None of these would repeat the crime and so would be sentenced to imprisonment.

I had been taking Telugu lessons daily. My teacher tried hard usually after I had been on parade for an hour and a half and after a good breakfast. I wasn't good at the language, he must have found me a disappointing pupil, but I tried.

In due course I went to Madras, sat for Lower Standard Telugu, and a Telugu I.C.S. Officer passed me. Social life followed and outings at the Madras Boat Club. Calling on the Inspector-General, he informed me of my posting as Assistant Superintendent of Police, Hospet, in the Bellary District which pleased me greatly. To celebrate I bought a second-had 12-bore gun and case.

Back at Samalkot I worked under the same conditions as an Indian and performed his duties, but in the evenings I was usually free and attended the

[16] a mat attached to a plank which is pulled to and fro – the punkah – puller sitting outside.

tiny Samalkot Club. It had a membership of four Scotsmen with their wives and an Anglo-Indian bachelor. There was also a small golf course. All five men were employed by Parry and Co. of Madras. True, whisky was unrationed and cost 12/6d a bottle, nevertheless, I think it would have been hard to find four English wives who would put up with such a restricted existence, for there was nothing else there and hardly a shop worth the name.

On my first Government holiday I went shooting for the first time. My 'bag' consisted of nine pigeons, a paddy bird or crane and a wounded partridge. John Kaye was much amused, but he had little leisure for organised shooting – whenever there was some game he just walked out in the evening, carrying a loaded gun.

My next post was as Circle Inspector on a Zamindari, or estate, owned by the Rajah of Pithapur. He was a pleasant man of about forty with the big moustaches sported by members of the warrior caste. He had a Dewan or Estate Manager who looked neither very reliable nor very trustworthy. In short a rogue.

For the King's Birthday, with the help of my Reserve Police Orderlies, I organised a parade, teaching the local policemen to march, counter-march and to fire a feu-de-joie. I was booted and spurred and gave the Dewan a sword-salute; he wasn't expecting a sword brandished so close to him – he flinched but was, I think, quite pleased.

My first inspection of a police station was hilarious. I did not know how to begin or how to carry on. I quite forgot to prepare a scheme in advance. Somehow I got through it and when it was over I wanted to shoot.

The Rajah Saheb had generously allowed me to shoot anywhere on his estate and a relation of his took me in hand. We went after deer. One night we found a small herd of fallow deer in a grove of trees. I could not see their heads, only brown spotted bodies. I picked one out and brought it down. To my horror it was a doe, possibly in the family way. I felt so guilty that I never attempted to shoot another fallow deer.

We sat up several times for panther and I managed to bag one. He was a young male five feet ten inches in length. I sent the skin to Madras for chrome tanning and mentioned the fact in my weekly report to the Inspector-General who seemed pleased. Evidently I was shaping up all right, for bachelors were expected to hunt for game, not women.

I cannot speak too highly of the system by which we performed, over six months, every duty which our subordinates had to execute. We had drilled in the ranks with sub-inspector cadets; we had drilled squads of recruits and so we knew our men and had done their work. A few of us British officers may have been overbearing, arrogant and therefore disliked, but there must have been real respect and affection for many others, for there was never any difficulty in recruiting and there were high-caste men in all ranks, even in the constabulary. Many of the sub-inspectors were graduates, while in times of political tension or war, the Government could depend on the provincial police. There were mutinies in the Army during the war, notably in the Burmah campaign; there was a serious mutiny in the Royal Indian Navy, but there was no Police mutiny until the very end and this occurred in Bihar, the most nationalistic of all the Provinces.

Some British officers preferred Muslims, some preferred Hindus, but when it came to a decision we were impartial, which was greatly appreciated by the Indians. Nor was there any instance of corruption. If any British official had accepted a bribe, woe betide him! None of his fellows would have spoken to him or to his wife and we knew it. Such isolation would have been terrible and I doubt if any man could have borne it.

District Administration – a Brief Description

The Indian district is not administered like the counties of Great Britain. The administration is simple and effective.

The head of the district is the Collector and District Magistrate (or, in northern India, Deputy Commissioner). He is in charge of the revenue and keeps records of every field and crop, road, path and well. [17] He is responsible for the district treasury, is chief magistrate and keeps in touch with all other departments.

His right-hand man is the Superintendent of Police, but one difference from Britain is that Magistrates and Police Officers are jointly responsible for law and order. So though the Superintendent has a sizeable force of men – at the end of the last war maybe 1500 – he has not the sole responsibility for keeping order and I believe it to be an excellent system.

The district courts consist of the Civil Court and the Sessions Court, the latter is presided over by the Sessions Judge who tries both civil and criminal cases and also hears appeals. Other criminal cases – chiefly offences against the person or property – are heard in the lower courts: a first-class court in charge of an I.C.S. or Provincial officer and a second-class court with a Stipendiary Magistrate, who also verifies important criminal cases before committing them to a higher court.

As the district is the size of a county or bigger, it is divided up into parts, as inherited from the Mogul Empire. Each part is called a taluq and the Revenue officer in charge is the Tahsildar.

Police divisions correspond and the Tahsildar's opposite number is the Inspector of Police. These are respected men, so the lesser towns contain the Tahsildar, a sub-jail and treasury and an Inspector of Police, whose office is adjacent in the police station. The Inspector has several other police stations in his charge.

The Sub-Collector headed a part of the District, a Sub-Division. The Assistant Superintendent was his colleague and 'opposite number'.

Men of the All-India services are not only better paid but carry more respect

[17] Every field, large or small is mapped and given a survey number.

than Provincial officers though they perform the same duties, perhaps they perform them better?

Other officials include the District Medical Officer; the Executive Engineer and maybe also a District Forest Officer. The remaining departments were under Provincial control.

Obviously the District Medical Officer (drawn from the Indian Medical Service); the Executive Engineer who is in charge of irrigation, roads and buildings and the Forest Officer are very important officials for terrible things can happen if health, irrigation or forests are neglected. Epidemics may spread, dams may burst and cause enormous floods or forests may be destroyed by goats, diseases or by fire.

Here I pay a humble tribute to the staff of the Government Offices in District headquarters. Office hours are from ten to five but the clerks rise early, wash, say their prayers, dress, then eat their morning meal at about nine, which the womenfolk have been busy preparing. They get straight down to work; now and again they drink sodawater, tea or coffee but there is no formal break or lunch hour. There is very little chat or gossip and they get through an enormous amount of work. Their pay is low for the first twenty years and their houses, by British standards, are small and airless. After Independence their rewards are even less, especially in the higher grades.

Large sums are needed to provide and maintain a district police force of 1,000 to 1,500 men. I was never keen on accounting and auditing but never had any trouble. This I attribute to the excellent system and to the efficiency of the accountants and clerks.

On the rare occasions that a clerk falsified an account and embezzled, a discrepancy would later be discovered and the Officer would have to make good the missing sum.

★ ★ ★ ★ ★

For a short rest I decided to visit Vizagapatum, where the Superintendent of Police and Mrs Martin had asked me to stay. They were an unusual couple. A.C. Martin was one of the old school and had married late; he was a trencherman and ate a full breakfast every day. Halfway through the morning he had a large cup of coffee with milk. For lunch he always had curry and rice and ate a normal dinner of several courses in the evening. He was only of middle height, but weighed (at the time) sixteen stone ten pounds and was a delightful companion. As an Assistant Superintendent he had spent years in the Agency, it was lonely but he loved it; for company in the evenings he would invite the Inspector – there was no-one else – while on other nights, with the help of night glasses, he watched the stars and knew a number of them by name.

His wife was considerably younger, weighed seven and a half stone and ate like a bird. There were no children and the marriage did not last, which was a severe blow to him. While staying with them I exchanged my old Hillman for a sturdy American car, a 23 HP Dodge.

The Club at Vizagapatum had seventy members and was the biggest for many, many miles. One thing that amused me was that the bar stocked seven or eight brands of whisky, for in the smaller clubs there was but one brand.

Two years later, when conditions had changed, there was some scandal in the bar. On Saturday night the usual consumption of Club whisky was eight bottles (not counting small amounts of other brands). The steward had got to like whisky and conceived the idea of pouring seven bottles into a pail and adding one bottle of arrack (or country spirits). He mixed them well, poured the liquor into eight bottles and so had a bottle to himself. No one noticed for weeks till a Scot with a delicate palate became suspicious of the flavour and persuaded the Club Secretary to investigate and so the deception was found out.

My six months' stay in a most interesting district ended with the annual District Sports. It was similar to Police Week at Vellore but on a humbler scale. There was running, jumping, relay races, a hockey match, revolver shooting, tug-of-war, games for spectators and at the end fancy dress and buffoonery, such as impersonating the Superintendent. So, for the prize-giving everyone was in high good humour. The Deputy Inspector-General presided, Dewan Bahadur Ramanuja Iyengar – 'Dewan Bahadur' being a title that ranked just below Knight Bachelor. I had met him at Vellore. He was short, plump and very fair-skinned. He was full of humour, Brahmin culture and self-assurance. He seemed genuinely fond of me. At 54 he had not yet learnt to swim and decided it was time he did, so we gave him lessons in the Club swimming pool, he retaining the sacred thread which Brahmins and the warrior caste must always wear from the age of seven.

By then my trials at Vellore were forgotten.

11

Assistant Superintendent

MY FIRST posting to an independent charge was a wise one – not to a large town with plenty of social life, dances, picnics and shooting parties – but to a small station in a good dry climate, with very little social life and quite good shooting. It was about 350 miles away.

The Government allowed a week to travel to a new posting, for one motored along macadam roads often badly worn. One crossed rivers, maybe over a causeway, maybe a bridge. In August 1938 I was not an experienced traveller and it was impossible to find out the road conditions fifty miles ahead.

The road I took led me to the Kistna river, which was then a mighty stream about two miles across. As it happened, the small ferry was waiting, an old one twenty-two or twenty-four feet long. In the stern was a platform big enough to take an American car, but only just. So I drove up two stout planks and the car was secured. There was no motor – the boat was propelled by a paddle-wheel on each side; four coolies to each. The coolies looked undernourished.

I was told there was a road on the far bank which was too far away to be visible, so we set off. After some time the men tired. Already the current had carried us nearly half a mile downstream and when the men stopped, we just drifted further. I was alarmed and ordered them to resume, which they did. We crossed slowly and eventually landed safely about two miles below our starting point. So we unloaded the car, the bank was rough but we managed to reach the road again without losing the silencer.

Car insurance was optional and most of us didn't bother; but I didn't risk my car on an old one-car ferry again.

That evening we arrived at a much smaller river without a ferry and though it was getting late I turned back to find another route, but my waterman thought I was being unduly cautious; he thought the powerful American car could plough through the river like a tank.

It was the last day of August when I arrived at Bellary, the district town. Formerly a cantonment of the Madras Army, it looked spacious and rather empty, or, put another way, not teeming with people like most Indian towns.

We found the Police Bungalow in the cantonment area and A.J. King, who was to be my superior, smilingly welcomed me. He was of medium height, sturdily built. He had fought with distinction in the trenches as an infantry officer and was a bachelor. He had not been wounded, but the terrible artillery bombardments had probably slightly affected him. For who could fight in that war and survive unscathed?

Before breakfast I sent my car to be serviced and in the afternoon was anxious to drive to Hospet, which was close on forty miles and on higher ground.

The country was unfamiliar, dry and brown with rocky hills a few hundred feet high. It did not look attractive before the monsoon, with no standing crops, but Hospet town made a good impression. The population was small, only 30,000, but it was clean and cared for; there were no mangy stray dogs or deformed beggars.

Mr Krishnamurthy, the Deputy Superintendent, was still in the official house, so we drove to the Rest House. Further, my small stock of furniture, pots and pans had not yet arrived. While the servants unpacked, I sat outside and heard little but the gentle cooing of doves. I knew no one in my subdivision of about 1200 square miles and there was no other European. I felt lonely, not elated at my first charge.

Next morning I drove to the official house which faced west, was off the road and set in a field. It was basically a small house of two downstairs rooms and two bedrooms upstairs, with bathrooms attached and verandahs on three sides. Behind was the butler's pantry, the kitchen and servants' quarters.

Beyond was a mountain, nearly 3,000 ft. high; while looking the other way one could see the valley of the Tungabhadra River and on the far side, the Nizam's Dominions, usually known as Hyderabad State. At the time, the river was unbridged and contained crocodiles. When villagers wished to cross to visit relations they used leather coracles, just like the old Celtic coracles.

As I took charge, met my Camp Clerk and signed the transfer papers, Krishnamurthy told me of a dangerous gang which had been active till the year before. It consisted of a leader and two associates, one being an expert with locks, the other a fast runner. They were responsible for nearly a hundred burglaries, a few robberies and some rapes committed by the leader of the gang. They terrorised a considerable area and were a sore trial to the police who were not able to charge them in a single case.

Eventually, a trap was set (not one taught in the Police College). An attractive young prostitute was chosen, given a sum of money and a bottle of drugged liquor. Her task was to entice the leader (the womaniser) and give him a tumbler of the liquor. This she did; the police arrested him while in a drugged sleep, paid the woman a further sum and soon rounded up his two associates. On their arrest, they were given a severe beating. Had I been the officer, they probably would not have done so, or at least not so severely, as I would certainly not have turned a blind eye to it.

The only charge which could be pressed was one under the Criminal Tribes Act, as they were registered members and obliged to report their movements.

I duly interviewed Rama, the leader of the gang in jail. He was short, dark, wiry and about fifty years old. he denied all knowledge of the long list of burglaries and insisted that he was loyal to the British Government. The gang was not active during the two years I was in the subdivision partly, no doubt, because of the 'lesson' they had been taught. Rama married a new wife, a girl of twelve. He could afford the expense!

My first month was very quiet. There was no serious crime; the Inspectors and Sub-Inspectors came one by one to meet me – they were a good lot. I began to take anti-malaria tablets which brought on some depression. The office work was completed by lunch time. After tea I walked my dog then had a whisky and soda, bath and dinner alone. For twenty-four days I didn't see a European. After dinner I would sit in the living room and there was no sound except, now and then, the clanking of the big wheels of the bullock carts on the nearby road. I had a kitten but it was too quiet. After a month I had an idea, going to the Hospet Bazaar I bought a good double-spring H.M.V. gramophone and the dealer got me records. The gramophone became a real friend and lasted many years.

For a week I toured my subdivision to get the hang of it and once while driving through a forest area I heard the cries of two or three peafowl. I had heard that a peacock is difficult to bring down, so, with the gun loaded with No 4 shot I crept towards the cries, looking intently at the foliage for the large bird, but could see no sign of one. Then, when my back was turned, with a flurry of wings he was off. This happened four or five times showing what a crafty bird he is and how adept at camouflaging himself in a tree.

Returning to Hospet I found a message from Mr King calling me in to Bellary. I thought how considerate he was and that night was too excited to get much sleep.

My first call was on Deputy Inspector-General J.S. Wilkes. It was a privilege to meet him, for he was a perfect gentleman, wearing what was then fashionable among senior officers: an eye-glass. If all British officers had had such perfect manners, Imperial rule might have continued for much longer. When I said Hospet was very quiet, he replied: "The Agency[18] tracts in which I served as a bachelor were a lot quieter." And he was right.

After my call I attended the Sessions Court. In the evening we went to the Mess of the Madras and Southern Maharatta Railway Regiment, which was on manoeuvres. The Commanding Officer was interested in my work as an 'up-country' official. Next evening we were invited to Retreat followed by drinks in the Mess.

Bellary was the most important of the four districts ceded early in the 19th century by Hyderabad State in lieu of payment for military protection. It was built round two rocky fortified hills on which grew some rather attractive thorny trees. A soldier once described it as "Two 'eaps of road metal and an 'orspital", but he maligned it. Years before an important meeting took place there.

In 1876 a severe famine hit Bombay Presidency and then spread to Madras, Hyderabad and Mysore. Bombay had a very able Governor, Sir Philip Wodehouse, who was making a good job of famine relief, for it was the first major famine since India had been administered by the Crown, (1858). But the Governor of Madras, the Duke of Buckingham, was out of his depth and his relief measures were costing a great deal of money. So the Viceroy, Lord Lytton, convened a meeting with the two Governors and their advisers. Lord

[18] A jungle.

Lytton, a man of great ability and charm persuaded the Madras Governor to adopt the Bombay pattern of relief works, instead of merely feeding the destitute.

From this, under Lord Lytton's guidance, an Indian Famine Code was drawn up which is still in force, but I never saw it in operation.[19] It was administered in drought-stricken Chittoor district the year after we left in 1948 and presumably in inland areas as well.

Not long after my return to Hospet, two murders were reported. The first was on the borders of Sandur State, a very small Maratha State within Bellary district and containing valuable manganese ore. The murder seemed to me a foul one: a clear case of a man murdering his wife to make room for his mistress. The accused was duly convicted by the Sessions Judge, E.E. Mack, I.C.S., but an appeal was expected to the Madras High Court.

As soon as I had verified the Inspector's investigation I sent off my report and began my second murder case. This involved a girl of twelve or thirteen who was being betrothed. A third murder was infanticide. The three crimes in a row unsettled me, I could not take my mind off them. I drank more whisky but slept badly. But I soon got used to grave crime and lost little sleep on its account.

Before Christmas I worked hard at inspection of police stations, as they had to be inspected every year. There was also the annual mobilization of the Reserve Police; this was important: to keep the men in training, especially in a law-abiding district like Bellary, where Armed Police were not often needed. Another aspect of my routine was the daily Telugu lesson. As a schoolboy I learnt to speak French and German but Telugu seemed much harder and the script, of course, was an added difficulty.

Touring was part regular routine and part variety. One is spared all the labour of packing. The Assistant usually camps for ten or more days at a time. He chooses which areas and stations he will inspect and there are usually convenient rest houses. The Camp Clerk makes out a tour programme and the local officers reserve the bungalows.

The cook packs aluminium cooking vessels into a wooden box. Another holds crockery, glasses and cutlery. Stores, whisky and beer fill another. A portable food safe is also taken. Oil lamps are necessary. The bearer (or butler) packs uniform, clothing and toilet requisites. He does not forget anything and, to be on the safe side, packs more clothing than is needed. he also takes a comfortable camp bed and mosquito net, for the beds in the rest house are probably hard as nails. An orderly packs the office records, typewriter and stationery under the camp clerk's supervision.

Early next morning an old 24 seater bus arrives and all the luggage is stowed on its roof. I take the car, with bearer, orderly and perhaps the cook. The camp clerk, another orderly and the waterman travel in the bus. We drive off and, after a couple of hours, camp is reached. A constable awaits us and we arrive at

---

[19] In time of war a district is placed on a war footing. In this case it is placed on famine footing and one man has complete control – the District Magistrate.

the bungalow. Perhaps half an hour later the bus arrives in a cloud of dust and stops by the bungalow, which is likely to be beside a grove of mango trees. Everyone knows what he has to do and sets to work with a will. Soon, the officer will be relaxing after his drive on a long chair on the front verandah or under a tree with a cool drink.

Camp life is simple: there is no fan because there is no electricity, no telephone and no fridge. If it is hot the watchman or a menial pulls the punkah. After allowing a decent interval, the Inspector calls. He is a calm, well-fed looking man wearing a smart red and gold turban, a buttoned-up khaki tunic and shorts, a well-polished Sam Browne belt, stockings and brown shoes.

He may be accompanied by the Sub-Inspector who looks less prosperous and has no Sam Browne belt. [20] A local dignitary or head-man may make up the third. The Inspector and I chat in English and I try to get an idea of the locality. Well do I remember my very first inspection at Tuni, when I was acting as Inspector. The men paraded before breakfast and I inspected their equipment, tested their drill and catechized them. After breakfast, the three-day inspection proper commenced.

But I had no idea how, so I called for the sub-inspector's service book. It showed that he had been recruited as a sub-inspector several months before I was born and there was I, a Probationer, trying to tell him how to run his station. The man was grave and dignified and did not bat an eyelid; what breeding he possessed! So I looked up all the headings of earlier inspections and managed to write a report, which, typed out by the clerk, looked just presentable. I would have liked to have read it ten years later by which time I had inspected more than a hundred stations.

Sometimes, one did not leave for camp after an early breakfast but in the afternoon, one would then arrive in the dark. The orderlies would immediately light a couple of Petromax pressure lamps, which give off an excellent light. In half an hour everything would be unpacked and arranged. The waterman would be heating a 4-gallon tin of water for the bath-tub; cook would be preparing a meal, the bearer would be laying out the camp bed, a white cloth or the dressing table, then the dinner table, while the officer relaxes with a bottle of beer or a whisky-soda if it was in the 'cold' weather.

The five or six servants and orderlies are all working for the officer's comfort. They give no thought to themselves until he has bathed and dined and all is put away. Only then do they think of their own needs. So, they turn in later than he but, promptly at 6 o'clock next morning, *choti hazari:* a neat tray of tea and perhaps a banana is placed at his bedside.

And if anything was needed in the night one had only to call and an orderly would wake and stand by saying, "Sah?"

Sometimes, especially if he is keen on wild life, a forest bungalow, set in the jungle, is chosen, miles away from a village. One can take pleasant walks with the dog along dirt roads or tracks and, having obtained a Forest licence, carry a gun and hope to see a hare, a chinkara (gazelle) or a jungle cock. Forest bungalows are usually small with one living room only.

[20] After Independence, the wearing of the Sam Browne was extended to Sub-Inspectors.

The nearby village is small, there is less faction and crime in Forest areas and inspection of the Police Station would take only two days. The hot weather would be chosen for these camps as the temperatures in the jungle are some degrees lower than the open plains.

Yet another type of camp would be more remote, with no Rest House. The Officer would then need a hill tent with single pole, a bathroom (or necessary) tent and two more tents for the camp office and the servants. These tents, being stored at District Headquarters, had to be sent in advance with a tent-orderly to erect and later dismantle them.

Camping in a grove of trees in the dry, clean air of the Indian plateau was one of the valued privileges of the British Officer. But there was no social life. So one invited a local official, the Inspector perhaps, who would talk of old times and of men long since retired. In the evening an orderly brought letters, files from the District office, a newspaper and a flask of ice. In those peaceful surroundings the cities and towns seemed remote, another world and not till the third year of the war did I have a portable wireless-set to tune in to the B.B.C.

After a day's work, bath and dinner, one was not quite alone, for behind was the quiet talk of the servants eating their rice or enjoying a smoke; a book on the lap, a dog at one's feet. Outside, the darkness, the shrill sounds of crickets and night birds. In the dry months came intermittent and almost human cries of the jackals. Why are the jackals so sad, as though mourning a loved one?

God made the jackals sad and the frogs to chuckle in the monsoon.

When inspecting a police station the whole object is to study the records and statements and then try to see behind them. Are the figures reasonably accurate, or are crimes and affrays being suppressed? Does the station-house officer serve the community or is he making money on the quiet? Has he the confidence of the people or is everyone mortally afraid of him? I once heard of a Muslim officer, promoted from the ranks, who not only always carried a loaded revolver, but was prepared to use it. I was shown the exact spot where he once shot a Gypsy boy who had the temerity to laugh at him. Once he fired at a newly arrived Police Sergeant but the Sergeant, being ex-Army, ducked just in time: he did not realise that there were purdah women in the room.

One thing was very clear; on the Sub-Inspector rested a heavy burden of responsibility. Three superiors were always sitting over him and constantly supervising his daily work.

After eighty years of organised policing in the Presidency there was no doubt that the incidence of property crime in the villages was light and that serious crime and unprovoked murder were confined to certain areas. For example, car doors could not be locked and my Dodge car had no ignition key. No one ever tampered with it. Cars were few and never stolen.

Touring was not, however, always gracious and efficiently organised. It was not the duty of the Assistant to register and investigate a crime, but when it took the form of a murder, robbery or rioting, he was informed immediately and he re-investigated, till satisfied that all possible steps had been taken; he then sent in a report to the Superintendent.

In these cases, the officer had to sleep where he could and I have spent the night in village school-rooms and have slept quite well in police lock-ups. Sometimes I was shown a small house, the family having moved out, for it would not be proper for women and children to share the house with a foreigner and a bachelor. Nor was it necessary for the Inspector to put pressure on the owner of the house – he moved out with good grace – such is Eastern hospitality.

In England one would send a thank you letter, but in India the host would take no payment and get no thank you letter. At the most, he would be in the Inspector's good books.

Only once were we stuck in a village without luggage. It was evening and several miles from a bus route when my car sighed to a halt for want of petrol. After only ten minutes' walk we reached a small village which was poor even by the standards of the Deccan, so there wasn't a drop of petrol to be had.

A peasant offered me his one-room hut, which was clean and airy. Soon, the village headman produced a string-cot and a wooden arm- chair. The villagers lived on millet cakes which have no taste, with dry chillis and onions. This I couldn't manage so my host offered me the yield of his cow in a pan – about a quart, which I gratefully accepted. Fortunately, the season was dry and not yet hot, there were no mosquitoes and I had a good night.

Next morning Orderly Hirelal produced half a gallon of paraffin which he funelled into the tank and after some loud misfires with black smoke, the engine started. They would not accept payment – it was the true hospitality of the very poor.

This gives an idea of the camping routine, but the heaps of office files, each fastened with pink tape, had to be read. Some were for information only; and there were many pages, carbon copies of investigation reports, each one numbered and docketed. From time to time there was a departmental enquiry into alleged misconduct by a subordinate. In the Army three or four officers sit for a court martial but in the Indian Police a junior officer sits alone, comes to a finding and sends the file to the Superintendent for orders, and if the procedure is found to be faulty, the latter returns it for a fresh enquiry. Under British justice the guilty may well escape, but the innocent man is very rarely punished. The system of appeals ensures this.

One of the junior Officer's routine duties was the supervision of shops selling muzzle-loading guns (for crop protection), powder, shot and fireworks. Most of them sold only fireworks, made on the premises. But there was little demand – one young man who had less than ten sales a month said he was only carrying on out of respect for his father, who had opened the shop. Another man probably put his finger on it when he said that business was bad because of the (British) Act fixing the minimum age for marriage at fifteen. What he mant was that many of the brides were under-age so fathers had to dispense with the fireworks. Perhaps I should add that in the East marriages take place at home and always after dark.

India is particularly rich in insect life. In the hottest weather the insects are asleep and the officer sweats in peace, but for much of the year the mosquitoes, the tiny eye-flies and house flies keep him company. Ants generally prefer the bathroom. So part of his office equipment is a couple of fly swats and a 'flit gun' to make a fine spray of paraffin with D.D.T. For few there can be who can concentrate their minds in a hot room or tent in the company of these trying little creatures.

> "All things bright and beautiful
> All creatures great and small .....
> ..... The Lord God made them all."

But it may be doubted whether Mrs Alexander would have written these lines had she experienced the 'stink poochie', this is a tiny beetle, like the ladybird, which sometimes alights on the wrist or forearm and leaves a horrid, putrid smell. The smell is not cured by soap and water and disappears several hours later. Fortunately, this poochie is not a common one.

The Assistant could get by on three or four hours' office work, but in the big Madras districts the Superintendent would spend an hour before breakfast: 9 a.m. to 1 p.m. and 3 p.m. to 5.30 p.m., often in the heat, bending over his files and however hard he worked, it was never finished. Some returned to their bungalow office after dinner, but I felt that too much work resulted in a weary, dried-up bureaucrat.

Bellary soon lost its attraction. My host, A.J. King, was most hospitable but was quiet and reserved and used to eating alone. But I had Christmas to look forward to: I had made friends with two Englishmen managing the Manganese mines of Sandur – a very clever chemist, Mr C.S. Fawcitt and a young engineer called Thomas Entwhistle. The mines, at an altitude of some 2,500 ft, were delightful at Christmas time. There were just the three of us – we ate well, drank well, played the radiogram, talked about everything under the sun and went for long walks through the jungle. Once, when I was alone with my terrier he was charged by a wild boar. I grasped the branch of a tree in case the boar went for me too, but when he caught sight of me he stopped short, glared and then trotted off. My dog got away.

One evening, returning after dark by car through the jungle - a fine panther stood in the headlights. It was the first jungle panther I had seen. This one was heavily built and darker than the common or village panther, which when full-grown weighs only ninety or so pounds. But there was no question of a shot for the shooting in the forest was the Rajah's prerogative.

Paradoxically, it is the sportsmen who look after the game best. They preserve the cover, leave them alone in the close i.e. breeding season and control the shooting.

Soon afterwards, in the New Year of 1939 – I stayed with the Deputy Inspector-General and Mrs Wilkes and really enjoyed my visit, for Wilkes was a well-read man and his conversation was always stimulating.

The New Year's Eve party was a big one and hilarious, given by the Conservator of Forests whose name was Clear. I drove back in the early hours. It was the best party I attended during my two-year stay in the District.

Returning to Hospet, a letter awaited me from my elder brother, Louis. He was nine years older and a brother I had always looked up to. After Cambridge he joined the firm of Reckitt and Company (later Reckitt and Coleman) and in 1938 was sent to manage their firm in Calcutta. I was very pleased to hear from him and he gave me the excellent advice to mix with Indians and so learn their point of view.

Well, I had one coming to me every day – my *munshi* or teacher of Telugu. He was Head Clerk at the Imperial Bank of India, a very nice man who duly got me through the Telugu Higher Standard. And I got to know a charming lawyer, a Brahmin who was also President of the nearby Congress Committee. I took a lot of notice of the petitions and representations he delivered as he always set out his case clearly and accurately. For some of the petitions were so exaggerated or even false that one could not act on them. I also attended when in Headquarters, the Indian Club, where we played tennis and the retired men – draughts. So, I got to know men such as the town health officer and engineers, the Government Sanitary Inspector, the Veterinary Officer, Inspector of Co-operative societies, bank officials and insurance agents. In those days all their wives stayed at home, such clubs were for men only.

These men knew their job and did it conscientiously. Not one of them was dissolute or corrupt and one could not help respecting them.

At one of the Hindu festivals evey workman or craftsman offers *puja* to his tools. Hirelal obliged by offering *puja* to my car. First he washed it, then placed a garland of flowers on the radiator and sprinkled it and the headlamps with red powder. Finally he repeated the prescribed *mantras* or prayers. When I saw it I smiled, but should have shown more respect for he was doing his duty as a Hindu.

The next day evening my legs were stiff from riding and so I watched the sun set over the Tungabhadra river. Caressed by a light wind the water purling, like silk. As the sun sank the big hills turned to pink and then to crimson; the wind dropped and the water became smooth and black till the landscape darkened under the still luminous sky.

Watching sunsets in the comfort of the verandah is one of the great pleasures of a hot country. But India is not a paradise. In the morning, I woke up with a very sore throat after drinking boiled river water.

My Officer, Mr King, was so painstaking and thorough that I grew impatient when, after sending him punishment rolls for his orders, they were not returned for three weeks. So I decided to make more use of my limited authority, especially the power to award punishment drill.

The delinquent constable had to report at midday when the sun was blazing down and I would take it myself. Carrying a rolled blanket, musket, fixed bayonet and ammunition he had to drill at the double, for part of the time holding the musket and bayonet over his head. After about twenty minutes without a pause he was usually pouring with sweat and close to exhaustion and I would stop. So punishment was swift, discipline was kept and the constable lost no pay. As soon as Mr King was succeeded by Mr Jakeman I cut down on the practice as Jakeman was prompt in all his office work.

My next trip to Bellary exposed my snobbery. I had been invited to stay by a young couple who were considered not quite 'pukka' both by British and Indians and I wondered whether to accept; but what decided me was their young English nursemaid who was plump and winsome. We slept in adjacent rooms with no locks on the half-doors. It would have been so easy to visit her but she gave me not the slightest hint or wink.

But I enjoyed my host's company – he had the catholic, open mind which always attracts me.

On 19 February I was in my office, reading and noting on files. Suddenly the date caught my eye – it was my 23rd birthday. I didn't celebrate it, but the news that I had passed the last but one of my exams - Telugu Higher and my confirmation as Assistant Superintendent, with an increment in salary – made me a happy and contented young man.

Being out on a limb of the Madras Presidency there were few travellers and usually I was alone, but twice I met couples who had elected to retire to a hill station and had a passion for shooting. One of them a family of three, the Rowes, had left the Nilgiri hills in their motor-caravan with two servants: they moved from one shooting ground or river to another. He had been an Army contractor; he had handled a rifle and gun all his life and was such an outstanding shot that he would only shoot a buck with his rifle as it leapt and bounded along. They and their two servants lived on a diet of river fish, wild duck, venison, wild boar, with snipe for the savoury course. They fed like a Maharajah.

Former Maratha chiefs in the Deccan had their own way of hunting blackbuck, by means of the *cheetah* or hunting leopard. First a *cheetah* had to be trapped, then tamed. To tame him a relay of drummers would watch him in his cage and start drumming as soon as he closed his eyes. After some six weeks without sleep the leopard was sufficiently tamed. With his head covered by a hood, he was led towards the herd of buck; as soon as the hood was lifted he streaked off, overtook the buck and broke its neck with one blow of his paw. Thus the buckskin was obtained without a mark on it. The sporting painter, Stubbs, depicts one in his famous picture: 'A cheetah, a stag and Indian attendants'.

12

War Clouds Gather in Europe
January 1939

BEFORE LONG I was summoned to Madras for my language exam. When my father visited Madras earlier in the century he would stay for up to ten days, but times had changed; my trips lasted about three days, making five with the journey.

At Guntakal Junction on the main line, there were two English girls waiting, one of them very pretty. They were the first young English girls I had seen for over a year – I hoped they were going to Madras, but as it happened they were on their way to Bombay, much to my disappointment.

It was quite a change having dinner in the restaurant car. A British couple, he with a heavy moustache, were very stiff in their behaviour – I found they had come from Africa. I made friends with an American banker who gave me all his Evian water to drink during the journey – a most generous gesture.

Whenever we junior officers were called to Madras we did not have to book at a club or hotel. One of the Police officers put us up. My host on this occasion was H.D. Latham, who was Deputy Commissioner, Law and Order. He had attended a rival school to mine – Sherborne – and I had stayed with him once before. He was a strong officer, a bachelor with high standards and was not particularly convivial.

During my stay I met a charming young lady, Miss Joy Westerdale, who had visited me in hospital. She was the daughter of a Superintending Engineer – of the same service as my father. Joy was a jolly girl and we got on very well. Her mother approved of me and did a little pushing which was, I think, unwise.

One night Latham, my host, took me to the Race Club Ball but I was not used to a large company of people and did not enjoy it.

After rowing on the Adyar river I left for Bellary by the night train and was quite happy to be returning. Little did one realise then that a tremendous war was less than nine months away.

After clearing accumulated office work, I went to 'camp' again, to a small town. The medical officer was a young and well-educated Muslim of good family. He was very good company but tried to put the case for Pakistan – a scheme of which we British officials were not at all in favour.

Other evenings I spent in the company of the Sub-Inspector, Srinivasan, a young Brahmin. He was a very intelligent graduate of Madras Christian College whose subject was English literature. I grew very fond of him but it was a mistake. His inspector, also a Brahmin, was less educated, became jealous and took it out on the young man.

Festival duty is the lot of all district officers and both Hindus and Muslims hold popular festivals or gatherings that attract huge crowds. In a big city or in the Ganges valley crowds can number hundreds of thousands but in the Deccan they are smaller.

The festival held at Mylar in the Bellary district is a good example: the central event is a prophecy. The prophet was a small man, old and lean from fasting. Big crowds, some 80,000 people, gathered. Plenty of liquor was available, also drugs. Prostitutes both male and female mingled in the crowds, while young men slapping tom-toms and blowing pipes stimulated the crowds to a pitch of excitement.

Government officials were there in force: eighty-five policemen; Revenue and Health officials who told them what they could do and what they couldn't. Areas for washing clothes, bathing and latrines were all designated.

The prophet was held in tremendous respect. Surrounded by young men devotees and wearing a large padded turban, he climbed up 'Shiva's bow' some 15 ft high, shouted a one-sentence prophecy and fell backwards on his padded turban. He was shaken but unhurt.

A ring of policemen armed with *lathis*[21] had to keep the devotees from mobbing him. They were hit on shins, wrists and shoulders pretty hard but were indifferent to the pain. Two or three young men then came to me and offered to wound themselves with hooks but I said the Government didn't allow it.

What was the prophecy? The year was 1939 and the prophet foresaw trouble but worded it, like the Delphic oracle, in general terms. He couldn't later be proved wrong for there is always trouble somewhere in that huge country.

If the police had not been in control, some sort of fight would certainly have broken out, but I am sure the villagers wished the Government would not interfere.

The annual festival at Kuruvathi which I attended for a couple of days attracts an enormous number of fine cattle, (mostly the Nellore breed, big and white with upstanding horns) estimated to number 25,000. In the dry weather of March the dust was something terrible. The central act was a piece of mesmerism: a young girl, fair and well-built was laid flat on a table and raised some four feet in the air. There was no doubt about it.

It is essential that the Government's writ applies everywhere, even to remote villages and hamlets not served by a road, otherwise they would become a haven for criminals. So the Revenue and Police must visit every village and hamlet even if it entails a two-hour walk each way.

Equally there must be co-operation on both sides of a border, if not criminals escape across the border as was formerly so common in Ireland. My opposite numbers were at Dharwar in Bombay Province and in the States of Mysore, Hyderabad and the little State of Sandur.

[21] Solid bamboo sticks

So, with my bearer and an orderly, we drove westwards to Dharwar, where I met the Superintendent, P.M. Stewart, a tall, quiet-spoken Scot and the young I.C.S. Sub-Collector, an Irishman called W.M. Gallagher, curly-haired and very good-looking.

He lent me his horse, a fine chestnut, and I had a good cross-country ride. On my return he said I hadn't had enough, so he sent me out again. Then we went for a walk, followed by dinner and sing-song.

13

Rowing Holiday

ONCE AGAIN the All-India Regatta came round and I was given leave for training in Madras followed by the journey to Poona, heart of the Maratha country and the future state of Maharashtra.

When the overnight train to Madras came to a halt at 6 a.m. I was half awake, so I stepped out onto the platform in pyjamas and dressing-gown. No one took any notice except a kindly Anglo-Indian railwayman who enquired anxiously: "Have you anywhere to go?"

A taxi took me the few miles inland to the garden suburb of Adyar where I arrived at 6.30. My host, B.S. Lawrence, received me in a silk dressing gown, he was expecting me and drove straight to a popular beach called Cathedral Beach, but instead of the usual crowd of bathers there were only a few men, so I said: "What has happened to everyone?" "Last week," he replied, "there was a big shark off the beach which killed two Indians." We had a good swim and saw no shark. (I was not afraid of sharks till, one day, north of Madras, I saw a big one, ten or more feet long, swimming less than twenty five yards from the water's edge.)

Three or four days later I noticed a marked change on the beach after our swim and asked my host: "Last week there was only a handful of chaps here, now there must be at least three hundred people. What has happened?" He replied: "It's because the new Governor (the Hon. Sir Arthur Hope) has arrived with his family, they find April in Madras oppressive so their two grown daughters are taken to the beach by an A.D.C. for a swim." Early morning bathing was popular again!

After tea, we began serious training on the Adyar River. We had dinner at the Connemara Hotel, I revelling in the air-conditioning. At the next table was a party of wealthy Indians and three Europeans – all drinking champagne and dancing.

One of the dancers was conspicuous: she was tall and wore a black dress; long reddish hair brushed her shoulders. Her dress was revealing but what was most remarkable was her brown skin which was darker than that of the Indian ladies present. Apparently she was Swiss and sunbathed every afternoon in her panties at the Gymkhana Club.

In the mornings I went shopping and made calls. We were not allowed beer for lunch or more than two cigarettes a day.

So, we took the train for Poona. After a night in the train we found ourselves on the Deccan plateau and I saw famine for the first time. The monsoon had failed and instead of cotton and millet crops there was bare earth and the cotton plants were dying from lack of moisture. In the villages the men were sitting about with nothing to do and little to talk about, women and children were not in evidence. The cattle looked gaunt but were being kept alive till the next monsoon, thanks to famine relief.

Poona is a flat and very large cantonment area with a river. We were put up at the Royal Bombay Sappers Mess. The Corps was not yet motorised and still had its mule transport. The Sappers had enough to do in peace-time for while many others snoozed in the warm afternoons, they were all busy in the workshops. For dinner, they wore smart white patrols and were clearly professional soldiers with little or no private income.

I made friends with a subaltern at the Boat Club who took me round Poona. It seemed a dull station, compared to the big cities of Calcutta, Bombay and Madras.

We should have done well in the Fours, but one of our crew was a bit of a playboy, which is unusual in the I.C.S. He was a good oar but wouldn't get up early. One morning we started out much too late and one of the crew got heat-stroke. We got through the first round, but were beaten in the second, much to my disappointment.

I met a fellow policeman of my year, H.S. (Wiggy) McGuigan, who was very good company and I couldn't help noticing a difference between a junior Police Officer and a Subaltern: the former was given a responsible job, while many subalterns had very little responsibility, at least in peacetime.

On our last day we were asked to lunch at the Poona Horse Mess. It was a good and lively meal accompanied by a vigorous discussion on Indian politics. We went on to have tea at the Poona Club, a very large one and then caught the Madras train, I being the first to alight en route for Bellary.

14

Hot-Weather Camps

"As a rule man's a fool:
When its hot he wants it cool,
When its cool he wants it hot
Always wanting what is not."

THERE WAS plenty of work waiting at Hospet and it was hot. Having passed in Telugu, I chose Hindustani as my second language, which the District Police Office made easy by posting a young Muslim as my camp clerk. He was very fair-skinned, had perfect manners and spoke, I thought, a pure and graceful Urdu, the sort of speech for which Lucknow in the north is famed.

One day I decided on a very early start in order to do a surprise check on the buses - their times and their documents. I told the camp clerk and two sub-inspectors, but then suspected that they leaked the information, so I put it off till later in the week.

When I did go, I set my alarm clock and left within a quarter of an hour – packed for a full-day's absence: such was the efficiency of Yelliah, my bearer. I didn't find much wrong with the buses but, calling at a Police Station by surprise, I found the Sub-Inspector dressed in khaki shorts, a smart checked shirt and a pork pie hat. I knew him to be a good fellow and so gave him a warning. Nor did I subsequently have to discipline him for any default.

As very few up-country Inspectors owned a car, the speed checks of lorries and buses devolved on assistant and deputy superintendents. The country roads were macadam, without a bitumen surface and were usually worn into ruts by the iron tyres of the numerous bullock-carts, with potholes from the previous monsoon so they were hardly conducive to high speeds.

My speedometer was a good one but for months I had not noticed any overspeeding. One fine morning I happened to follow a bus travelling, according to my meter, at 31 to 31.5 mph, so I stopped it and charged the driver, who showed surprise. After the sub-magistrate had found him guilty on my evidence, I suffered pangs of remorse, thinking that his speedometer might well have read 30 m.p.h.

Never again did I order or authorize the prosecution of a law-abiding man for a trivial offence and I firmly believe that a warning in such a case is appropriate as it encourages respect for the Law, which surely is the aim and desire of British justice.

After a night's halt at headquarters I set off for a quiet camp during which there was time for some shooting. En route we saw two gazelle fawns, beautiful creatures, and a group of peafowl. These are very hard to shoot, for their strong wing feathers protect their bodies from the shot. When, weeks later, I managed to bring one down, I was surprised to find that a plucked peacock looked exactly like a small Norfolk-reared turkey; but my cook failed to hang it and it was very tough.

One evening I sat up for a panther on a rocky hill with a tethered goat as bait. Nestling between the ancient rocks were bushes and prickly-pear. While sitting still, I saw many birds, a humming bird, peafowl chicks; monkeys and a majestic peacock, standing erect on a big rock only 20 yards away. He saw me and watched, then with a swift take-off disappeared. But no panther came for the goat. The easier way is to beat one out of the jungle, but this needs a number of beaters and not less than three rifles.

The southern part of my subdivision sloped up to the Mysore Plateau. There was a village at 2,000 feet where the clear morning air was invigorating. It was half-way to the Manganese mines. I did not camp in the rest house, for there was none, but in the village serai. It was small but spotlessly clean and recently whitewashed; the little verandah was hung with plants. A white-painted gate kept out any stray dogs beside which, to my astonishment, stood an English streetlamp. I suspected that it had been whitewashed out of respect for the British visitor.

The local gentlemen arranged tennis. Afterwards, we sat under the stars with cigarettes and cool beer. My host was charming and gave me great pleasure. Dinner was brought which was beautifully cooked, one of the sweet dishes which I enjoyed was made of potato, spices and butter.

Next morning, we walked for an hour to the nearby railway line where the Inspector had arranged for a goods train to stop; servants and luggage were taken aboard and I was given the little guard's van.

Soon the train stopped at its terminus. I did not know the Kanarese language and the man who interpreted for me was a Malay, working for the Railway. The station master complained about an unwelcome visit by a drunken constable who, no doubt, I later punished.

We walked to the village – about three miles away – my orderly, Hirelal and I, with a cooly carrying my suitcase on his head.

Then we climbed up some 1200 ft to the Manganese Mines, by which time I was sweating profusely. The Manager, Mr Fawcitt, greeted me on arrival with the words: "Well, Bob, you look thinner than when I last saw you."

We sat down with tea, biscuits and cigarettes and listened to the whole of Beethoven's Pastoral Symphony, but I, for one, was watching the clock, for I knew that at noon, and not before, his tall butler would bring in bottles of beer and glasses.

That afternoon he took me to one of the open-cast mines. The place was thick with red dust, the miners' clothes and faces were red and colourful. By means of a rope railway the ore was conveyed to the aforesaid railhead 1200 ft below.

Mr Fawcitt watched a man trying to split a boulder. He watched for some minutes, then called the contractor and said, "I thought you said that man was a good miner." The contractor was covered with shame – the Manager's soft rebuke being much more effective than abuse.

In the evening we discussed the European situation and the Nazi menace. Mr Fawcitt, the senior of us, was very definite that he would fight for his country and that the Nazis were a danger to the whole world.

Next day I went down to the plains and after finishing my inspection, drove to Bellary for the farewell party of Mr and Mrs Wilkes. It was very hot; when I arrived I drank a glass and a half of cold water and some six large cups of tea. Later, a tumbler of lime juice and at the club two large glasses of beer. At last my thirst was satisfied. Next morning there was a farewell photo and badminton at the Club. But I was sad – I felt I might not see the Wilkes again, for such is life in the services, you get to know people, you make firm friendships, then they are broken up. The Wilkes left for good a couple of years later and I never saw them again.

I didn't stay for it was the beginning of the month and I was expecting Mr Fawcitt and Entwhistle at Hospet after they drew cash for the Mining Company.

We sat on my first floor verandah with its view over the river to Hyderabad State; we drank superb beer, Beck's Master Brew and listened to Dvorak's Fifth Symphony. At dinner, we drank a bottle of Graves. To me, sitting and talking with two friends was much more satisfying than being in mixed company with acquaintances, but a necessary preparation is intervals of solitude.

It was May and getting hot, over 100 degrees, the heat took the stuffing out of one. This time I was camping under canvas two miles from the road, even the two-mile walk was tiring. A hot wind was drying everything up and driving the dust before it. The furniture inside my hill-tent had a film of dust which my servant dusted off twice a day.

Next morning the men paraded, but I was not satisfied with their drill, perhaps I was crochety. In the late afternoon the Inspector took me for a walk and we watched the villagers digging holes in the dry sand of the river bed in order to collect a few pots of brownish water. Then I watched the light dying out of a leaden sky with the wind tearing across the Tungabhadra river and covering the shrunken stream with dust.

The middle of the day was worst – without fan or punkah, a 'cold' lunch was warm. The sweat trickled down and formed pools in the elbow joints and behind the knees.

From there I moved to a small town – Harpanahalle, as the Parliamentary Secretary to the Minister of Health was attending the jubilee of the local school. There were two sets of rooms in the Rest House and naturally, I occupied the smaller set. The place was full of Congressmen, clad in spotless white *khaddar* or homespun and wearing Gandhi caps. Two of my Congress friends paid me a vist: B. Anantachar, the local President and Nagana Gowd, District Board President. We drank some beer and the evening passed pleasantly for I really enjoyed the company of these cultured Indian gentlemen.

Part of the ceremonies consisted of sitting in a hot marquee and listening to one speech after the other. After an hour I was nearly melting with the heat, so excused myself and went to the small club where some officials were playing tennis. Later that evening there was a drama. Next day an Indian breakfast and lunch party, with seated musicians playing in the background. The food was, of course, served on the floor; the guests sitting cross-legged before a banana leaf on which the food and sauces were placed. No plate, no cutlery, brass tumblers, no mess and very little washing up.

The ethos was Hindu, which meant that most Muslims would not feel at home. After the drama I sent my compliments to Sub-Inspector Srinivasan, the English graduate, who came to share my beer. Two days later he came again, but he said something which, with my Christian upbringing, I did not like. He was thinking of marrying a second wife which, of course, was perfectly respectable in Hindu society.

Our next stop was by a small hill-fort. But on the way we came to a fine plantation of palms, bananas and mango trees - a most welcome splash of green, moreover it was comparatively cool under the trees, so we pitched our tents under them.

Hundreds of forts were built in the Deccan during the 18th century as the Mogul power declined. It was something like England during the reign of King Stephen.

The land-owner of *Sowcar* was only too delighted - such is Indian hospitality. He invited me to his house and as we drew near there was a muffled sound of bugles, then, God Save the King played on his gramophone. I had walked two miles in the heat, the perspiration pouring off me, but there was nothing for it but to stand to attention till the last of the three verses and the last flourish were over.

Tea was then served to the accompaniment of songs from Hindu films. Afterwards my host took me to see the little hill fort which was situated on his land. More tea was served on returning to his house, but after one cup, I asked if I could have a bottle of beer, which was graciously provided.

I stayed for three days as the sowcar's guest and it was a pleasant change – but the air was very heavy and a storm threatened. We saw it arrive: a tremendous wind raised a great cloud of dust, followed by rain, driven horizontal by the force of the wind, then hail. My terrier was miserable - battered by the hail – but I enjoyed every minute of it.

Next day I took my rifle to search for blackbuck, but the dry weather had driven them away – we didn't see one, instead we saw another storm – a livid cloud thousands of feet high and advancing slowly. It made the whole plain livid. Gradually, it merged with a rain-storm over the distant Sandur hills. May is a trying month in the plains.

Whether one shoots anything or not, a long walk with a gun along shady jungle tracks is refreshing to both body and soul. There was a full morning's investigation at a small town called Kottur, near a fine stretch of Reserve Forest.

As the hot sun began to sink, orderly Hirelal and I set out in the car. After half an hour's walk into the forest, I spied a jungle cock (very like our bantams). Up came the gun and I fired a round of birdshot. Immediately, loud crashing sounds broke out from a thicket twenty yards or so to our left: a herd of wild boar had sprung to life and were charging and grunting for all they were worth to safety. There were tuskers, sows and young ones – all sizes and higgeldy piggeldy.

It was a lovely surprise, for though boar have a distinct leathery smell, we had not seen, smelt or heard a thing.

★ ★ ★ ★ ★

Walking to a remote village near the Mysore plateau, two aged men were on the outskirts, talking. "What are they saying?" I asked. The sub-inspector replied: "One was saying 'Who does this waste land belong to?' The other old man answered 'To the Rani'".

Rani means Queen – it was a clear reference to Queen Victoria!

If one's car stops in the middle of nowhere it is an accepted fact that one or two men will shortly appear from somewhere. One warm day, near another remote village, as my borrowed Ford tourer chugged along the track, men and women hearing the unusual noise, suddenly popped up in pairs from the adjacent bushy crop. Evidently, they were enjoying a short break from tedious field work but if I was surprised, the station-house officer beside me kept a stiff upper lip, just like an Englishman.

15

The Vijayanagar (City of Victory) Empire

AS THIS city was situated only a few miles from Hospet I give this short account of an Empire which was the most powerful to emerge in South India. It arose from the persecution of Hindus by Tughlak, Emperor of Delhi. The city was founded in 1336 by military men. Twenty years later, one of them – Bukka I – made himself King.

A Venetian traveller who visited the city a hundred years later described it: the site – very rocky, the circumference of the city walls – 60 miles. The standing army: 90,000 men, later considerably increased. The palaces showed Islamic influence but the temples were pure Dravidian. The king kept 12,000 women, for prestige; out of these 2,000 to 3,000 were in the harem, all of whom agreed to be burnt as a sacrifice at his death (this rite – *sati* – reached its climax during the Vijayanagar empire). With this example it is not surprising that polygamy was widely practised and that there were many dancers, courtesans and jugglers at the Court. Sati was finally made illegal by Lord Bentinck, Governor-General, 1833-35.

An inconspicuous but probably unique feature in the capital is an oblong opening in the ground with a stone stairway descending to a plain underground chamber. No foreigner would ever guess its purpose - it was where the King, in perfect secrecy, would consult his chief advisers, take his big decisions, and so foil the enemy's spies at his court.

The greatest king was Krishna Deva Raya who died in 1530. By this time there was a prosperous trade with the Portuguese in Goa. The king was a devout Hindu and merciful towards the vanquished, unlike his contemporary rulers. He endowed temples, subsidised Brahmins and patronized writers and poets. Nevertheless, the people were oppressed and heavily taxed for the empire was governed for the rulers' benefit. Following his death the empire declined under less able rulers.

There was no enemy to the south but the Deccan to the north was divided into four Muslim kingdoms and fighting with them was almost continuous. Finally, the four kingdoms formed an alliance in order to crush Vijayanagar.

Battle was joined in 1565 at Talikota, near the River Kistna. The Hindu army was immense, but not well led – it comprised 900,000 infantry, 82,000 cavalry, 2,000 elephants[22] and some artillery. At once a considerable body of Muslim mercenaries defected, which disorganised the Hindu Army. But, as is often the case in Indian history, the artillery proved decisive.

[22] A number of these would have been shipped from Siam.

The Muslim guns, supported by cavalry and elephants, fired a sort of shrapnel with devastating effect; the king was captured, beheaded and his head placed on a pike at which the huge Hindu army broke ranks. 100,000 Hindus were killed in the battle and subsequent rout.

After the crushing defeat, the city lay undefended. For three days there was looting by nearby gypsy and robber tribes. When the Muslim armies arrived on the fourth day a terrible massacre took place with an orgy of destruction lasting several months. Very few escaped but some of the royal family took refuge at Penukonda, a hill-fort in Anantapur district and it was they, who in 1639, granted the East India Company a charter to build a fort and factory on a site later called Madras.

A number of times I visited the remains of Vijayanagar, much of which, built of tough granite, is in good preservation. No one will live there – so terrible was the massacre of 1565 – not even wanderers. Shepherds will pasture their flocks but at dusk they depart on account of evil spirits, for the population of about half a million was almost wiped out.

As the empire was constantly fighting, there was little development of Hindu culture: theology, philosophy, music or literature. So when the city was destroyed, little was left to posterity. Not since the invasion of Timur (Tamerlane) at the end of the 14th century had there been such destruction.

By and large the territory covered by the empire subsequently became the Mogul Province called the Carnatic.

★ ★ ★ ★ ★

Before long I was no longer the only Britisher in Hospet. An ex-Army Sergeant had come as engineer to the Indian-owned sugar factory. I spent two evenings with him and liked him more and more.

On the King's birthday – 8 June – I had a pleasant surprise: the Superintendent of Police (A.J. King), the District Medical Officer – Major Myers and J.L. Ronson, Probationary Assistant Superintedent of Police, arrived unexpectedly. Once again while sipping beer we watched the splendour of the sunset, but they didn't stay.

Not long afterwards I drove to Bellary for my half-yearly revolver practice under the eye of the Sergeant-Major. Calling at the club, King and I found only one member there, the new Sub-Collector, a North Indian by the name of Dass, who rather surprised us by his strong views. "Gandhi," he said, "wants to put us all into bullock carts. I would prefer tanks." Another time I remember him saying, "We need to take Constantinople." (He didn't say Istanbul.) When I asked why, he answered, "It is necessary for defence." One Government holiday when we had nothing to do, we went to the Railway Refreshment Room at Hospet. Dass was a well-bred and courteous Indian, very much one of the upper class. He didn't air his views much, but after his third whisky he said: "You know, Bob, everything you British have done for India, we could have done ourselves: the canals, railways, roads, factories and so on. We could have sent our young men to study at European Universities, but there is one thing we could not have learned for ourselves." "What is that?" I asked. "To decide a case without taking bribes." After that statement by a young I.C.S. officer, one of India's outstanding men, I never had any doubt that British rule had been worthwhile. No doubt after Independence there was some reversion to earlier practices. But during my last year in India I came across an instance of a young C.I.D. Inspector in Bombay, a Roman Catholic, who refused a huge bribe by a smuggler of gold. It was reported to Pandit Nehru, the Prime Minister, who ordered him to be promoted to officer's rank.

★ ★ ★ ★ ★

Something to look forward to was my annual visit to Dharwar, Bombay Province. After some hours of driving we reached Hubli, a big Railway town and were surprised to find a well-laid asphalt road as good as any in England. Dharwar had had rain, it was green and pleasantly cool in contrast to Bellary which was bone dry. The Assistant Superintendent of Police was doing his duty, which was playing hockey with his men. So I found Gallagher, the Sub-Collector, who was lounging in his office, apparently twiddling his thumbs. We drove to his bungalow and I met his new bride - she was charming and seemed a woman of exquisite purity. We had tea, played with the dogs, then got ready to go to the club, where we found an excellent supper of ham, bread and butter and fruit salad. There was a ping-pong tournament and much laughter, even some good natured brawling. G.C. Ryan, Assistant Superintendent, was there and afterwards at his house we had a long talk, he asking many questions about the Madras Police. (Later, he was awarded the King's Police Medal for gallantry: arresting a dangerous armed outlaw.) I couldn't see him in the morning as he had been called out to a murder case, instead I had a late breakfast with P.M. Stewart, his superior. Later in life, we were both ordained – he in the Scottish Church, I in the Church of England.

Gallagher was most generous with his horse and I rode him twice. I met another charming lady, who offered to find me a cook – there didn't seem to be a suitable one in Bellary and what good cook would want to work for a rather solitary bachelor?

Another visit was to the Criminal Settlement at Hubli, one of the projects for reforming the criminal tribes in which the Bombay Government was very interested. It was managed by a Swiss, a strong character and his French wife. After touring the Settlement they gave me a grand high tea.

The formal meeting had been arranged between the British and Mysore police officers. It ended my visit to Dharwar and I returned to camp. For a change I decided to visit a nearby town by bicycle. It was 17- 18 miles each way and I was tired on my return – one doesn't have much energy in the heat.

Once again, I arranged a border meeting, this time with the Chief of Police, Sandur, a very small State. I found him a young and somewhat dissipated-looking Maratha – but most friendly and courteous; we got on well. Then I drove on to the Mining Company for a night's stay.

After clearing up the arrears of work in Hospet, Clarke, the engineer at the sugar factory and I went on a shoot and we did well, getting chinkara (gazelle), pea-fowl, hare and partridge. My orderly, Hirelal, was delighted and I cannot say how delicious the gazelle was in the eating and what a change from the local mutton.

Junior officers were allotted two orderlies for office and personal duties, one of whom would be a driver. Superintendents had four orderlies and if the telephone needed to be manned day and night – two more. So in thirteen years I had quite a few of them, but none meant as much to me as Hirelal of the Bellary Reserve Police.

When I asked him about himself he said he was of Rajput descent which meant he had pride and self-respect. He did not have a driving licence but was quite knowledgeable with a car and could change a wheel in no time. He knew no English, we conversed in Hindustani. He spent very little time with his wife, never asking for leave to go home and what he loved most was for us to go out together in search of game, he sometimes taking his own gun, a muzzle-loader, or carrying mine if I tired during a long walk back. (He never tired.) He hadn't been taught to ride but he was Rajput and afraid of nothing and would ride my horse for miles back to his stable and Rembrandt was no ageing hack, but a thoroughbred race-horse. What was most remarkable about Hirelal was his attitude to an order. An order to him was an order and must be obeyed. If he took a message to a clerk, a sub-inspector or a village headman, they had to do what I said. He would not accept any excuse or delay – they had to jump to it. I knew he would make any sacrifice for me.

Few British men and very few British women could stand the summer heat which, even on the Deccan plateau, reached 108 degrees. By June I was very weary but was working for my first Hindustani exam. This meant a train journey to Madras, where I sat the written paper and passed, but failed in the oral, which was really the more important part.

It was amazing how a few days in Madras revived me; good, nourishing food, exercise on the river, meeting friends and attending the annual Boat Club Dinner at the Connemara Hotel.

My host was one of the senior officers of the City Police. After a day or two he was called away during breakfast and when I returned at tea-time his wife was lounging on a settee, drinking champagne with her boy friend. I was shocked, though it wasn't the first time I had seen this sort of conduct.

That evening I had the pleasure of taking out a young lady of 18 or 19, a charming blonde, to a dance. This was a rare treat for me and does wonders for a young man's morale. To round off an enjoyable few days, my friends Gordon and Valerie Marshall came and saw me off at the Railway Station. So I left, thinking what very kind people there were in the world; part of the kindness was the hospitality we junior men received from the older officers stationed in the city.

16

The War Looms Closer

THE NEWS from Europe was disturbing and in a little over a year I would be
qualifying for home leave. As it happened August was unsettled, with unusual
rain and cloud which increased my sense of foreboding. Mr Fawcitt came as
usual to draw a month's cash and I much enjoyed having him to lunch and tea.
He had intended to return to the Mines after tea but I persuaded him to stay the
night.

Mr L.A. Bishop, our new Deputy Inspector-General, had arranged to meet
Mr P.M. Stewart of Dharwar at a Rest House in my sub-division. We had a
cordial border meeting and then joined Mrs Bishop, Mrs and Miss Stewart for
a superb lunch.

Mr King was calling me in to see him once a month and before going I stayed
by a large artificial reservoir near a village called Daroji. For two days there was
thick cloud and a terrific wind but not a drop of rain. The Rest House was by
the lake and the blast was incessant. However, on the third day the wind
subsided and the water was calm enough for me to paddle my canoe.

This time Mr and Mrs Bishop were my hosts. There were several young
people in the station. Mrs Bishop gave a grand dinner party and next morning
a trip was arranged to the ruined city of Vijayanagar, usually known as the
Hampi ruins.

I didn't want a big breakfast but a pair of kippers was brought and I was not
allowed to decline them. I did not enjoy the drive but after walking several
miles I recovered from the kippers. Lunch was served in the Rest House and for
the rest of the day I worked hard with Mr Bishop going through disciplinary
cases and appeals, which he decided with exemplary fairness.

I went straight into camp but the news from Europe was so serious that I
returned to Bellary. War seemed imminent and I felt very sad. I was greatly
looking forward to long leave and to watching my younger brother, Charles,
competing at Henley in the Grand Challenge Cup.

Back in Hospet I worked my way through a heap of files and cases, among
which was a case against Sub-Inspector Srinivasan, the English graduate
whom I liked so much. Alas, he turned out to be less than honest.

A murder case was reported on the borders of my sub-division. I drove as far
as possible by car, bicycled 18 miles along soft, dusty tracks, investigated and
bicycled back, which was very hard work. My reward was a bottle of beer.
Then the District Medical Officer, Major Edis-Myers, I.M.S. arrived at the
Rest House. He talked about his work and seemed glad to, as he had no
Assistant to whom he could talk freely.

An hospitable Indian landowner then asked us both to a shoot. We left in an old, open American car as darkness was setting in. Using our lights I managed to bag two hares then both the headlights and the petrol gave out. So we left the car and walked towards a police outpost, which took nearly two hours. We were about to spend the night there on string cots when the car arrived in a blaze of light.

By the end of 1939 I was close on 24 years of age and was getting adjusted to the solitary life. I wanted to improve my knowledge of Hindustani, which though not spoken much in Bellary, was the *lingua franca* of India and also was reading Dunbar's History of India with great interest.

★ ★ ★ ★ ★

When His Majesty's Government declared war on Germany, the Viceroy, Lord Linlithgow, without summoning his Council or consulting the Provincial Prime Ministers, declared war on behalf of India. This was a grave mistake and the Congress Ministries which controlled most of British India, resigned en bloc. Some said, however, that this decision had been taken before war broke out. So Section 93 of the Government of India Act (1935) came into operation and the Provincial Governors assumed power, ruling with the help of a few senior I.C.S. Advisers.

If I expected more effective rule as a result, I was disappointed and could not think why more was not done to alleviate poverty. It seemed to me that the older and wiser men got, the more cautious and timid they became.

A prominent Congressman gave a splendid dinner at the Railway Refreshment Rooms at Hospet for there was no hotel and no 'big house' in the town. It was a substantial meal but very well cooked and a cousin of his waited on us; it was, of course, an all-male party, for only in upper-class Indian society did ladies join in.

One day a report was brought to me of a small bomb which had exploded in a field near Sandur State. Bomb cases had to be investigated by an assistant or deputy superintendent, but my investigation showed that it was non-political; the bomb was made by a farmer exasperated by the damage done to his crops by wild boars.

It was while staying at the nearby Rest House that I met a very unusual type of Anglo-Indian, a Railway official. He was big, overweight, thick-skinned and overbearing. I did not like him and wondered why he was staying in the Rest House when Railway officers each had a comfortable saloon for their touring. Normally, I got on very well with Anglo-Indians. Europeans regarded them as part of India, but Hindus, particularly, resented them and treated them as foreigners, so it behoved them to be tactful and most of them were.

Until the setting up of the Wireless grid after the war, the telegraph, still manually-operated in up-country post offices, was by far the quickest means of communication and was used extensively by government and people. It was not perfect – what system is – but was pretty reliable. For example, of the many cypher telegrams I received as a district officer, all were deciphered without difficulty. One important telegram, sent en clair by my superior and received by me at Vizianagram, was misleading and I suffered for it, but I did not suspect the Post Office of carelessness.

A.J. King, my Superintendent, received a telegram from a villager over thirty miles away. The message read:

"Sir, come immediately. They are murdering me."

17

Mysore Dassera or Durga[23] Puja

IN OCTOBER 1940 the monsoon was in full swing and it was time for the Festival for which Mysore is famed.

Driving through the monsoon is hazardous and twenty-five miles out, my car stuck in the soft bed of a stream. But in India men always appear and are only to willing to help a traveller so we were soon out of it.

We reached the Rest House at Davengere in Mysore State close to an open-air cinema that kept me awake till the early hours; then the crows woke me at dawn. It was not at all like stopping at a P.W.D [24] Rest House, quietly situated outside a village, and I left the town feeling jaded. Perhaps my driving suffered too, for late in the afternoon I collided with a half-grown buffalo who rolled over and over. This I reported at the next police station but the sub-inspector was not much concerned. Oil was escaping from an oil pipe, sending unpleasant fumes into the car but we reached Mysore safely.

The hotel I stayed at was most comfortable, it was sheer joy to have a full-length bath in a white-tiled bathroom for it was some months since I had used other than a hip-bath.

Next morning was not so pleasant as some Indian gentleman wanted my room. I was rather put out but gave way reluctantly and soon found another room at the Mysore Race Club.

There I met several British people, some of whom I knew. We decided to visit the big hydro-electric dam – the Krishnarajasagar Dam, fourteen miles out of Mysore. It was built entirely by Indians and compared with the best in British India. The great lake was full, excess water roared out of the sluices and formed a fast-flowing river. Below the dam, beautiful formal gardens had been laid out with a row of seven fountains as the centre piece.

No doubt Mysore looked its best for the Festival but it certainly was an impressive State. The Maharajah was an old man, a Rajput, small, saintly and dignified. His Prime Minister, Sir Mirza Ismail, was a most capable administrator, but it was less democratic and more efficient than Madras. Mysore lies mostly between 2,000 and 4,000 ft and the climate suits everyone.

The City is well laid-out with broad boulevards, grass verges and wide footpaths lined with flowers and trees. Most of the Government offices are in a massive white-painted secretariat, a satisfying blend of western style with Hindu towers and cupolas.

[23] Durga – the Goddess of War.
[24] Public Works Department

The Palace is enormous and the main gate reminds one of the Gateway of India at Bombay. It was guarded by household troops who never went on any active service and who looked more like faithful retainers than soldiers. Bodies of smart, dismounted cavalrymen marched here and there. The State Cavalry wore dark breeches, white tunics and blue striped turbans; the Lancers wore khaki and blue. It was cool enough for the Infantry to wear not cotton drill but barathea tunics and Bedford cord. Now and then an elephant walked by, his head, trunk and limbs decorated with floral designs in chalk.

The highlight was the State procession. Grandstands were provided for the visitors' comfort. Most of all I enjoyed the ride past of the Lancers, mounted on black Walers and carrying their lances and gay pennants. Behind came the state landaus, the silver coach looked like one of our royal coaches and was drawn by a pair of big, black horses, while an Indian coach was shorter and higher, with an ornamental roof. The nobles sitting in it were some five feet from the ground and it was drawn, not by horses but by a pair of magnificent white oxen, some 4 ft 6 ins at the shoulder with great high horns. One didn't see their bodies as they were caparisoned i.e. covered with embroidered coats.

Lastly came His Highness in full Indian regalia: his great elephant was caparisoned in white and gold, head and eyes decorated and tusks gleaming; on his high back a gilded howdah with pillars and roof. There, more than twelve feet above ground sat His Highness the Maharajah in full state. I could not take my eyes off him, but think the Maharani Sahib was beside him, suitably veiled in accordance with Rajput custom.

Next day His Highness held a great Durbar. The scene was one of a magnificence at which former travellers to India must have marvelled. A broad flight of steps led up to the dais. On the right sat some two hundred of the leading state officials, all dressed alike: white and gold turbans, black buttoned-up coats and white and gold scarves.

In the centre stood the throne: gold and sparkling with precious stones. In due course His Highness arrived in a carriage. He was dressed in cloth of gold from his turban down to his slippers and the whole was set off by diamonds and sapphires.

A great crimson carpet surrounded the throne and the background was of Indo–Persian design in simple colours of gold, white and two shades of blue, all in superb taste.

Guards of honour flanked the forecourt and before him was a wrestling ring. After a display of wrestling, first by big men and finishing with boys, all of us guests were presented to His Highness by an A.D.C.

As the war had not yet hit us in India, the dress was still formal. The I.C.S. were mostly in morning coats, ladies in long dinner dresses, Army and Police Officers in either full dress or ceremonial uniform. There were also a few Royal Navy and R.A.F. Officers.

Each of us was presented by name and bowed to His Highness. Some bowed deeply and respectfully, but I noticed some of our ladies (?) who were too ill-bred to bow or curtsy to an Indian, even a Maharajah, and merely inclined their heads. His Highness took no notice and hardly moved for an hour. As they passed him, another A.D.C. gave each of the ladies a large bouquet of flowers.

So we returned to the comparative simplicity of the Race Club. It was rather late and one of our party, the wife of a Railway Official was in an ugly mood. The superb pageantry seemed to have unsettled her, or was it only hunger; her behaviour was disgraceful and her husband and grown daughter must have been most embarrassed. A dance followed which was enjoyable as there were enough partners to go round.

Next morning, two of us went to take photographs of the City. An officious Police Inspector tried to stop me photographing the Palace, but I refused to listen to him. Soon dozens of people with cameras arrived and the Inspector had to allow them in.

We returned by night to the Krishnarajasagar Dam. It was flood-lit and out of this world. Waterfalls were illuminated from the back with pale blue light. Tall spouts of illuminated water pierced the darkness. Small, wide fountains of deep-red water looked like fires. There was so much light that it showed up the colours of the flowers in the many borders.

The sound of waters and the playing of many fountains muffled the talk of the numerous visitors. It was a dream garden.

Another spectacular show was the torchlight review at the Summer Palace. Much as I regretted not seeing it, one couldn't see everything, so I resolved to return for the next Dassera in 1940, little realizing that by then the War would be total.

★ ★ ★ ★ ★

Next morning a party of us drove to Seringapatam. It is an immensely strong fortress, lying between the two chief cities of Mysore. It has a permanent place in Anglo-Indian history being the scene of a famous siege in the year 1799. Mysore was then ruled by a strong and able Sultan: Tipu Sahib, the son of Hyder Ali who, as an able general, had usurped the throne of Mysore. Hyder Ali fought the Marathas but they were too strong, so he claimed the support of the British and when this was refused, became our bitter enemy and ravaged the country to within forty miles of Madras, till General Sir Eyre Coote defeated him. Tipu continued his father's anti-British policy and intrigued with the French, sending his ambassadors to France and engaging French officers and ships.

Finally, it took an alliance between the British, the Marathas and the forces of Hyderabad to control his aggressive designs. As part of the subsequent peace treaty of 1792 he had to surrender two of his sons, who were interned in Vellore Fort.

He resumed hostilities seven years later and was defeated in open country and one of the senior commanders was Lieut-Col Arthur Wellesley of the 33rd Foot, the future victor of Waterloo, who was then thirty years of age. Defeated in the field, Tipu Sultan took refuge in the fortress of Seringapatam. General

Harris [25] was in command and Col Wellesley took part in the storming of the mighty fortress. Tipu was killed in the assault and so died the Tiger of Mysore. He was buried within the fortress and a fine mausoleum with twin minarets guards his tomb. The visitor wonders how so strong a fort could be stormed. It was the artillery bombardment by siege guns that proved decisive.

Following the defeat of Tipu Sultan the rightful Rajput dynasty was restored and continued until the abolition of the Princely States. Relations with the British were cordial and the Maharajah leased part of Bangalore to the Government of India as a Civil and Military station or cantonment. This was where the Madras Sappers and Miners had their Depot.

On the way home I stopped at Penukonda in the Anantapur district with the Sub-Collector, J.C. Griffiths, I.C.S., who was a big, blond, rugger-playing Welshman. He was a lonely bird like me and most hospitable; his guest room was beautifully furnished with rosewood furniture. We spent the evening drinking whisky, then singing, though he was not a musical Welshman. Later, after Independence, Griffiths and I got to know each other very well, as one does when there is little social life.

★ ★ ★ ★ ★

Attempts to stamp out bribery in the East are doomed to failure for small gifts or services to low-paid officials have been the custom from time immemorial, they can be compared to lubricating oil. It is the bigger amounts, the real bribes that are such a menace.

In the 17th and 18th centuries, as is well known, many East India Company merchants and factors made fortunes by dishonest or very dubious means (the Nabobs), but in the 19th century the tide began to turn and from the Imperial period i.e. 1858, corrupt officials disappeared. Any enquiry into this phenomenon must take account of the influence of missionaries, chaplains and of the numerous God-fearing Evangelicals in the Civil Service as well as the Army. For the Army was a reservoir of manpower for the new Services, especially the Engineers, Police and the Railways, e.g. the outstanding officer and administrator of Madras was Major-General Sir Thomas Munro, who died in 1827 when Governor.

A Superintending Engineer, Mr Nightingale, told me he was once approached by a wealthy contractor who was keen to obtain a major contract on a construction site. Nightingale soon guessed what the man was leading up to, so he said: "Every man has his price. I have another four years' service, so my price is four years' pay plus twenty years' pension and doubled for loss of face. Shall we say 12 lakhs of rupees (Rs. 120,000)?" The contractor did not pursue the matter.

Later in the war it appeared that garrison engineers were fair game for Army contractors and there was a sad case in Calcutta of a British garrison engineer convicted for accepting a bribe of Rs. 1300 – a mere £100.

[25] Later Lord Harris of Seringapatam

18

Meetings in Hyderabad State and Bombay Province

A.J. KING, MY Superintendent, left with a very good name and the Bellary police named their club after him. His successor was A.R. Jakeman, who had been educated at Crypt School, Gloucester and was very proud of his Cathedral. He was a gin drinker and heavy smoker but this had no apparent effect on his health. His mind was keen and he quickly reached decisions on cases and punishment rolls. Incidentally, he had served in Aden, which was formerly administered by the Government of India.

Two Probationers had been posted to Bellary for practical training; J.P.L. Gwynn, I.C.S., an Ulsterman of good family, very devout and abstemious; the other was J.L. Ronson, a Police Probationer, from Kent.

December was approaching and I still had two further meetings to arrange – one with my opposite number in Bombay Province, the other with the Superintendent of Police, Kopbal, in Hyderabad State.

After only an hour's journey by train, which, in India is nothing, I was welcomed at Kopbal by a grave, elderly, courteous Muslim. He wore a fez and the long coat which is de rigueur in much of India, it resembles the former frock-coat but is buttoned high. His subordinates were all in uniform: trousers, tunics and Sam Browne; all wore the fez. It seemed very different from Madras or Bombay – it felt as though I was in Egypt.

In the afternoon we had our meeting at his office. I was greeted by a bugler and the guard turned out and presented arms. The agenda was in two languages, beautiful Urdu for them – English transcript for me.

Afterwards we played tennis at their Club. I played indifferently, but did better at ping-pong. Finally, a game of corinthian bagatelle for two hours! Although Hyderabad State has a majority of Hindus, the district and non-gazetted officers were nearly all Muslims and all had old-fashioned formal manners.

After a bath and change I was taken to the bungalow of a Muslim gentleman. A pretty good band was playing in the garden, there were fourteen to dinner round a long table loaded with superbly cooked Muslim dishes, of which I tasted about a dozen.

One one side of me was a big man, who turned out to be a doctor and a Christian, on the other side was a Muslim headmaster with a Ph.D. of Dublin; they had so been placed, obviously because of their command of English and my indifferent Urdu.

I woke next morning to the sound of the Police band practising and a subadar, or Indian Officer, drilling a company of men. So I got up and joined them on the parade ground.

At eight o'clock I was invited to the Collector's bungalow and was offered a substantial meal of Muslim dishes. After which I needed exercise and was given one of the police mounts, an Indian horse of about 13 hands.

A Jemadar escorted me; he was a magnificent old man who looked like a relic from the Napoleonic wars. Of aristocratic appearance and aquiline of features, he had superb bushy whiskers and eyebrows. His manner was most courteous but not in the least servile. He acknowledged my slightly higher rank but was an officer and he knew it. I enjoyed his company immensely and wished I could have known him longer.

The Superintendent Sahib had a lunch of cold dishes ready for me but ate sparingly himself. Finally, he accompanied me to the Railway Station and I departed, feeling great respect for a perfect and most hospitable gentleman. Only one thing I did not like: to see under- trial prisoners in leg-irons, which I never saw anywhere else.

The last 'frontier' meeting was in the Province of Bombay. Taking the train to Gadag I was met at the station by a smart Sub-Inspector with the Superintendent's car. According to British custom one arranges for visitors to be met and a man of Sub-Inspector's rank was glad to welcome an officer. We did not go in for the elaborate and time-wasting procedure, later insisted on by Congressmen, of all the district officers and officials going en masse to meet a Minister or Party dignitary.

So, we drove to the Superintendent's bungalow and were received by P.M. Stewart, G.C. Ryan, his Assistant and Davies, the Assistant Superintendent of Railway Police.

After tea we watched a football match at the Lines and as it got dark early, the next item was a camp fire with a film showing police methods in America.

Early next morning a duck shoot had been arranged. We drove to a small State called Sangli which gave the appearance of being peaceful and well-administered for it was large enought to be viable. Our bag was small: 14 wild duck and a few other birds but I thoroughly enjoyed the outing and had no time for organised massacre.

A formal meeting followed in the Police office and I returned to Hospet, refreshed and ready to tackle the heap of files waiting on my desk.

Christmas 1939

Christmas was usually a slack period in the middle of the short cold weather season. The first part of my short leave took me to Madras where I had arranged to buy a City Police remount. The horse I fancied went to another, so I took 'Rembrandt', a thoroughbred brown gelding, who was too highly strung for work in the City. He was a grandson of Solario, nevertheless I got him for only 130 rupees. or ten pounds exactly, as horses were cheap as the result of mechanising the Indian Army.

I was booked on the night train to Trivandrum, capital of Travancore State, where I was to meet my elder brother, Louis. The train was metre-gauge and slow and it felt pretty warm in the compartment.

The hotel at Trivandrum was cool and comfortable: there were very few Europeans as they preferred to go up into the hills to the coffee estates and enjoy blankets at night. Being so close to the tip of the sub-continent we felt we had to visit Cape Cormorin, a place sacred to Hindus and therefore marked by a temple. Looking south, one sensed the vastness of the Indian Ocean, looking north one saw the beginning of the great Indian land mass, an enormous inverted triangle.

We returned to Trivandrum, which was a pleasant city, cleaner than most and inhabited by a strong minority of Christians, not recently converted but of ancient lineage. For the oldest Indian Church is Apostolic, the Mar Thoma, founded by St Thomas.

Next day we headed northwards to Cochin State. The Malabar coast is quite different from the East Coast: the rainfall is very heavy and one is continually crossing salt water inlets; streams and rivers flowing down the Ghats. [26] It is green, with luxuriant palm, banana and other trees.

Malabar is an important district with a large population and the people (Malayalis) are people to be reckoned with, one reason for their sturdiness is that the system of land tenure is the freehold. The women are buxom and it is probably the only part of the country where matriarchy is found and where a wife can divorce her husband. With water so plentiful they all bathe twice a day and both Hindus and Moplahs wear clean white clothes.

Malayali-run hotels and tea stalls are found far from Malabar. One story goes that when Captain Scott reached the South Pole he heard a voice behind him. It was a Malayali offering him a cup of tea. Cochin is a small State on the Malabar coast: whose chief town, Calicut, gave it name to calico.

I had a 12-bore gun with me in a locked case and it was checked by a Cochin Customs official who declared that it needed a State licence. So I tried to get one on being told that there was a Customs Inspector two and a half miles up-stream. A hired canoe took me to the spot but he wasn't there, which meant leaving my gun with the Customs.

My cousin and Godmother, Mrs Harrison-Jones, had often spoken to me of Cochin, where her husband was Manager of Aspinall & Co. and where she spent eleven happy years.

We drove to the Club which is beautifully sited on the beach. We sat on a verandah, listening to the wavelets dancing up the sands and to the music of the breeze as it hummed through the foliage, fine as maiden-hair, of the casuarina trees. Beyond, graceful Arab dhows, with their scissor-shaped sails, glided over the Arabian Sea.

The sun sank into the sea, dusk fell; the moon rose, shimmering the water and lighting up the beach. By then I was in love with Cochin.

In the morning we explored the old town, found an old Dutch church

(26) Mountains

bearing the inscription 'Renovatum 1729'. The rest of the day we spent at the Malabar Hotel. There were a number of people there: Royal Air Force, Royal Fusiliers and Royal Indian Navy; there were businessmen and shipping agents and we met Grant, the grand old man who was Manager of Aspinall's.

The distinguished master-mariner, Vasco de Gama, who landed at Malabar and gained a foothold for Portugal, died at Cochin in the year 1525. His grave is a very simple one.

Next day we were on our way again and as Cochin is an island, my brother's Chevrolet station-wagon had to be driven to the car ferry. We were heading for Coonoor in the Nilgiri Hills but never got there as the transmission of the car gave trouble and we limped into Coimbatore and put up at the Club. In the morning I had a streaming cold and my brother's most capable servant, Abdul, a Punjabi, looked after me as they always do.

In a day or two both the Chevrolet car and I were fit to travel and we set out, visiting on the way the Mettur Dam. The dam itself is impressive: some 2,000 yards across and 180-200 ft high and forms a lake more than fifteen miles in length from the waters of the Cauvery River. Eventually the water serves to irrigate millions of acres and also provides electricity over a wide area. For instance the high- tension cables reached as far as Vellore, about 150 miles to the north. The Vellore transformer reduced the voltage which was perfectly steady, unlike, for example, nearby Chittoor which was supplied from a power-house that was insufficient at peak periods.

We reached Vellore without incident and stayed at the Police Mess. There was only one officer there – J.P. Moore, the last European to join the Madras cadre of the Indian Police. He was unusual in that he was Irish Roman Catholic and English was his second language. He proved most affable and said he had been a journalist in London, presumably working for an Irish newspaper. The poor fellow came to an untimely end, for though he was extremely particular, one day he somehow drank unboiled water and died of enteric fever.

I took the opportunity of looking up Dr Miss Birnie Siebers, one of the finest women I ever met. Tall, fair haired and good-looking, she worked at the Medical Missionary College. She set her face against marriage but eventually took pity on a missionary, a widower, who was a good fifteen years older.

From Vellore I accompanied my brother to Madras where he had to meet his agents. We hadn't had a Christmas dinner and looked forward to a New Year party at the Connemara Hotel, but as it was very quiet we went on to the Gymkhana Club where we met a number of my friends. We returned to our hotel at 4.45 a.m. but that didn't stop us getting up betimes. I accompanied my brother on his business visits and he came with me to the Police Horse Lines to see my horse who seemed very frisky. I arranged for him to be railed to Bellary.

19

The Joy of a Horse

AFTER SAYING goodbye to my brother I returned to Bellary to find that Gwynn, the I.C.S. Probationer, was finding even the pleasant Deccan winter too warm. He had a new English saddle and bridle which he didn't want and generously sold them to me at the English price which was well below its local value.

Rembrandt arrived safely at Hospet and I managed a ride, but had to leave the next morning in order to see an Inspector who was having frequent affairs with women, also a Head Constable who was notorious for taking bribes: there wasn't much crime in Bellary district and there wasn't much bribery, but officers had to be on the watch for it the whole time.

I duly returned, greatly looking forward to a ride. I did manage one, but next evening Rembrandt had a strong objection to being mounted, he waltzed about and let fly, he wouldn't stand for a second. So I said "All right, no dinner." As the days went by he calmed down but needed so much hard cantering that his master got a stiff back and had to call in the old masseur from the bazaar. But I persevered and slowly tamed him until one day he condescended to trot. Rembrandt made a big difference to my life for with good servants, a dog and now a horse I was very happy.

After a month of work and language study the examination fell due. Travelling on the train were P. Crombie, I.C.S., Mrs Crombie who was a lovely person and an Indian I.C.S. officer. He was a bachelor and after a couple of drinks said he was thinking of marriage. He had little time, he said, for love matches, "that was old fashioned." His plan was to marry a plain girl with a big dowry, live with her for a month, then send her back to her parents and live with the beautiful woman of his choice. My guess was that his sentiments were partly bravado and that when the time came he would marry an attractive young lady with a dowry, for as a good-looking young I.C.S. man he was most eligible.

After the exam. was over I spent the mornings and afternoons rowing at the Adyar Boat Club. One evening we went to the Connemara Hotel with dancing and cabaret, but I wasn't adjusted to City life and could not let myself go – a feeling that all those Britishers who have lived in lonely places will know and which is a common cause of too much imbibing at parties.

On the Friday I called on the Inspector-General, F. Sayers, C.I.E. and Mrs Sayers, who were most friendly and gave a very pleasant tea.

Next day was the local Regatta on the Adyar River, an event always attended by the Anglican Bishop, Bishop Waller, who was respected and was said to smoke the biggest pipe in Madras. After the Regatta, my brother and I went on to the Gymkhana Club, but again I found the crowd of strangers overpowering.

Sunday was the end of my short leave: a jolly swimming party at the Gymkhana Club and a lunch party, given by G.S.W. Marshall who was the heavyweight in the Boat Club 1st Crew and his charming wife, Valerie. Later, he took me to the Yacht Club from where we had a most enjoyable sail in his dinghy.

I took the late train back and had Peter and Mrs Crombie again as fellow passengers.

On my return I found a telegram announcing a gruesome double murder, so went straight into camp; it was 1 February and camping near the Tungabhadra River was still pleasantly cool.

Kelso, the new manager of the sugar factory at Hospet asked me to dinner, with him was a fine-looking young man, another sugar engineer from one of Parry's factories.

Next day I had them to lunch and as the last course, my servant produced what he had been carefully saving up: a pate-de-foie-gras and Bath Oliver biscuits.

My next camp was a routine inspection at a small town. Close to the inspection bungalow was a large reservoir, well-filled with water. I had my canoe and took a gun in case of a couple of shots at duck. When resting quietly I noticed a crocodile slowly swimming towards me. He came to within 25 yards, I only had No. 4 shot but for fun fired both barrels, aiming at his eye. I expected a great swish from the mighty tail, but unexpectedly he sank like a stone. Later I saw him again and trailed him until it was dark.

It wasn't often that a dinner party took place in a Rest House, but that evening six of us sat down. It was another shooting family who provided peacock soup, river fish, teal, followed by a sweet and snipe on toast. But the conversation was monotonous – shooting – till I managed to shift it slightly to other sports.

Next day a personal enquiry was arranged: a Muslim constable had made allegations against a superior and swore by Allah and the Holy Koran. As, however, he had no other witness or evidence I found him guilty and he was punished by a reduction of grade and pay.

Returning to Hospet in the afternoon I was delighted to find the two men from the Manganese Mines sitting on the verandah. As Tom Entwhistle was expecting to be called up, he had grown a fine blond moustache. Before the war he was not a bit keen on fighting but the Nazis changed all that.

We listened that evening to most of Beethoven's Ninth Symphony. At six a.m. I joined in a rapid march of about nine miles, returning to a late breakfast after which we played the remainder of the Symphony.

My next engagement throws a light on village administration. In England everything is done by committee, but in the East, administration is more personal and every village has a headman who has duties both towards law and order and the collection of revenue. For the latter he is assisted by the village accountant who keeps the revenue maps. From time to time vacancies arise and the appointment of successors rests with the Sub-Collector of the division, who presides with the police officer at his side. The Sub-Collector was N.S. Arunachalam, I.C.S., a Tamil who could no more speak the local language (Kanarese) than I could, so he spoke through an interpreter. He quickly made up his mind but I had an opportunity to object to a candidate.

Every year district police sports were held and it would take a lot to postpone them as they were a popular social event. The armed police do not compete against the district police who have little time for sport. The men of my subdivision did not do well except for the Hospet Circle (of six stations) which won the tug-of-war. The judges were Mr and Mrs P.M. Stewart of Dharwar, Bombay Province and a Railway officer. The Presidency Police Band came from Vellore under my friend, Mr Taylor, and they played as well as ever.

Mr and Mrs Bishop gave a dinner party and dance and I partnered Mrs Bishop who was a very light and graceful dancer.

The Collector, A.D. Crombie, I.C.S. and Mrs Crombie gave a large dinner party and dance for the whole station. But it was young Mrs Peter Crombie who attracted attention, beautiful, dignified and natural, all the bachelors tried to dance with her. At the end I organised a sing-song with the Bandmaster, Mr Taylor, at the piano. As couples got up to dance, a waiter would remove one's half empty glass and bring a fresh one after the dance. That night, the sweeper was given a bottle of the whisky, gin and lime remains and pronounced it "Very good *sharab*" (i.e. wine).

A recent arrival at Bellary was a Mr Tony Mango, a Greek representative of the prosperous Anglo-Greek company, Ralli Brothers. He gave me a basket of home-grown vegetables, which was most acceptable as I did not keep a gardener and was out on tour for a good fifteen days a month.

Next day I drove back to supervise Mohurram, a Muslim festival which can easily provoke Hindus. It made a great deal of noise but passed off peacefully. This was followed straightaway by a double murder in a village, the murderer ran amok but was caught and overpowered.

To my great pleasure, my brother Louis wired that he was coming to stay, so I returned to headquarters. Arrive he did, at two in the morning, covered with dust but very cheerful.

As he had not seen the Hampi ruins, of Vijayanagar, we went there soon after breakfast. Though the victorious Muslim armies spent five to six months looting and destroying the city, it was hard work breaking down tough granite buildings with sledgehammers. They destroyed palaces, the royal stables, the royal baths, an aqueduct and the massive stone bridge over the Tungaghadra River, but at one end a giant statue of the bull of Shiva remains and at the other end of the boulevard stands the main temple on a hill, undamaged. The fact that it was the secular buildings which suffered is to the credit of the Muslim commanders.

Travellers have recorded its magnificence, the abundance of gold, rubies and pearls: as in the reign of King Solomon silver was of no account.

Carved on the outer wall of a building is a frieze showing a line of chorus girls high-kicking with bare legs, thus anticipating by centuries revue choruses of London and Paris. But the former were more daring in that they also swung their bare breasts in unison. The Moguls would not allow such dancing and nautch girls had to be decently clothed.

My brother was full of enthusiasm and after lunch in the heat, wanted to climb the temple hill, but I dissuaded him. Instead, we paddled my canoe on a nearby reservoir.

Next morning we rode my horse in turn, but Rembrandt wasn't fit, oats not being obtainable. Months later I discovered that the syce or groom was helping himself to part of the horse's rations, the horse- beans.

To entertain my brother I took him to a Gypsy village - and asked them for a dance. The women, colourfully dressed with wide skirts and many ornaments, obliged us with grace and gusto and we gave them ten rupees, a quite adequate reward, but they were crafty and didn't smile, in the hope of getting a few more rupees.

There was an elderly contractor living in Hospet, who invited us to lunch; he had worked with the British and was more British than Indian. We began with beer, then sat down to chicken palau (or pilaff) with a moderate curry, followed by a sweet. We were given cutlery but his family used their fingers, quite noiselessly. In accordance with Hindu custom, his wife served us. It was a most enjoyable meal.

At one of the villages called Ittigi there was no rest house, so I camped in the police station in the middle of the village. In the evening I sat in the yard and observed the stars and the moon. I listened carefully to the village sounds and conversation, which I couldn't follow, while bullock carts rumbled by, their wheels clanking; to the cries of children, the lowing of cattle and now and then the popping of a soda-water bottle.

In the conversation I could recognise place-names, which were all of the locality. And not once did I catch the name of the district, provincial or national leaders. I could also tell that their conversation was quite free from indecency or malice. They were good, loving people.

There were black-buck about in the cotton fields and I went stalking three times. My rifle was a .300 Remington Express, but it was too light and I never had much success till I changed it for a heavier weapon. But stalking before breakfast is a grand pastime, though I am sure the village leaders were disappointed that I brought down only one.

Soon after my 24th birthday I decided to paddle my 2-seater canoe fourteen miles upstream to the next camp, which required practice.

The current was swifter than I had thought and the first two miles, through narrows, were very slow, then into a broad sweep of river thickly lined with trees. At dusk, there was a great kerfuffle, flying foxes started their screeching and night birds gave sudden piercing cries. Now and then a fish leapt, one weighing several pounds leapt high into the air and hit the water with a resounding smack. Was it a crocodile after him? But I was tiring, turned back and was relieved after some time to see the lights of my camp brilliantly reflected in the water.

Two Indian gentlemen, the District Health Officer and the Doctor had come to call, but I was too exhausted to receive them. I had only paddled about seven miles so the 14-mile trip up-stream was definitely off.

★ ★ ★ ★ ★

Once again the Mylar Festival came round. The Sub-Collector, N.S. Arunachalam, was already there in a similar tent to mine. I called on him as he sat at a table laden with gifts of fruit and some tins of cigarettes.

All went well, but I reproached myself for relying on last year's arrangements and not checking them thoroughly. This year, 1940, the prophecy was a brief one and all too obvious: "Clouds over the world."

Mylar was miles from anywhere and after it was over our tents and luggage had to be loaded onto bullock carts which took ages, but the pace of villagers and their bullocks cannot be hurried.

When we reached the market town a telegram was waiting. It was an invitation to take part in the All-India Regatta. So I typed an application for casual leave and sent it by 'runner' on a bicycle. I then left camp with my faithful orderly, Hirelal. It was very hot. We cycled 17 miles along tracks deep in dust and I arrived, de-hydrated. First I drank tea, then tumblers of lime juice, finishing with a well-cooled pint of Alsopp's beer.

My camp was a pleasant one by the river as it swept round – clear and sparkling, unfortunately it wasn't safe for bathing. There were few insects and I watched the silvery moon as it glided behind the trees growing along the bank.

Next morning we continued our journey on bicycles, Hirelal carrying a quart flask of cooled water for me and a water-bottle for himself. After 12 miles along tracks I stopped for a drink: no good swallowing it down, you fill your mouth, swill it round, wait until it is warm, then swallow. In this way a sharp thirst is slaked.

I offered some of the cooled water to Hirelal: he put his head back and poured half a pint down his throat – much more refined than me swilling it round the mouth.

At our destination a camel was tethered, so I went for a ride on him along the tow-path. I was looking forward to the comfort of my bungalow and above all, to electric fans and to seeing J.P.L. Gwynn, but he wired to the effect that he was delayed so I prolonged my camp for a couple of days and finished the inspection. Well may the reader ask: 'But why all this rushing about in the great heat?' Secretariat officials all retired to the hill stations for three or more months but we district officers did not and worked almost as hard in the hot season and subordinate officials could not say: 'Now we can relax and take things easy till the hot weather is over.'

It was good to be back; I had not met one of my kind for more than ten days.

At the sugar factory I met a tall Englishman, J.M. Sweet, an old Cliftonian who was a Deputy Conservator of Forests. He was very pukka and spoke little. I met Sweet again at Poona but he remained aloof as before.

I was very pleased to have the company of J.P.L. Gwynn. He was different from most of us: he was deeply religious and kept a well-used Prayer Book at his bedside and his Irishness made him warm towards Indian Nationalism and freedom.

Meanwhile, I was waiting for my casual leave to be sanctioned. The evening before it arrived two Brahmins called: one was very orthodox, the second was my favourite vakil or lawyer. Though he was the leading local Congressman he would enjoy a bottle of beer and a cigar. He was a Liberal in the best sense, a Congressman all could like and respect.

Leaving in the morning for Madras I called at Bellary specifically to discuss with Jakeman, my Superintendent, the case I was working on against a Sub-Inspector whom I believed to be corrupt. Then I called on the Dy. Inspector-General, L.A. Bishop and Mrs Bishop. I was indeed fortunate to have these two officers as my superiors.

My next stop was the neighbouring district about a hundred miles on, where I had arranged to stay with a young Indian officer – Krishna Menon – who was Principal of a Police Constables' Training School. He was easy to get on with, with pleasant manners, but one evening was not enough to get through to him, for he clearly had his own opinions but was too polite to air them.

Next morning we reached Ranipet, a small station, dominated by Parry's sugar factory. I called on an engineer I knew but instead of a British engineer found a tall, military-looking man, with blue eyes and steel-grey hair. He introduced himself as Dr Otto Stern and gave me a good lunch – such is Eastern hospitality. Later I got to know him well. He was Austrian, had served as a cavalry captain in the Austro-Hungarian Army and what he didn't know about horses was not worth knowing.

We drove on and reached Madras Boat Club for tea, weary but happy.

20

Regatta and Recreation

A WEEK was devoted to strict training and outings on the Adyar River before breakfast and after tea, for the afternoons were hot. I met a very nice girl and took her out twice. She was not very happy though, probably because her parents' marriage was in difficulties.

Joy Westerdale asked me to dine with her parents. She was a jolly girl, but one of the guests could not but attract attention, Paddy. She was tall and walked like a queen. All her movements were deliberate, her voice well modulated and her speech dignified. After dinner, we went to the Connemara Hotel, but after a couple of dances with Joy and one with Paddy, I went home to comply with training rules.

Then was the start of the Regatta. My pair lost in the first round to a pair from Calcutta University. Our main race was in the fours in which we drew a strong crew: the Calcutta Lake Club. I was stroke, my friend Gordon Marshall was behind at No. 3, Madras led most of the way but not by much. Then the Lake Club gave a fine spurt near the finish and won by half a length. The time was much faster than the prevous race between Bombay and Poona Boat Clubs, so it was defeat with honour and we were no longer in the contest.

A young married woman called Peggy Bindon introduced me to two charming girls, Margaret and Pamela. They were close friends and liked to be together; I tried to find another man to make up the party, but probably without much enthusiasm.

It was the first time I had ever taken out two young ladies. After dinner we saw a film, Shaw's 'Pygmalion' and finished up at the Connemara. There was a small cabaret including a dancer who danced the hula-hula. At the end she invited a man to dance with her, but no one came forward. So my brother Louis volunteered. It was hilarious because he forgot to take the cigarette out of his mouth and once the dancing began he couldn't get rid of it.

We stayed late and I took my guests back to their respective homes. For the next few days of leave I had Margaret and Pam to myself. We went to the air-conditioned Connemara, danced at the Gymkhana Club, then to the Regatta finals on Saturday, which were attended by the Governor and Bishop of Madras. The best race was the Sculls between Major Waters, of Poona, and Sen, a Bengali. Sen was in the lead, but Waters pressed hard and drew up inch by inch till he won by a mere canvas. It was a magnificent race.

⁜ ⁜ ⁜ ⁜ ⁜

One evening, when Pam arrived she looked a picture. A light green skirted gown set off to perfection her soft, pink complexion and fair hair in which she had placed a red rosebud. We were a party of six including my brother and began with dinner at the Connemara. We went on to the Gymkhana and finished at the Madras Club for more dancing.

To cool off we decided on a walk along the harbour arm, then I persuaded Pam to come for a quiet bathe from one of the beaches. We sat in the sand. It was night, stars twinkled brightly and light clouds drifted across the moon. I was entranced by the deep blue sea rolling, curving and breaking into white foam.

Pam was also quiet. I don't know whether the sea moved her as much as it did me, for she was like a fairy, light and graceful.

For my last day I arranged a lunch party in a private dining room at the Connemara Hotel. We were ten in all and I kept their signatures on the menu:- Pam, Ian, Blue Eyes, Bottle-nose, N. Dunn, Flatfoot, Snow White and Soapy.

A subaltern was attracted to Pam but I managed to shake him off in order to take her and Margaret to tea at a place called Moore's Gardens. And so I took them home, saying how very much I had enjoyed their company; bade farewell to my friends Valerie and Gordon Marshall and finally, to my brother Louis. His parting message was "Don't get engaged just yet."

So ended the best leave I had had for four years. The drive home was long and dusty and I thought of those delightful girls and of Peggy, the kindly married woman who had introduced them and who helped us to get on so well.

At a hot, dusty station in the Anantapur district I hoped to meet a colleague, J. R. Le Fevre. I found his camp and sat in the shade under the flap of the tent till he returned. He was hospitable, working hard and obviously rather lonely. He was younger than I and was still adjusting to the lonely life.

So I pushed on to Anantapur, headquarters of the district. While driving round Madras I had forgotten to have the car serviced – near our destination the gearbox ran out of oil, we crawled the last few miles and put up with D. Crossley, the Superintendent of Police and Mrs Crossley. They were a kindly North Country couple and I enjoyed playing with their little girl – as a bachelor one rarely had anything to do with children. In the evening we played a round on their golf course; nine holes, brown fairway and sandy 'greens'.

Early in May, while camping by a big reservoir, I gazed on one of the sights of the Indian plains – a spectacular sunset. The day was overcast and a variety of rainclouds filled the sky – the lightest was pale pearl, ranging to a deep shade of grey. The water, reflecting the sky, was grey, but a shaft of light from beyond it gave it some brilliance while the gentlest of breezes ruffled the surface just enough to add sparkle.

The distant bank of the reservoir was dotted with trees and above them was piled up the cumulus – clouds that had already shed much rain but were good for more.

The sinking sun shed a brilliant crimson glow that coloured the base of the cloud-mass and painted the edges with gold. The crimson grew deeper, then paled away to pink and finally died away. Night began to fall but suddenly a rift formed in the clouds showing once more the fiery mass of the sun. It seemed like a battle between light and darkness, but as the darkness gathered the sun blazed forth for its last fling before the night.

Back in Hospet and to office work. It was good to ride again, but the air was so hot one felt thirsty after barely an hour's ride.

While working in the office a visitor arrived and who should it be but Peter Gwynn, just back from a short Easter break in Goa. Soon I was listening to tales of ancient Goa and its many churches. But he was more serious and scholarly than me – I could never have spent the Easter break attending services and visiting churches. Gwynn by then had a horse and to go for a ride together was a great pleasure.

Goa, the largest Portuguese enclave, had a character of its own. As early as 1510 the Portuguese Viceroy sanctioned mixed marriages, so that Indo-Portuguese men could supply manpower. Thirty years later the King of Portugal signed a decree ordering all Hindu temples in Goa to be destroyed and shortly afterwards the famous missionary, St Francis Xavier, an early Jesuit, arrived in Goa. These factors explain the dominance of Catholics in the Colony.

The only Mogul Emperor to destroy temples was Aurangzeb and the Portuguese were the only European power to do so. When in 1565 the Muslim armies plundered Vijayanagar, the temples were spared. I cannot find any excuse for this cold-blooded act of destruction by a Christian power.

★ ★ ★ ★ ★

We expected our two friends from the Manganese Mines and Tom Kelso, Manager of the sugar factory. For once, we had entertainment for them; four Punjabi wrestlers performed, one a very big man. After the exhibition we collected Rs. 20 for the four of them, with which sum they were more than satisfied.

We decided to call at the Railway Refreshment Room, where we found a young Englishman drinking alone, he was the Assistant Traffic Superintendent at Guntakal Junction. But it was so warm, despite the overhead fans that we all repaired to my place for dinner. Dinner for six was an event for my little household. Kelso became more than a little excited and talked of fighting for King and Country.

Early next morning was my day for the Town Police parade. Later we were again invited by Thandu Mudaliar, the retired contractor, who gave us an excellent meal. After a rest at my bungalow, four of us set off with servants for the Manganese Mines in two cars.

My Dodge car climbed alright till we reached Sandur, the little State capital, then it gave up. So we piled into the Chevrolet, servants, luggage and all. The going was quite steep and with the heavy load it soon boiled. So we waited, eating lumps of ice to keep cool and popped some ice into the radiator.

We arrived before dark and were pleased to find the air (at 2,500 ft) fairly cool.

The next evening we drove along forest roads to watch for game and on the way back we had some luck seeing several peafowl, cock and hens; a wild cat, then after dark, a pair of wild boar. They turned towards the headlights, blinked with surprise, walked up to within ten yards of the car then turned and trotted back into the jungle.

So four days passed quietly, a temporary relief from the great heat. At Sandur I called on the Police Officer. We then began our descent. On the way down we saw a sad sight: many acres of scrub jungle burnt black by a forest fire.

At Hospet we were surrounded by servants, Gwynn's and mine, each set consisting of butler, cook, waterman, sweeper; my two orderlies – and Peter's two Revenue peons. My well-bred Muslim Camp Clerk was the senior and all addressed him with respect. Though there wasn't nearly enough work for them, there was no drinking or quarreling. They were perfectly behaved and all got on well. I mention this as Indians are able both to work hard and to relax when there is no work to do.

Among the imports that were disappearing was the popular Rose's Lime Juice, which the ladies liked to mix with their gin. But Rose's also recommended it to young bachelors as a remedy against the morning after. The advertisements showed them in the morning, hanging their heads after failing to drink some the night before, or lying wearily in bed when it was time to get up. Abdul, the bearer, would say to a fellow servant. "Sahib no drink morning tea. He complain that mosquitoes are stamping their feet against the mosquito curtains." Or: "Sahib not well. He say his tongue feels like old mango stone in dust of bazaar. So I tell him: 'Drink Rose's Lime Juice at bed time and you will feel better in the morning.'"

21

Hot Weather Camp Near Mysore

A DISTANT police station, at a place called Arisikere, not a good village, but a poor one and divided into two factions. Once such a feud becomes established it is almost impossible to cure – something like the Montagues and the Capulets. As there was no road, I rode along cart-tracks for twelve or more miles. There was no Rest House and a small house at the edge of the village had been placed at my disposal. It was hot and airless, not having electricity. I worked to an accompaniment of boys repeating their lessons, donkeys braying, village dogs barking, babies crying, little children playing, women drawing water and sometimes quarrelling, crows squawking and the little grey squirrels screeching, which was very trying.

The local landowner wanted prestige. This, strangely, he sought by desiring to take in procession a god, or idol, in a palanquin carried sideways! This was offensive to the other faction and had to be prohibited. So I called on him and found him very charming: he garlanded me, sprinkled rosewater, served tea, biscuits and sweet meats and a bottle of English beer. He played Western music, then when I was feeling good – his daughter made the request: to carry the palanquin sideways. After such hospitality I was most embarrassed but had no alternative but to refuse.

One evening I rode Rembrandt in order to visit three villages, but wasn't looking at the time and started back too late. In a short while it was dark. There was no moon and not a star in the sky; the blackness was complete.

The return journey was about seven miles along tracks. As I could not see anything I left it to Rembrandt. He walked at quite a good pace, stumbling occasionally and in a couple of hours, to my astonishment, I suddenly saw the hurricane lantern on the wall of the house. I don't know how Rembrandt found the way and he was shrouded in steam. I hugged him and was so pleased that I gave him my bottle of beer. The groom and I were very proud of Rembrandt that night.

It might not be out of place to mention that catering for a touring officer, miles away from any road, wasn't easy, especially in the hot season. Flour and stores were scarce – also fresh fruit and vegetables – while a salad was out of the question.

Though no one would live in the ruins of Vijayanagar following the massacre hundreds of years before, a temple car festival did take place at intervals and in view of its history, officials could not take risks. The temple car is a very high wooden structure, 40-50 ft high, with four huge solid wooden wheels, eight or more feet high. It is dragged by two stout ropes by hundreds of young men with much noise: strident music and shouting, women throwing rosebuds, posies and even bananas. When in motion, great care needs to be taken to keep people away from the wheels.

The evening before I rode to Hampi, the nearest village, through great crowds in gala dress, the women favouring crimson saris. Jakeman and I stayed at the Rest House and were on duty all next morning for the dragging of the temple car with much shouting and the shrill cries of the women. Further it was hot and dusty. After a break for lunch I returned for the afternoon – Jakeman's presence not being necessary. After more heat and dust I felt overcome and handed over to the Inspector, rejoining Jakeman at the Rest House. All went well, for the Inspector was a respected Hindu.

Next morning I drove to Bellary for my Urdu examination and in the evening called at Jakeman's. He had a well-watered green lawn and there four of us sat and relaxed. It was so refreshing after all the dust and heat to see soft green again – to one side was a fishpond and we spent a delightful evening listening to a gramophone and dining on the lawn.

My ten days leave in Madras had been my best spell of leave and these two days spent in Bellary, which seemed modest enough, were in fact the end of an era, for supplies of stores and drink were running out – the ships from Australia were loaded with troops and military supplies.

Near Hospet a new barrage across the Tungabhadra River was on the drawing-board. This brought the Chief Engineer (Irrigation) and as he remembered my father he kindly sent me an invitation to dinner at he P.W.D. Rest House. F.M. Dowley was a big, tall and good-looking Irishman and I much enjoyed his company.

The War Reaches India

In May 1940, the Nazi war machine was forcing its way across Europe: first Holland, then Belgium, Luxembourg and France were prostrated. I listened avidly to the news, but the Indians and those round about took little notice.

I went to Kudligi, a local headquarters for the Tahsildar of the Revenue Department and the Police Inspector. I was alone and the Inspector sat with me in the evenings. It was a good year – rain was falling, the reservoirs were all full, the frogs were croaking happily, the hedges were sprouting green. Insects were plentiful – ants, moths, flying beetles and, of course, the mosquitoes were breeding. It is important to protect the ankles and forearms from the tiny malaria mosquito which stings painlessly, produces no noticeable swelling and yet can cause a high fever.

The Inspector and I toured the villages by car and on foot. I wanted to know what the villagers thought of the war. So I put my questions and the Inspector translated into Kanarese. It was soon clear that the reality of the terrible war had not yet penetrated. At that time many villages had no wireless receiver, so they depended on an Indian language newspaper. At one village only two miles from the road, villagers turned down a suggestion to take a newspaper, for this would have to be posted and they felt two miles there and two miles back for the postman would be too much trouble.

In June I paid my last visit to the Manganese Mines. Instead of having no cares in the world we were listening to the daily war- bulletins and I had been warned of a transfer. The jungle was cool, fresh and green, but poor old Fawcitt was ill. I did not know his age but he had been in India for many years and his health had given way. He was suffering from a severe attack of malaria and bronchitis and his coughing was pitiful. Much of the manganese ore which was exported from Goa went to Belgium and with the fall of Belgium, the mining had to be severely curtailed. What with this and their beloved Manager seriously ill, the entire mining community was afraid. It was impossible to feel cheerful – the tale of the General Sandur Mining Company appeared to be drawing to its close and without mining royalties the outlook for the State would be bleak.

On my return to Hospet, a telegram ordering my transfer was waiting. I sat up late trying to leave everything in order, while my butler supervised the packing. Jakeman took charge of my subdivision by telegram.

My stay at Hospet had only lasted for a couple of years but they were years full of movement and variety. And it was my first charge with responsibility for law and order and some 300 policemen; well over 1,000 souls with their families. With few exceptions they had been loyal and disciplined; they had put up with my peculiarities; they had helped me to overcome the difficulties and discomforts that went with the job and had taught me a great deal. I had no family – camp clerk, servants, orderlies and subordinates were my family. Now I had to leave immediately. There could be no farewell tea party with garlands and mutual expressions of regard – no last words. It was a great wrench.

Yelliah, my butler, orderly Hirelal and I drove to Bellary. For the next two or three days I felt so low that I thought we were going to lose the war, for it was shortly before Dunkirk. One of my colleagues, A.E. Spitteler, was there and also far from his usual cheerful self. Then the depression cleared and I never again had the slightest doubt that we would win the war.

So ended two of the most enjoyable and carefree years of my life.

22

Transfer to a New Post

THE REASON for my hurried departure was the new war-time sense of urgency which finally reached India towards the beginning of 1940. My posting was to a town in Vizagapatam District on the East Coast; it was called Vizianagram, a former cantonment. The journey was back along the route we had taken nearly two years before from Cocanada and thence we would proceed north to Vizagapatam.

We left on 19 June 1940 loaded up with luggage, the furniture and furnishings following by goods train and arrived at Kurnool, a remote District town about 10 a.m., in time for breakfast. The Railway Refreshment Room was the obvious place and there a curious incident occurred. The platforms were deserted except for two Army officers. The first was tall, very handsome with a well-cut uniform, obviously a regular from a good regiment and was marching up and down. The other was ordinary looking, with ordinary uniform, obviously a war-time officer. The regular was having nothing to do with him and as the latter was sitting on a chair outside the refreshment room, I asked him in for a bottle of beer. He smiled but declined saying, "No thanks, the train will be coming at any moment."

So I sat down to breakfast of cereal, sausages, eggs, coffee, toast,marmalade and beer. When I had finished and paid there was the R.A.S.C. Captain still waiting for his train. So I had a good laugh.

We drove up the road, up to 3,000 feet. Then had a splendid drive down the Giddalur *ghat* i.e. hill road. There was thick green, but dry, jungle on either side for mile upon mile without a break, as far as the eye could see, more than twenty miles; it invited a walk with a gun and a shikari (or hunter) as guide.

After the rains, hundreds and hundreds of bright yellow butterflies were flitting around. Giddalur was the name and as I drove this ditty went through and through my head:

> 'Git along little dawgie
> Git along, git along
> Git along little dawgie,
> Git a-long.

Kurnool is a magnificent district for those who love the forest with its wildlife and solitude. Modern civilization can hardly touch it.

Living in small settlements on the slopes of these hills is an interesting tribe of aboriginals. Having lived in the forests from time immemorial they, not surprisingly, considered the forests to be their property; no doubt former Indian rulers left them alone, but the British rulers with their logical minds did not agree. The Chenchus are a simple lazy tribe, much addicted to arrack, which they distil and to quarrelling among themselves. Their weapon is the bow and arrow which they can use with deadly effect. Taking cover in the jungle they would attack and rob innocent travellers and pilgrims. Special officers were appointed to try and reform them, but the task proved too great. However, in 1950, when political offenders took to the jungle, Chenchus proved their skill as trackers and several wanted men were duly apprehended. (Vide History of the Madras Police, 1959)

About 20 miles before my next halting place a slow puncture developed. Every few miles my civilian driver pumped it up. Then I told him to change the wheel but he replied "No Sahib, it will last out." But he was wrong – as we approached the town the tyre went flat and ripped.

There was a small rest house, it was stuffy inside after the cool, jungle-clad hills of Kurnool. I was jaded and went to the Railway Refreshment Room which was up to the usual high standard. I had a good wash-and-brush-up and tea. The evening was heavy and dull and I went to bed early.

In the night I was woken by the sound of torrential rain so I dashed out to garage the car. In the morning it was much cooler; a nearby Sub-Inspector called to see if he could be of help and obliged by booking a railway truck to take us and the car across the Krishna (or Kistna) river, for I was not going to risk a country ferry again. So we drove off; en route a stream, swollen by the rain, proved just too deep for us to cross, but this is never a problem on the Indian highways, soon a few strong men pushed us through a foot and a half of water. Guntur district is the chief area for the tobacco industry – there were British planters growing the crop from Virginia seed and one of these planters was the father of two Indian Police Officers – E.S. and P.M. Treasure.

I had stopped at the next Railway Refreshment Room, when a car-load of American missionaries arrived, having been on vacation at Kodaikanal, a hill station in the south. We pressed on, crossed the Krishna and reached the important city of Bezwada, a commercial, religious and Railway centre. The same party of missionaries soon joined me in the Refreshment Room; I had bought a book, a bottle of Gilbey's whisky and a tin of cigarettes so I offered cigarettes to the one male missionary, but he didn't smoke. I then offered him whisky, but very reluctantly it seemed to me, he said "No thanks, I guess."

There is a marked difference between Catholic and American Protestant missionaries. The Catholics: French, Belgian or Italian priests gladly accept a cigar, cigarettes or a drink. The Protestant men are allowed to marry and have children but are not allowed to drink or smoke. I only remember one Catholic priest who declined an offer of a whisky and soda: he was an ascetic Irish priest, a rather rare type.

That night a box of matches – not Bryant and Mays – exploded in my hand, then a party arrived late in the adjoining suite: a man, woman and half a dozen children who didn't settle down. Next morning I found he was a Muslim Police Superintendent.

The Godaveri River is not on a par with the Ganges, the Indus and the Brahmaputra, but it is no mean river. Rising in the Western Ghats it flows south east for some 800 miles and fans out into a very fertile delta. Being miles wide in the lower reaches, all through the monsoons (S.W. and N.E.), it is only crossable by a long Railway bridge and for half its length it flows through the heart of the Telugu country.

The car was put on a truck and we took the train across the great river and got off at Rajamundry. From there it was not far to our destination: Cocanada, where I knew a couple living near the Club House. It was about 8 p.m. and I asked his butler if I could stay the night, assuming the answer would be "Yes, of course." But I was mistaken. Mr R. didn't see me but sent a note saying "This house is neither an hotel nor a rest house." I mention this because such a refusal was quite exceptional. It was the only instance I experienced, in thirteen years, of hospitality being refused to a traveller.

The Cocanada Club was deserted so I rang the Manager of Parry's sugar factory and distillery, and he fixed me up in no time with the Collector, a Mr Woodhouse.

Next morning, one of the local Sub-Inspectors called. I had worked with him in Cocanada three years before. He was a fine fellow and I was pleased to find he was doing well in a responsible station.

The next stage was to Waltair, the Government headquarters of the very large district of Vizagapatam. Until 1936 there were two more Madras districts north of Vizagapatam but they were then taken in order to help form the new Province of Orissa.

Driving along the trunk road I could not help noticing the tall and shapely Telugu women as they walked along carrying a basket or a pot on their heads, a contrast to the peasant women of Bellary and round about, who were mostly small and lean.

We arrived at the bungalow of the Acting Superintendent of Police, C.E. Lonsdale and found him alone, his Canadian wife and children being in the hills. [27] He brought me up to date on the war news which was serious and was listening to the bulletins three times a day. While staying with him, France collapsed, but there was nothing we could do except follow the news. Life went on and it was important to keep up morale.

Lonsdale took me to the Bengal-Nagpur Railway Institute where we watched a pretty good exhibition of boxing which made me want to put on the gloves. Then he introduced me to a charming and hospitable couple called Kennedy, next day I called on Mrs Hume, wife of R. Hume, a tough and able Scot who was the Deputy Inspector General of Police for the Northern, Telugu, Districts.

Amongst others I met was an I.C.S. Probationer, D.J.C. Crawley, 'Dismal

[27] After the war Lonsdale was ordained in the Diocese of British Columbia

Desmond', a nickname chosen only for reasons of alliteration, for he was a cheerful young man without a care in the world.

Lonsdale took me along the busy road to my destination; large quantities of produce from the hinterland were being taken to Vizagapatam Port, not by lorry, but in strings of bullock carts, so driving was slow.

By great good fortune my brother Louis was passing through, having motored from Calcutta.

23

Change of Life Style

VIZIANAGRAM AND its environs were not typical of British India, for it was a big estate owned by a Rajah – cricketers may remember that, before the war, the Captain of All-India was the Rajkumar of Vizianagram. When I lived there the palace was occupied by caretakers and every day I saw a band of twenty or thirty professional beggars walk to the palace for alms and they were given alms. But without the Rajah, the place seemed only half alive.

Some years before, it was the scene of the murder of a young Probationer called Holme. The Inspector-General, Sir Charles Cunningham, took charge of the investigation and it was found that Leonard, a Senior Assistant Superintendent was having relations with a Mrs Woodward, the Bank Manager's wife; Mr Woodward was a hard-working and blameless official. Then Holme, a Probationary Assistant Superintendent of Police was posted to Vizianagram for practical training. Mrs Woodward kept Leonard but preferred the younger man and one night a shot rang out and the young man was found shot through the head. He had been visiting Mrs Woodward. His skull was sent to Sir Bernard Spilsbury, the forensic scientist in London, but evidence was hard to find. It transpired that Mrs Woodward required her waterman to attend her when she took her evening bath. She would soap herself, then the waterman would pour warm water over her, but he was cleared. Of course, Leonard was strongly suspected but all they could pin on him was the burning of love letters. For this offence – the suppression of material evidence – he was duly dismissed.

My job was a new one as the Madras Government had decided to raise two more companies of Armed Police, each of 255 men. One Company was to be raised near Madras by a keen young officer, P.F.S. Murray, the other by me. My officers were an experienced Sergeant-Major, Mr Gover, late of the Queen's Bays (5th Dragoon Guards); an ex-Army Subedar of similar rank and Police Jemadars – one for each platoon. Men were arriving daily – some from District Armed Reserves, some were older men – ex-Army – and many were recruits.

All were to be housed in empty barracks. No families were allowed and my first task was to choose a contractor to feed them.

It was interesting to try a number of samples of rice of various qualities and prices and of varying cooking times. A jolly Anglo-Indian Deputy Superintendent of Police was camping there. He had a grown daughter who had fine dark eyes and a buxom figure. She was musical and we got on well – she accompanying at the piano, I singing; but they were soon gone.

British India, as already indicated, was then being governed not by elected Ministers but by the Governors, with the help of senior I.C.S. Advisers.

The Adviser in charge of Law and Order, J.G. Rutherford, C.I.E., paid us a visit and inspected all the men; he was tall and handsome. It was hot and sticky and, foolishly, I wore Review order: gabardine with collar, tie and Sam Browne, which was most uncomfortable.

Between us we weeded out over a hundred men as being either too old or unsuitable. I was sorry to see so many go, but men were arriving every day and they were soon replaced.

My next task was to find a suitable Urdu teacher and a very respectable Muslim was soon found. A party of young Europeans from Calcutta offices who had been called up were travelling in high spirits to the Officers Training Establishment at Belgaum in the South Deccan. I joined them over drinks, but had a severe toothache developing.

Next morning the train arrived at Madras Central Station and I took a taxi to the bungalow of D.C.T. Cameron, one of the Deputy Commissioners of Police who was my host. I called on my friends, G.S.W. (Gordon) Marshall and Valerie and learned that he, a chartered accountant, was expecting shortly to be called up.

With two colleagues, Ronson and Le Fevre, we spent a quiet evening at the cinema and saw Deanna Durbin and Herbert Marshall in 'Mad about Music', Herbert Marshall being a favourite of mine.

Next morning I reported for the Urdu exam which took place in the imposing building of the Public Services Commission. My chief difficulty was reading Urdu manuscript which is cursive. However, the examiner was indulgent and in due course I learned that I had passed.

At dinner I was most interested in the tales told by P.F.S. Murray of his time in the Malabar Special Police. This is a force designed to control the Moplahs of Malabar, a spirited Muslim fraternity with a fair amount of Arab blood in them. The Moplah Rebellion of 1921-22 was a political–religious one. It was handled gently to begin with, unlike Amritsar. I merely state the facts which show how difficult it is to pass judgement:

Amritsar 1919	Moplah Rebellion 1921-22
300 and odd killed	Several thousand Moplahs killed.
1,200 wounded	Several thousand Hindus killed
2,500 brought to trial	by Moplahs, often after torture.
No army casualties	48 Police and Army killed; 139 wounded.
	43 Government offices and police stations looted.

The Regiments that assisted the Police were the Leinsters and the Dorsetshire Regiment; a George Cross was awarded to one of the latter and the Regimental Museum in Dorchester contains relics of that rebellion: some murderous steel weapons and a large war drum four to five feet high, which must have drummed up the latent fanaticism of the Moplahs.

From then 1922, to the end of British rule, there was no serious disturbance in the South and Army garrisons were reduced to five.

Next day a senior Police officer gave a dinner party which was followed by a visit to the cinema. When a party of City officials go to the cinema, a clerk informs the manager, who reserves the required number of cane chairs at the back, he meets the party at the door, escorts them to their seats, while during the interval, whisky and soda is served. So a pleasant evening is passed.

My dentist in Madras was a big German, grave and very professional. He duly removed a wisdom tooth. Afterwards he took me to his sitting room and served a 'krug' of good German beer. He carefully chilled the krug with crushed ice, emptied it, then slowly poured in the beer. "Never," he said, "should beer be kept in a fridge or diluted with lumps of ice."

After making certain calls, including the necessary calls on the Inspector-General in his lovely office facing the sea, I went to Adyar. Paired with F.F. Coldwell, we won the Double Sculls. A friend of my brother's, Walter Grantham, had asked me to dinner and dancing at the Madras Club. Walter by his manners, rather than his looks, attracted the most charming and elegant women. We danced first at the Madras Club, then at the Gymkhana.

Next day after a bathe, I called on H.M. Hood, I.C.S., Chief Adviser to the Governor. He was extremely able but spoke little, he was a listener. Mrs Hood was a charming and admirable hostess who remembered my mother.

Petitions

No book about India during our rule can fail to mention the important part played by the written petition, a practice which we inherited from the Moguls. It was the chief means by which people scattered over a wide area brought their requests or grievances to official notice. As most of the population was illiterate the writers were mostly lawyers, clerks or the village scribe.

The petition is in parts; the address – honorific; then the circumstances; the request and the doxology. Petitions in varying numbers were received by office-holders every day and many were in the Vernacular.

Shortly before the war, a Calcutta businessman showed me the following choice example, in original:-

To the Manager
XYZ Company, Calcutta

Most respected and honoured Sir,

By the grace of God and your Honour's kind help I am the father of nine children. What to do to make ends meet and keep both the ends together?
Thus I pray for an increase in my menstrual remuneration and this I beg in the name of J. Christ Esquire, whom your honour most closely resembles.

I have the honour to remain,
Kind Sir,
Your most obedient servant
C. Lall Dass

It happened during a dinner party in Vizagapatam. The dining-room was in the middle of a large bungalow with four bedrooms opening off it which had half doors i.e. open top and bottom. Two of the guests, a married couple, were staying the night, he having just rejoined his wife after an absence of months. When the coffee was brought the man drank his, excused himself and, to her evident surprise, led his wife away into their bedroom. Eyebrows were raised but nothing was said. If the butler noticed the incident as he most probably did, he would have been highly amused.

The Collector and District Magistrate of Vizagapatam was an outstanding one: C.H. (Chris) Masterman, I.C.S. Mrs Masterman had organised a fete in aid of war funds at the Collector's office and for some reason the electric fans were not working. I had on my best suit and found it stifling. There were no refreshments but that delightful couple, Mr and Mrs Kennedy asked me to dinner and to stay the night. Eventually, it felt cooler – it was August and preparing for the monsoon. After dinner they took me to the Club, where we played billiards and from there on to the Railway Institute for dancing but it was too hot for us. Only Anglo-Indian couples could dance in that sticky heat.

I woke up to see the morning sun shining on the garden, and beyond, the sea breaking on the white sands and beyond that the deep blue waters of the Bay of Bengal. I couldn't stay in bed or sit drinking tea, but went out and had a refreshing swim and walk along the beach.

Afterwards I called on S.W.W. Wright, the regular Superintendent of Police who had previously been at Vellore and who had relieved Lonsdale.

Before lunch we had another bathe with Gilbert Kennedy and met John Burton, a most attractive young man who was Assistant Traffic Superintendent on the Bengal-Nagpur Railway.

After tea I paid my official call on the Deputy Inspector General, R. Hume, who was evidently very keen on pre-Great War infantry, the sort of job I had. He was somewhat disappointed in me but without transport, workshops, without signalling, Bren guns or tear gas or games I found it a dull job.

The Public Works Department had chosen a vacant bungalow for my use in Vizianagram with two bedrooms, but it needed repairs and re-painting. While this was being done the Manager of the Imperial Bank of India, Neville Smith, kindly put me up for a month; his wife was away and I think he was glad of some company. A lot of agricultural produce was handled in Vizianagram and he was a busy man. Once a week he inspected stocks of produce, on which as security he granted loans. He was a man of very regular habits as befits a bank manager and as soon as he returned in the evening, the butler would bring him a bottle of very cold soda and a glass on a salver. He would pour out the soda and drink it straight off but I didn't think it was good for him – I always drank cold drinks slowly.

The routine was simple: early morning parade for one and a quarter to one and a half hours, then breakfast, followed by inspection of the Lines. Office work never took more than a couple of hours. During the day, an hour with my language teacher; in the evening, parade with a route march once a week. August-September evenings were a warm time for route-marches, but we all enjoyed them and the men would sing Telugu songs as they marched.

One evening during parade there was a remarkable storm. A sudden terrific wind drove the rain horizontally, a lake formed at one end of the parade ground, which was churned into waves. After each blast of wind the water raced back over the flat ground but the next blast pushed it on again 'till the ground was left bare. It was like the strong east wind which pushed back the Red Sea for Moses and his tribes. Then, suddenly, the wind dropped and left the parade ground a shallow lake. India is full of surprises – it is never dull for long.

Neville Smith had suggested that I call on the local Baptist missionaries, but I wasn't keen. Anyhow, I did call on Dr and Mrs Daniell of the Canadian Baptist Mission. Dr Daniell was out when I arrived, so I met Mrs Blanche Daniell. She was short, fair and most charming. She had a piano and soon she was playing – I singing. I thoroughly enjoyed myself and before long I was staying with them as my bungalow was not yet ready and Mrs Smith was expected. The Daniells were delightful hosts and on Sunday I attended their Chapel service. She also told me that I must not drink whisky or beer in the reception rooms but that I could do what I liked in my bedroom. So I had my peg of whisky alone.

One evening I returned, wet with perspiration, after a route march. She looked at me and said, "My, you are wet through. You must have your bottle of beer. You deserve it." So I had it on the verandah, openly.

During that month the Battle of Britain was in full swing. My father used to write to me once a week from Bristol and previously I had not been more than three weeks without a letter from him. But six weeks had passed without a letter and I became more and more worried. A cold fear gripped me one night that something had happened to them. I was very distressed. So I knocked on their bedroom door and told them my trouble. She told me to lie down and stroked my forehead, then she fetched a milk drink. Soon I calmed down and felt better. My fear was quite irrational, but fear is not rational. About a week later a letter arrived, the lost letters were probably lying in torpedoed ships on the sea bed. If ever the Daniells see these lines I would like them to know how greatly I appreciated their kindness and hospitality.

During my stay in Vizianagram there was little social life but plenty of time. I read history, Asian and European. I practised my singing, had plenty of exercise, but no shooting and I had left my horse with a friend. I did, however, enjoy the company of a small community of Scots people who ran the nearby Jute Mills. They were all from Dundee – about a dozen in all – including wives. I was especially friendly with one couple: Ian Campbell who was a big, strong engineer with dark, curly hair and a moustache. He was a splendid fellow and when he returned from work he dropped into an easy chair and rested, his wife waiting on him. Next morning he was rested and ready for another day's hard work. Even on a picnic, I noticed, he drove the car, he carried out the heavy hamper, then the ladies did all the rest. Each knew where he stood and it worked well, though it wasn't our English way.

During the fateful August of 1940 we were tremendously cheered by the successes of the Battle of Britain. Nothing would make us miss the 9 o'clock news and we eagerly scanned the front page of the Calcutta 'Statesman' for details of enemy and Allied losses. The news was simply great.

One Sunday morning, two couples from the Jute Mills drove into the little Clubhouse and we drank to the Royal Air Force. The Campbells then drove over to Bank House. Neville Smith as usual was at his desk, but we made him give up. We played jazz records and drank pink gins.

After Neville and I had lunched, a great storm arose; first the sky was darkened by thick cloud then the water cascaded down. It was as though millions of little taps in the heavens had been opened and very soon the ground was awash. The rain overcame all other sounds and noises and one's senses were lulled.

After tea the two of us tried to play golf but the little course was mud and puddles and we gave up.

That night the manager of the cinema showed an Indian film in aid of War funds. It was a rather threadbare cinema but the film was certainly entertaining. A film star played the part of a courtesan; she was very provocative though of course she remained fully clothed. It was her eyes and eyebrows, her mouth and the little movements of her hands and hips that did it. Strangely, the part of her mother, who was her manager, seemed to have been played by a man. We stayed for a couple of hours, left for a short walk and returned for the conclusion. Indian films give good value for money.

Another week, Mrs Smith and Mrs Campbell of the Nellimarla Mill entertained me for tea. Afterwards I met Mr Smith at the Mill and was taken round. The power house was impressive – spotlessly clean with all the metal parts gleaming. Turbines were screaming, dynamos humming and generating high voltages.

It was very interesting to see the jute canes turned into yarn, the yarn woven into cloth and the cloth into gunny-bags, which of course were much needed for the war effort.

So we returned to the bungalow; Smith had a good radio, he got Beethoven's Ninth Symphony from Saigon, but there was some distortion which marred the magic of the symphony. The music reminded me of the Manganese Mines, where Mr Fawcitt was able to play symphonies superbly on his radiogram. The Smiths gave an excellent dinner, the best I had enjoyed for some time. Eventually, they walked back with me along an avenue of trees bathed in moonlight; we crossed by a bridge the river swollen by monsoon rains and over to my car waiting by the roadside.

On my return there was a letter to say that my younger brother, Charles, had been posted by the Colonial Office to a district in Tanganyka. I would have been very pleased if the decision had been the other way – a Commission in the King's African Rifles and I think he would have too, but he wasn't given the choice.

One evening most of the little British community foregathered at the club – twelve in all, with one child – we started with a round of golf – that is 9 holes. Young Master Lorrie entertained us with some recitations, until he announced that he had a tummy pain and couldn't go on. The more I saw of these friendly, natural Scotspeople, the more I liked them.

I hadn't enough to do, but could go over to the Daniell's where Blanche was always willing to accompany me on the piano. One evening they invited me to a missionary dinner and afterwards we played charades, an entertainment which television has since killed.

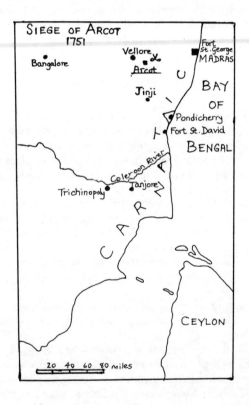

24

August – November 1940; to the Carnatic

THE WAR at that time still seemed far away. The Germans were occupying the Rumanian oil wells, the Italians invading Greece; the Navy very active in the Mediterranean; a Presidential election campaign being waged between Franklin Roosevelt and Wendell Wilkie. Wilkie was an attractive man but Joseph Kennedy, the Irish-American Ambassador clearly didn't want his country to declare war. It seemed at the time that almost everyone in Britain was enthusiastically behind King George and Winston Churchill.

In August, a sticky month, the Deputy Inspector-General, Mr Robert Hume, arrived for a two-day inspection. The Force was far from settled, older men in their forties were being discharged and recruits enlisted in their place. Hume decided on re-organisation ; I had clearly understood that it was being raised for riot duty and crowd control, but he wanted to see them drill like Guardsmen. I could not disagree or argue with him. On his second night he wanted me to sit down with him in front of a bottle of whisky. But I couldn't. The air was heavy and full of little flying creatures and felt like a blanket. I easily got a headache, hence my refusal to drink with my superior.

Week by week the Congress were expected to start a civil disobedience campaign. The weeks passed but the Congress were in two minds.

My Scottish friends asked me to join them for a picnic in the Agency. It was high up and pleasantly cool but sitting in the back seat of a big American car unsettled me and I could not do justice to the splendid fare. It was almost like a picnic in the Scottish Highlands. We looked for aboriginals but they were few and we saw none.

At the end of the month I made an appointment to see the District Medical Officer but he did not discover the cause of my malaise. My host was John Burton, the cheerful young Railway Officer who tried to improve my faulty golf swing. He was as good as a tonic.

As usual, good food and cheer made me feel much better – for there was plenty of social life at Waltair with seventy or more members of the Club. One day, I met a Norwegian ship's captain, a very fine man and heard first-hand news of the war at sea. He was accompanied by his Indian ship's doctor, who seemed wholeheartedly for the Allies.

There was a local beauty called Daphne Dennis-Smither who made my heart beat faster, but no doubt there were others too, whose hearts went pit-a-pat in her company.

In October a telegram arrived from Mr Hume which either wasn't clear or I misunderstood it. As a result he arrived unexpectedly and was very annoyed and so was I. He was sure that rice was being misappropriated at the Mess but couldn't find a leakage. I guessed that he had had a complaint from some informer. He left in a bad temper and a week later I got warning of a transfer.

The routine went on. One night we marched off at midnight and returned at 7 a.m., to my surprise at 4 a.m. it felt quite cool.

An officer a year or so senior to me had been appointed in my place, A.E. Spitteler, but he wrote that he was ill and had to postpone his departure. Meanwhile it was Hallowe'en and quite an elaborate party was held at Nellimarla Jute Mill. Mrs Smith, the Bank Manager's wife was there with Neville, her husband.

Early in November Spitteler turned up. I wasn't expecting him for several days, so my butler and I hastily began packing.

A farewell party and photograph was held that evening and next morning we were ready to leave: my butler, driver and I.

The two companies of Special Armed Police were not a great success. The Madras Company was well-trained by P.F.S. Murray, but he was a most energetic young man and got very bored. When, a few months later, Happell, the Inspector-General, twice refused his petition for a transfer, poor Murray was desperate – he took his revolver and shot himself. So ended a very promising young officer.

One aspect of my six months with this Force deserves a mention. We were continually weeding out unsuitable men, but I did not have one case of serious misconduct. There was no drunkenness, no violent quarrel, no disease (and there was no lack of prostitutes). The good behaviour of the men was one reason why orderly-room and office work took less than three hours a day. Another reason was a first-rate Sergeant-Major, Mr A. Gover. I do not think a full company of European or African soldiers would have behaved so well in the circumstances.

My posting was as Assistant to Mr G.F. Harrison at Vellore with responsiblity for nearly half of North Arcot district. My stay at Vizianagram had not been a very happy one and I was not sorry to leave.

At this point it would not perhaps be inappropriate to mention astrology and its bearing on travellers. Astrology originated in the Babylonian Empire and spread to Persia and thence to Hindustan. It is an integral part of the Hindu way of life. Its main application to travellers is that each day has an auspicious hour for starting a journey and an inauspicious one. One of my colleagues once began a journey of transfer, like the one I was making. His camp-clerk begged him to postpone it: "Do not start now, Sir, the hour is very inauspicious." But Mr F. pooh-poohed the idea, set off on his 300 mile journey and, within a month, one of his children died of a fever; he remembered his former camp clerk's warning. Thereafter he never went on a journey without enquiring the auspicious hour, which varied from day to day. He was the only European I met who did. I must have travelled at the wrong hour many times but did not ever have any serious accident or mishap – touch wood. According to the

Times of India, Pandit Nehru and his daughter Indira (Mrs Gandhi) regularly consulted their astrologer, but no astrologer warned Mrs Gandhi who walked, unsuspecting, into the bullets of her assassin.

We made slow time to Vizagapatam harbour where half a dozen ships, including a Japanese cargo vessel were moored. The black hulls, the smell of tar, paint and salt brought back memories of my boyhood, when I used to gaze on the shipping in Avonmouth Docks, but the muddy waters of the Severn estuary could not compare with the luminous blue of the Bay of Bengal.

From Vizagapatam the trunk road led to Rajahmundry on the majestic Godaveri river. We drew up at the house of J.L. Ronson. He was out but soon drove up in his open American Ford. Then the Asst. Collector, Dass, arrived and we had dinner. I remember the parched red soil of his bungalow compound for no rain had yet fallen.

A Sub-Inspector called and took charge of my loaded car in order to put it on the train. Next morning we were up before dawn and Ronson drove me to the Railway station in time to catch the early train. I admired the great river and hoped one day to become Superintendent of Police, East or West Godaveri so that I could explore by houseboat the mysterious blue hills and coconut groves of its higher reaches.

After breakfast on the train, we crossed the Kistna, also by train, and alighted on the left bank.

We resumed our journey by car and reached the Pennar River in Nellore district without incident except for a puncture. But with carts drawn by bullocks and shod with iron shoes even the best tyres are liable to pick up a nail.

Once again it was necessary, in view of the high level of the water, to cross the river by train. We left the driver to look after the car and alighted on the far side before him and so we took a little cart, or tonga, drawn by a pony. The pony was small and took dainty little steps and after a mile I hailed a passing 'bus and asked the driver to take us to the Judge's Bungalow. I had had a long day since 5 a.m. but a warm bath followed by a bottle of cool beer put me right again.

From their imposing two-storied mansion (or bungalow) I was welcomed by my hosts E.E. Mack, I.C.S. and Mrs Mack. I told them that I was born in the Mission Hospital at Nellore (and baptised by the visiting chaplain from Madras, the Rev. W.K. Bazeley). My father had sent his gardener to the hospital and when he returned with the news of my safe arrival my father tipped him a rupee, which during the Great War, was a handsome tip.

The Macks had arranged a dinner party. The Deputy Superintendent of Police, M. Krishnamurthi Naidu, whom I liked and respected, was the first to arrive. He stood 6' 2", which is tall for a South Indian and was unquestionably straight and loyal. In fact I have liked many members of the Naidu caste, they were not of the warrior caste, but of a lower one with traditions of military service. The next guest was the local priest, for Mrs Mack was Roman Catholic.

The table was loaded with glasses, silver, flowers and sweetmeats and a full dinner followed. Next morning, I was dressed long before my hosts. No breakfast was announced, but at 10.30 a huge meal was served: 'Brunch'. I was hungry by then and did full justice to it. It consisted of cereals, ham and eggs, fish molee with rice and vegetables; toast, butter, marmalade; tea, coffee and fruit. It certainly set one up for the day, which in our case meant heading south for Madras.

The trunk road was badly worn by the heavy war-time traffic and we were shaken up for mile upon mile. Then I spied a shady avenue, a good place for a halt. A couple of grown girls were standing, baring their fine bosoms to the breeze, but they soon covered them up again. I walked up and down to shake off the stiffness and not long after we started up, we had our second puncture of the day. We had no more spare tubes and as it couldn't be repaired on the spot I left the car with the driver, with instructions to get a lift and buy another tube from the next town. So my servant and I boarded a 'bus which took us to the centre of Madras; soon we were in the Madras Club and next morning the car arrived.

The Country Clubs

A certain amount has been written about these by persons who have never actually been an ordinary member. I belonged to the Madras Club, probably the oldest in India, the New Delhi Club, to district clubs and a very small one with nine members including wives.

The Madras Club was then open to British members of the Services and of the Army, Navy and Air Force; also to British in commerce, industry and banking, but not in trade. Each member had to be elected and if an applicant was 'black-balled', no explanation would be given.

Lingering on in the atmosphere were the shades of John Company – in the spacious, high-ceilinged rooms, the pots of green ferns, the slow overhead fans. Talking if any was in low tones. The ladies had their own saloon.

My friend, E.W. Bouchier, had only one ambition: to work in the Provincial Secretariat and live in bachelor comfort at the Club and so I would have a peg with him in his room. He was very civilised.

The servants were dressed as in the heyday of John Company – long, white robe, like the Egyptian *gallibieh* fastened at the waist with a coloured sash and the head covered by a flat white turban. Barefooted, they moved almost noiselessly and were the best servants I have been privileged to meet. As a tribute to them I recall an incident.

Having arrived the evening before, I had just sat down for breakfast when a very young servant, hardly 21 years old, brought me a slice of chilled papaya, a kind of melon. "How did you know I wanted papaya?" I asked. "Because last time Master have breakfast you have papaya." And the last time was a weekend six months before.

The Club was very grand and set in spacious grounds, but the district clubs were much more modest. For example, the Vellore Club was situated in a bungalow with only a few large rooms, a wide verandah and pillared portico. There was a hard court, a billiard room of one table, a drawing-room for dancing or supper parties, a committee room and a double bedroom. Bridge was usually played on the verandah or, in colder weather, indoors. One feature of all such clubs was the coloured prints of hunting scenes and some humorous cartoons dating back to Edward VII.

When I first joined Vellore nearly half the paying members were Indian members of the Services and we all got on well together, though the Collector, a Brahmin, did not attend regularly – he found it too boring.

There were two club nights a week, the Police Band playing on the bandstand some distance away. The men wore dinner jackets and white drill trousers for coolness; the ladies wore long dresses as there were mosquitoes for at least half the year. Sometimes the mosquitoes were so bad that they put their feet and ankles in a cotton bag.

At the set time, the band played the Madras Police March, which was Kinloch of Kinloch and dismissed; the members then returned to their bungalows for dinner, which had been cooked, then placed in a hot cupboard and so could be served at a moment's notice. Some bachelors did not have dinner until 10.30 p.m. but the servants did not mind too much, they expected to be on duty for sixteen hours with a couple of hours off in the heat of the afternoon.

A large country club such as the Waltair Club did not make a lot of difference, only that there was a much wider choice of friends. One of the local residents who kept away from it was the Deputy Conservator of Forests, a Mr Wrench. He had little desire for company and was known for his good looks and his elegance. No hair of his head was ever out of place and he dressed for dinner in black jacket and bow tie every night, even when he was in the depths of a Reserve Forest. Nor did he take only one black tie to camp, his bearer had to pack several. I should have liked to have met him but never did.

So to the Madras Club bar, on a Thursday evening in November 1940. Many men have foregathered: the senior Civilians; Army, Navy and Air Force Commanders. No ladies are present and the men are mostly discussing official business and reaching agreements.

Sir Frederick Sayers, the Inspector-General of Police was there with a number of other officers as he was retiring next day after a long service of 33 years. Sir Frederick had been kind and understanding to me; it wasn't a very jolly party – I gathered he had been crochety for months – but I knew he had suffered for years from migraine.

The Madras Club was founded in 1832 replacing a much humbler institution. It had a Saturday night custom of serving stewed prunes with custard and a glass of old Madeira wine. The custom was in memory of a siege of Madras by the French, when rations became short and the only items in plentiful supply were dried prunes and Madeira. The only siege that fits is that of December 1758 when Comte de Lally, with fresh reinforcements, laid siege to the town and heavily bombarded Fort St George, causing heavy casualties. But Governor Pigot and Stringer Lawrence defended stoutly till, after two months, a British fleet sailed into view, whereupon de Lally raised the siege and returned to Pondicherry.

My Dodge saloon car was getting old after eight years' hard service so I decided to sell it and was looking for another – but there were very few for sale. Finally, I settled for a dark green Morris 8 saloon only a year old. Though small it performed very well, even on bad roads.

The nights were very dark as, on account of mounting tension in the Far East, the City was blacked out. I looked up Pamela, my girl friend of the year before. We went to a couple of dances and to the cinema, but somehow the magic had gone and we parted company.

On 12 November my servant and I drove off in the Morris car. The monsoon that year was a good one and the potholes were all puddles. At Arcot, the causeway was deep in water and needed great care; further on, the road was almost under water. So we arrived at Vellore and drew up at the bungalow of the Superintendent of Police, G.F. Harrison and his charming wife, Margot, whom I have been privileged to count as my friends ever since.

As North Arcot district was at the heart of the Carnatic Province where the idea of a modern empire first germinated, I include this short historical note.

The East India Company, chartered by James I, was by no means the only trading corporation in the East. There were French, Portuguese, Dutch and Danish ports and factories – all in a maritime situation. The Directors of 'John Company', as ours was called, were chiefly out to make profits and pay dividends. They were parsimonious, grudged military expenditure and there was no question, with their 1500 souls all told – of their entertaining imperial designs.

The first European to dream of an Indian Empire was probably Dupleix, Governor-General of the Compagnie des Indes at Pondicherry. He was a statesman and an astute one, not above breaking his word. He saw the Mogul Empire disintegrating and Imperial Governors setting themselves up as princes, as in the Deccan (Hyderabad) and the Carnatic (Arcot). He did not expect the warlike Marathas to take their place.

Trade flourishes when there is law and order, but in the first half of the 18th century there was no law and order in India. It was a time when strong leaders and adventurers prospered. About 1740 the Marathas were spoiling for a fight and threatening the British settlements at Madras, Bombay and even Bengal, so the Directors were forced either to fight or quit. The Dutch traders withdrew from Negapatam to Java. This left the two strongest companies – British and French. Dupleix saw his opportunity and was the first to raise a colonial army of Sepoys, trained and officered by Europeans. (The Portuguese had done this earlier but only on a small scale.)

Dupleix did not wish to get involved in the War of Austrian Succession (1740–48) but his hand was forced when, in 1746, a British Squadron appeared near Pondicherry sinking French ships. So Dupleix conceived the bold plan of capturing Madras, first persuading the Nawab of the Carnatic to remain neutral and promising to return Madras to him. Then a Naval expedition was fitted out in Mauritius and commanded by Admiral de Labourdonnais. He sailed to Madras roads, bombarded the Fort and town for two days, when the small garrison surrendered.

Dupleix revoked his promise to the Nawab, but did not hold Madras for long as, by the Peace Treaty of Aix-la-Chappelle (1748) Madras was returned to the East India Company. So Dupleix lost his prize and made an enemy of the Nawab.

From 1750 Dupleix had the best general, the Marquis de Bussy; first he captured the strong fortress of Gingee (or Jinji) which was believed to be impregnable. Then he pushed northwards and by force of arms and astute diplomacy he gained the whole of the Deccan and set up his residence at Hyderabad. This made Dupleix master of almost the whole of southern India and British prestige sank to its lowest ebb. Meanwhile, due to assassinations and Carnatic politics there were two claimants for the throne of Arcot: the young, fair-skinned Muhammad Ali, who was the Nizam's choice and who was backed by the British. The other was a close relation – Chanda Sahib – a fine soldier who was backed by the French.

In 1751 Muhammad Ali was chased into the Fort at Trichinopoly, which was still held by the British. Determined to capture him, Chanda Sahib withdrew most of the Arcot garrison and invested Trichinopoly Fort, together with French troops. (See map, page 110.)

This was Clive's hour. With no hope of relieving Muhammad Ali and the garrison in Trichy Fort, Clive offered his services to Governor Saunders, who was at Fort St David. After consultation Clive resolved on the bold plan of attacking Arcot, the heart and capital of the Carnatic, so that Chanda Sahib would either have to abandon Trichy or sacrifice his capital.

Thomas Saunders, the wise and resolute Governor, backed Clive to the hilt with most of his garrison: 200 British (in heavy red coats), 300 sepoys, eight officers, half of whom had been civilians, a surgeon and only three guns. Later he sent two more 18-pounder guns.

With these Clive, not yet 26 years old, attacked and occupied Arcot Fort in a severe thunderstorm. The Fort, a mile in circumference, adjoins the town and so lacks a clear field of fire. As expected, Chanda Sahib raised the siege of Trichy and invested Arcot with 10,000 men. His son, who was in command, mounted assault after assault on the somewhat dilapidated fort, but all were repulsed. On the 50th day he launched a last, furious assault. Clive, with little ammunition left, had to serve one of the guns himself; but it was the end: the attackers and their elephants fled – for a relief force from Madras was arriving and a force of friendly Marathas was on the way.

Clive fought and won four more battles and so prevented the French from regaining Arcot. Not long afterwards Dupleix was recalled in disgrace by his ungrateful country. Never did Indian soldiers fight more gallantly than at Arcot and the succeeding battles. To Clive, a man of genius, the lesson was clear. Hitherto, John Company had been waging war against the French for their survival. Afterwards, Clive dreamt of an Indian Empire.

But how did the unhappy Company Writer become the Hero of Arcot?

Five years previously he had escaped from the French at Madras to the Company's southern fort, Fort St David. There he became a subaltern under the Company's Commander, Major Stringer Lawrence, an able and seasoned

Royal officer. And it was he who perceived Clive's genius, who trained him and made him his second-in-command.

Stringer Lawrence, to quote Bence-Jones, 'bluff, portly, a fighter and loved by his men, who called him the Old Cock', is regarded as the father of the Indian Army.

Chanda Sahib, a gallant officer, was murdered and Muhammad Ali was left as undisputed Nawab, which was a pity, for he grew up hopelessly extravagant and a great source of worry to the Company: borrowing money left, right and centre. He even sent magnificent diamonds to Queen Charlotte and Lady Clive after the accession of George III. His descendants were styled 'Prince of Arcot'.

The French Government had an advantage over the British – the possession of Mauritius in the Indian Ocean, where ships could be repaired and provisioned.

In order to avenge the capture of Calcutta and Fort William, together with prisoners, a fleet sailed from Madras in October 1756. Ending with hazardous navigation up the Hugli River, the journey through the N.E. monsoon took six weeks. Jointly in command were Vice-Admiral Charles Watson and Col. Robert Clive, also in the force was Col. Eyre Coote of the 39th Foot, a seasoned professional soldier of whom Clive was probably a little jealous.

The army of the Nawab of Bengal, Suraj-ud-Dowla, numbered close on 50,000 men, including 50 medium and heavy guns, French gunners, armoured elephants and fierce Pathan cavalry. They took up a position in a semicircle on the open plain. Clive disposed his force of only 3,000 men, mostly veteran sepoys, eight guns and no cavalry along the Hugli river. He hesitated to engage so strong an army but Coote, knowing the enemy was not united, persuaded Clive to attack. His guns kept up a fierce cannonade for four hours, heavy rain fell, their powder got wet and the enemy line broke. The Nawab fled with the Company's army in hot pursuit. So Clive won his second decisive battle but a much easier one than Arcot.

Suraj-ud Dowla was murdered, another Nawab was installed, Clive became his overlord and the master of Bengal, the richest Province of India. It took another five years to consolidate, by which time Bengal with Bihar became the nucleus of a British-Indian Empire, with Calcutta the seat of the Governor and later, in 1773, the seat of the first Governor-General, Warren Hastings.

To guard the capital, Clive began the building of a new Fort William, much larger and stronger than the former one and, joining forces with Admiral Watson, the French fort and factory at Chandernagore on the Hugli was bombarded and taken. Again the ships' officers showed their great skill at navigation.

By now the French had been well beaten by land and sea, but they refused to accept defeat and their opportunity came in the South when a soldier of fortune, Haider Ali, usurped the throne of Mysore, two years after Plassey. Haider Ali was uneducated but able and ruthless; his son, Tipu Sultan (the Tiger) was a bold French-trained commander, a militant Muslim, arrogant and cruel. His British prisoners were ill-used and some were persuaded to embrace Islam. They hated the British, gained more territory, and ravaged the country up to the walls of Madras; only Sir Eyre Coote was their match. He defeated Haider Ali with terrible loss at Porto Novo (1781).

The French supported them with many good officers, including the ageing Marquis de Bussy, and with ships. In 1782 Tipu Sultan succeeded his father and soon was extending his frontiers and intriguing with the French. Then came the French Revolution. Tipu sent envoys to Mauritius who persuaded the Governor to become his ally. This was too much for Cornwallis who went on to the offensive, which was continued by his successor, Lord Wellesley, till the Tiger was trapped and, brave to the last, was killed on the ramparts of Seringapatam. (vide Chapter 17, end)

French hostility continued at sea when warships, based on Mauritius (then called Isle de France) intercepted, sank and plundered scores of East India Company ships in the Indian Ocean, but on account of the war against Napoleon, the Navy could not be spared in any strength until after Nelson's great victories of the Nile and Trafalgar. Finally, ships of the line were spared and a strong combined force was assembled at Madras and in 1810 the smaller French ships were sunk or blown out of the water off Mauritius by the heavy guns of the Royal Navy. No longer was Mauritius a thorn in the side of the East India Company and the French-speaking people of the island, Royalist in their sentiments, duly became loyal subjects of the Queen.

The Compagnie des Indes was disbanded well before the Revolution; in its service were two brothers named de Chazal, [28] from the elder of whom I am directly descended.   They were strongly attracted to the island of Mauritius and retired there about 1763.

The Dorset Regiment, Primus in Indis

Clad in red coats, white leggings and wearing a black hat, the first Royal Regiment to be sent to India was the 39th Foot. It had been raised in Ireland in 1702 by Colonel R. Coote, and three years after they landed in India in 1754, they fought in the Battle of Plassey. Among the congratulations was one from the Nawab of Arcot, who sent them a ceremonial staff which is now in the Regimental Museum.

The 39th Foot, after Plassey, was awarded the Battle Honour 'Primus in Indis'. Just fifty years later, the 39th Foot became known as the Dorset Regiment; later the 54th Foot was amalgamated to form the Dorsetshire Regiment, an Infantry Regiment as fine as any in the British Army.

Closely associated with the Dorsetshire Regiment, now joined to the Devons, is Sherborne Abbey where its old Standards may be seen.

The Company's armies were not the same as the Royal Army as promotion was only by seniority, there was no purchase of Commissions. Many died or were killed but few retired as there were no pensions. So Brigade Majors were usually Captains, seasoned Majors often commanded a battalion and a Colonel could command one or even two brigades.

[28] Francois de Chazal de la Génesté, believed to be a Naval man, and his brother Régis, an Army officer.

25

North Arcot

NORTH ARCOT is a splendid district for a District Officer. Low-lying towards Madras, it slopes gradually up towards the Mysore plateau and the Javadi Hills to about 3,000 ft. It has excellent camps: jungles and beautiful valleys; it has an exciting history, at Arcot for instance, the window-bars in the rest-house consist of old flint-lock musket barrels. Vellore Fort was very well preserved and within it, two large buildings, then used as police barracks, were the 'mahals', a term applied to palace buildings, for they had been used to confine two of the sons of Tipu Sultan of Mysore.

The one mutiny of the Madras Army erupted in Vellore Fort in the year 1806. The Welch Regiment was decimated and, while I was there, a battalion of that Regiment arrived, mounted the Quarter-Guard, flew the Regimental Flag and sounded the retreat in memory of 1806. A short account of the Vellore Mutiny will be found in the Appendix.

I was fortunate, not only in my Superintendent, but also in the Brahmin Camp Clerk provided for me. He didn't dress in the old fashioned way: dhoti, shirt and coat, but: shoes, khaki stockings, khaki shorts, shirt and a short coat. He was quick-witted, with a keen sense of humour and never got excited. I think he much preferred touring to the daily grind of the District Police Office. I also managed to get my favourite orderly, P.C. Hirelal, from Bellary. They, with my faithful butler, Yelliah, made my household a very happy one.

The little community at the Vellore Club had shrunk. When I first joined, there were fourteen members, five years later there were ten. The Collector and District Magistrate was Khan Bahadur Ahmed Ali of the Provincial Service. He and his brother, Mahomed Ali, who was in the Indian Police, traced their descent back 200 years to the rule of the Nawab of Arcot. He was an excellent district officer and both the Harrisons and I got on very well with him. He was a strict Muslim; once at the Vellore Club, he partook of a trifle pudding, not knowing it contained sherry and said "What a delicious pudding." So the ladies said nothing and gave him another big helping.

My quarters were quite close to the Police Mess and the Reserve Lines which meant that I spent much more time with the Reserve Police than at Hospet.

I remember my first field-day with them. We left by lorry early and then climbed a rocky hill. The top was in the cloud and I filled my lungs with the moist, cool air and enjoyed the sight of mountain grasses and shrubs; we could only see a short way and it was a pleasant feeling. We then retreated down the other side and exchanged signals with the 'enemy'. Finally, we marched back ten miles to the Lines.

That month I did two more marches, one in the competition for Armed Reserves called the Stevenson Shield, and another with a special Reserve platoon which was available only to the Inspector-General. This platoon was in fine fettle, we covered the ten-mile march in under two and a quarter hours, they then did well in target-shooting. They got the best marks in the Province and so won the Shield that year. I have no doubt that Harrison rewarded them.

One afternoon I borrowed Harrison's mare, a 'Waler'. She had a hard mouth and tremendous strength. She pulled and pulled, though the going was soft after rain, 'till my arms ached and I wore the skin off my upper calves.

For a month I really enjoyed the social life, for I did not have to work later than 5-6 p.m. The Harrisons took me on two or three snipe shoots, trudging through the paddy fields.

After being on escort and protection duty for the Governor, the Hon. Sir Arthur Hope, he asked two Indian Officers senior to me and me to his Railway saloon. After a short while he sent them away, which I don't think they liked very much and kept me for a talk. An A.D.C., the Earl of Shannon, was with him. Soon the A.D.C. got on to his favourite topic – racing – on which I was very ignorant. But I was interested to hear how he had once owned my horse – Rembrandt, that he nearly won a race, but his jockey beat him so hard that he was soured for racing.

One rainy night during the monsoon I returned to the Mess after a dinner party and noticed a snake curled up on the front verandah, fast asleep. As I wasn't sure what to do I woke the waterman whose duty it was to sleep on the back verandah when no one was in. He looked at the snake, took a stick and chased him out into the night; he was about a yard long. It was the first and last time I saw a snake actually in a house.

On 2 December I went to camp in the rain. One night that week I felt strangely cold; it was fever so I was driven back to Vellore and to bed.

After a few days, I went to the Club and there found one of the finest officers I have ever met. He was the Chief Recruiting Officer at Bangalore, his name: Major E.G. Phythian-Adams, formerly of the Madras Infantry: King George's Own Pioneers. He was visiting Army pensioners, of whom there were many thousands in the district. He was not only extremely handsome but exuded friendship and humour. He loved the men and would embrace retired Indian officers. He was also an authority on the history of the Carnatic and of the old Madras Army, saying that it had been spoilt by the posting to it of inefficient and overweight officers from the North. The fact remains, however, that the British conquest of India began in the South and after Law and Order was established only a few battalions were needed.

Stout men were a feature of earlier Anglo-India. For example, before the Great War, out of sixty five or so British officers in the Madras Police, three weighed over twenty stone and one weighed twenty-three stone. Daily and substantial meals of meat or fish curry and rice probably had much to do with it. By my time curry and rice was confined to Sunday lunch and stout men were rare but Indians, especially the poorer ones, respected and liked big, heavy men.

Phythian-Adams was a bachelor and one of his close relations was Dean of Carlisle Cathedral. Thereafter I helped him as much as I could and after 20,000 recruits had been enlisted from North Arcot, he invited me to dinner. We dined alone at his house in Bangalore, waited on by a faithful old soldier and a splendid dinner it was with claret, port and cigars.

Although I hadn't quite recovered from fever, I began inspecting and went for it hard – one station after another.

The town of Ambur was near the Mysore border and contained a strong minority of Muslims. The Rest House was a fine one, set in the midst of a plantation of jungle trees; one afternoon a monkey raided the larder and managed to steal my precious half-pound of Australian butter. So I shot the thief, the only monkey I ever shot, because it is sacred to Hindus and must not be killed: even when they steal precious grain or seed corn they must be left alone.

Muharram is a sad Muslim occasion. I had had some experience of it at Hospet, but it was on a small scale. The Muslim minority at Ambur was about a third and when this third is a spirited one, rioting is a strong possibility as the Muslims' fervour rises and they ignore the feelings of the Hindus.

Basically, it is a commemoration of the deaths in battle between Hassan and Hussein, the Prophet's great-nephews. We British do not think much about the past, but to the Irish, Jews and Muslims, the past is very real as they re-enact past history. The Inspector and I spent many hours patrolling, watching and receiving reports. But there was no untoward incident.

At this Muharram I saw fire-walking for the first time: a good fire was made in a shallow pit 12–15 ft long. The fire was allowed to die down 'till the embers glowed pink and it was very hot standing near. Two youths arrived with bare legs and torso. They were blessed by an old man, then, shouting "Din, Din, Din", they trotted through the soft embers, leaving black footprints and raising some steam. They were unharmed, but had been prepared, I was told, by sitting for a full two hours in a tub of cold water. I had noticed that they were trembling and thought it was nerves, but they were shivering with cold. Another feature is the tiger dance, with young men painted with stripes.

I had two enjoyable rides, one was a long canter across fields and jumping over the low field bunds or ridges. The other was up a hill above Ambur, which looked deceptively peaceful from a height. In the other direction, to the west, was a long vista of hills and jungle with the sun setting, as it were, in a sea of gold and crimson. In England we have no extensive natural forest left, even the New Forest is patchy and intersected by roads. May the great areas of Indian forest long continue for they are a priceless asset.

After long days of keeping the peace I felt like a quiet camp. The rest house at K.V. Kuppam was perfectly quiet with doves cooing and cattle lowing in the distance. That night the moon was full, the forest and forest glade were bathed in silver splendour.

But I was not left to work at files and case diaries for long on account of a gruesome murder which I prefer not to describe. It involved a slim, attractive young woman, who refused to sleep with her husband.

From this camp I rode to a village called Vrinchipur, mainly to see the temple which is notable for its enclosing walls – hundreds of feet long, broad in proportion and 30 ft high. They consisted of great stones, perfectly fitted together without mortar and absolutely plumb, the mason's art at its very best.

At this time a certain caller came to see me every three or four months. Later, I realised that he exemplified the frustration felt by the sons of the best families. He was fair-skinned, big and strong with a robust personality. Probably a Brahmin, he had a very good brain. He had all the qualities needed for one of the top jobs in the All-India Services. In fact, his job was inferior to the services both in income and prestige: he was the area representative of Canada Life Assurance, a Company well established in South India. But though he tried hard he failed to tempt me – I was already insured with Equity and Law of London, as were a good many Civilians.

26

A Romantic Christmas Week

MY CHRISTMAS holiday was almost entirely taken up with a beautiful American girl of about my age, her name was Betty Bailey. We met at a dinner party and were quickly attracted to each other. We saw each other every day and after only three or four days I thought I was in love with her

George Harrison saw that it was serious and gave me excellent advice. "Don't rush into an engagement: for your pay isn't sufficient to marry on!" I am sure too that my butler, Yelliah, was against it. He did not want a mem-sahib to come between him and me.

After a week of Christmas festivities and picnics we both went our way but corresponded frequently – she replying to my letters almost by return of post. We corresponded for some months, but I could not keep it up.

After returning to headquarters, my next tour took me to a Railway centre called Arkonam, towards Madras, where I had the privilege of meeting a very fine Church of Scotland Minister. His name was Silver and he headed the Scottish Mission there. He was of middle height, well-built with a clipped moustache. He was most courteous and full of humour. The Rev Mr Silver and Mrs Silver kept open house and I attended three or four happy tea-parties at their home. His hobby was Carnatic history. One battlefield at nearby Sholinghur, which took place during the Mysore wars, was not shown on modern maps. But by studying ancient maps and documents he determined the site and duly dug up old cannon and musket balls.

So I rode on to Sholinghur, but the District Board rest house was little used, infested with mosquitoes and smelly, a playground for monkeys. Soon afterwards, the District Board Engineer arrived with his wife and several young children. He worked at his files with his clerk until 11 p.m. Then on his entering the living room the children got excited and kicked up a row.

I couldn't do a full day's office work next to a strange family, so next day I moved to a charming little Forest bungalow with a single living room.Though my father was a P.W.D. engineer, I have no hesitation in saying that the Forest officers had more taste for beauty than the Engineers, their Forest bungalows were beautifully sited and planted with trees.

Next morning I was called before dawn and combed the jungle for spotted (or fallow) deer. There were numerous tracks of both deer and wild boar but they were mostly stale. I spent hours in the forest, but only saw a doe bounding along a ridge and returned very tired.

In order to involve the people in our war-effort and also to raise money for Spitfires and comforts for the Indian Army, war-meetings were arranged in most if not all the towns.

One such meeting took place at Ranipet with platform, loud-speakers, decorations and plenty of seating. I had to make the second speech and felt very nervous. The first was a good one by the Manager of Parry's Factory, mine was typical of a beginner: too long and above the heads of most of the 2,000 people who attended. Afterwards, at a dinner party I had the pleasure of meeting a Brahmin official I knew, highly intelligent and cultured, his name was Ramaswamy Ayyar. The Ranipet meeting was followed by another at Palmaner in Chittoor district to which Harrison and I needed no second invitation, as Palmaner was 2,000 feet up and cool, with light jungle all round as far as the eye could see. Mr and Mrs Harrison, their two daughters and I occupied the rest-house and were a happy family.

My duties took me back to Ranipet; on the Sunday Dr and Mrs Stern invited me to bathe at the Parry and Company's swimming pool, followed by lunch at their house. He was usefully employed by the Company as an engineer but on account of his Austrian nationality and military background, he could not travel outside Ranipet without a permit. But they had no time for the Nazis and were perfectly harmless.

During my first year at Vellore there had been cases of bubonic plague. This time on my return from Ranipet there was a small outbreak and once again the whole population was promptly vaccinated. It is quite a potent injection, most work stopped and I was laid low for a couple of days.

It was a privilege to serve under such good officers as Ahmed Ali and Harrison. Ahmed Ali had an old-world courtesy which derived from the Mogul Empire.

One day he sent me an invitation to lunch saying he needed me to witness a document. So I arrived at his residence and was welcomed. Already there was Philip Hatfield, manager of Parry's factory at Ranipet and Mrs Hatfield. Then George and Margot Harrison arrived. Half an hour later the butler announced lunch and we had a leisurely meal of palau and dry curries. We chatted over coffee and cigarettes on the verandah, till Ahmed Ali asked the three male guests to his office, where a clerk was waiting with a deed relating to a purchase of land by Parry and Company. Ahmed Ali and Hatfield signed, Harrison and I witnessed and it was all over in a minute, but with the accompanying lunch party for seven, it was the occasion for gracious hospitality.

Ahmed Ali was nearly twenty years my senior and he taught me much. Once he said: "Don't think you can improve the system. Many able men have produced it over the years. Your job is to make it work."

At one time he was usually the last to arrive on club nights and I asked him why he couldn't come earlier. His answer was: "I have been receiving callers, village elders." "Why don't you send them away at six or half-past?" I asked. "Because they come for a purpose and often they talk of this, that and the other, then at last they come to the point. If I sent them away at six I would miss the important thing." A lesson I never forgot.

There was a prosperous merchant of Ranipet, a devout Muslim of simple tastes, who devoted himself to works of charity in which he was quite impartial, for Hindus and Christians were treated the same as those of his own Faith and no supplicant was sent empty away. The Mother Superior of the Convent school, who was a Frenchwoman, told me that whenever she had a special need, she went to see him and always received a generous donation. He was the most respected man in the town.

★ ★ ★ ★ ★

The reader may think that government and district officers were united in a common purpose – upholding the Raj and keeping Indians in their place! But we were men capable of making up our own minds and we frequently grumbled against the Provincial Authority. And one of the purposes of the Clubs was surely to enable their members to let off steam.

While the Provincial Secretaries and heads of departments, certainly in Madras, often disagreed with far-away Delhi, by and large the European community, as also the educated Indians, were often critical both of Delhi and of the India Office.

Mr Churchill, great war leader though he was, had not noticeably changed his views on India since he was a subaltern in Bangalore. While the Secretary of State for India, the ageing Leopold Amery, did not seem to us to behave like a Cabinet Minister at all but rather as a Permanent Secretary. And while the India Office was efficient in all administrative matters, in the political sphere it seemed, under Amery, more dead than alive. Not even the loyalist 'Madras Mail' paper had any praise for Amery.

As for the Viceroy he was splendid but remote. He reigned from his Palace, he laboured at his desk, he was a regular worshipper at the Church of Scotland, but he could not mingle with the people. He crossed the face of India, but all anyone could see was the long white Viceregal train. For the tradition of the country is personal: the durbar or levee, the *darshan* or audience, the tribal assembly or *jirga*.

When war broke out in Europe he had declared war on behalf of India without consulting his Executive Council, or the Provincial Prime Ministers or even, apparently, his private secretaries and not even Sir Stafford Cripps, the War Cabinet's emissary, could win them round.

By February 1941 I knew I could not manage a long Indian summer and applied for two months' leave which was promptly granted. I camped again at Ambur, organised a parade of police and civic guards followed by a war meeting which was well supported. I visited some of the Lutheran missionaries, who were Americans of German origin and in the increasing heat of March returned to Vellore to prepare for leave; but within hours of my return, while drinking coffee after lunch, an express constable brought a message of riot. I changed, collected a few things and my revolver and drove to the scene as fast as my Morris 8 would allow. But Harrison in a bigger car overtook me and we soon found the village. The Sub-Divisional Magistrate also arrived and we spent a long time with the Inspector and a police party clearing the crowds, putting out fires of which there were quite a number and taking precautions at nearby villages, where trouble could spread.

The Inspector had quelled the riot by ordering the few police to open fire when the crowd became insulting (a man exposed his genitals). One man was killed and several wounded. I saw one young man with a neat hole in the lobe of his ear where a musket ball had passed through; but he was unperturbed.

No one knew how the rioting began, which was quite usual. It was only a small riot and soon after finishing my report I handed over charge.

Soon after I took leave a rebellion broke out in Iraq, led by the pro-Axis Prime Minister, Rashid Ali. It was quelled by the 10th Indian Division sent from India under the command of General Sir Ouvry Roberts. In view of the strategic importance of oil, this Division was then ordered into Persia and Syria.

27

Two Thousand Miles to Srinagar

APRIL 1941

FOR MY leave I chose the fabled State of Kashmir. It was a four-day journey at the quickest but I wanted to see something of Mogul India and the North. Travelling second class during the long journey to Agra I had pleasant companions, a captain in the Royal Inniskillings and a Parsi civil servant; Indian trains were and probably still are remarkably cheap and reliable. They get you there but not at breakneck speed. Fifty-five m.p.h. on the broad gauge would be fast, so one can enjoy the countryside. Metre-gauge trains are somewhat slower, and better for poor passengers who travel on the roof.

The most interesting part of the journey was the Vindhya Range, the extensive jungles of the Central Provinces and the deep valley of the Narbada River. From the train it looked fascinating country. I much regret that I never got to know the Central Provinces – the background of Kipling's Jungle Books. The Vindhya Range, running from east to west, is 900 miles long and the natural boundary between north and south.

AGRA

The first Emperor, Babar (1483-1530) made it his capital and began to beautify it. I went to a modest hotel and as soon as the sun began to sink took a *ghari* or little carriage through the long, broad avenues of the cantonment. I was not expecting great things and feel sure, as I approached the Taj Mahal, that my pulse was normal. I got out to view the building from a distance.

Walking along one of the outer walls I noticed that the long sandstone blocks were fitted together with a thin lamina of stone between each block – what a refinement! Then to the great arched gateway.

A framed picture of the Taj taken from the front hangs in scores of thousands of homes and I wondered how large it really was. I viewed it from the left side then from the right and walked slowly up the central avenue. It was like being introduced gradually to a splendour not of this world. About half-way or 150 yards from the steps I was overcome: its perfect form, its surfaces, delicate as eggshell and the great dome – set off by the central arch – turned my knees to water. Walking towards the west, the perspective gradually changing, I felt in the presence of God and wanted to remove my shoes and so welcomed a notice on the western plinth of the mosque to this very effect. The inlays were of deep red, dark green and yellow and represented trees and flowers – coral, cornelian, jasper, malachite and lapis lazuli.

The polished marble floor of the mosque is divided into spaces, one for each worshipper. I walked its length, having it to myself and gazed up at the splendour of the ceilings. These designs, I felt, were of human execution but of divine inspiration.

Just then the peace was shattered by a group of sightseers making loud remarks with coarse laughter. Their behaviour was outrageous, but I did nothing. I should have lectured them, as naughty children.

A young Hindu lady entered. She was fresh and graceful as a lily – she too was deeply moved. Then her husband entered, looked round briefly and beckoned her away. And she, being a dutiful Hindu wife, after a short pause, obeyed her lord; for obedience is *dharma* for the Hindu wife.

An attendant came in and chanted in his clear tenor voice: "Allah, illa Allah, u'lla Akbar." The words echoed in the dome, the echo lasting fifteen seconds, then died away.

I wandered round again, taking in less and less, strolled back along the central aisle, but was so overcome I could take no more.

That evening after dinner at my hotel, I took another *ghari* and returned, hoping to see the Taj by moonlight; but the moon was veiled and there was only a faint light which the creamy marble reflected dimly. I vowed to try and return on a clear night to enjoy a second kind of beauty, that caused by the 'Fair, still companion of the night'.

Fatehpur – Sikri

A visit to the city of Agra demands another to the capital, founded by the Emperor Abkar in 1569. He wished for a son and begged a local saint, Salim Chishti, to pray for one. His prayer was granted and a son was duly born to a Princess of Jodhpur, (a Hindu) named Salim, after the saint.

The Imperial buildings are sited on a low hill and enclosed by a high wall of deep pink sandstone. They are very varied and bear the impress of the Emperor's original mind. One enters by a huge archway with pointed arch. The mosque has an unusual feature: the wings are a blend of Muslim and Hindu styles – for Akbar was no religious bigot. To his spiritual guide, Shaikh Salim, he erected a superb shrine. The Imperial stables have roomy stalls for camels.

The Ibadat Makan is a council and debating chamber of unique design: the Emperor's chair was placed on a platform, supported by a central pillar some 15 ft high, so he sat well above and could see all his councillors or those he received in audience. For he was minded to discuss religion with representatives of other faiths and developed a theology of his own in the hope of uniting his subjects in a common faith. For he was truly Emperor of all Indians, Hindu, Muslim or Christian.

As a reminder of the harshness of 16th century justice, outside the court-house a strong stone ring can be seen. When the Emperor was in court an elephant would be chained to the ring and whenever he sentenced a criminal or other offender to death, he was straightaway placed at the feet of the beast, which was trained to crush him. There was, of course, no court of appeal above the Emperor's.

The Golden Palace

The Queen's apartment is of moderate size but exquisitely contrived. On the wainscoting are carved birds, lions and tigers which the Koran does not permit and which have since been defaced by fanatics, for only fanatics would mar such beautiful work.

The courtyard of the Panch Mahal (a unique five-storied building) is designed for the game 'pachis' or 'twenty fives', similar to draughts. The Emperor and his Queen seated opposite each other on thrones played it, the pawns consisting of attractive slave girls. Another smaller building was for the purpose of playing hide-and-seek with ladies of the harem.

The young Prince Salim had his own palace and it contained of all things, a Hindu temple; a harem and a spacious durbar hall for the reception of visitors. Evidently, relations between the Muslim rulers and their Hindu subjects were pleasantly relaxed.

Akbar's own palace is of quite modest proportions and in superb taste, for he abhorred vulgarity. The whole complex is kept in excellent order, though three and a half centuries old, for the climate is very dry and the city has at no time been attacked or vandalized. Perhaps the shortage of water is a reason why Fatehpur was abandoned as the Emperor's capital.

Agra Fort

Like Seringapatam and others it is immensely strong, but whereas Seringapatam served a mainly military purpose, Agra Fort was rather an Imperial residence secure from all possible attack. The smooth pink sandstone walls rise to a height of 70 ft and are interspersed with mighty bastions. There is also an outer wall, a mere 40 ft in height which forms the moat. Six rows of embrasures for cannon and muskets pierce the inner wall. It is so strong that no enemy has dared to attack it.

Within are barracks, military buildings and residential blocks, some in pink sandstone built by Akbar, others built later by his grandson, Shah Jehan, who preferred white marble.

Jehangir 1560-1627

The Prince Salim, later the Emperor Jehangir, had his own palace. Here again are to be seen a Hindu-Mogul blend of architecture, but Jahangir was less gifted than his illustrious father. He provided himself with a large harem and was a heavy drinker, which Islam does not of course permit. A story which may be apocryphal is that he couldn't find a drinking companion who matched his capacity until his agents found one in the Persian Gulf – a British sea captain – whom therefore they brought to the Court. Jehangir's drinking habits set a very bad example to the Court. He was a kindly father, but like other weak men, could also be very cruel to his enemies.

He was artistic and a patron of miniature painting. He planned beautiful parks and gardens, like those in Srinagar which, however, no longer have the massed flowers such as roses and tulips, which he loved.

Jehangir married a remarkable lady as his Empress. She was the Court beauty, though 34 years of age and a widow. Besides her remarkable beauty she possessed charm, intelligence and taste. She rode and hunted with her husband. She took part in State matters and came to share the sovereign power. Her name even appeared on the coinage:- Nur Jehan – Light of the World.

The Portuguese had little idea of getting on with the Moguls, which was a great help to the East India Company and Jehangir was pleased to receive at his Court the first British Ambassador, Sir Thomas Roe, together with his chaplain.

The Dewan-i-Khas must not be missed. It was the pride of the Moguls – a sumptuous council chamber, but to describe it needs a more skilful pen than mine.

Shah Jehan, Fifth Emperor 1627-1666

Who loved more than any previous or subsequent Emperor. His great love was Mumtaz Mahal (Jewel of the Palace) and he never ceased to love her. On her death in childbirth, he poured out his grief into a memorial which he built regardless of cost – the Taj Mahal. One may say that it was wrong to tax heavily many millions of people to commemorate one man's love, but in doing so, he created what is surely the most beautiful building in the world. He outlived her by 35 years – including close on eight as a prisoner in the Palace. He occupied a tower overlooking the ramparts and it was from there that he gazed upon the Taj, communed with her soul and there, attended by a loving daughter, that he died. His remains are laid beside those of his Queen.

These are some of the glories contained in Agra Fort and there are others too outside the Fort, such as the Great Mosque, a building and court of imperial proportions, beauty and dignity.

The bazaars are famed for the skills of the craftsmen, jewellers, glass workers and smiths, but I did not visit them.

For seven miles, from Agra to Sikandara, are numerous mosques and ruins, but Akbar's tomb at Sikandara dominates, for the Moghul Emperors provided themselves with tombs more splendid than did any European emperor. Akbar's tomb or mausoleum is a building of considerable size set in a walled park with four gateways. The building itself is several stories high with many cupolas. The materials used are red sandstone, black, white and yellow marble – the top storey of white marble being added by his grandson – Shah Jehan. I did not think the finished result would have met with Akbar's full approval – it is too ornate for his taste. A plain, domed chamber houses his simple marble tomb, devoid of decoration or inscription. This surely is a hallmark of greatness?

In the park a herd of black-buck was grazing; big, hefty chaps with very dark coats, long horns of 24 ins. or so and well spread out. I stalked a few and got close enough to hear the little belch or cough they give before they scurry off.

Next day I paid one more visit to the Taj. It was about 8.30 a.m. and early enough for the morning sun to gild the great domes, which more than ever seemed delicate as eggshell. As I walked back along the main avenue I saw a young Indian lying on a bench, holding a notebook and pencil and absorbed in his thoughts. Was he composing verses? Or working for an exam?

So I took the train to Delhi. There were many soldiers on the platform and I had difficulty finding a seat. Eventually, a small Englishwoman with a baby and dog showed me a seat. She turned out to be the padre's wife. I was glad to be of some use, minding the baby, the dog or lifting her luggage.

It was later in the war that a senior R.A.F. officer was the guest of a high-ranking American at the latter's Mess at Agra. He said to the Britisher, "Have you been to see Fatehpur Sikri?" "No, not yet," was the reply. "Then you sure must go." He spoke quietly to a junior who was nearby, who left them and in less than half an hour, a roar was heard and a four-engined 'plane taxied up and stopped in front of the Mess. "Let's go," said the American and the 'plane flew them to Fatehpur Sikri.

28

Old Delhi in the heat

AFTER TRAVELLING some 1300 miles and much sightseeing – I arrived at Delhi with a heavy cold and hoped I did not give it to the baby on the train. But Indians are so understanding: I went to bed and though I was a complete stranger, the hotel servants took charge of me for two days. I then went out to visit the most impressive sight in Old Delhi.

The Red Fort

At that time the entrance – the Lahore Gate – was guarded by British sentries, the walls of the fort rising up to a hundred feet. Walking through a high tunnel perhaps 150 yards long, one emerges in the wide open space inside. The style resembles Agra Fort, the stone is the same pink sandstone. An interesting feature of the Palace is the outer gateway with a gallery for drummers and pipers to herald the arrival of visiting dignitaries.

The Dewan-i-Am

Or audience chamber lies opposite; at the far end stands a magnificent throne faced with carved and inlaid marbles. The background design contains birds and plants in coloured semi-precious stones. Behind the throne is a chamber separated by a stone screen, so that the Empress and her ladies could see and hear without being seen. It was also used as a court and Mumtaz Mahal, wife of the Emperor Shah Jahan, would listen to the cases being heard and frequently persuaded the Emperor (and Judge) to reduce his harsher sentences.

The Royal Baths

In the hot weather of northern India when the mercury rises to 115 deg. and higher, daily baths in a pool are as beneficial as exercise. The Mughal Baths in Delhi must be unsurpassed: picture a great hall of cool marble decorated with flowers and plants in coloured stones; where the water ripples through carved and gilded channels: where hot water, cold water are laid on and, to finish, a supply of rosewater to perfume the skin.

Shah Jehan and his wives used to bathe together, then, when refreshed, pray together in a small chapel. Nor were the children forgotten: they had their own shallow pool of carved marble.

The channels were not only for water: they were also used betimes for milk, sweetened with honey. And of course there was no shortage of servants to clean away the sherbet from the channels.

The Dewan-i-Khas

Or Hall of Paradise, I will not attempt to describe adequately. It is a hall of incomparable, yet tasteful richness, carved overall with gold and coloured marbles and semi-precious stones. Through it the stream of water flows and ripples till finally it enters a large, shallow basin in the shape of a rose and inlaid with gold and coloured stones.

This surpassed any of the royal chambers at Agra except the Dewan-i-Khas.

The last of the pavilions built by Shah Jehan is a hall of rest and recreation. By means of numerous fountains and water-courses the outside world is hushed and a cool, moist atmosphere is created as a relief to the intense heat of the north Indian summer.

The water-course runs over a shelf supported by little arches. Each arch was to contain a flower pot by day, while at night the pots were replaced by little lamps, a lovely idea. So the Mughals, Shah Jehan in particular were not only great patrons of art but were served by outstanding architects, designers, builders and stone-masons.

Aurangzeb 1618-1707

The last of the great Mughals – the Emperor Aurangzeb – usually depicted with a white beard – was the third son of Shah Jehan. But the Mughals had no real family life and sons were often disloyal to their fathers. Aurangzeb succeeded in capturing his father at Agra before seizing the throne. He showed his old father no mercy.

Naturally, Aurangzeb was greatly feared and mistrusted. His reign was a difficult one – his sons emulated their father's treachery, while Aurangzeb's harshness towards his Hindu subjects was in marked contrast to the more tolerant attitude of his predecessors. This harshness led to a strengthening of the Rajput States and to the rise of the Maratha power which was only defeated a century later, and with difficulty, by the British.

Aurangzeb was quite different from his predecessors, he soon settled down to a simple and strict religious life. He dressed simply, with a single great jewel in his turban. He married only three wives. He was very religious and followed every precept in the Koran. He stopped the playing of music at Court and did very little building, being preoccupied with wars and revolts.

In administration he did not spare himself. He did however build the Moti Masjid or Pearl Mosque in the Red Fort in Delhi. It is very small, designed for a few worshippers only and surmounted by three little domes, like pearls. The interior is cleverly contrived: a series of ornate arches gives an illusion of much greater size. It is a gem of a building.

Aurangzeb's weak points were his intolerance of the Hindu majority and like Louis XIV his contemporary, his reluctance to delegate. When he died the Empire fell apart.

Thousands of Muslim boys are named Sikandar (Hindustani for Alexander the Great), likewise Akbar, the Great Mogul. A number are named Jehangir, but few bear the name Aurangzeb.

(Shah Jehan is a title and means king of the world.)

The Delhi Ridge and the Mutiny 1857-58

A vast, largely level plain stretches from Calcutta to the Punjab and Delhi is flat, but a few miles to the north stands the historic Ridge. It was here that a decisive battle was won in 1398, when the Mongol – Timur – defeated the King of Delhi, advanced to Calcutta and returned to his capital – Samarkand – with vast booty. His name is alternatively – Tamerlane (Timur the Lame) and he was the forerunner of the Mugul Dynasty.

The Ridge also featured during the Indian Mutiny and on its summit stands quite a humble monument commemorating the 249 British soldiers killed and 3605 wounded. Though the Mutiny left a deep scar, especially on British men and women, the number of British casualties shows that it was not a general mutiny, but affected one of the three armies, the Bengal Army. [29]

India was, however, changed irrevocably. The Crown assumed responsibility for government. Queen Victoria duly became Empress and the attitude of the British population grew more suspicious: for example, as the Mutiny started on a Sunday, British troops habitually marched to church with their weapons. To their great credit the Queen and the Prince of Wales were above colour prejudice and took great pains to reduce it: the Queen's Indian orderly officers becoming a familiar sight and symbol.

The Ridge is covered with light scrub jungle and I saw a splendid peacock sitting quietly on a rock, his six foot tail resting elegantly behind him. Also a pair of partridges, which are different from the partridges in the south. I was glad the Army showed respect for the past and did not allow sport on the Ridge.

The Jumma Masjid

Or Friday Mosque is the pride of the Muslims of Delhi. They say it is the most famous mosque in the world, but to this the Arabs would never agree. Built by Shah Jehan, it holds 20,000 worshippers.

[29] This army was not recruited in Bengal but largely in the former Kingdom of Oudh, capital Lucknow.

It resembles the big Mosque at Agra. The guardians of the mosque have various treasures, the chief one being a hair from the beard of the Prophet. Also slippers and letters of nephews and near relations of the Prophet.

A footprint in hard rock is claimed to have been made by the Prophet himself (which is hard to believe). Other features which the tourist shouldn't miss are a fine park, the memorial to General John Nicholson, a Company officer and a hero who was killed during the Mutiny near the Kabul Gate.

Another of the gates is the Kashmir Gate, where during the Mutiny, intrepid British Sappers blew their way into the Fort; the extent of the breach, some twenty yards across, being clearly seen in the masonry.

St James Church

This is the memorial to a very fine Cavalry officer, Colonel James Skinner, who raised the regiment named Skinner's Horse. The church has immensely thick walls and is quite cool inside. It is closely associated with the Regiment, many of whom are buried there. Outside the building in the courtyard there was a rather gruesome relic – a metal dome which originally stood on top of the church – the dome had a number of bullet holes which it received in the Mutiny. Colonel Skinner, whose mother was a Rajput lady, was a brilliant cavalryman and loved his troopers as he did his own children. He became a legend. The architect was Colonel Robert Smith of the Bengal Engineers and one reason for the foundation was because Anglo-Indians were not then admitted to European cemeteries, partly for lack of room.

These form a selection of the buildings and antiquities of Agra and Delhi.

New Delhi
and the Ruins

The garden city, designed by Lutyens, I will for the present pass over. Likewise most of many ruins of ancient palaces, forts and mausoleums of five successive capitals.

The Qutb Minar

This is a tall, round tower, started by Hindu Kings of Delhi in the 12th century who built the first four storeys. It was completed by the Muslim Viceroy of North West India, Qutb-ud-din, who began life as a slave. He was the founder of Islamic architecture in India and completed the Minar, which attains a height of 238 ft. It is interesting that while the entrance (built by

Hindus) faces South, all the upper windows face East i.e. the direction of Mecca. The tower is decorated overall with texts from the Koran.

Purana Qila (The Old Fort)

An ancient fort, close to the present Old Delhi, is a remarkable ruin. No one knows how old it is, but it must have been built originally by Hindu Kings. It contains several buildings, one of which is a fine library of red-sandstone, built by the Emperor Humayun. While descending the stairs, Humayun fell and received fatal injuries. His Queen, Hamida Begum, must have been devoted to him. For returning from a pilgrimage to Mecca she brought some 400 holy men to perform his funeral rites and then raised a great tomb over his remains. It resembles the Taj and may have been its prototype.

Love will always find a way

This tale which has been handed down gives a glimpse of the Moghal Court. A certain princess, some seventeen years old, but not yet married, liked to be carried out of the Palace during the hot season in her litter in order to enjoy the light evening breeze. To do this she had to pass through a bazaar. One evening, she spied a handsome young tailor sitting cross-legged in his shop and bent over his sewing. The next day she passed that way again and, by Allah! he was handsome! A third time she gazed on him through the lattice-work of her litter: this time her mind was made up – she must have him. But how? How could a princess still unmarried be closeted with a man and one far below her station?

So she confessed her passion to her faithful nurse, the one person she could trust implicitly. Her nurse opened her eyes wide with horror – her Baby must not think of such a thing! But the princess pleaded and so the nurse consulted one of the palace officials, Kasim, who was related to her. His reply came at once; "Impossible! how could any unauthorised man get past all the Palace guards?"

The nurse returned to her charge and repeated his reply. But the princess refused to accept it. "There must be a way", she cried.

So Kasim pondered and pondered. He walked all round the ramparts. He studied all the points of entry, but all windows were barred and every entrance and exit was guarded, even the one used by the scavengers. Gradually, however, an idea came to him. Every day, water from the best well was drawn, boiled in great iron cauldrons, then, with the lids fastened and bolted, they were carried into the Palace.

He then went to see the young tailor and prevailed on him by threats and a sum of money to crouch in one of the cauldrons and be covered with water up to his neck. Several times this was done and each time the young tailor, wearied by their embraces, returned safely to his abode. Then word reached the Emperor that a man was being smuggled in the royal water butts!

Next day, he stood by a side gate as the water was being carried in. He watched the coolies very carefully and noticed that one water butt appeared to be heavier than the others. So he asked the overseer: "Has all the water been boiled?" "Yes, yes, your Majesty." Then pointing to the cauldron which he considered was the heaviest the Emperor asked: "And has this one been boiled?" "Yes, yes, your Majesty." "I am not satisfied," was the Emperor's reply, "Boil it again!"

At the Woodlands Hotel where I stayed, I became friendly with a young American who was employed by the Caltex Oil Company. I found him extremely intelligent, quiet and refined. We talked a lot about India, which I happened to know rather better than he. There was also a young businesswoman from the Philippines. They both lived in the hotel, but neither had made any friends and found Delhi rather lonely.

Walking before breakfast in the Civil Lines I was impressed by the number of men walking to keep fit. One I saw each morning was probably an Army pensioner, white-moustached, lean, fit and hard. Another was a very stout Indian, trying, no doubt, to keep his weight down. I was pleased to see the large number of horses used for riding or for traps and carriages. And Sikhs, whom I was not used to, looked very handsome and well-dressed.

Delhi is sharply divided into old and new, old Delhi is very mature and the people mind their own business. They are used to strangers and accept them without emotion. Beyond New Delhi, for mile upon mile, stand the remans of almost forgotten Empires.

In the West one rarely sees an ivy-clad building abandoned to nature; our old abbeys and castles are carefully preserved. India is rich in old temples, forts and palaces and growing richer, following the dissolution of the princely states. Some are maintained, others not.

The ruins beyond the present capital are one of the most extensive in Asia – an historical romance. I saw them at a later date and include them in a later chapter.

So after a week's stay, I left Delhi, still in April, without any breeze; fine dust suspended in the air and obscuring the sun was parching to the nose, throat and eyes, especially those accustomed to a less dry atmosphere.

✴ ✴ ✴ ✴ ✴

From Delhi Main Station I caught the mail train for Rawalpindi, headquarters of the North-Western Army. The distance was 450 miles and again I had pleasant company in a second-class compartment. One was a Jemadar from Peshawar, that is an Indian Army officer with a Viceroy's commission. He was a very good fellow, risen from the ranks. The second was Anglo-Indian, originally from Madras, who was employed by Military Telegraphs. The third was a magistrate and Revenue officer of the same grade as myself. He was the best educated of us four, with many generations of culture behind him. But his views were unusual: he said he preferred British and Germans to other Europeans and also declared his preference for paternal British rule, rather than shared rule or dyarchy.

When reserving a sleeping-berth at Delhi I had also booked a Retiring Room at Rawalpindi Railway Station. So a suite of two rooms and bathroom, swept and dusted awaited me. As there is always a Refreshment Room on the same platform there is no need to go to a hotel.

After tea, bath and dinner in these well-appointed Rooms I tried a local cinema. The stars were Paul Muni and Bette Davis. I did not choose one of the best seats but was happy to sit among British soldiers who were a good lot: pink, cheerful and well turned-out. In front of me, sat a sergeant with his Anglo-Indian wife and children.

Returning to the several Retiring Rooms I met another occupant, who much to my surprise, was a Brahmin office manager from Bellary district in the South. He said he found his north Indian clerks "rather slow".

From Rawalpindi was the final stage of my long journey: 205 miles by road to Srinagar, capital of Kashmir State. One books a seat in a large American car.

Army manoevres had begun the night before and some miles out we passed formations of men and motor transport. The springing was soft and the vehicle swayed round the bends. I felt queasy, one of the passengers was sick. I did not then know the secret - to skip breakfast and carry a flask of brandy.

We climbed up to Murree at 6,000 ft, then descended into the Jhelum valley. At one short stop an old Muslim played delightfully and with real feeling on a small stringed instrument; he played Indian tunes and, for my benefit, Scottish dances!

Lunch was provided at a travellers' bungalow in the Jhelum valley. We sat on the long verandah and were served a delicious meal of river fish, mutton chops and tomatoes. In the garden, trees cast a dappled shade, birds chirped in the branches and from below us came the music of the swirling river.

As we drove up the valley the people changed from virile Pathans to the gentler, poorer and artistic Kashmiris. Whenever the car stopped a crowd of boys and loafers shouted and competed for bakshish. I was rather rough with them but my fellow passengers were pleased to have protection.

April in Kashmir is as beautiful as April in England and the well-watered valley was full of apricot blossom. So we reached our destination – Srinagar – an old city built largely of the material close at hand and abundant - pinewood. I reported to the agent who took me to a small houseboat a few miles out on the Dhal Lake and found it spotlessly clean and tastefully furnished. I loved the sweet scent of the wood and the gentle heaving whenever a boat passed nearby. In the clear water could be seen water-plants and fishes darting about.

29

Life on the Dhal Lake, Srinagar

FOR A few days life was dull and the rain fell. I did not know anyone but spoke to a middle-aged couple in the next houseboat. They were from Calcutta and were keen fishermen.

Then I met a charming girl, Jane Holdsworth, whose father was a senior I.C.S. officer in Madras. The Holdsworth's were most hospitable and treated me as one of the family.

We went for walks; rode small, hardy Kashmir ponies and sunbathed at the club which was beside the lake. It was lovely to see and smell the blossom: almond, apple, pear, mulberry, cherry, peach and laburnum. We lay on sprung mattresses on *shikaras*: long narrow boats paddled through waterways by three or four men in the stern. All round us the Himalayas rose up, thickly forested with cedar on the lower slopes, while above the 10,000 foot contours the snows shimmered in the sunlight. Kashmir resembles Switzerland but on a grander scale.

In the evening the setting sun casts blue shadows, then gold and pink lights. The lower slopes above the lakes are ideal for walnut trees, which provide an important trade in timber, furniture and of course nuts for the Christmas table.

Once, in Srinagar, we looked at all the handicrafts: walnut ornaments; rugs and woollens. I also saw for sale a wide selection of skins: tiger, a huge ten-foot panther skin, black panther, wolverine, grey leopard and lynx; but those were for the tourists.

The British behaved quite differently in Kashmir: the burdens of administration were forgotten, British reserve melted, friendships were made easily and caste distinctions, such as between civil and military almost disappeared. There was a number of married women, their husbands baking down in the plains and it was not surprising that officers, on leave from the war, made overtures which were not always repelled.

We heard of an unusual court case. An Englishwoman of about thirty was staying alone on a houseboat. She could afford to hire her own *shikara* and went daily to the club and to parties. In the day-time she went about with bare back and short skirt. One night, she was assaulted by the men who paddled her shikara. She was highly indignant and filed a case against them: they were charged with attempted rape. Their defence was interesting:

"We have been employed by Miss......... for weeks. She always goes about with bare back and arms and we all assumed she was a prostitute. One night we thought we would take our pleasure and were very surprised when she resisted us!"

The Mogul Emperors did not like the heat of the plains any more than the British. They loved Kashmir and several of their buildings remain. One is a small palace on a hill, where the Emperor used to rest with just a few of his many womenfolk.

Everyone has heard of the Shalimar gardens. They are one of the Mogul gardens in Srinagar planned by the Emperor Jehangir: built on four levels so that the shrubs, lawns and flower-beds have plenty of running water. The Mogul taste was for formal gardens and pavilions were provided for rest and refreshment. One is named 'Abode of Love' and is next to fountains with no fewer than 150 spouts which of course drown all sounds from the outside world. The Emperor Jehangir was a keen patron and designer of gardens.

In the East (excluding Far East) there appear to be three countries where art, music, buildings and gardens combined to enhance the Royal pleasure: Turkey, Persia and India.

At a dance I joined up with a colleague, F.J. McLintic, who was recruited the same year as myself and had also sailed on S.S. Viceroy of India.

After a while McLintic decided to move into my houseboat. He was a very professional officer and soon was enlightening me on the growing Muslim-Sikh tensions in the Punjab. He thought serious trouble was inevitable and deplored the apathy in the Government of India and Army H.Q. The shining exception, he said, was General Auchinleck, the Commander-in-Chief.

Srinagar in May was warming up and all the young people foregathered in the morning to swim and sunbathe; there was also water-skiing. Mac and I had nothing to do but enjoy ourselves: all the work on our small houseboat was done by an elderly Kashmiri and his grown-up son.

One morning the Holdsworths proposed a climb up a hill to a nearby fort. It was picturesque and still manned by sepoys armed with muzzle-loaders and guarded by 19th century field guns. this was typical of many of the States, which were delightful but clearly couldn't survive for much longer in the modern world.

As the month of May progressed more young people arrived. I met a brother of Captain Stewart, Indian Medical Service, whom I knew at Bellary. There was a plump Swedish girl, called Bubbles, and I was attracted to an intelligent brunette, Maureen Anderson.

One night after taking Maureen home, I went out in the shikara in the moonlight. The water was perfectly still with wisps of steam. All round the Dhal Lake houseboats were moored, their lights reflected in the water. There were lights up in the Fort, while a few miles away a delicate chain of lights led up to the Temple on the hill. Above, the mountains loomed: huge, impassive, brooding over the midnight scene.

I listened to the music of the water, parted by our bows and the gurgling from the thrust of the paddles. It was extremely satisfying and I don't doubt that after landing I dropped straight off into a deep sleep.

One day McLintic and I discovered in Srinagar a small Mogul garden. We entered through a pavilion and then walked on to a formal garden with green lawns, fruit trees, flower beds and borders. Beyond was another pavilion and a courtyard at a higher level. The garden was watered by a spring at the far end housed in a little pavilion. People were resting on the green lawns or in the shade of almond, apple and cherry trees. We tasted the spring water, which, unlike boiled water in the plains, was cold and delicious.

Afterwards we climbed up the Temple Hill which took less than an hour; on the hillsides grew an abundance of dog roses, wild hyacinth, a reddish sorrel and a mauve flower we didn't recognise.

Our object was to view of the Vale of Kashmir, 84 miles long by 24 miles wide. The valley is a gently sloping plain to the south and half of it was under water. The air was very clear but the far distance was muffled by clouds, while to the west rain was falling.

After feasting our eyes we turned to the Temple and noticed that the electricity had been installed by the late Maharajah of Mysore in token of his friendship with the Maharajah of Kashmir. A Sadhu or holy many showed us round and duly accepted a modest tip and a couple of cigarettes. Among the visitors I noticed one, whom one wouldn't see in much of India: a tough old Indian gentleman, dressed in mountaineering garb with a rucksack and two dogs.

On the way down I picked flowers: sorrel, honeysuckle, also acacia, which was growing from out of a private garden.

That evening we went to see the film 'Rebecca' and we agreed that it was the finest we had seen for years. Afterwards we were paddled back to our houseboat, the night being dark. The Dhal Lake was a brilliant, glossy black, but all along the shore houseboat lights were reflected, like liquid gold.

One day a colleague, Sydney Plew, Mac and I fetched Jane Holdsworth and hired a car to take us up the Sindh Valley, a tributary of the River Jhelum.

On the way, we saw pony caravans, which looked as though they had walked out of the Old Testament. The people were nomads, dressed mainly in black, the women hooded. The younger men had fine black beards, the older men dyed theirs red with henna.

We climbed slowly up the valley till we reached a torrent of water rushing down from the snows and over stones and boulders, so we took off shoes and stockings and waded across. It was icy cold and our feet got numbed, very refreshing.

The valley is thickly forested and high above we could see the Sindh Glacier. After a good English breakfast McLintic wanted to light his pipe, but couldn't find his matches. He asked several Kashmiris but not one had a matchbox – they were very poor. Finally, a train of little ponies descended – a colonel and his wife had gone for a week's trek into the blue and of course – the colonel's good Punjabi servant produced a box of matches from his pocket.

At one stage a big flock of sheep blocked the pathway, Sydney Plew shouted to the shepherd, who said it was impossible to clear a way for us, so Sydney and I did it ourselves, for we were police officers and could handle a crowd.

Lunch had been organised by the Agents and was perfectly cooked: trout with potato salad and peas, with a bottle of beer each. We were delighted with the lunch and after a rest we dammed a little stream, only seeing one other person. He was a Kashmiri, educated and well- dressed being employed in the Archaeological Department.

One evening I was sitting with a good-looking Army officer in the Srinagar Club and we were watching the dancing. A tall, stately Indian lady in a rich sari was conspicuous among the dancers; my companion was very taken with her. "Who is she?" he asked. "Why, that is the Princess of Berar," I replied, "her husband is the Heir Apparent of Hyderabad." "What a marvellous dancer," he said. "I wish I could have a dance with her…. My father met her father-in-law when he was a war correspondent in the first war. Do you think I could mention this and ask her for a dance?" "Certainly," I replied. "Have a go." He took a pull at his drink, drew himself up to his full height and walked over. A minute later he returned. "What did she say?" I asked. "She said: 'I am sorry I don't dance with people to whom I have not been introduced.'" My friend was crest-fallen.

By the end of May the forty or fifty houseboats moored round the Lake were full. There were a lot of young people and someone proposed a picnic in a 'dunga', which is a kind of barge.

Fourteen of us went out in it with ample supplies of food, drink, nuts and cherries. Some servants came and sat in the stern. We didn't need them but they didn't want to be left out. We played records and sang, but it had one drawback, after drinking beer Sydney Plew and I were uncomfortable. So we changed and went for a swim, it was rather a cold day and we didn't get much relief. But soon afterwards we disembarked in some gardens and then were able to enjoy our lunch.

Later it became colder, blankets were produced and we lay under them. I found myself next to a tall, lanky girl. I knew her as a rather serious person and we talked about horses; there was some 'horseplay' in the boat but Audrey didn't seem to be that sort. Months later, I was told that she was in trouble: she was in mixed company and suddenly tore her clothes off and hugged a young man. Evidently she was highly sexed and being a well-brought up Service daughter, became repressed beyond endurance.

Years later I heard of a similar case - a Church of England missionary, a quiet bachelor who had lived alone for ten years, when walking in a bazaar, suddenly ripped his clothes off and assaulted a woman.

★ ★ ★ ★ ★

The Walar Lake, which was said to be the largest natural lake in the whole country, was the objective of another picnic. Six of us got into McLintic's car and we drove for thirty miles and had a good view of the lovely Mansabal Lake, calm and blue with a village nestling among trees. We lunched by a torrent and, after washing up, rested under the trees. The mountains, clothed with evergreen forest, rose steeply up to a snow-covered massif – dazzling white against the deep blue of the sky.

Maureen rested in the crook of my arm and I felt very happy. Later, she and I went for a walk. We came to a paddy field and squelched through it. We jumped over some streamlets then, just as we were about to wade through the mainstream, a large snake appeared making straight for her. As her Indian experience was largely confined to Dehra Dun this was the first snake she had seen and was pretty scared. So we turned back and joined the others, who, no doubt, had a good laugh. We reached the Lake, but it was not nearly so beautiful as the smaller one.

It was an indication of the bad roads that McLintic's car stopped on the way home for lack of petrol. However, a rickety old bus passed and we boarded it. When we came to a wooden bridge, the passengers were asked to get out and we crossed on foot. I then managed to get Maureen next to me, in the gathering dusk put my arm round her and life felt very good.

At the height of the season the club arranged a fancy-dress dance. As I didn't know what to wear, Maureen, another girl and I drove into Srinagar in a tonga, a small pony-carriage. Maureen decided I should go as a caballero. "But what exactly is a caballero?" I asked. "You will see," she replied. So she helped me to buy some cloth and accessories such as ear-rings.

She proved to be excellent company, was well read in modern history and was curious to know how I came by a French name. That evening though I probably looked a freak, I did not lack for partners but got on best with Maureen Anderson.

At the dance was a number of very young subalterns with various moustaches, some soft and limp. Not one had had any responsibility or heard a shot fired in anger. Then a Naval Lieutenant arrived. He looked a real man, strong, disciplined, efficient. His destroyer had been in the Dunkirk evacuation and he had made more than twenty crossings without any solid food. Soon afterwards he was back at sea. When his ship docked at Bombay, his skin had gone yellow and his Captain ordered him to take leave.

A great-hearted woman took charge of him, introduced him to various girls and herself danced with their partners. McLintic had his partner whisked away three times and was somewhat aggrieved.

Most people who travelled as far as Srinagar liked to go a little further – up to the highest hill-station in the country, Gulmarg, which is 8,500 ft up, as in June even Srinagar can be pretty warm. So Jack McLintic, Sydney Plew and I settled our bills and Jack drove up to Tannmerg, the end of the road. For some reason unknown to us Sydney delayed his departure.

As we got out of the car, poor and rather dirty coolies swarmed round us, desiring us to hire ponies while they would carry our cases, for the usual way to reach Gulmarg is by pony. Much to the disgust of the pony-men Mac and I left on foot. It was a long pull up the wooded slopes but the scented mountain air was balm to the soul.

We arrived at our wooden guest-house which was owned by a Mrs Baldwin. She had expected three of us the day before and she only got two, a day late, but never complained.

Next day, I kept a light tweed coat on all day, which was a great treat.

At the club, I met a man who rejoiced in the name of Goodale, then a delightful couple called Rushton. He was the son of an Indian Police officer and she the daughter of an I.C.S. officer, both of the Bombay Province. After his education at Rugby he joined the Calcutta office of the Eastern Bank, one of the great British banks.

I hired a hardy, mountain pony to take me back to Mrs Baldwin's and returned by the longest route, cantering over the turf; but he had a mouth like iron.

Next morning after breakfast Mac and I hired ponies to ride up the mountain. The slopes which, in the winter would be ski-slopes, were dotted with little wild irises and buttercups; higher up was wild gentian, above that rhododendrons and anemones, white, yellow and pink.

We saw a party of Indians tobogganing down a snowdrift, both boys and girls in the party. Only North Indians would do that, the rest never see snow.

As we sat for sandwiches a long vista of the Himalaya was before us - one mountain, Nanga Parbat, with triple peaks soared up to over 26,000 ft, its summit lost in cloud and I marvelled to think that from there the Himalaya extended as far as Burma.

We climbed further to 13,000 ft and sunbathed behind a rock, yet close by was a five foot deep snowdrift.

The descent was long and very tedious, but after a bath we felt sufficiently rested to go to the hotel for a drink. There we met Bubbles, the Swedish girl and her friend – we made a small party, so next day we decided on a picnic to a place with a Dickensian name: Ningly Nullah.

We set off on small ponies and it was like a story: we walked through a long green corridor flanked by the tall Himalayan cedars. There were cool streams to cross, flowers and mossy banks. Here and there, forest clearings were blue with forget-me-nots. So we stopped by a stream and ate our lunch. There was one snag, however, there were fleas in the bank of the stream. It was McLintic's last day and he wanted it to last as long as possible, so Bubbles and I walked on ahead.

As Mac left, several arrived, including Sydney Plew, Maureen Anderson, Jane Holdsworth and her mother. So Sydney Plew joined me at the guest house and I found him as good company as Mac.

It was here that I met two subalterns of the Guides, not knowing what a crack Regiment it was; they were both modest and unassuming. The Corps of Guides consists of both infantry and cavalry and the officers used to be interchangeable.

They are the only Regiment to have their own church. Built at Madan on the Frontier it is still cherished and in use by Christians from Peshawar. Also they introduced khaki cotton uniform during the Mutiny and so set the pattern for the whole of India and beyond. Their fame was based on their professionalism, morale and the fighting qualities of their hand-picked men. In the heat of May 1856 they rode 580 miles in just over three weeks and then joined battle.

One did not find them adorning Government Houses or Residences, nor did I meet any on the Staff, though there must have been a few. Both William Hodson who raised Hodson's Horse and General Sir Sam Browne, V.C. were from the Guides, while the Battye family, from London, provided no fewer than ten of its officers.

By then I was fully adjusted to the altitude. I organised a dance and even got complimented on my dancing, for the first and last time, but Maureen was not yet adjusted and couldn't dance much. The best dancing was at Nedou's Hotel as it had an excellent band which they hired, the Punjab Police Band, whose bandmaster was a Mr Chapman, a fine musician who had trained in the band of the Seaforth Highlanders.

After a picnic up the mountain, we arranged to meet at Nedou's but Sydney Plew took Jane Holdsworth to the cinema. I was seeing the Rushton's every day and got to know them well. They introduced me to yet another girl but it was my last day.

So we finished up at the cinema – Charles Laughton – and as we walked back I drank deep of the cold mountain air, for next morning it was down, down to the plains my boy. As I walked down the path I reflected how lucky I had been all through my six-week stay.

At Tannmerg I waited an hour for the taxi, warding off the flies attracted by the waiting ponies. So the long drive of well over 200 miles began, easy for the first half but full of twists and turns in the second. We stopped again at the romantic rest-house by the swirling river Jhelum.

Rawalpindi was dull and the light yellow, for there had been a duststorm. A man I knew in Madras, Bob Hargraves, asked me to dinner at his Mess – the Frontier Force Rifles, after which we went to a cinema and laughed at the Marx Brothers. By the time I left him, the heat was oppressive so I took a cold bath before retiring. One did that sometimes in the heat, a warm bath before dinner, a cold bath before bed.

Next day I caught the Frontier Mail to Delhi, the compartment being a two-berth one. My companion was a big Sikh, a Recruiting Officer seconded from the Income Tax Department. He had breeding, intelligence and education, an ideal companion for a long journey.

The Tughlaqs

As McLintic was in the New Delhi Police he had me to stay with him. I wanted to see the oldest ruins, which are fifteen miles out, the early-mediaeval city called Tughlaqabad. It is a long time since a Muslim army invaded Sind in the 8th century and added it to the domains of the Caliph of Baghdad. But the important Muslim invasions began about 1000 A.D., the chief object being plunder. It is worth mentioning the cruel and bigoted Mahmud of Ghazni, an Afghan, for he is held to be the original cause of the religious feuds between Hindu and Muslim, which reached such a terrible climax in 1947-8.

Muslim kingdoms were established in the Punjab in the 12th century, but the ruins of Delhi begin with the Tughlaq dynasty founded in 1320 by the son of a Turkish slave and a Hindu woman. He ruled an empire which extended from Peshawar across peninsular India to Bengal and as far south as Mysore. But the slave-Emperor proved a bad ruler. He oppressed his Hindu subjects and a revolt in the south led to the founding of the Vijayanagar Empire.

The Delhi remains are decayed but the massive fort, the palace, the harem, mosques and offices are easily made out. Opposite, stands another palace built by the Founder's son. For wherever there is a zenana or harem, there one is sure to find jealousy and intrigue.

From the Tughlaq remains, McLintic's driver drove slowly for mile upon mile, some fifteen in all, past the ruins of past kingdoms and empires, slowly crumbling away. For not one of these dynasties lasted more than two hundred years. No one at the Delhi Durbar of 1911 foresaw that the mighty British Indian Empire would soon begin to decline. But it followed the historical pattern and was to last barely 190 years. (The Mogul Empire lasted just about 200 years.)

After this feast of antiquities we called for McLintic at his office and drove to Maiden's Hotel in Old Delhi. In the large dining-room, not being the season, there was only one other guest and several waiters.

Mac showed me over the large New Delhi Police station, which had been designed, with the rest of the city, by Lutyens. I had never been in a big City police station and found it palatial, being particularly impressed by the showers and flush lavatories.

So I was driven to the railway station. Punjabi servants are very loyal but can be slow to adjust to strangers. But Mac's Punjabi driver had been most courteous and helpful. I was very pleased with him and tipped him a rupee, the cost of forty cigarettes.

30

The Rise of the Marathas

"Breathes there a man with soul so dead,
Who never to himself hath said
'This is my own, my native land.'"

AFTER LEAVING the North the train takes one through a major Maratha State. The rise of the Marathas during the reign of the Emperor Aurangzeb makes a fine story, so, before I alight at Gwalior I will try and give the reader some idea of these remarkable people, whose exploits are still legendary in Maharasthra.

As already indicated, the harshness of the Emperor Aurangzeb towards the Hindus inflamed the most warlike of them at that time, namely the Rajputs and Marathas.

As early as 1664 Shivaji, a Maratha chief, had seized and looted the East India Company's Fort and factory at Surat, north of Bombay. Years later he tried again, but this time the Fort held out. In 1707 the Emperor Aurangzeb was defeated by a Maratha army, took flight and died. Shivaji was a great man and big enough to respect the rights of Muslims and Christians.

The Marathas come from Central India and near Bombay, and their head was not a king but a Brahmin – the Peshwa. Also in Central India there roamed a cruel and lawless tribe, the Pindaris. Between them: the cavalry led by Shivaji, the supporting infantry and the Pindaris terrorised central India. Later, a high officer, called the Sindhia was granted a kingdom which further strengthened the Maratha Confederacy. Henceforth he is styled the Maharajah Sindhia.

The Marathas conquered much of what later came to be called the United Provinces and extended their power as far south as Tanjore. Their armies, with the help of French and other European officers, were re-organised on western lines and no power could stop them.

By the year 1758, the year after Clive's great victory at Plassey, the Marathas reached the height of their power and ambition: advancing north, their confederate army captured Delhi, Lahore and beyond, while their rule in the south remained firm. But the Afghan King, who was a fine general, was alarmed. "The Marathas," he said, "were the thorn of Hindustan." After prolonged skirmishing, which weakened the Hindu army, the Afghans attacked at Panipat, near Delhi, and defeated them with a great slaughter, no prisoners being taken. But the victorious Afghan army would not stay to garrison the Punjab plain and returned to their highlands for they did not receive their pay.

The battle of Panipat was decisive in that the Marathas never fully recovered from their huge losses. However, their armies fought continuously, living off the country and so causing untold misery in the villages.

The Confederacy no longer held together, they fought among themselves and some even fought for the British. So the Governor-General, Marquis Wellesley, decided to take a strong line and put his younger brother, Major-General Arthur Wellesley in command. For many months Wellesley had been organising and training his forces; he cleared the South Deccan of mounted freebooters; he captured the strong fortress of Ahmednagar by storm, then encouraged by this success, he searched for and found the army of Maharajah Scindia with that of an ally, the Rajah of Berar, at Assaye in the plains northeast of Bombay. The year is 1803.

The Marathas, as usual, had a large number of cavalry, over an hundred guns, infantry consisting mostly of North Indians with not a few European officers and commanded by a German from Hanover. Wellesley's Bombay regiments were more than a day's march away and though heavily outnumbered, he promptly attacked and duly won a brilliant victory, captured most of their guns and small arms, but not without considerable losses to his redcoats:-

The 78th Regiment of Foot in kilts and tall black headgear fought magnificently and with perfect discipline. They richly deserved the battle honours and the Highland Light Infantry, as they are now called, bear on their cap-badge the title: 'Assaye'.

Who can doubt that the future battles in the Peninsular War were won on the plains of Maharashtra?

The Maharaja Sindhia retired to Gwalior with its strong fortress. This was considered impregnable, but in a subsequent campaign it was brilliantly captured by Col Goddard of the Bengal Army. Later, a magnanimous Governor-General, Lord Cornwallis, restored it to the Maharajah Sindhia. The Maharajah showed his gratitude by supporting the British, particularly during their fiery trial – the Mutiny. For his services his gun-salute was raised to 21 guns, so placing him on an equality with the major State of Hyderabad, Kashmir, Mysore and Baroda, (another Maratha state). The Marathas settled down after the British conquest, for military men do not bear grudges for long and a Regiment was raised which has become famous: the 5th Maharatta Light Infantry. The strength of an infantry Regiment was eight battalions.

A most remarkable and surely the finest of all the Maratha Rulers was a lady of peace, Maharani Ahalya Bai of Indore. She reigned for 30 years till her death in 1795 and was so revered that she was accorded the Hindu title 'Avatar' or incarnation of the Deity.

I drove to the main hotel, the Hotel de Gwalior which was a stately one, built in the Mogul style with cupolas of pale sandstone. It was almost empty at that time of the year. The rooms were high and spacious, each bedroom had a tiled bathroom and the service was excellent. For instance, when unpacking my clothes and putting them away, the room-boy took out some items which needed washing and noticed that one end of pyjama cord had disappeared and put it right.

The Fort was the first place to visit. I took a buggy or tonga driven by a Muslim youth, whose Hindustani was not grammatical (to notice this made me feel good).

The Fort is built on a ridge of sandstone nearly two miles long and 300 ft high – an acropolis. As one walks up there were some fine Buddhist figures carved in the rock, the largest a good 50 ft high. The gateway was guarded by a few sepoys. Placed on the ramparts were some light cannon with a couple of magazines close by for the shells. The interior, like Vellore Fort, contained a school and office blocks. At one end, high above the plain, as on a cliff, was the picturesque Old Palace, built in the 16th century. There was no guide, but a dear old boy with white whiskers showed me round the palace. We saw the royal apartments, a pavilion for the ladies and the dungeon. The doors were low and as we came to them he spoke the only English words he knew: "Please mind yo head!"

The tonga driver took me round the town, centred on the Civic Square, then on to the second Palace. There was hardly anyone about but I found a very handsome official with a long, grey moustache and asked him: "Is the Maharajah in residence?" The Maharajah was a plump and well-favoured young man in his twenties. But the official didn't think I was respectful enough and replied with great dignity: "The Maharajah Sahib is not in residence!" I returned to the hotel and sat down to a bottle of beer in the lounge, there was no one else and I didn't see another guest till after dinner, when an Englishman arrived.

Next morning one of the hotel staff, a courteous young Maratha, took me round the second Palace. It was a very large building - painted white. Most of it was used as offices, for the young Maharajah didn't like it and had built himself a new palace of modern design. So there were three palaces in the capital.

The Durbar Hall was on the first floor. A red-carpeted staircase led up to it, but what caught my eye were the bannisters, made entirely of glass. The columns were of twisted glass and at the turns were cut- glass newels.

The Durbar Hall itself was conventional, hung with portraits and contained a huge red carpet, over a hundred feet long and all in one piece. The banqueting hall held three long tables and the billiards room, four full-sized tables.

Beyond the palace was a park, guarded by a huge bronze cannon well over 20 ft long; I forgot to ask the cannon's name, no doubt it was a Mogul gun.

To continue my journey south meant catching the midnight train. As it happened, two trains left at midnight and having little sense of direction I took the wrong one, which was going to Delhi. I managed to get off after only a few miles, with difficulty found a tonga and returned to the Hotel de Gwalior in the middle of the night.

It was a long, hot and tedious journey of nearly 1,000 miles. There were five of us in the compartment: two young Madrasis, a veteran Gurkha subedar, an officer; and a very good type of Sergeant in the Royal Signals. As I happened to mention to one of the Madrasis that I had no wireless set, he said he had some influence in the bazaar, promised to get me one and was as good as his word.

From Central Station a taxi soon dropped me to the Madras Club, to a bath and clean clothes. My Morris car which had been in the care of a sub-inspector, arrived clean and serviced. I met one of my colleagues, F.D. Paterson-Morgan who had been posted as A.D.C. to the Governor. I had wondered how he would get on as he was deeply religious, a teetotaller and a humourist, but he was getting on well.

After shopping in the markets, I called on the Inspector-General and met there for the first time, a man with a considerable reputation, a Jerseyman called W.F.A. Hamilton. I expected someone tall, dark and handsome, in fact he was tall and of average appearance.

Later, when I got to know him well, I decided he was one of the outstanding men then in the Indian Police and yet he had failed the entrance exam. at his first attempt. Examiners are never infallible.

In the evening, with friends, I had a long and refreshing swim in the warm sea, my first sea swim for many months. I even watched the sun-set from the water.

After my first year at Vellore, a new Probationer arrived, P.F.S. Murray. I had not seen him for four years, he was as full of energy as ever and enthusiastic about his time in the Malabar Special Police.

He and I and another had a busy evening, first at a cinema, then dinner and dancing. There were many people there and I noticed that most of the women were pale and rather listless. Pam, my former flame, was an exception: she was very sensible and abstemious.

At the Gymkhana Club I danced with a young woman in a silky dress. In the tropics partners do not cling to each other, but this young woman clung so that I could feel very curve as she swayed to the music; I did not care for her dancing. Next morning I left for Vellore, which was only a morning's drive.

31

Back to the fields and plains
Cowdust

WHEN THE sun begins to set and the bullocks wend their weary way, stirring up the dust on the field tracks, then mother, cooking beside their little cottage, looks up and cries to the children: "Look! Father is coming home."

It had been a marvellous holiday. I felt mentally and physically refreshed, was happy to be back and my colleagues gave me a welcome. Naturally, there was plenty of work to do: finding out all that had happened in the two previous months, reading up the cases still under investigation and attending daily parades of the Reserve Police. In the Office: catching up on auditing, for it was part of the assistant's duty to audit the various sorts of bills which control expenditure. Not least I had the pleasure of fetching my horse who had been in the care of the former cavalry officer, Dr O. Stern, at Ranipet. He was in fine fettle.

As yet there was no Army unit to strengthen the membership of the Vellore Club, which was reduced to nine members, different ones from 1936–37, and we were a happy family.

On Saturday evening the Police Band was playing merrily from the bandstand, after they dismissed I brought out my portable gramophone. I wonder what the Collector, Ahmed Ali and his wife made of my music but I think they enjoyed the Band.

One morning I held a parade for all local Sub-Inspectors, Head Constables and the Civic Guards, as part of preparation for war or disturbances. Afterwards, a deputation of Hindus came from Wallajah, a nearby town with a strong Muslim minority. Their spokesman was a lawyer who first praised the war effort, then extolled the British Raj, then the deputation came and garlanded me. Just before they left I learnt the reason for their visit; I promised to look into their complaint, which had been presented with such tact and finesse.

The last months of 1940 were a time of Civil Disobedience and there is a world of difference between disciplined *satyagraha* or non-violent resistance and militant picketing by say, miners. In this campaign it was the object of prominent Congressmen to be jailed as political prisoners. So it happened that a Congress leader wrote to Harrison, the Superintendent, to say that on such a day, time and place he would court arrest.

The venue was the flat maidan or plain in front of the Fort. Harrison said we would arrest him ourselves and travel there in my small Morris car. The crowd numbered several thousands and the Congress leaders were on a raised platform in the middle. We had to drive along a crowded road beside the maidan and the men and youths closed in all round us so that we had to stop. They looked menacing, as though to say: "We don't need *you* here!" After a while, Harrison somehow broke into a broad grin: the whole attitude of the crowd changed, they broke into big smiles and let us through.

As the elegant, white-clad Congressman saw Harrison and me approaching, he shouted anti-war slogans. Harrison tapped him on the shoulder, took him to a waiting van, which drove to the Central Jail where the Jailor was expecting the important prisoner.

My next camp was arranged at Arkonam, the railway junction and concided with the arrival of several troop-trains carrying Italian prisoners, captured during Wavell's great advance on North Africa. They were being escorted to the big Prisoners-of-War Camp in Bangalore. I spoke to an Italian who understood English; he said they had been suddenly surrounded by Australians. "What did you think of the Australians?" I asked. "Sir," he replied "they are not gentlemen."

To reach the next camp involved driving through several villages; I passed through them leisurely and got the impression that they were not interested in the world's troubles: in India – deadlock between the Congress and the British Government; in North Africa, Europe and Russia – war.

After inspecting the police station, I assembled my canoe and paddled on the reservoir. It was July and the water was shallow, but there was a profusion of pelican, cranes, water-crow, some duck, black and white kingfishers and two kinds of snippets, one with long pink legs.

I rode my horse to a nearby village where there was an old Roman Catholic military chapel, for the French were fighting in these parts between the 1740's and 1750's.

Day by day I was waiting for the promised wireless set and eventually it arrived. What joy! But it was a disappointment, I could get very little out of it and couldn't hear the B.B.C. (As soon as we returned to headquarters, I took it to a wireless dealer and was told it needed a separate aerial which he supplied, and from then on it worked well.)

After a parade by the local police, a war meeting was arranged. The Headman was a smart and very efficient man and all went well. Another meeting followed at a nearby village: there was no support, no enthusiasm; maybe my translator was no good, anyhow I returned feeling I might have been addressing a field of artichokes.

A fine camp had been pitched in a grove of mango trees: hill-tent with small bathroom tent for me; kitchen tent and servants' tent behind. A crowd of villagers was waiting as I dismounted and they gaped at me as though I was a strange animal. It was good to be in a tented camp – no traffic, no noise, no telephone, no electricity; water was brought on a small bullock cart; there is something cosy and friendly about a tent, provided it is not too small and is in a good situation.

Next day, after office work I held a village meeting assisted by an Indian gentleman – who was a 'Rao Sahib' – a title something like the M.B.E. It wasn't much use describing the progress of the war, so I told them stories (the Rao Sahib translating) and when I had no more I told the children to sing – and there were dozens of small, dark brown faces singing together – a Hindu hymn.

Touring can be delightful, even in July, but the supplies of food were very limited, and the heat and lack of fruit and vegetables did not suit me.

The Sub-Collector, T.M.S. Mani, I.C.S., invited George Harrison and myself to assist him at a selection of village headmen. Mani, a Brahmin, was a loyal officer. For there were a few up and down the country holding Government positions but showing a marked sympathy with the Congress. (Irishmen will know what I mean.)

It was noticeable that Mani gave preference to candidates who had contributed to the Governor's War Fund. One of these candidates had been missed out: he owned a small cotton-spinning factory, but no one had asked him to subscribe. So he was asked and duly contributed handsomely, but wanted it to be kept quiet in case the Congressmen got to know!

I was told that the day before, Mani had spoken strongly at a war-meeting and called the audience a lot of cowards. This was courageous of him, but an objector threw sand in his face, which is much more unpleasant than tomatoes for the sand would be fine and full of dust.

After returning from duty in the Town, I sat down to what was a luxurious evening: whisky and soda, an overhead fan and my wireless working splendidly.

Two days later I heard the joyful news that after a fierce onslaught, the German motorised columns invading Russia had ground to a halt.

The reader will gather that Ranipet was a key town. I went there again partly for the inspection of Wallajah, where a battle had been fought between the British and French.

At Dr Stern's house I drank a bottle of Nilgiri beer and became violently ill. It took three days before I got my strength back, but I rode twice to Wallajah, the second time for a joint meeting of the mixed population. I think I was a little pro-Muslim, for several Hindus spoke out strongly and the meeting achieved nothing.

Once again I rode out to give a talk on the war. The Headmaster of the High School was present and afterwards made some complimentary remarks to me, which was encouraging, as I had worked hard for both meetings.

The Training College at Vellore had then a fine Principal, D.C.T. Cameron, who was a born schoolmaster. One evening he and I were alone at the club and we had a long talk. He complained of the hypocrisy of the Government in respect of the two main communities. He much preferred the Hindus and disliked the obstinacy and fanaticism of many Muslims, recalling the fanatical cries to be heard each year in Kurnool of "Din, Din, Ali, Din." I respected his opinion. But before deciding what was the best line to take with regard to Muslims, I thought one must have lived in northern India – the Punjab, Sind or the N.W. Frontier.

One morning, a telegram reported a strike at a cotton mill, so I dashed out in a taxi, with a large Madura hound I had recently acquired (the hound could crunch bones, as though they were toast). I could not keep him for long – he needed a full-time handler to control him.

With the hound on a leash I had the ring-leaders arrested and locked up, met the management and organised street-patrols with a show of force. Then there was a welcome shower of rain, the situation became calm. I had a pleasant ride under a grey sky, with wisps of mist floating about, the greys blending with the greens of the trees.

That night I attended the Sacred Heart Festival at a village composed mainly of Christians and Muslims, the Christians being poor and ignorant. After Mass, a bearded Indian priest blessed three chariots fitted with canopies. One held an image of Christ, one of the Virgin Mary and the third one of the Pope. A procession formed with powerful pressure lamps, drummers and pipers, followed by a crowd of women in new saris. The procession then moved to a continuous background noise of rockets. I wondered what the austere Muslims thought of it all.

On my return to Vellore, a letter was waiting from Sydney Plew announcing his engagement to Jane Holdsworth. I was surprised, as I hadn't noticed any romance between them when we were staying at Gulmarg. I wrote her a letter of congratulation and she replied, describing her work in the Defence Department, New Delhi. It seemed that nearly all the assistant superintendents I knew were married or engaged and I was nowhere near marriage.

But there was no time for gloom in my lively subdivision. A report came to the effect that a Revenue official had been stoned and injured. The culprit had been arrested and charged, but it was a serious matter so I rode out to the village, told them off and then moved on to Ambur, which was surprisingly cool.

Several American missionaries of German descent lived nearby and I met them all. One of them asked me to stay and I accepted. Most of the next day I was left alone with his wife and I much appreciated their trustfulness. For it is not much fun being told (and this did happen) "I'm sorry Mr de Chazal, I have to go out for several hours, so I'd be obliged if you would kindly leave." I took her out for a long walk, climbing a hill where we had a magnificent view of the forest which stretches up to the Mysore plateau in the far distance.

As the hot weather reaches a climax in June and July, clouds begin to gather, the temperature drops a little but the humidity increases. There is no work to be done in the fields and tempers can flare up easily. In the first nineteen days of

August 1941, five murders were reported in the subdivision. In the first, near Wallajah, the body was cremated before the police arrived. In another a man was found sitting up on his small verandah. He was dead and the police thought he had died of heart failure, but the post-mortem revealed that he had been skilfully murdered. In another a prostitute near Arcot was strangled and her gold jewels removed. For three weeks I was supervising the investigation of these and other cases, travelling from one village to another and writing reports.

At Vellore there was an annual festival which attracted holy men from all parts of India. They wore saffron robes and had long hair and beards. Sometimes they were near naked and a number were addicted to drugs, which showed in their eyes. One procession numbered about a thousand and they had loud musical instruments. I was on horseback and they were moving so slowly that I tried to chivvy them, like a sheepdog with a flock of sheep. But it was no use: their reaction was to move even more slowly.

Another huge crowd formed in the Vellore Long Bazaar, it was headed by youths doing all kinds of strange dances, what, later, would be called 'freaking out.' They meant no harm, but a big crowd is always a danger, for it can change its mood very quickly by auto-suggestion. We stood by and watched for day after day.

Afterwards I joined the Collector (Ahmed Ali) and Harrison who were staying in a rest-house to plan the Governor's forthcoming visit.

I drove slowly along the routes, for it would be my job to pilot the Governor, driving in front of his car. When everything was buttoned up I took a few days leave, heading for Bangalore.

It was a relief to drive up rocky hills, some covered with green jungle. My destination was a town called Hosur, where J.P.L. Gwynn was Sub-Collector and I stayed with him in his handsome, white bungalow.

He ate light meals which left me rather hungry. Hosur was close to the border of Mysore State and as soon as one entered the State there was a fine, broad, asphalt carriage-way. Why was it then that the State road was much superior to the road in British India? The probable explanation was efficiency. In Mysore there was a very efficient bureaucracy. In Madras, the upkeep of most roads was entrusted to locally-elected Boards, the District Boards.

Arrived in Bangalore, I had a good lunch and marvelled at the variety of flower-creepers such as bouganvilea and garden flowers: dahlias and zinias in full bloom; in the sun-baked plains were no flowers.

Some friends took me to see the Italian Prisoners' Hospital where I met a young serviceman, D.T. Piper, whom I knew at school. Then we had a grill at Lavender's Hotel.

I walked in the City Gardens, which are irregular in shape – which I really preferred to the formal Mogul gardens and met A.R. Jakeman of Bellary who was also taking a few days' leave. I took two British Cadets to the United Services Club and they watched men and young women bathing – these Cadets knew no girls. We parted after tea at the Cadet College.

32

Governor's Visit

PLEASANTLY REFRESHED, I drove back to Vellore in preparation for the impending tour.

After hours of piloting the Governor and supervising his protection, I returned to his headquarters, tired and thirsty. One of the A.D.C.'s, a Captain Brett, offered me a gin and lime but I needed a long drink and asked for beer – half a pint came, which I soon finished and longed for another, but the elegant Brett didn't really approve of beer.

During lunch I sat next to Bryant, the Governor's Private Secretary. After lunch, superb madeira from the Government House cellars was served. I really enjoyed it and noticed that our Sub-Collector, T.M.S. Mani did too.

That evening the Governor attended the cinema, where a large crowd of sight-seers had collected. My former superintendent, A.J. King, was there, also on Governor's protection duty. After the show, His Excellency asked us in for a drink.

I liked the Governor (The Hon Sir Arthur Hope) very much. He was a Guardsman and stood 6ft 6ins and there was no nonsense about him.

The next day, being a government holiday, we rested and after tea, I left for the next camp.

It began with a war meeting at which I met a local merchant who had given Rs 10,000 to the War Fund, a large sum. One afternoon, I rode out to a small prosperous village called Mailpatti. It was clean and peaceful, I saw no beggars or stray dogs. Some hospitable farmers invited me to a drawing room, a servant bringing Ovaltine and delicious oranges.

It was dark when I left and got into the saddle. So often the moonlight is clear and harsh but, that evening, the light was softened by a haze and its colour was old gold.

I moved on into a tent, pitched by an out-of-the-way village, but was so bothered by gaping boys who had not seen a touring British officer before, that I left for an old rest-house with a thatched roof, an excellent thing in the heat. By then a big stack of files was waiting which kept me busy for three days, together with the writing-up of inspection notes of two stations. These I wrote in longhand, which the Camp Clerk typed – one copy for the station, one for the Supdt. of Police, who forwarded it to the District Magistrate and the Deputy Inspector-General. Some District Magistrates read them, some merely scanned them for points of interest.

Leaving the villages I moved on to a town called Gudiyattam with a mill and a cinema and which was the headquarters of a Tahsildar, (a Revenue officer) and his opposite number, the Police Inspector. These being warrant officers were greatly respected by the villagers, especially if they happened to be Brahmins. I stopped at villages en route to make enquiries about crime and the crops. A long departmental enquiry against a policeman took up much time and patience. Lastly, a war meeting. I was getting used to these and was able to use notes instead of a full script.

One more camp was enough, for only the Gudiyattam rest house had electricity and ceiling fans. So I returned tired after a satisfying tour.

One of the charms of district life was the variety, for nearly all the Madras districts had hills, jungle, rivers or sea. I had camps of up to 4,000 ft in Chittoor district and the jungles are always cooler than the open plain. However one couldn't always stay in the best camps – the flat plains had a bigger population and deserved their share of supervision.

But it was always pleasant, after two or three weeks' touring to return to one's house, to fans, a fridge and more varied meals; to one's own furniture, books and pictures. Then, after some time one went on tour again to inspection and the charm of being without a telephone. The bearer has constant practice at packing and unpacking and hardly ever makes a mistake.

I went to the club but the others left early and Duncan Cameron, Principal of the Police Training College and I were left, his wife being in the hills. We were like a pair of bachelors.

The farrier arrived before breakfast next morning and I watched him do the cold-shoeing. I was out twice for meals that day: breakfast with Duncan Cameron and lunch with Mr and Mrs L.A. Bishop who were staying at the Mess while on tour. My relationship with them was a very happy one.

It was only a short stay in headquarters. With the horse newly shod, I groomed and saddled him myself and set off in late afternoon, trotting along the verge of the main Bangalore military road and therefore mostly straight and lined with trees. It was interesting to meet sundry wayfarers and I spoke to a group of Sikhs, the leader speaking perfect English. They were taking a crated aircraft to Bangalore.

The countryside was parched. After parades and war meetings at two centres with two nights' halt, I rode back. But what a change: the ground was waterlogged, all the dust had turned to mud and the air was moist and fairly cool.

That evening the Band was playing in the Fort for a small dance; there were two or three European women, several Anglo-Indian women, the wives or daughters of Sergeants, one of whom was young and attractive. But the Fort is rather enclosed and I found it too hot for dancing.

Next day more rain fell. It was club night; only Cameron and I were there so we had dinner together and decided to have a long walk on the morrow after the day's work. Behind Vellore is the town reservoir and after the rain it was overflowing into the watercourse, by which could be seen a variety of stone: limestone, laterite, blackstone and granite. So we walked up the watercourse to the reservoir. A week earlier the water level measured 7 in. on the gauge. That evening it stood at 27ft 5ins.

As the only bachelor I was persona grata at the various bungalows and decided to call at the Jail Bungalow. Major Clements, Superintendent of the Central Jail, was a very good chap, but he looked over-age and so did his wife. No doubt on account of the war he had agreed to serve another two years, for by the age of 53 or 54 European men and many Indians were ready for retirement, the maximum age in the Services being 55.

I gave a dinner party followed by a sing-song at which Cameron excelled for he knew screeds of Gilbert and Sullivan by heart.

The first years of the war were superficially quite peaceful. British bureaucracy was having its last innings, ruling efficiently without elected Ministers. But under the surface, there was ferment and the two main communities: Hindus and Muslims, were growing apart. In the Punjab, the vigorous Sikh community had its own objectives, but they did not affect the rest of the country. The big problem was that M. A. Jinnah, President of the Muslim League, was putting Muslim interests before those of India and he was a strong leader, dedicated to his cause.

Meanwhile, the German Army had recovered the initiative and was advancing into the Russian heartlands. Where would it all end? Lord Halifax (formerly Lord Irwin, Viceroy) could see no future peace without effective Anglo-American collaboration.

33

Last months of uneasy peace

A GOOD monsoon having begun in October 1941, all the reservoirs were filled to overflowing and the paddy fields were like a lake. I sat on the verandah in the evening with rain pouring down. The rain brings happiness, for it spells good crops and, louder than the sound of the rain on the roofs, was the frogs' chorus. How they survive the hot weather is a mystery, but come the monsoon and they are in fine fettle.

The air is much cooler but the high humidity does not suit the liver. Between rains, the sun beats down and great piles of creamy cumulus stand motionless in the sky.

L.A. Bishop (Deputy Inspector-General, Central Range) and Mrs Bishop returned to the Mess and threw a lavish cocktail party one rainy evening. After most of the guests left, Harrison, Cameron, John Kaye (formerly at Cocanada) with their wives remained. We sang, dined, then danced. Dorothy Bishop was a beautiful dancer but was much too thin, the climate didn't suit her. She could not have weighed more than seven stone, less than half her husband's weight, but she outlived him.

The morning was wet and overcast. In the middle of Reserve parade Harrison drove up and announced that five political detenus[30] had escaped from Vellore Jail.

The next few days were hectic; first, telegrams were despatched far and wide, for the Police Wireless Grid was not yet installed. The Town Inspector, with Harrison and me, investigated the means of escape. The telephones were ringing the whole time, Harrison was getting worried and peppery. One or two only of the escapees were arrested.

A Job in a Convict Settlement?

In a country where murder is quite common, the death penalty remains, but many convicted murderers were sentenced to "Transportation" and this meant serving a life-sentence at the Criminal Settlement at Port Blair, chief town of the Andaman Islands in the Bay of Bengal.

About August 1941, I was asked if I would like to accept the post of Police Officer at Port Blair. It would be a pretty lonely job at a place which was a fit subject for the pen of Somerset Maugham; but the pay was attractive. I would

---

[30] Political prisoners, detained by a District Magistrate or the Chief Secretary to Government.

only need to take my personal servant, the cooking and other domestic duties would be performed by convicts of good behaviour. For recreation, there was good sailing and excellent fishing and these were tempting.

I accepted, through the Inspector-General, for a period of two years. But this apparently routine posting was held up, for the Government of India did not send a reply. Early in December – less than three months later – the Japanese swooped down on Pearl Harbour and destroyed the U.S. Pacific Fleet. Before long they occupied the Andaman Islands prior to their invasion of Burma. I was more than glad I wasn't there.

★ ★ ★ ★ ★

The ending of the monsoon was the time for the Inspector-General's annual inspection of the College. Cameron was ready for it and was going to ask for two improvements, the first priority being re-turfing of the parade-ground. But money was short and he could not take it for granted, so he ordered all squads of recruits, when they saw the Inspector-General approaching, to mark time. The dust was terrific and the old man (about 52 years old) coughed and spluttered. After evening parade he needed a quarter of a bottle of whisky to wash down the dust.

Cameron also wanted a very dark record room, i.e. archive, set in the thickness of the Fort walls, to be electrified. So he took the old man there at midday, from blazing sunshine into blackness; he could see nothing and cracked his head on a low beam.

At the end of the three-day inspection, the Acting Inspector-General, Alexander Happell, asked: "Is there anything special you need this next year?"

"Well" replied Cameron, "we would like the parade-ground re-surfaced and re-sown."

"You shall have it" Happell replied. "Anything else?"

"Well, all these years we have had to put up with no electric light in the record room and there is no window for oil fumes to escape."

"I entirely agree. You must have electricity. Send me the estimates for both works."

While camping at Ranipet, which is close to the Fort at Arcot, I gave a party in the Rest House to the local people who had been so hospitable. We sang and Dr Stern and I gave a hearty duet of the Volga Boatmen.

Though there was no longer a garrison at Vellore, the Fort and the two police training establishments gave it an atmosphere similar to that of a cantonment. And the Band, under Mr Taylor, compared favourably with a good military band, for Mr Taylor was a fine musician and conductor, and I reckon we were very lucky to have him.

The annual sports were very well organised and a large crowd from Vellore town and Ranipet came to watch them and take tea. Mr Hatfield, Manager of Parry & Co., Ranipet and his wife were my guests; two others were unable to come at the last minute. After dinner, we returned to the Fort for dancing.

After a day's rest I set off for camp on my horse, only fifteen miles away. But

I was wearing new jodhpurs which had never been washed and was very sore at the end. Two days later I had to go to Ambur, seventeen miles away. I wore shorts under my new jodhpurs, but they were no help. So I gave up riding for a week while the sores healed and had my jodhpurs thoroughly washed. However, one of the missionaries, a Dr Leckband, could ride and he enjoyed exercising Rembrandt.

I got on well with the Lutheran missionaries, one evening they organised a picnic with two cars, a servant, cotton rugs, a charcoal fire and a gramophone. Appropriately, our host played Chopin Nocturnes.

The town of Gudiyattam was not a peaceful one. I had my best Inspector there – he had the Indian Police medal – and he warned me that feelings were running very high. One way to prevent trouble was to enforce the Police Act, which required all meetings and processions to be licensed. So I sent an express message to the Sub-Collector, T.M.S. Mani, requesting him to issue an Order, but as his reply was delayed, I anticipated it and enforced it on my own. Mani was a good magistrate and his approval duly arrived.

Sometimes an officer cried 'wolf' but the wolf did not appear or give tongue. I was very careful not to cry 'wolf' without good reason and so never experienced any difficulty in obtaining restriction or detention orders from the magistrate concerned.

The Inspector and I went off to the scene of a murder, which took place in a delightful valley of the Javadi Hills. A marriage had been arranged between a young man and a virgin; but the young man had other ideas and was opposed to the marriage. As his parents and hers were determined it should take place, he – in despair – murdered her. The relations became very excited when we examined them and it wasn't easy to obtain a coherent story.

We returned in the Inspector's car – a tourer with a hood. I sat in it without wearing a topi and next day had heatstroke. Howbeit, there was a very pleasant Rest House to retire to, and it was cool both day and night – everything was green – trees, hedges and grass. Beyond, the pale green millet crop was growing well in the fields, but there was no meat available so I shot three blue pigeons for the pot.

The cold weather was beginning and soon I was ready to ride to the next rest-house. The rain had stopped, the ground was drying out and I had a pleasant ride through jungle on both sides, rising to about 1,000 ft. The road surface was quite soft, fit for a canter and my orderly, riding a bicycle had a job to keep up; he was a Muslim and helpful for practising my Hindustani.

The rest-house was evidently little used. Forest trees had been planted in the compound, some resembling our silver birch which shivered in a breeze.

The sun rose at about 6.15 a.m. and I watched the deep orange ball as it rose above the hills, shedding its golden light on the grass and tree-trunks. I had slept under a blanket – for the first time since Kashmir and it was a treat to drink early morning tea. Soon, I was walking into the forest with a gun, but this forest was under the control of the village, not of the Forest Department. The village authorities allowed cattle to graze through it and I saw no sign of any game.

Returning, I saw a knot of villagers in the compound – they heard I had a wireless set and asked if they could listen to it. So I tuned in to Trichy and we picked up a veena recital; but the camp clerk said afterwards it was too classical for them.

Next day, they re-appeared. We got popular Indian music, which they enjoyed. So I left them and went for a ride, during which a woman sitting in a cart took fright and hid her face in the floorboards – she thought I was a devil. The Sub-Inspector duly collected the villagers and I tried to deliver a talk on the war. But they were so innocent they couldn't follow it at all and I gave up.

My colleague, Le Fevre, wrote me a long letter – he had spent his leave visiting Rawalpindi, Lahore, Delhi and Bombay. I wrote to the Rushton's in Calcutta whom I had met and liked in Kashmir, but they didn't reply and I guessed that he had been called up. By this time the Germans were only sixty miles from Moscow.

A few miles out of Vellore stands a steep, well-wooded mountain called Kailasa-giri. I rode to the foot of the mountain and walked up the steep path – 3½ miles long. I reached the top very tired, but it was well worth it on account of the splendid view: one could see half the district – stretching out like a map towards the 3,000 foot-high Javadi Hills.

I found ruins of a small fort, some Hindu carvings, two small reservoirs and ruined houses. I wished I knew their history, but India is so full of history that much is not recorded.

Another time when walking near the top of this mountain I spied a tarantula spider on a tree trunk. He was quite frightening, seven to eight inches across and hairy and I kept my distance. I never saw another, though in the well-watered forests along the West Coast they are doubtless less rare.

I have always loved woods and forests and to walk through the many kinds of trees was a delight. There was plenty of sandalwood but several of the trees I couldn't name.

34

War Clouds Mass in the Far East

BY 1 DECEMBER 1941 the war was coming closer and closer. My brother, Louis, had been called up and was on his way to Belgaum, Bombay Province for his officer's training. How I wished I could join him!

That same week, Winston Churchill warned Japan of the folly of going to war. If they did, Britain and the United States would declare war on them – but it was pure bluff. Six months before, it was clear, even from ordinary newspapers, that Japan was a threat to peace in the Far East; yet no reinforcements had been sent to Malaya, presumably the cupboard was bare.

Suddenly, early in December, Japan went into action with her devastating onslaught on the American Fleet in Pearl Harbour, with a loss of 2,000 Americans. A wave of indignation swept the States. Even Colonel Lindbergh, the pacifist, declared it was a just war. So Pearl Harbour united the disunited States.

Churchill ordered two of our great ships, H.M.S. Prince of Wales and H.M.S. Repulse to Far Eastern waters. But it was a forlorn gesture, for without escort vessels and with obsolete air cover they were soon sunk by Japanese dive-bombers. It was a terrible blow to Churchill and to our morale and the traders in the bazaar were quick to notice our weakness: they began to stockpile food grains and prices rose sharply. Formerly, Burma was a granary for rice, but with the ending of Burma rice-exports, the danger of looting the Vellore stocks of grain, supplies for perhaps a third of a million people, was very real.

Ahmed Ali, the District Magistrate, with the newly arrived Superintendent A.V. Patro, a Hindu and the son of Councillor Sir A.P. Patro and I decided to tour the bazaars and warn the merchants against hoarding. I snatched a quick breakfast and then attended an Inspectors' meeting, called to meet the threat of looting. On 23 December I rushed to Gudiyattam to supervise arrangements there. By Christmas Eve the situation seemed calmer and I accepted an invitation to dinner at the American Medical College – turkey and pumpkin pie.

Holy Communion at the church, followed by an invitation to breakfast. Then a full lunch at the Cameron's who had their two fine boys with them; while the Clements at the Central Jail naturally wanted a guest and I felt I couldn't refuse. I tried to eat my third dinner but it was difficult. In the morning I decided that of the two – overeating and over-drinking – the former was the worse! But I soon forgot Christmas, for in the afternoon I was called out to supervise a large crowd which had collected in Long Bazaar. The fear of looting persisted, the District Magistrate and the Superintendent again warned grain-merchants against hoarding.

Foot-patrols were sent out to all the likely trouble spots, including nearby temples and mosques. The Special Branch men were dispersed. We did everything possible. Had rioting broken out, the District Magistrate and the Police would have worked perfectly together. There was no outbreak – so often it happens when no one is expecting it, but this time we were mobilized.

The scare over for the time being, on 30 January the Camerons invited me to spend a night up on the nearby mountain of Kailasagiri, lit. Paradise Hill.

We drove to the foot, walked up the steep path, then had a hearty breakfast. We bathed in one of the large ponds, had lunch and tea and went for a good walk. I teased Irene Cameron saying: "With all this exercise, we will soon run out of food." But Irene was a good housewife and she knew it. We slept under blankets and rose early for it was cold and brewed up tea to warm ourselves. After another walk we decided to return. So ended the year 1941.

Despite the war, festivities continued, this time at Ranipet. A Swedish engineer had arrived there who had a daughter with any amount of sex-appeal. She needed a driving test and I was the one to test Europeans. She turned up for the test with her beautiful bosom outlined and shorts about two inches long and thought that would do the trick; but I wasn't happy about her driving and failed her. A month later she re-took it, this time decently dressed; her driving had improved so I passed her.

There was a dance and she was there of course. She looked ravishing. I hadn't seen such a desirable girl for a long time; but her conversation was so boring that I lost interest.

A farewell party had been arranged for Dr Galen Scudder of the American Mission Hospital, a much respected member of the Scudder family; but the party could not take place, as Dr Scudder and Dr Leckband (from Ambur) had left two days earlier than expected for Rangoon.

The District Magistrate (Ahmed Ali), Patro and I then camped together at Arkonam. Ahmed Ali, Harrison and I had formed a brotherhood – I being the youngest. This continued with Patro and there was no better way of keeping the peace than such close relationships between Magistrates and Police, and I did enjoy well-cooked Muslim food provided by the hospitable Ahmed Ali.

The purpose of our visit was to attend a War Exhibition Train, which was touring along the broad-gauge railways. It gave us a much better idea of the new, mechanized Indian Army and the demonstration which impressed me most was by the Corps of Transport: a 30 cwt. truck was dismantled by a section of sepoys till all the parts lay flat on the ground, even the radiator. This took six minutes. Then, they re- assembled it and drove off in seven and a half minutes. I would never have thought it possible and felt it reflected great credit on their instructors, for the sepoys had only a couple of years' service.

From the Exhibition Train it was back to Vellore for a Servicemen's Reunion - in practice a Military Reunion. Someone had laid on clowns for their entertainment, which some of the Army officers rather disapproved of – I certainly thought it odd. But the Tamils are less serious and formal than North Indians; if someone is too pompous, the Tamil will probably burst out laughing. They gave us a substantial tea, I was a fool, but ate it out of politeness, for later a rich palau and curry was laid on by them at the Police Mess.

Colonel and Mrs Franks, who had come for the reunion, said they would like to visit the Fort and the temple. I had met him in Bangalore and found him off-hand, so I declined to show them round and sent a clerk instead.

Muslim festivals usually begin at the new moon and my next engagement was again Moharram at Ambur.

I decided to ride the thirty one miles and Rembrandt was in good form. He started at a canter, trotted much of the way and finished at a canter. March in Vellore is very warm, but Ambur was still cool with quite a nip in the air at six in the morning.

As usual, I enjoyed the company of the Lutheran missionaries. Mrs Leckband and her eight-year-old son came to tea so I hired a pony and gave the boy his first riding lesson, which he enjoyed.

But Mohurram, at best, is tedious for those who supervise it. Processions started at eight in the morning and continued until late at night. The drums throbbed with hardly a pause. There was the 'tiger' dance when youths painted with stripes emulate a tiger hunting. There was a mock battle with single-sticks, to commemorate the ancient battle between Hassan and Hussain. "Ya, Hassan. Ya, Hussein" they shouted. There was also fire-walking.

For a break, I rode up a nearby hill on Rembrandt. It was a lovely ride and next day I persuaded two of the missionary men to walk up with our supper in a knapsack.

The village police station at Kauveripak(where Clive won a battle against the French) was due for inspection so I stayed in the rest-house, close to a large reservoir with hundreds of wild duck resting well away from the shore. Next morning I rose early and tried to approach them in my canoe before, as I thought, they were wide awake, but with a great flutter of wings they took off and landed at the far end of the lake. So I tried again, half an hour earlier but they flighted just before I could grasp the gun.

I tried once more, this time my puppy wanted to share in the fun, he sitting on the foredeck. Suddenly all the birds took off, I grabbed the gun which went off, blowing a small hole in the side of the boat just behind the dog. He got the fright of his life but I fired the other barrel with one hand. The recoil rocked the canoe and the paddle fell overboard. Holding the trembling puppy in one arm I recovered the paddle and propelled the boat slowly towards the shore, keeping one eye on the hole which was just above the waterline.

The pup soon felt better and returned to his perch when a wave rocked the boat throwing him into the water. I grabbed him by the scruff and we disembarked without further incident. Puppy ran off barking to his breakfast and the servants and I had a good laugh.

35

Business as usual and bad news

WITH THE Japanese advancing rapidly from the North and down the Malayan Peninsula, with our Far Eastern Fleet hopelessly outnumbered, with the great shore batteries of Singapore useless, it could have been expected that morale in South India would have faltered, but we can suppress fear and present a calm front, perhaps better than other Europeans or Americans.

There were still stocks of food and drink and social life continued almost as it had a year earlier when the war was still remote. Dancing went on - for we weren't going to stop for the Japanese!

During January and February 1942 I was camping in the forests of North Arcot. My portable wireless had been packed, but somehow the aerial had been left behind. There were two bicycles in the camp, so I connected them and clipped the leads to the spokes. The Nine o'Clock News, which by then was a matter of obligation, could just be heard and one evening (14 February) I heard the announcement of the fall of Singapore. I was alone and did not share my shock with anyone. Singapore was the eastern bastion to India and Ceylon and its capture was a disaster.

It is worth mentioning that two years later, I was shown a report prepared in 1937 by a distinguished head of the Malayan C.I.D., Mervyn Llewellyn Wynne. He was an excellent linguist and uncovered a Japanese plan to attack Malaya from the North East, and their agents – which included Chinese Secret Society members; prostitutes, Japanese photographers and barbers – would act as spies behind the lines.

The report was submitted to his superior, the Colonial Secretary, Singapore, who did not believe it; did not forward it to the General Staff Branch, but returned it to Mr Wynne. This was part of the master-plan put into operation less than five years later in December 1941. Mr Wynne knew that he was a marked man and, before the surrender, was evacuated to Java, where he died.

The fall of Singapore marked, in India, the beginning of intense preparations for it constituted the most serious external threat in British-Indian history. Even I was affected, for a letter arrived from the Superintendent, Special Branch, Madras, to say that he had recommended me as his personal assistant. My Superintendent, A.V. Patro, thoughtfully suggested that I took a few days' leave, as the Mohurram Festival was over. So I left for Madras, stayed with George and Mrs Harrison and enjoyed the social life which was only possible in large cities.

One morning, in Mount Road,[31] the main thoroughfare, I met some Naval Ratings. I assumed they were Royal Navy Ratings and then noticed 'R.A.N.' on their capbands. It was the first time I had seen Australian sailors, who were on shore leave from their auxiliary cruiser. They were so pleased that I had taken them for Londoners.

One engagement I enjoyed was dinner at Mr Justice Wadsworth, a High Court Judge, who in his younger days had camped with my father, then a senior Executive Engineer. His hospitality was superb, his daughter charming. We then went dancing.

His Majesty's Government was, at long last, alert to the political unrest in India and, partly to meet American criticism, the War Cabinet sent out Sir Stafford Cripps with a new set of proposals. But it was too late, the Japanese sun was in the ascendant. Sir Stafford had no authority to negotiate, which was a serious defect. The proposals were rejected by the Congress on Mr Gandhi's advice, who said: "The proposals are like a post-dated cheque on a failing Bank."

Before long, my posting to the Special Branch was gazetted. Rembrandt was entrusted to a friend, my light furniture was stored in the Fort and I arrived in Madras about the time that carrier-based Japanese dive-bombers launched a heavy attack on Colombo.

When I rang my superior, W.F.A. Hamilton, he insisted on putting me up. He took me to the Office where we worked with only a short break for sandwiches. At dusk I heard the powerful sirens reminding everyone of the blackout. Hamilton said I was in the Auxiliary Fire Service and took me to a fire station.

Very early next morning, the shriek of the sirens shook me out of sleep. While I was groping in the dark for my clothes, the well-trained Hamilton appeared wearing a tin hat and accoutred with axe, rope and revolver. We waited in the slit trench outside but there was no noise except the scream of Army and A.R.P. vehicles and an occasional whistle blast by an A.R.P. warden. At dawn we both went to our fire station. We were received by a short man accoutred for fire fighting, who turned out to be D.D. Warren I.C.S., a Secretary to Government and a very senior man. Hamilton, using his field glasses, saw two Japanese fighter-planes out at sea. Then the all-clear sounded; it was, after all, only a reconnaissance by enemy planes.

That afternoon was cloudy, with peals of distant thunder, which must have frightened some people, thinking it might be Naval gunfire. From 7 p.m. to 11 p.m. I was on shift daily in a Fire Control Room, which was hot and airless. The Japanese were active, there being bombing raids from aircraft carriers along the east coast. The worst raid in the Province was on Vizagapatam Port, where there was no anti-aircraft battery. So six or seven Japanese bombers took careful aim in two raids, hitting several ships, but mercifully not an ammunition ship. The lack of retaliation by our Forces made a deep impression

[31] The long street leads to St Thomas' Moumt, where the Apostle St Thomas, is reliably believed to have been buried. His memorial is the ancient Mar Thoma (St Thomas') Church in south India.

on the population: they lost their confidence in the British and some two-thirds left the city that night, including all the harbour coolies. So Gurkha soldiers cheerfully unloaded the ammunition – tossing shells from man to man. It is a terrible thing when the Government is powerless against enemy attacks.

It was the general feeling in Madras that "it would be our turn next", all the Services were put on 'red alert' and all civilian traffic gave them precedence. The City was bristling with guns and planes, but the Japanese wisely left it alone and went for less defended ports. Such is the reality of war.

On the afternoon of 11 April, W.F.A. Hamilton, Oscar Burrell, (the Deputy Commissioner of Police, Law and Order) and I were called to the residence of the head of the C.I.D., Mr L.A. Bishop. In strict confidence he told us that Madras was going to be attacked and invaded.

Burrell and I went to the Madras Club and dined together in state. We had the best of everything; but the people there did not suspect anything and were gliding over the dance floor as though nothing was wrong. Next morning, I went to Mr Bishop's residence to wait for orders. A council of war, chaired by the Governor, had decided that the City should be evacuated. Government departments were to be stripped down to a skeleton staff and the office staffs and records were to be removed to various districts inland. It was decided to move the Special Branch Office to Vellore under my charge. So I drove straight back to Vellore. There were other officials there from Madras, who were en route to southern districts and some young women for the hills.

A Test Case

Tucked away in the Nilgiri Hills was the sole cordite factory supplying the Indian Army. It was well guarded and the surroundings were a prohibited area. One day, a constable from a detachment of the Madras City Armed Police found a British Sahib walking in the prohibited area with his dogs.

The following conversation took place:-

"May I see your identity card, Sir?"

"I don't have it on me. Don't you know who I am?"

"No, Sir."

"I am Col. – the Hon'ble the Resident in Hyderabad."

"My orders, Sir, are to stop any stranger and check his identity card."

But the Resident, a very important man in his State, was fuming, he took the man's number and reported him to the Commissioner of Police. He, Mr R. Hume, saw clearly that the Englishman was in the wrong and issued an order promoting the man to head constable (three stripes) for meritorious execution of duty.

No British officer would have punished the man and Mr Hume's order would have a very good effect on morale; but I regret to say that hardly any Indian Officer would have acquitted – they would deem it politic to agree with the Resident and censure the constable.

36

Invasion Scare: In Charge of Special Branch Office

MY JOB was to find a building for the office and as many houses as possible for the clerical staff. The office manager and two or three others were Anglo-Indian, the rest over thirty in number were Indians. The houses had to be fairly small so that they could afford the rent. But Hamilton was a man of action, small things couldn't stop him, which made my task much easier.

As the Vellore Club had recently been wound up, I chose it for the office, but I rushed about too much and before long had to retire to bed with heatstroke.

At first, there were some delays and growing pains but Hamilton and I sorted them out and soon the files and papers were moving smoothly, the most important and secret matters being handled in Madras.

In the June Birthday Honours, the Inspector-General, A.J. Happell, was dubbed Sir Alexander. He was a sound, but not outstanding officer. He looked older than his 53 years, for as a young man he had served in the Agency and became very ill with black-water fever and dysentery at the same time.

To celebrate the honour done to us, L.A. Bishop gave a large dinner party. There was a number of Provincial Service Officers present who were somewhat over-awed, so the dignity of the occasion was not spoiled by over-indulgence, which our Chief would not have liked.

I managed some sailing with J.R. Le Fevre, an Assistant Commissioner of Police; swimming at the Madras Club and returned to Vellore after two and a half days.

For company, I had my beloved horse and Officers of the nearby 10th Anti-Tank Battery, Royal Indian Artillery. The C.O., a Major Hewitt, was the soul of honesty and decency, but ignorant of India and liable to say the wrong thing, which was a disadvantage, for he had high-caste Indian subalterns under him including a blue-blooded Rajput. This officer had beautiful manners and did not show his feelings if offended by tactless remarks.

After the fall of Hong Kong on Christmas Day 1941 atrocities committed by drunken Japanese soldiery terrified European women as far away as South India and there was an actual instance of panic in the hill station of Kodaikanal, which has no escape road, in the month when invasion was expected any day. The wives of the two leading officials were responsible.

To protect military information Censor stations were set up in the major ports. The Madras Censor was a Lieut. Colonel and the censor is no respector of persons. One fine morning a packet addressed to a European of some standing arrived on the desk of a junior clerk, a well-brought up young Anglo-

Indian woman. Opening it she found six long packets inside, but not knowing what they were she took them to a more experienced clerk, a married woman. "Don't you know what these are?" said the latter. "They are french letters." "Well in that case" came the reply, "I'll take them to the French Translator."

Day by day and week by week we waited for news of the invasion. But it did not come. Years later, while serving in Delhi, I was told the explanation.

Trincomalee, in Ceylon, was the principal Air-Force base for the southern part of the vast Bay of Bengal. One Saturday, a reconnaissance pilot spotted an entire (Japanese) fleet consisting of a battleship, two carriers, cruisers, destroyers and a number of troop transports; the fleet was off the Andaman Islands, latitude 13-14 deg. N. Back he flew to his base4 and reported. Signals in cipher were immediately sent to Delhi and Madras. But a vital mistake was made in transmission: the fleet was, in fact, steaming North but the signals to India said West. Hence the discomforture of the whole Madras Government and the rapid reinforcement of Southern Army.

The hot weather at Vellore in 1942 was a scorcher and I used to return to the Mess exhausted, sitting outside to catch the slightest breeze. Meanwhile, the Madras Government were recruiting new staff, among them some young men of high calibre. One of these was a Police Probationer, Eric Tracey. He held first-class honours and had also represented his College of Madras University at cricket and athletics. He was an Anglo-Indian and gradually rose to the top of the tree. There was also at the Mess undergoing Police training a young Arab prince, a powerfully-built young man with perfect manners; later I entrusted my beautiful horse, Rembrandt, to him for four months. I paid for two months in advance, expecting to pay the rest on my return; but Tariq would not advance money for the fodder and the poor animal languished. I could not forgive him.

J. J. E. Morgan, Frontier Constabulary, R.I.P.

One of my contemporaries at school and just two years younger, was a tall and extremely good-looking Welshman – Jeffery Morgan. He had a splendid presence and physique and was the outstanding athlete of his year.

In the spring of 1937 he consulted me about his preparation for the Indian Police. In the cold weather he duly arrived and was posted to the Punjab and North-West Frontier.

A few years afterwards Morgan was leading a patrol of the Frontier Constabulary at Bannu when he and his men walked into an ambush and were killed.

It was particularly sad – he was such an attractive and outstanding young man. Of the several men of my acquaintance who died in Indian service, his loss was the hardest to accept:

> "The flying bullet down the Pass
> That has for text 'all flesh is grass'."
>
> (Kipling)

The former garrison church at Vellore was served at monthly intervals by a Chaplain from St Mary's Church, Fort St George. I liked to put him up and go with him to Evensong. The congregation were mostly Anglo-Indians and Indian Christians. One evening the preacher was the new Bishop of Madras, visiting his large diocese. He was the Right Rev A.M. Hollis, who was later elected as the first Moderator of the Church of South India.

While visiting Madras to take instructions, I stayed with Le Fevre and his stable companion, J. Pare, I.C.S., when a fourth man arrived. He was tallish, slim and clean-shaven, one of the last to be recruited to the I.C.S. He did not impress me very much but there was nothing about him to cause offence. He was normal except perhaps in one respect: instead of running a second-hand car like the rest of us assistants, he preferred a solo motor-bike. And when he retired to sleep on the verandah he had the machine propped up beside his cot.

I thought no more about him till about a year later, I learnt that while on short leave he had jumped off the upper-floor balcony of a hotel. The finding of the enquiry was kept confidential – maybe it was disappointment over a girl.

Prolonged heat or muggy weather or the effects of an illness could aggravate depression and for a European to make good he needed not to be too subject to 'highs and lows' and preferably not an introvert. This was the second suicide among the few young British Civilians in Madras, the first being P. F. S. Murray of the Police. It is the parents, thousands of miles away, who suffer most and the head of the department who informs them has a most unenviable task.

As part of my training in war-time security, Hamilton sent me to a course at Bangalore in July.

It was organised and led by Major R.J.A. McInerny and was for Army, Police and Air Force officers. McInerny soon showed himself to be very efficient. (A year later, we met again and went trekking together in the Himalayas.)

I became friendly with a regular major in the Camerons who had fought through the Burma campaign, the long retreat, but found him disillusioned. I also became enamoured of a beautiful, charming young lady but she turned out to be a young war-widow, still mourning her husband. It was a long time before I forgot her.

The war was won by our leaders, by our efforts and by morale. Social life was vital for morale and I cannot praise too highly civilians who entertained large numbers of Servicemen. Among them in Bangalore were J.M. Green, Commissioner of Police, Civil and Military station and Mrs Green, who were selfless in their hospitality.

August 1942 was a very trying month throughout India; the monsoon was preparing and a violent political storm was gathering. The storm broke on the 15th of the month with the arrest of Mahatma Gandhi in Bombay, together with all the Congress High Command. The reaction was immediate: rioting broke out in Bombay and within days, spread over India. Dozens of railway stations were burnt and looted. Scores of police stations were attacked and policemen burnt alive. The police opened fire on a number of occasions – while anti-British feeling blazed in several areas.

Madras Province suffered much less rioting and bloodshed probably because the local Congress leaders had been arrested and detained during the night of 14–15 August, on Hamilton's strong recommendation.

North Arcot district was calm, but one day I saw a whole train-load of Congressmen from the Central Provinces on their way to Madras for detention.

During the months I was manager of the Special Branch office, I lived at the Mess, as all the houses were occupied. This suited me very well, except when the Deputy Inspector-General was there on tour. L. A. Bishop was like a father to me, but his place had been taken by C. R. Charsley. Charsley had served in the Great War as an infantry officer. He was no fool, but was quite unsuited to Indian service. He did not like Indians and was much too outspoken. Further, he was bitter because he had been relieved of his appointment as A.R.P. Controller, Madras. It was very boring – listening to his disparagement of Indians – especially their music.

He could however make the most delicious coffee. He had a podgy dachshund called Blitz. One day when we were out walking, an elephant walked towards us. In Madras city, where Blitz grew up, elephants are not seen among the traffic. Blitz looked up, and up and up, then put his head down and trotted on. We agreed that what Blitz had said to himself was:

"No, I don't believe it. I don't believe it!"

Charsley could be pretty relentless towards a bad 'un but he repaid loyalty. Some years before, he handed over charge of one of the Godaveri districts before going on long leave. He and his wife were staying in Colombo waiting for a ship to take them home, when a telegram arrived from his headquarter Inspector saying he was in trouble – a charge had been framed against him. Charsley caught the next boat-train, reached Godaveri, enquired into and sorted out the charge, then returned to Colombo. Four days' travelling in all, at his own expense.

Knowing something of the circumstances, I did not think the Inspector entirely innocent, but though I would not have interfered, I admire Charsley's loyalty to his loyal subordinate.

In November 1942 a Bank official of thirty or thirty-five was posted as manager of the Imperial Bank of India at Vellore. His name was G.H. Cobb. There had not been an English banker at Vellore for some years. As a bungalow became vacant I moved out of the Mess and invited Cobb to stay while his Bank House was being renovated. I wasn't able to offer him a whisky but he had a bottle, which made a pleasant start. Unfortunately, while staying with me he had an attack of dysentery.

Cobb had been Bank manager in Patiala, the Sikh state in the Punjab and related how the Maharajah Sahib invited him on some of his shoots. Once, deep in the jungle, a liveried bearer asked: "What would the Sahib like to drink?" Cobb, for a joke, replied: "An iced Martini, please." To his astonishment, the bearer brought him an iced Martini on a salver. (It was Somerset Maugham who said: "The world is divided between those who drink Martinis and those who don't".)

When the Maharajah went duck shooting he provided all the cartridges. One day Cobb fired about 120 cartridges, but said the noise and the fumes gave him the worst headache he had ever had.

At this time I was keenly interested in a young lady called Mildred, I didn't get to know her well, but was quite upset on hearing of her engagement to a Lieutenant of the Royal Indian Navy.

Partly in order to forget Mildred, I took a few days' leave for Christmas, staying with J.M. Green, Commissioner of Police, Bangalore. On Christmas morning we attended the Garrison Church; also in the congregation was the General Officer Commanding, Lieut.-General Sir Noel Beresford-Peirse with his Colonels, Brigadiers and ladies; but the padre did not impress me.

After church, Mrs Green took me to a very cosmopolitan cocktail party. I remember talking to a large Parsi lady, who, after her second drink, said she was much looking forward to Independence, even if it involved a bloody civil war. Naturally, Independence, or Swaraj, was a beautiful dream to the nationalists and I didn't disagree with her.

In the evening, the Greens gave a Christmas dinner for the Army and R.A.F. Provost-Marshals and for the brave little wife of a British prisoner-of-war. Mrs Green complained that she had been kept awake into the early hours by British servicemen singing and shouting their way back to barracks. To which the R.A.F. officer replied: 'Yes, I'm afraid these disturbances are apt to occur during Xmas'.

I took two of my friends, Walter Grantham and Marcia, his fiancee, to dinner at the Club and a cinema. My subsequent behaviour shames me: that night I lay awake into the early hours thinking of Mildred and next morning I called on Marcia before breakfast. She was still in her kimono but was perfectly charming. I told her of my disappointment over Mildred, which I had kept entirely to myself. It was very rude of me to absent myself from breakfast at the Green's and to call on Marcia so early. But I had only one day's leave left and felt so much better for confiding in an understanding woman.

A few days later, Cameron gave a New Year's Eve party at the Vellore Mess with an excellent buffet supper. Mildred was there, I hardly spoke to her and seeing her did not upset me too much.

37

New Year, 1943

"It does not matter whether the cat is black or white
as long as it catches mice" – Deng Xiaoping.

THIS IS the day when all the subordinates call with a token gift: a garland of
roses and two limes, some oranges perhaps, or a small fruit cake. You
exchange pleasantries and wish each other a happy New year. The Rules
permit the above gifts but no more. At the same time the officer gives New
Year tips to his servants and orderlies.

On a visit to Madras I met Sir Denys Pilditch, Director of the Intelligence
Bureau, New Delhi, the highest rank in the Indian Police. He was staying with
Sir Lionel Gasson, the new Inspector-General. Sir Denys was tall, slim and
very distinguished, but not such a forceful personality as Sir Charles
Cunningham, my first Inspector-General, who was short and plain, but a
tough and extremely able officer. Later, I was to serve under Sir Denys.

At the Connemara Hotel I got to know an older man, a very fine Lieutenant
who had been a Territorial. He was a Scot, with thick brown curly hair and
moustache and was a real man. He described a little-known operation, a
German invasion off the West coast of Scotland on 16 August, 1940. As the
landing craft approached the shore, oil was sprayed on to the sea, and then set
on fire with incendiaries. Drastic, but in that month we were fighting for our
very lives.

★ ★ ★ ★ ★

Living in the southern part of North Arcot district was a remarkable person,
Miss Ella Maillart, a Swiss athlete who had represented her country in the
Olympic Games. I got to know her and found her excellent company. She was
studying certain aspects of Hindu civilisation. Previously, she had crossed
China on foot with Peter Fleming, as recorded by him in his 'Journey though
Tartary'. Ella had the trim figure of an athlete, a masculine mind and
handwriting. She was able to mix with tough and virile men because she had as
much stamina as the best of them and was a person, rather than a woman.

Once she asked me: "Could I spend the night at Vellore so that I could catch
the early morning train? I only need a grass mat to lie on." "Certainly," I
replied, "I can easily arrange to sleep elsewhere." Evidently she didn't like my
reply, for she never came. She just wanted a cot on the verandah and had no

patience with Anglo-Indian notions of respectability, but I had to accept them.

Those who come to work in India should realise that the men who are most respected are the fakirs, the holy men (and sometimes women). The men wear long hair and beards, hardwood beads round their neck and saffron-coloured clothes. They own no property and accept whatever food is offered them. My father knew one who was a remarkable ascetic, the sort who could lie on a bed of nails. But most of us didn't know quite what to make of them; one wondered if they were all holy.

Early in 1943 I had an invitation to visit an Ashram[32] at a place called Tiruvanamalai not far from Jinji. My host, a Dutchman called Mees who had known my brother at Cambridge, received me, he was an inmate and of course wore Indian dress.

He was a follower of the holy one, the Maha Rishi, whom he revered; he had no time for Mahatma Gandhi. I stayed at the Rest House and next morning Mees took me to the huge Temple with its four great towers and vast courtyards which were very clean and tidy. At his little 2-roomed house he talked sadly of Holland, over-run by the Nazis; then we walked to the Ashram. The Rishi was seated on the dais of a large room with a few men near him. The floor of the room was carpeted, Mees salaamed to the Rishi and we sat on the carpet.

The Rishi was a south Indian of average height and about sixty years of age, he was very spare, like Gandhi and bare above the waist. Evidently he ate little, his white hair was clipped short and he had white stubble on his face. On his forehead were smears of sacred ashes and a crimson caste-mark. Under black and well-formed eyebrows were his remarkable eyes – they shone clear, intelligent, gentle and wise, the eyes of a religious thinker.

Brahmin disciples chanted from the Vedas. When they had finished the Rishi was gazing into the distance, deep in thought. Some twenty or more people were sitting on the carpet before him. They gazed and could not take their eyes off him and nor could I. After an absence of some ten minutes, he returned, his eyes gazing intently. He did not say a word. After twenty minutes perhaps he dropped his head, closed his eyes and dozed off. The spell was broken.

His disciples included men and women, Indian and European – all in Indian dress. They were searching for truth and a faith. Presumably the Rishi spoke sometimes and being South Indian, doubtless he spoke very good English. I express no opinion on the value of the Ashram – but could not doubt that the Rishi wa a true ascetic with unusual powers. Such men are few.

After lunch with Mees, I left by car for a Hindu fort built on a long hill, a commanding situation. It was a stiff climb up steep steps. At the top there were old cannon and a fine view over the plain. I spoke to a small Brahmin, a romantic, who discoursed eloquently on the former glories of the Vijayanagar Empire, the Madura Kingdom and of Gingee.

Gingee, or Jinji, was fortified in the 17th century by Shivaji as the main Maratha stronghold in the south. It is so strong that it held out for over seven

[32] A religious community.

years against the best of Emperor Aurangzeb's generals, which stout resistance was very demoralising for the Mogul Army - a victory gained at too high a price. In the following century it was occupied by Tipu Sultan. That this fortress is scarcely mentioned in the guide-books is evidence of the great wealth of impressive buildings in the country. Unfortunately, I had to leave it all too soon as my throat was getting parched after the climb and there wasn't a drop of water to be had. Knowing this, the kind Sub-Inspector met me at the foot of the hill with a flask of piping hot, sweet coffee! My thirst remained.

They took me to a small railway station and I caught the little metre-gauge train. At nearly every station wives were weeping as they said goodbye to their sepoy husbands who were returning to their units.

It was two years since I had taken regular leave. With the invasion of Burma, the threat to South India disappeared. I felt it was a suitable time to apply and was granted four months.

My last few weeks before leave were hectic. To avoid trouble I agreed with all Hamilton's directions and remarks, which was boring. Towards the end we had extra work preparing for the return of the Special Branch office, records and clerical staff to Madras, my manager Mr Andrews, being most helpful.

For the Governor's visit, two Deputy Inspectors-General came to stay at the Mess; Hamilton came for a day and we all went to the Fort to hear the Governor's (the Hon Sir Arthur Hope's) speech; but I thought that too few of the general public had been invited. All my friends were there and I was able to say goodbye to them.

Next morning my servant and I were driven to the railway station. It was only an hour's run to the junction at Arkonam. The Rev Mr Silver sent his car and Mrs Silver gave one of her usual delicious teas. Afterwards, a missionary took me to see the new airfield, built for the invasion of Malaya. The runway seemed huge – two miles long by 100 feet wide. Close by, the R.A.F. groundstaff were playing a game of soccer, half of them stripped to the waist.

In my compartment of the train was a tall Rajput who said: "I am a medicine merchant. Much of my business is in aphrodisiacs and this leads to more business, because often when I advertise and sell my aphrodisiacs they write back asking for V.D. killers!"

38

Peninsular Journey

HAVING SO much enjoyed some weeks in Kashmir two years before, I did not hesitate to write to Cockburn's Agency in Srinagar to book me a houseboat. But, as I had four months' leave, it seemed a wonderful opportunity to see something of Central India, the rural heart. So the journey was first over the Western Ghats to Bombay. It needs 25 tunnels and 22 bridges to reach the crossing point at over 2,000 feet.

My friends Rosemary and Bill Coltham put me up and let me wander about as I would.

I met several people but enjoyed the company most of C.W.E. U'ren, a bachelor who was head of the Special Branch. His flat was on the sea front, cooled by delicious sea breezes. After a leisurely dinner, he played the piano which made a delightful evening.

Bombay was fascinating and one obvious difference from other major cities was the Parsi community: their well-dressed and be-jewelled women and thin old gentlemen in shiny black hats. The parts close to the sea looked very prosperous, one of which was Malabar Hill, which I thought the finest residential area in the Plains.

U'ren was not hopeful of the future and foresaw serious trouble breaking out after the war and when the Mail train steamed slowly out from Central Station, my companions who were Gujerati traders were all reading anti-Government newspapers, which confirmed U'ren's forebodings.

The train stopped at Ratlam Junction in Central India, where I had to wait for a connection. There was a palace, for it was in Princely India, and I was very taken with the lovely pastel shades of the women's saris. They also wear a tight bodice which holds their bosoms high and firm even into old age.

A *puja* or festival procession was moving along the street, attended largely by children and women in their best saris – a tasteful harmony of colour.

From Ratlam was a slow journey to Neemuch, which is on the edge of Rajputana. I was expecting to be met by an Indian friend, but he did not appear. So I decided to call on Mr Tregenza, Commandant of the Crown Representative's Police. He received me cordially, inviting me to lunch. I found him rather lonely; he was a widower and hadn't seen his only son for several years.

Such was the hospitality of this out-of-the-way station that an invitation came from a Captain Buss for me to visit the Club where his superior, Major Jack Bazalgette and Mrs Bazalgette had asked me to dinner. He was second-in-command to Mr Tregenza. They were a most charming couple and many years later I met him, of all places, in the Anglican church in Istanbul.

They showed me a small British fort which had contained the local Europeans and which had been besieged during the Indian Mutiny – this was about as far south as the Mutiny extended.

Captain Buss then drove me to the station, from where I caught a train to Chitor. The Railway Retiring Rooms there were appalling, but I soon forgot the discomforts.

Chitor is a household name in Rajput history. The fort is associated with Maharajah Kumbha, one of the most illustrious of Rajput Rulers who lived in the 15th century. Kumbha was a conqueror, the builder of no fewer than thirty-two forts and many temples. He was also a poet, musician and a patron of the arts and he was murdered by his own son!

A young Brahmin offered to act as guide and he seemed quite impressed when I accepted a drink of water from an old woman: the water was in a brass pot and I poured it into my mouth, knowing that if the rim touched my lips it would defile the pot. We saw a very traditional old Rajput, a priest, who had whiskers, each nearly two feet long – I saw him pull them out.

Chitor was also famed because, in the 14th century, all the Rajput ladies in the fort committed *sati* i.e. immolated themselves, rather than be captured by the Muslim invaders. Everyone knew their heroic deed, though committed over six hundred years before.

The Fort hill is three to four miles long, half a mile at its broadest and rises 500 feet above the plain. A great number of buildings are to be found within, chief of which are two towers, one 80 foot high and the other 120 foot high; also the remains of Maharajah Kumbha's palaces, built in the Rajput style.

The temples were not Hindu, but Jain and the impression was of a number of layers, crowned by a sugar-loaf dome. The temples are adorned with numerous marble statues of voluptuous nude women – puzzling to the foreigner as Jains are considered to be strict and ascetic. The high Tower of Victory, which is in the Jain style and covered with carvings, was built by Maharajah Kumbha after he defeated a Muslim Sultan.

The Jain religion, dating from 6th century B.C. is dedicated to *ahimsa* or non-violence and to the sanctity of all life, even of tiny insects, so it is strictly vegetarian. Its stronghold is Western India, where its monasteries are found. Mahatma Gandhi was clearly influenced by Jainism.

Chitor needs at least a whole day's visit and space does not permit of an adequate description. It lived in the past and its atmosphere gloried to past splendours. I bought a humble but attractive memento – a pair of upturned Rajput slippers.

The last leg of my journey to Delhi was in a compartment containing a mother, fat and autocratic; three daughters between six and twelve years old and a little boy of two or three, wearing only a short shirt. Mama took very little notice of the girls, but petted the little boy, frequently stroking his private parts to cause a little erection. I thought they were of the bania or money-lending caste.

So ended my long and interesting journey from Vellore to Madras, to Bombay, across Central India and Rajputana to New Delhi. My brother, Louis, had passed out of the Officers Training depot at Belgaum and was then attached to Royal Signals Intelligence. So, naturally, I stayed with him in his bachelor quarters at Mandi House[33] in New Delhi for I was travel-weary and glad of a couple of days' rest.

We spent his free time at the Gymkhana Club, bathing, and relaxing by the pool. A full Colonel under whom my brother served had just returned from the Persian campaign. His wife was a lovely person, with a heart of gold, a priceless wife to any commanding officer.

There wasn't much motor or taxi traffic in Delhi. With petrol strictly rationed, most of the traffic consisted of tongas and bicycles, which were ridden by nearly all ranks. Most of the soldiers were either British or American, the latter were much better paid and usually had the best, including the girls.

The mail train to Lahore, capital of the Punjab, was much more crowded than two years earlier. As I had corresponded on an official basis with the Superintendent of the Special Branch, I had written to ask if I might have breakfast with him.

The express arrived at the usual time, 6.30 a.m. It was customary for a host to send a car to meet a guest but I did not see one. So I took a taxi and had an interesting drive past one of the large parks. Many Indians like to walk before breakfast, but there in Lahore it was different: hundreds of young men were running round the park, others were doing press-ups; knees bend or wielding clubs – several hundreds were hardening their muscles. I had not seen such enthusiasm before. But, as I discovered later, the Punjab Police knew vey well what it was all about – the Punjabis believed or hoped that the British were on their way out, which would leave the Muslims and Sikhs as the chief rivals for power. Now and again a Sikh soldier would desert with rifle and ammunition – which was then stored in a Sikh temple. They felt in their bones that there was bound to be a showdown. In the event, after Independence, it was much worse.

About seven o'clock I reached D..'s house. He was not yet dressed; later, he appeared groomed and very elegant in a well-cut silk suit and so we had breakfast. D ... was one of a certain type; he did not want to get mixed up with processions or rioting, with noise, heat and dust, nor explore the wilds. He was an office man and wrote good and clear English.

Two years before I reached Srinagar by the usual route: Lahore to Rawalpindi by train and from there to Srinagar by long-distance taxi. But there was an alternative route available in the summer months only, which was Lahore to Jammu by train, a town just inside Kashmir State and from Jammu a long-distance bus to Srinagar.

Jammu town seemed remote and was very quiet. There was a good hotel but only one other guest, a Forest officer, British and domiciled in India.

[33] Most of the Princes had a house in New Delhi; this one belonged to the Rajah of that name. All were let to the Defence Dept. for the duration.

Next morning I caught the bus which was of about 26 seats. We began to climb the Himalayas; Scotch firs appeared, then glimpses of snow- covered mountains. At about 5,000 feet stood the first Himalayan pines. Another 1,000 feet up and we reached a wooden chalet which said 'TEAS'. We stopped but it was disappointing, a kind of Indian transport café.

From there it was downhill, but the valley had almost vertical sides and we could see, thousands of feet below a fast-flowing river – the Chenab. We were down to 3,000 feet again and most of the passengers got off. The bus went on and crossed the Chenab on a narrow wooden suspension bridge.

At 7 p.m. there was a stop; I was all for stopping for the night, but the local State Rest House was reserved for senior State officials. The engine was pulling badly, but we pushed on, slowly. Then we passed what, for the passengers was a common sight, but for me a strange one. It was a gang of coolies, fair-skinned men of Gilgit in the north of the State. They were dressed in filthy clothes, caricatures of footwear and were bent double under heavy loads. Their features were slightly Mongoloid and they looked like beasts of burden – rather inferior ones - yet they seemed cheerful. I was told that they were returning from Dalhousie in British India. I felt indignant, but what would these men do if their loads were carried on mules or lorries?

The light faded as we crawled up a narrow mountain road. One false turn and we would be hurtling down the mountainside and into the river. We stopped at a spring: the water was cold and delicious. I filled my water-bottle and the driver carefully poured some into his radiator.

So we reached our halting-place, a wooden rest-house, at 9.15 p.m. We had not stopped for lunch, I didn't care for the tea and was hungry, but within half an hour dinner was served.

I had travelled through burning hot plains but here it was beautifully cool. I slept on a borrowed blanket, in thick pyjamas, a dressing gown, with my only blanket and a Kashmir shawl. The men couldn't have been kinder – they didn't have much but were generous to a fault. And this is what the traveller can expect in India, provided he behaves as a guest in their country.

Next morning was cold and grey. The 'bus had had a good rest and we began to climb the barren mountainside. I wore khaki drill slacks and a blazer and it felt cold. As it grew colder, the windows were closed, then small snow-drifts appeared, followed by bigger ones. At 9,000 feet, the top of our ascent, we drove through a tunnel in the mountainside, long, dark and dripping wet. At the end of the tunnel was a big snowdrift, so we drove through a short snow tunnel. Standing on the far side was a cluster of officials, policemen and coolies shivering in the cold, for the snow tunnel had to be kept clear and the road swept free of snow and stones. They said that the road had only re-opened to traffic the week before.

I wasn't sorry to be going downhill again and the 'bus duly drew up in Srinagar after its two-day journey, the few passengers left shook me warmly by the hand and we went our way. Years later, my wife and I crossed the Syrian desert by bus, but it was not nearly as interesting as this journey through a Himalayan Pass.

39

The Vale of Kashmir

"Here with a loaf of bread beneath the bough
A flask of wine, a book of verse – and thou
Beside me singing in the wilderness
And wilderness is Paradise enow."

AT FIRST I recognised no one but soon made acquaintances. The first was the
wife of a District Forest Officer I had met at Dharwar in the Deccan. She
introduced me to a golden-haired dream of a girl. I had not been thinking of
girls and this one bowled me over; her dancing was divine but I felt awkward
and made no progress. Two weeks later, I met her mother, who was so
different I could hardly credit it: she was dark, fat, with little beady eyes and a
deep voice, almost like a man's and was enough to put any young man off!

For a change from Srinagar, I arranged to go on a walking tour with the man
who had organised the Security Course I had attended in Bangalore
– Major R. J. A. McInerny.

The Agents in Srinagar made efficient arrangements for a ten-day trek,
providing a Kashmiri butler, who was also foreman, with tents, furniture and
bedding. All this was carried on the backs of a string of little ponies which were
attended by a few coolies.

I never had a dull moment with Ralph McInerny. We would walk all day up
the Sindh Valley with a sandwich lunch. Then the tents were pitched and chairs
set out, soon a good tea was prepared and drunk while admiring the scenery of
wooded valleys, a fast-flowing river and way above – the majestic snow-
covered peaks. Then, with glasses of rum and lime we yarned till dinner was
ready. And so back to Srinigar, refreshed.

There was a dance at the Residency and I found a partner. Ralph was there
with a most elegant married woman called Bunty Nelson – she was wearing an
eye-glass which someone had given her. But one thing I objected to was the
modern habit of stealing partners – I lost mine twice including the last and best
dance.

One evening an incident took place the likes of which I never heard of
anywhere else. Four burly Americans challenged the British to a drinking
contest and four Scotsmen accepted. The Americans were extremely confident
and drank spirits, beer and aperitifs. The Scotsmen stuck to whisky and soda.
Within four hours the challengers had to give up while the Scotsmen were
sober enough to march away in step. It was considered a victory for common
sense.

One day I noticed Charles Filmer, a Squadron Leader and one of my brother's friends, sitting alone in a hotel. He was bored, so we decided to go on a trek together, this time up the West Lydda Valley. It was a more advanced trek than the Sindh Valley, but Charlie Filmer wasn't as fit as Ralph McInerny and we had to go a little slower.

We climbed to a wooden hut at 12,000 feet. Charlie was tired and had gone far enough. But I was attracted to the glacier above us and felt fine. So I went on alone; I reached the glacier, my legs going like pistons and the cold air whistling into my lungs. At about 13,000 feet there were crevasses and the surface snow was melting. Prodding the snow in front with my stick I went on. I heard the tinkle of water in an ice-cavern below me, then a rock suddenly got loose and fell. As it happened the rockfall was some way away, but it made enough noise in the stillness and I froze, suddenly realising the danger I was in and decided to turn back. I would never repeat it – it wasn't fair on my companion, but it was thrilling and the highlight of our ten-day trek.

That evening we were joined by a dear old gentleman – Sir Lancelot Graham, late Governor of Sind Province whose capital is Karachi. He admitted that he had been bamboozled by a dangerous rebel, the Pir of Pigaro, who successfully deceived the authorities by contributing handsomely to the Governor's War Fund.

The next day I was weary, but we walked down to Pahlgam and there met three American lady missionaries. They gave us a splendid tea, next day we asked them back to our tent and sang American plantation songs.

So, down again - from the pure, cold air of the Lydda Valley - to the capital. Evidently the hot weather that year was a severe one for Srinagar was warm, dusty and fly-blown.

Walking along the streets one saw a variety of people – no Pathans, but some of the Brahmins were pink-cheeked and blue-eyed, they could well have been mistaken for Englishmen in disguise.

To pass the time we took tea at a small Italian hotel whose owner sang charming Neapolitan love songs to his guitar. When he played 'So deep is the night' we joined in. And there were also White Russians for two of their young women danced regularly at our lakeside club. One was blond and natural while her companion had jet black hair, an olive skin and grey eyes. Her frock was cut low and she wore a pectoral cross of Russian design. In her tow was a very young subaltern, who two weeks later looked pale and ill. She then switched to an older man, a tough Welsh captain. He, however, was no fool and extricated himself after a few days; for she was dangerous.

But we were finding the air too warm and decided to return to Gulmarg, the highest hill-station in the whole country.

It is not only high up but unsophisticated and it caused British people to throw off their inhibitions. For instance, my very first evening I made friends with a young lady and we got on as though we had known each other for weeks. Several more young people arrived and we formed a party, doing everything together. Priscilla, my partner from Srinagar, was there. She was only seventeen and always willing to dance with me, but I also became friendly with Bunty Nelson, who was probably fifteen years older than I and had a sparkling personality. Perhaps I poured out my heart to her, anyhow afterwards I felt I hadn't a care in the world.

Our group of young people decided to go on a long day's trek up to Appelwat, a frozen lake at 13,000 feet, where there was a large, one-roomed wooden hut. We were tired after climbing over 4,000 feet and drank hot tea laced with rum. Later we cooked an enormous mixed grill.

After washing up I thought that bed was the next item, but some were still playing the gramophone. Then the men undressed and lay down, we turned our heads to the wall while the girls undressed – what a lark, I thought. But we were so tired we all slept like logs and didn't wake up till 8.30 a.m. After breakfast, I settled for the party with the caretaker, who, I thought, was overcharging and had a row with him. My brother, Louis, who was a born diplomat, ticked me off and said it should have been settled more amicably. So we began the long walk down the mountain.

Engaged for the season at Nedou's Hotel was the Punjab Police Band, they had a British leader and knew all the popular war-time dances. They gave great pleasure, none more than when they played a slow fox-trot such as "We're going to have a White Xmas" for the last dance of the night.

A few days before our leave ended, Louis and I accepted invitations to a picnic down below – on the lake by Srinagar. It made a very long day and returning rather late, I walked back up the hill to Gulmarg too fast, the sweat pouring off me. I did not change soon enough and caught a severe chill.

The journey back to Rawalpindi and from there by train to Delhi passed without incident. For part of the journey I had the pleasure of Ralph McInerny's company, who had been posted to Sicily. He was a fine linguist, and I believe, went into business in Lisbon after the war.

During a short stay in New Delhi I called at the Intelligence Bureau, part of the Home Department. There I met G.C. Ryan, one of the Assistant Directors whom I got to know when he was my neighbour at Dharwar, near Bellary district. I met two or three others and the Director, Sir Denys Pilditch, asked to see me. We talked for a few minutes on this and that and I attached little importance to meeting him, for the Bureau, in effect, faced North-West: the turbulent Punjab, the constant fighting along a roughly-defined and mountainous Frontier and , beyond, Afghanistan, where Russian penetration had been feared for over a hundred years. So most of the staff came from the Northern Provinces. Later, I realised that he had in fact summed me up.

From Delhi I pushed on to Madras, a two-day journey. At the Madras Club I had a suit quickly laundered and then took a taxi to call on the Inspector-General. I knew my temporary job in the Special Branch was finished and had no idea what would come next. But after seven years' service I was to act as superintendent in a short leave-vacancy of two months: the Inspector-General posting me to Tinnevelly in the far south.

We were allowed a week for the move, which meant two days' shopping in Madras, two more at Vellore to collect my servant and luggage – no furniture was needed as the bungalow at Tinnevelly was left furnished.

One day's journey by road took us to Madura, a large district town in which I was interested as my father had been Executive Engineer there and both my elder brother and sister were born there. Of the three great complexes: the Temple, the Madura Cotton Mills and the Palace, the latter was, I thought, the most attractive.

Tinnevelly has a good deal of character; it is bounded by sea on two sides and by the Western Ghats on the third; its climate is equable and less hot than inland.

The people are all Tamils and dark-skinned but bigger and more vigorous than further north, reaching six feet and over sometimes.

There is no doubt that they are a very old people who feature in ancient mythology. A certain member of them crossed the Straits and settled in Ceylon (Sri Lanka), forming a community long before Tamils were brought in last century to the new tea plantations.

The history of Tinnevelly is turbulent and the district contains more criminals than most. Missionaries have evangelised many of the castes and ten per cent were Christian, which is well above the average for India. The Tamils are an intelligent and quick-witted race.

Once during the war, the Governor's lady while visiting a girls' school in the Tamil country put the following question: "Can anyone tell me the difference between pence and pennies?"

A girl of twelve promptly stood up and replied:

"Pence, Madam, is the plural of penny. Pennies is the male organ of generation."

40

Criminal tribes and a promotion

IN BRITAIN if the incidence of crime is heavy, it reflects on the character of the local inhabitants. But in India, the population may be law-abiding and crime may occur almost daily, because a criminal tribe operates in the vicinity. Such a tribe doesn't do any regular work – they are hereditary criminals. The best known of them were the Thugs, who were professional stranglers. And it is to the credit of the British that they overcame the scourge of 'Thuggee', thanks largely to the work of Sir William Sleeman (1788-1856), who is still largely a household name.

Being hereditary professionals, men from these tribes become highly skilled. In Kurnool, for example, there is a tribe which is expert at bending and removing window bars, which they do, using a deer-hide thong and a tourniquet. Others are expert with locks and can open all but security locks. Pick-pocketing in a crowd is obviously a skilled operation, also removing necklaces and jewelry from sleeping women. And the thief never keeps hold of the property, it is immediately passed from one to another till it is spirited away.

Confidence tricks are also common: the criminals entertain people with acrobatics, magic or jugglery, while their mates pick pockets or burgle houses. The smear trick is a good one: the criminal chooses his victim, smears his clothing with human excreta then says:

"Please, Sir, your cloth is dirtied."

The horrified victim then goes to a tap, removes his coat and his cloth and while he is busy scrubbing, the criminal has removed all valuables.

When my parents were at Madura it was necessary to pay a watchman from the nearby Criminal Tribe, the Kallars. Provided you did, your property was safe and when a young Assistant Superintendent of Police was posted to Madura he was told he would have to appoint a 'Kallar' watchman on RS.10 per month. "Me, a Policeman!" he replied "You're joking!"

One very warm night he put his watch on a bedside table and slept out of doors in a cot with mosquito curtains. He had two sheets and a pillow. Later, he woke up: his watch, the curtains and the sheets had gone.

To remove the sheets they tickle you on one side with a peacock feather – you roll away, then they roll the sheet under you and repeat the tickle on the other side; but to remove a pillow is risky.

Another trick was to go to a post office or bank when money is being paid out or in. While the customer is busy counting, the thief drops two or three notes on the floor and says: "Sir, you are dropping your notes." While the man stoops down, the thief whips away the wad of notes, slips them like lightning to his accomplice and then joins in the search.

Great efforts have been made to control these tribes, registering them, re-housing them in settlements, providing work. The Salvation Army and the London Missionary Society have done noble work in South India, also the Provincial Government of Bombay. But the problem is a thorny one, for the more spirited tribesmen resent other people interfering with their way of life which they have followed for thousands of years. Immemorial custom in India is sacred.

In an attempt to tackle the problem, the Madras Government gave orders to recruit some of the Kallars of Madura district into Government service. I had one in North Arcot district; a sub-inspector who was robust and hardworking, a good man and I rewarded him. Later, I knew of another Kallar, who was recruited as a deputy superintendent; but the combination of criminal forbears and temptations was too much for him: he became notoriously corrupt.

The Rope Trick

This of course is the celebrated trick attributed to Indian magicians. My father was keen to see it and whenever he came across magicians he enquired if they could perform it. At last he found one: "Yes, Sahib I do it for you". "Not now", replied my father, who wanted to invite his friends. "Come to my bungalow, the Executive Engineer's Bungalow, at 5.30" and gave him five rupees. "Afterwards, I give you five more".

My father at once sent out invitations by his office peons. On the lawn – chairs, a table, matting and a backcloth were provided. The guests duly arrived. Drinks were sent for, they waited and waited, but the magician never came.

Tinnevelly

A fine station, the residential part across the river being called Palam-cottah, with churches, colleges and schools. The Club was a large one, too big for the period as there was no longer a garrison. The bungalows were old, which means airy and spacious and set in large gardens or compounds. There was a chaplain for the Anglican church and the services were attended mostly by Indian Christians. I called on the Bishop, the Right Rev. Stephen Neill, D.D., who was an outstanding Tamil scholar, as well as a theologian in his own right.

It was not a district for a weak man. Fortunately, I felt very fit after two months' leave and was determined to show a firm pair of hands. In a short time some ten or twelve punishment files came up for a finding. I found the charges proved in most of them and ordered several dismissals, reductions of rank or cessation of probation. There was, of course, the right of appeal to the Deputy Inspector-General, who, like an appeal Court, could reduce, uphold or reverse a punishment.

Soon afterwards, three prominent officials arrived on tour. Two were

Governor's Advisers – one British, one Indian. The third was Sir C.P. Ramaswamy Ayyar, the distinguished Chief Minister of Travancore State, who was a brilliant lawyer, a Brahmin. He was not an idealist but a practical administrator. He always wore traditional Indian dress but kept an independent position between the British and the Congress Party. He was also noted for his pursuit of women. His hosts would watch their womenfolk very carefully when 'Sir C.P.' was around, for though he was about sixty years of age he was still considered dangerous. He was fair of skin, like most Brahmins, with heavy black eyebrows and rather prominent eyes. I was privileged to sit next to him at dinner at the Collector's house and found him very good company.

My first camp was at a Forest Rest House, quite a large one, near Ambasamudram in the foothills of the Western Ghats. It overlooked a small river of clear water, flowing swiftly past tree-hung banks. A little further upstream there were rocks, short stretches of rapids and yet further, a beach of pure yellow sand – an ideal spot for a picnic. There was one other visitor, E. R. Ward Close, the Superintendent of Police for the South Indian Railway, with his wife, who stayed in their travelling saloon.

One of my next camps was near the beach at Trichendur, which is not far from Cape Cormorin. It is close to a rocky outcrop on which stands a well-known Temple. Very little had changed for hundreds of years: some extensions had been built and the invention of electric power had resulted in a beacon being placed on the top of the temple tower, which acted as a lighthouse and could be seen some ten miles out at sea.

The district officer visits many villages – too many to remember, but one village I visited in Tinnevelly deserves a mention. It was occupied by a tribe of fine-looking men – some of six foot and over. So I appealed for recruits and said good employment awaited them in the Army. The Inspector translated – but a stony silence ensued. 'What is your reply?' I asked. An elder said: 'Sir, we have our lands here, our women and our children, our flocks and our herds... Why should we join the Army?'

Afterwards the Inspector told me, 'These fellows never want for anything. If they do, they simply steal from a nearby village.'

I had been working hard and was fatigued, but the sea-air, bathes and freshly-caught fish soon revived me. It was here that I heard the news of my father's death. The Inspector was very kind; I spent the day quietly but there was nothing I could do except write to my mother.

Next day was work as usual – we went to a nearby salt factory, where an organised crowd of workers and others had collected and were demonstrating noisily. I took a detachment of Armed Police – fine upstanding men and ordered the crowd to disperse. I was prepared to send the armed men into the crowd (their bayonets were fixed) but happily, they dispersed. If I had muffed the operation and the crowd had rioted, so requiring a volley of bullets, I might have been commended and been awarded a medal.

The next camp was at Tuticorin where I stayed with the Sub-Collector, G.C. Wyndham, I.C.S. I had met him before and we got on well. There was also a Fire Officer, recently sent out from England.

As it happened, before long a fire was reported. I travelled in the fire engine and the Indian firemen, newly trained with a gleaming new engine, soon put it out. It was September – a sticky month and I nearly fainted with the heat of the fire. There is a large Roman Catholic community at Tuticorin but I did not have time to call on them.

George Wyndham was heir to the Williton Estate in Somerset and later became a much respected squire. But in my time such men were rare in the Indian Services and Army; almost all were drawn from the professional and middle classes. The I.C.S. were recruited mostly from Oxford, Cambridge and Dublin; Forest officers from the Oxford School of Forestry, the rest from public schools, good grammar and high schools and the minor public schools.

Another such member of the I.C.S. I knew was an Indian – for a time the Sub-Collector at Hospet. I do not remember his name, it may have been Nair and he came from an estate in Malabar. Unlike the vast majority of us he didn't depend on his salary. He was a good, impartial Magistrate and Revenue officer but showed no keeness to climb the ladder of promotion; promotion could take its own time. Most Indian members of the I.C.S. not only supported a family but also fifteen, twenty or more relations. Nair had no such burden and while we British picked our servants from the servant class, Nair's were his caste-men, family retainers and of course they all eat the same food. He was above us socially but closer by far to his retainers than we to our servants, though we could get very attached to them.

I noticed one of his household, a fair-skinned, healthy-looking lad of fifteen or sixteen. He was willing enough to work but didn't seem to have a regular job. So I enquired and was told: 'He is my cook's son. He had never been away from home and when he heard I was posted to Bellary district he asked his father if he could come too. His father spoke for him and I agreed'.

It was indeed a happy household, like the households of many village squires up to the Great War and some after it.

September 1943 was not a testing time as far as South India was concerned, but the possibility of a Japanese invasion remained and so A.R.P. precautions were being taken.

I made a point of visiting a Coast-guard station beyond Tuticorin – the land was flat, muddy and very salty. Not a tree or bush could grow. The sea beyond looked immense, but it was deceptive – for about 120 miles beyond lay – Ceylon.

The general effect was depressing and I felt sorry for the Indian coastguards who had a monotonous job and told them that their vigilance could save India from Japanese raids.

So I returned to Palamcottah. The regular Superintendent, – G.H.P. Bailey – was returning after leave. I had to bring up to date the confidential files of a large number of subordinates, which took days. I was also waiting for my next posting – not having any idea where it would be. Finally, a telegram arrived: a posting to the Intelligence Bureau (Home Department) New Delhi – about 1,700 miles away!

October 1943

There were a few days to prepare for the long journey and, wisely, the Home Department did not specify the date on which I should report. As the train took me northwards it became clear that the monsoon that year was a heavy one. The fields became wetter and wetter till in North Arcot the countryside was almost under water.

I stopped at Vellore to arrange for my car, horse and personal luggage to be despatched to Delhi. On the way to Madras, great stretches of country were under water. The Madras City power station was affected by floodwater and the telephones were not working, but it was pleasantly cool and I attended an enjoyable dinner party given by one of my colleagues, H.R. Longhurst and his wife.

Next morning my servant called me before sunrise. After breakfast, we drove to Central Station, the train was waiting but there was no sign of its departure. A passenger helped pass the time with dance records played on a gramophone. Eventually, the train steamed out with a long blast of its whistle.

We steamed only slowly and less than 40 miles out we had to stop. Floodwater had swept away both the ballast and embankment, leaving the lines hanging. However, a relief train was waiting further on. So, carrying our luggage we walked over and piled in, but, only a few miles on, stopped at a small station in Nellore district.

Nearly all the 200 passengers were Indian Army, with some British wives and small children. The Regular Major in charge did not know what to do, so though I had less seniority than he, I decided to take charge. Walking to the nearest village I found a police station and a large house occupied by American missionaries. I sent the British women and children to be looked after by the missionaries, while the Sub-Inspector went to the bazaar and organised a good meal for the sepoys. It arrived some hours later and it was a pleasure to see them all sitting cross-legged on the platform tucking into a substantial meal. I also collected some milk, eggs and paraffin for the handful of British men – for there was no light in the train.

Some hours later, about 10 p.m., a Railway Officer arrived with thick meat sandwiches and a pint of tea for each of us. He also told us the reason for the second hold-up – the flood had bent or strained the girders of a railway bridge.

Next day, we set off cautiously but, once out of danger, our Mail train was treated as a troop train so our progress was very slow. We finally reached Delhi early in the morning and two days late. I was dozing and failed to get off at New Delhi station, unlike Yelliah, my intelligent servant. I awoke fully only at Old Delhi and was happily reunited with him an hour later.

After a few days, I received an invitation from a colonel's wife to dinner, followed by dancing at the Gymkhana Club: she and her daughter had travelled on the train.

41

Imperial New Delhi

THOUGH DELHI was the historic capital, the East India Company had little choice but to establish its capital in Calcutta.

When the Delhi Durbar of 1911 was being planned, the British Empire – brightest jewel of the Crown – was expected to last for a long time and with the Punjab annexed and settled it was secretly decided to transfer the capital to Delhi. King George V made the announcement at the opening of the Durbar and it was greeted with great joy by the crowds, but understandably, caused resentment in Bengal.

Sir Edwin Lutyens was entrusted with the planning of the great project; building began before the War broke out but soon ceased and New Delhi was not completed before 1931. It is a fine city of wide, tree-lined avenues with plenty of light, space and air. It was kept spotlessly clean: there were no beggars, hawkers, stray dogs, mosquitoes and few flies – so efficient were the Health Inspectors.

It is joined to Old Delhi by the Kashmir Gate. Its principal feature is a broad vista, formerly called Kingsway, two miles long, the road passing under a grand arched gateway and leading up to the heart of the city: the two great Secretariat blocks of pink sandstone, the circular Central Assembly Building, and above, on a small rise, Viceroy's House . But, owing to the gradual slope, only its great central dome is visible from the vista.

Our Director visited the House or Palace for his weekly audience but the rest of us never went through the massive iron gates with their splendid Punjabi guards. I understand that it was larger than Versailles, that it contained no fewer than 340 rooms, including huge public rooms – durbar and banqueting halls and the ballroom. The staff included the mounted bodyguard, a police detachment, the bandsmen, clerks, grooms, gardeners, tailors, drivers, mechanics; all manner of domestic servants; orderlies, messengers and the Viceroy's printers. These added up to the best part of 2,000, not counting women, children and dependents and all living on the estate.

So grand was the building that one visitor said that to "arrive at the foot of the steps leading up to the portico, was like arriving at the steps of St. Peter's."

Mark Bence-Jones commented wittily on it as "unique among Indian Government Houses in having enough accommodation for even the largest of house-parties." (quotations from Palaces of the Raj).

For the office accommodation, residential, recreational and shopping areas of New Delhi I have nothing but praise, but the grandeur of the Viceregal Estate, the enormous expense of its construction, upkeep and maintenance is another story.

The year 1943 was the year of the terrible Bengal famine. Previously, the Provincial Government could make up any deficiency with rice from Burma, but in 1943 Burma was occupied by the Japanese. There was no Famine Code operating in Bengal at the time and the Provincial Government, with a weak Ministry, failed to tackle the shortage and the dealers forced up prices to beyond the reach of the labouring classes.

It was most regrettable that the Viceroy, Lord Linlithgow, did not visit Calcutta, nor did he order help from Central Government. In October of that year he laid down his office and was succeeded by Field Marshal Lord Wavell.

In extenuation it should be said that Lord Linlithgow's term of office was due to end in the spring of 1941, but Churchill asked him to stay on another year. The spring of 1942 was at the height of the Japanese menace and Churchill again asked him to stay on – for another eighteen months.

Towards the end of 1942 I saw the six-foot six-inch tall Viceroy at the Madras Club. The long hours he spent at his desk had given him a stoop and his eyes were the eyes of a very tired man.

In October 1943, Wavell stepped up from Commander-in-Chief (and Defence Member of the Viceroy's Council) to Viceroy and the first thing he did was to fly to Calcutta and see the famine situation for himself. Then, without any palaver, he commandeered stocks from other Provinces and ordered the Army to distribute the grain. So the famine ended and honour was restored.

At the height of the famine, peasants poured into Calcutta and Europeans tried to feed starving people in their street: but they discovered that these would starve to death rather than eat the wrong food. Such is the hold of caste laws.

It was impossible to say how many died of starvation: estimates varied from one and a half to three million out of a population of sixty million. [34]

Now and again, I saw Lord Wavell riding before breakfast without an escort, or, in the hot weather, in slacks, bush shirt and medal ribbons, striding about the Secretariat; or on some ceremonial occasion in top hat and tails in an old Rolls Royce; or, wearing a silk suit, reading the lesson in the Church of the Redemption, or dressed like a squire at the Point to Point. Humbly, I salute a great man and servant of India.

It was about a year later that Lord Wavell held an Investiture in the Red Fort of Old Delhi. We were arranged in a large rectangle on benches sloping down to the dais, so everyone had a good view. Out of a number of decorations awarded, one stuck in my memory.

[34] A similar great famine in 1769–70 led to the appointment of Warren Hastings as Governor (President) of Bengal.

It was during the Italian campaign that a grenade landed in a trench occupied by a section of Madras Sappers and Miners. The subedar, or Indian officer in charge, leapt onto it and held it to his stomach, shouting to his men to run. Not one of the latter was hurt in the explosion.

After the citation was read, the little Madrasi widow appeared, escorted by two Indian officers. In the crowd she looked so small and bewildered. Lord Wavell pinned the George Cross to her sari, whereupon Lady Wavell stepped forward and folded the little woman to her motherly bosom.

The Intelligence Bureau and the Finger Print System

The former developed out of the Thuggee and Dacoity Department formed in 1835. The Thugs were a caste of professional murderers, skilled with rope, thong and poison, who were a terror over a large part of India. The Dacoits were robbers, usually in a gang. The department was in effect a Criminal Investigation Department, (vide "To Guard My People", by Sir Percival Griffiths, published by Benn).

In 1877 the Department was expanded to include the collection of secret and political intelligence, both within India and on the North West Frontier. Ten years later Special Branches were separated off; these at first were very small, but they grew slowly, were expanded during the Second World War and grew even larger after Independence.

A Central Intelligence Bureau was established in 1904 and later moved to Delhi. But no story of police work in India should fail to mention the Finger Print Bureaux.

In the 19th Century much thought was given to the character of finger-prints, especially by Sir William Herschel and Sir Edward Henry, both of the Indian Civil Service. But the problem of their classification was solved jointly by two sub-inspectors of the Bengal Police: Aziz-ul-Haque and Hem Chandra Bose. By 1895 the first Finger Print Bureau was set up in Madras by Inspector E.A.S. Iyer and two clerks who had been trained by Sir E. Henry.

The Home Office in London were keenly interested and the year 1901 saw Sir E. Henry appointed Assistant Commissioner of Police in the Metropolis and so he introduced his own system to Scotland Yard. Later, he became Commissioner.

Similar pioneering took place in respect of Footprints especially in the Punjab, while early this century in Calcutta, C.R. Hardless developed the science of identifying handwriting and the training of experts.

From the Madras Special Branch I had corresponded with most of the Assistants in the Intelligence Bureau and knew them all by name. I was the eighth assistant director and as the days went by I found that its scope was wider than I realised. For instance we were in touch with Consuls-General in Nepal and Central Asia, with East Africa, London and even Canberra.

My duties had nothing to do with politics, which were under an Indian Deputy Director and two Assistants (Ryan and Beveridge). My duties concerned foreigners, chiefly of enemy origin and precautions were necessary due to the long history of intrigue: by Frenchmen in the 18th century, by Russians after that and also by Germans, who in the Great War plotted an armed uprising in Bengal.

As in the United Kingdom, certain of these aliens were detained in special camps. A number lived under restrictions, others had few or no restrictions, such as those who had spent many years in the country, or who had married British wives. The first two categories were under continual review.

While reviewing case-files one day I was surprised to see the name of an educated Englishman, the Rev. Verrier Elwin. An anthropologist, he settled in the Agency tracts or deep jungles in Central India and learnt the dialects. He lived in a hut, cut off from civilisation married a young woman of the tribe called Gonds and gave up his former way of life, devoting himself to research. He is the author of several learned books.

There were other scholars in the country who lived lonely lives but they kept in touch with a responsible official. Verrier Elwin did not bother; no doubt he was respected by men of science but had no sponsor and British officers in the Special Branch kept him on the books not because they had any ground for suspicion but because they could not make him out. After careful consideration, I decided that he was harmless; as an Englishman he was unique.

Two other assistant directors, G.A.J. Boon, W.F.M. Davies and I shared a room on the third floor of the Secretariat. George Boon had been A.D.C. to the Governor of the United Provinces and married Enid Smith, one of a distinguished family who served in the I.C.S. and Police. They were my best friends in the Bureau. Davies was the son and brother of officers in the Royal Irish Constabulary. Though I had served an apprenticeship I was trained further to appreciate the paramount importance of truth and accuracy. Nor was an assistant director permitted to express an opinion, he could only marshal facts from which any conclusion he intended could be drawn.

Every morning each of the two main Deputy Directors would receive his Assistants in his room for 'prayers'. My deputy director, William Jenkin, also controlled a special section which included three Army officers. This section, then very secret, was concerned with the activities of Indian soldiers captured in Malaya, who were persuaded by Subhas Chandra Bose, a friend of the Nazis, to fight against the regular Indian Army in the second Burma campaign. These men, who numbered some 10,000 were mostly unseasoned soldiers. They gave Indian Intelligence and the Field Security Police a good deal of work, but, militarily, they were a failure. Their chief value was in anti-British propaganda.

For details vide 'On Honourable Terms' edited by Martin Wynne, published by BACSA, Putney, 1985.

But we kept to our subjects and knew little about the work of the other sections. This was also the case in the Madras Special Branch and during my four years in Civil Intelligence, I did not hear of a single leak or breach of faith, which speaks volumes for the system and for the integrity of the Indian staff.

Below the officers' rooms were the records, office staff and secretaries' room. All the secretaries were male; I had a young Muslim, who became my loyal friend and I was able to keep him till we left. I also got to know the office staff well, partly by having them to tea, a few at a time of a Sunday afternoon.

I had not been in the Bureau many months before I felt that certain reports received from Calcutta were not being taken seriously enough. The reports concerned the activities of the Chinese, whose numbers had increased significantly since the Far Eastern War began. So I called for reports and digests of overseas Chinese, especially in Malaya and found that their behaviour and organisation followed a particular pattern. For instance, a Chinatown was a closed community with a leader, in this case a very well-educated Consul-General, a career diplomat. The police might find the body of a Chinese who had been murdered, but they could find out nothing about him, not even his name. Or, there would be a shop purporting to trade, but trade was desultory, evidently something else was going on, but what? To the foreigner, the Chinese could be inscrutable and there were no literate Chinese in any Indian police force; Calcutta had to rely on two or three Chinese-speaking Englishmen.

As the Germans and Italians in India were all under good control, I took an interest in the Chinese and after some months was able to prepare a detailed report and had the satisfaction of finding that it was read by my two superiors. For a Secretariat receives large numbers of reports but not all are taken seriously.

They were a closed, secretive community, quite unlike Indians and though no doubt there was smuggling[35] it should be stated that, by the end of the war, not one Chinese was found to be working for the Japanese, nor did any Chinese indulge in anti-British activity.

Despite New Delhi being six hundred miles from the sea, H.Q. Royal Indian Navy, were moved there from Bombay in the second year of the war. It was much smaller than General Headquarters but for smartness there were none in the capital to touch them. This was especially noticeable in February when the cold weather ends; on a given day all ranks discarded blue trousers and put on white drill, retaining their blue jackets. Next month, when the Admiral decided that the hot season had arrived, all changed into tropical uniform: white shirt, shorts, stockings and shoes and it was quite a dazzling sight to see them all trooping into their offices.

The Indian Navy, run down between the wars, recovered rapidly from 1935 – when Hitler began to threaten the peace. A measure of their wartime quality is that, before Independence, it was forcibly split into two – ships and personnel being divided between India and Pakistan, yet the two small Navies grew and prospered.

[35] Such as beauty preparations, perfume and other luxury goods for the elegant ladies of the Kuomintang.

42

Life in the Secretariat

"The unwearied Sun from day to day
Does his Creator's power display
And publishes to every land
The work of an Almighty Hand"

BETWEEN NINE and ten in the morning thousands of brigadiers, colonels, majors, captains and so forth; deputy secretaries, assistant secretaries, undersecretaries; thousands of office superintendents and clerks, A.T.S. and Women's Auxiliary Air Service bicycled to their many offices in or near the two great Secretariat buildings. The Home Member under whom we served, was Sir John Thorne, I.C.S. from the Madras cadre, I had the utmost respect for him and as I had met his daughter at home I was invited to his house. Sir John was so lacking in 'side' that he rode a bicycle to his office and even to the Palace for his weekly interview. The Home Secretary, Mr. Conran-Smith, later Sir Eric, was also from the Madras cadre.

I kept my car for a few months, but the petrol ration was so small that it wasn't enough to keep the battery charged. My horse, Rembrandt, duly came by rail, but he was in poor condition, his groom or syce was a lazy one and Rembrandt never fully recovered. Both my north Indian and south Indian syces were somewhat of a disappointment.

In the hot weather all we British lost condition – we sat in our offices for seven or eight hours, with a short break for sandwiches or tea and some days it was an effort, in a temperature of 105 degrees or more, with high humidity, to bicycle back two miles after the day's work.

I was a district officer, used to touring all the year round, so to have a steady routine – the same month after month – was monotonous. Only once did I persuade my Deputy Director to let me tour.

I was keen to see the work in Calcutta. The journey cost the Department nothing as I had no difficulty in flying on a R.A.F Hudson. The Deputy Commissioner in Calcutta concerned was Kenneth Tolson and I asked him if he would arrange accommodation. I thought he would put me up, but in the event he arranged for me to stay with the Commissioner of Police, Mr R.E.A. Ray, which I enjoyed, for his residence was an old mansion built by the East India Company. By modern standards it was very big and also cool - with large rooms, high ceilings and polished stone floors. Like my first Inspector-General, Sir Charles Cunningham, Mr Ray was unimpressive to look at and little interested in his appearance. But he was fearless and very able – he needed to be – for Calcutta was bursting at the seams, the second city of the British Empire.

Tolson was very co-operative – I was the first assistant director who took seriously his clear and concise reports on the Chinese.

★ ★ ★ ★ ★

After staying some time with the Ryans I decided to accept the offer of a comfortable tent at the Gymkhana Club. It was a hill tent, pitched on a brick floor, with a small bathroom tent. With it went a room for my servant in the servants' lines.

For seven years I had not known any cold weather. The temperature fell to 30 degrees F that winter and I caught the 'flu and lay in my tent, cold at night, for over a week. Each day, Gerald Ryan called to see me on his way back from the office, which I greatly appreciated and Barbara Warner wrote twice.

Meals were in the Club dining room; tea could be taken in the grounds, or in the tent if it was cool. And the club food was nourishing and varied, further, there was a ration of one double whisky per day and a bottle of good Indian beer per week. There were tennis courts and a fine, big swimming pool: a tremendous asset for those who had been living up-country.

The Imperial Delhi Gymkhana Club was part of the garden city designed by Lutyens. In 1911-12 he could hardly have forseen the numbers of potential members there would be thirty years later, but his plans were generous and it was surprising how the club coped with a two or three hundred percent increase in membership. There were fifty or more resident members and several hundred non-resident.

Set in grounds, close to the golf-course, the principal rooms were two dining-rooms, one very large; lounges, ballroom, kitchens, offices. In the grounds were living-quarters, tennis-courts and the servants' lines. The Secretary was an Englishwoman, the Steward was a Delhi man. Having after months of waiting obtained a tent, it was only a matter of longer waiting to achieve living quarters.

Since Hindustani is the dominant language of Delhi it followed that domestic terms differed from those I was accustomed to. I soon picked them up but had a little difficulty with one: the sweeper/scavenger who is addressed as 'jemadar'. But jemadar in military parlance means an officer, like second-lieutenant. Then I understood: it is a charming way of giving the most menial of servants and a Harijan some dignity.

There was plenty of social life, but for every British woman there were several British and American men, so the women were almost danced off their feet. But I was very fortunate. At a mid-week dance I met a young woman of eighteen or nineteen – Barbara Warner. Her father was a mature, pipe-smoking man, a superintendent in the Burma Police. Father, mother and daughter had done the long 800 mile trek along the Ledo Road into Assam. Father and daughter were close friends and both were working in the Burma office in New Delhi.

Barbara and I got on very well indeed. Her parents trusted me completely and never interfered. We danced together at least twice a week and neither of us wished to dance with anyone else. She had a gift for friendship. Had it continued for a couple of years it would probably have ripened. But it was not to be.

The Warners lived in war-time married quarters. Somehow, there was no proper light in the bathroom, only a table-lamp. One evening, Barbara had her bath about dusk. The sun sets quickly in the East and by the time she finished her bath it was getting dark. She switched on the light and was killed instantly – the light had a two-point plug. She was their only child and her parents were heartbroken.

> "Yestreen, when to the trembling string
> The dance gaed thro' the lighted ha'
> To thee my fancy took its wing, –
> I sat, but neither heard nor saw." (Burns)

The following winter Lord Louis Mountbatten arrived, the most glamorous of all the brass hats. His good looks and his charisma even won over American Generals, one of whom had fully expected his job. With Lord Louis, came Naval Staff Officers and hundreds of Wrens – good-looking and pink-cheeked – straight from Britain and they soon had us officers eating out of their hands. One of them, a Scotswoman, attracted me greatly, but she already had a boyfriend.

Lord Louis did not take to Delhi – there were too many Commands and Departments and soon his entire Command was flown to Ceylon.

There are always those who criticize foreigners on principle and one sometimes heard criticism of the Americans; but most of us respected and liked them. It was the American Army Engineers who built the Ledo Mountain Road from N.W. Burma and they did great things in the Burma campaign, supplying much equipment from Calcutta and we could not have re-gained Burma so soon without their help.

The Intelligence Bureau had close relations with a group of three American staff officers; one of whom was a big Texan, a schoolmaster by profession. All three were able men but I made special friends with the Texan and often worked in his room, which was much quieter than ours. That British and Americans combined well to defeat both Nazis and Japanese is testified by this anecdote which I quote, by kind permission of the Secretary, Clifton College.

One day there appeared in the office of the local American Commandant an Englishwoman of about forty and her daughter of about twenty. They complained that a week before, Sergeant K, an old friend, had visited them and, since it was late, they lent him their bicycle to ride back to his billet. He promised to return it next day but had not done so and they had no bicycle. The mother added: "We don't mind that we are both pregnant by him, but we want our bicycle back". A stern order was issued and the bicycle was returned forthwith.

In order to make for smooth relations with the General Staff, a liaison officer was posted to the Bureau and he became my best friend after my brother Louis.

George Adrian Carroll was Irish by birth, and a grandson of a captain in the Bengal Army. He joined the Indian Police after the Great War and was posted to the Central Provinces. After twelve years' service, during which he was awarded the King's Police Medal for gallantry, he was chosen to be tutor to the Rajah of Khetri, a vassal state of Jodhpur. A short man, he was very neatly made and possessed of a natural courtesy. His manner towards young men was fatherly and the Rajah of Khetri became, in effect, a son to him.

When the young Rajah came of age, the Maharajah of Jodhpur chose Adrian as his Finance Minister, but when the war reached India he was called up for a special appointment as liaison officer with the rank of Lieutenant-Colonel. Our friendship was ended only by his death in 1973.

Of course I saw my brother every week. He was only a G-3 or Captain in Signals Intelligence. He was not a bit interested in promotion and once before going on fourteen days' leave he told his Colonel that some of the things they were doing were "not cricket." Soon after he returned from leave he was promoted to second-in-command at their Bangalore station, which I thought, was one up to the Regular Army.

As the heat of summer made a tent very uncomfortable I shared temporarily a small house with George Wyndham, I.C.S., whom I had met in Tinnevelly district. He was then Assistant Secretary, under the Viceroy's Private Secretary. I could see it was a very interesting job and while the Burma campaign was going so well his department, like several others, was planning for the future. However, they were attempting the impossible – they planned for a united India, but the divisive forces of the Muslim League proved irresistible and all their plans had to be scrapped.

★ ★ ★ ★ ★

When eyes were tired from hours of reading, one would look out of a lofty window of the Secretariat and rest them on the broad, two-mile long green vista of Kingsway. War-time traffic, mostly bicycles and horse-drawn gharries moved slowly and the scene was very peaceful. It was easy to forget that the struggle for Independence was going on, that the Muslim League were straining towards their dream of Pakistan, that husbandmen were toiling in the heat, or that an Indian Army was locked in battle in Burma and the Arakan.

It is in late autumn that Divali, the Festival of Lights and Hindu New Year is celebrated. In New Delhi, open and spacious, it was a house here and there only, but cross the divide into Old Delhi, where Hindus form the majority and the city is bathed in light. Not by harsh, neon strips and signs but by innumerable little saucers of oil with a floating wick, which the women place on the cornices and window ledges of their homes. Buildings might be picked out by electric bulbs, or trees hung with old-fashioned lanterns.

The origin of the festival is lost in time but many connect it with Lakshmi, goddess of wealth. Cakes and sweetmeats are made and given and visits are paid to relations. It is the most beautiful of all Indian festivals and the only common note is that male votaries of Lakshmi like to throw dice and hope for a win!

43

Holiday at Simla
Christmas in Lahore

THE HOT weather in northern India is pretty extreme. One day in June the temperature reached 117 degrees F with a minimum that night of 92 degrees; those were the dog days. But the Government wisely gave us short or 'casual' leave and at the end of that hot season I chose to spend mine at Simla, which figures so largely in Anglo-Indian history. The train leaves Delhi about 9 p.m., and early next morning reaches Kalka in the Himalayan foothills.

I had booked a taxi and was happy to share it with two other men who had no transport. One spoke Italian and described his work in one of the Italian P.O.W. camps. He thought it a great pity that uncultured staff had been posted to these camps, thereby missing a great opportunity.

Driving up in the cool, pine-scented air was one of the finest pleasures imaginable. Arrived at Simla, which is 7,000 feet up, I engaged two porters and walked up-hill to the Club, but the hardy porters, taking a short cut, were there before us.

As one would expect, the United Services Club was very comfortable, with wainscoting and leather chairs. In the dining room hung oil paintings of past Presidents, including Lord Roberts and two old boys of my school – Field Marshals Haig and Birdwood. The waiters were Goanese and wore smart red waistcoats. The food was good, only sugar being strictly rationed. For the first time for years we had cheese with our lunch, it was made by the Benares Hindu University and bought by a keen-eyed secretary, for cheese is not made elsewhere. I did know one girl, Elizabeth Ogilvie, daughter of a Madras Civilian and took her out to lunch at a Chinese restaurant, she was good company and later became engaged to my friend, Tony Shaw.

An acquaintance, Bill Lovatt, was also staying at the club and asked me to Sunday lunch at the club annexe which is beyond Mashobra, for which we hired bicycles. In return, I asked him, his girl-friend and a cheerful married woman he knew to dinner and dance at the Cecil Hotel. I gained a little face by having a dinner jacket, Bill had only a blue suit. But I felt dizzy during a waltz, not yet being adjusted to the altitude. Next day, the married woman sent me a thank-you note, a courtesy which in war-time was not much observed.

The cinema was very much a small-town one, but we saw a good film of Madame Curie, my host at dinner being a colleague, Chris Everett of Lahore. My last day was a Sunday and I asked Chris Everett, Lovatt, Patricia, his girl-friend and one or two others to lunch at Mashobra. Mashobra is a famous beauty spot seven miles from Simla. Built on a spur it consists only of an hotel, Wildflower Hall and the Viceroy's Retreat with magnificent views over the Himalayas, rocky crags and evergreen forest.

So my short leave ended. This time I took the train, and as we glided down I thought of the good fellows I had met. As the light faded in the valleys, the dark green pines turned to black and the moon, rising above the trees, shed her golden light.

Early in October, Robert Bailey of the Guides Cavalry took Tony Shaw, a young Civilian of the Malayan Service and me for a special ride of his along the banks of the Jumna River. Tony had a hired mount and slipped off, remounting almost as quickly, which made us roar with laughter. We battled through elephant grass nine to ten foot high, waded through large pools and had a lovely time. And it was that day that the wind turned and the cool, North-East monsoon began to blow, fresh from Tibet, the temperature dropping no less than eight degrees.

E.J. Jenner, Superintendent of the Special Branch in Bombay, wanted me to visit him, which I was more than willing to do. This needed my deputy-director's permission; W.N.P. (later Sir William) Jenkin was a man who liked to be at his desk for twelve hours a day and had no use for touring. He didn't refuse but thought I should put it off for two or three months. So Jenner decided to come to me to sort out certain problems. He was tall, dark-eyed and very handsome and I much enjoyed having him as my guest.

On Sunday mornings I began to take a picnic lunch and tea to the banks of the River Jumna. There, one could escape the city and relax in the shade of a thorn bush, (there were no trees) far from traffic and noise. I would watch tortoises on the river bank, read, listen to the birds and the gentle ripple of the water. Then bicycle back, refreshed. In the evening I found spiritual refreshment at the Church of the Redemption.

In the cold weather, the Delhi Hunt began the hunting season. The quarry was Indian jackal which is about the size of a fox and similar in behaviour, with a strong scent. The Master, Captain Codrington, was a veterinary surgeon from Gloucestershire, respected and liked by all and the pack consisted of at least twelve couple of good English foxhounds.

I would get up before dawn, then wrap up well before meeting Adrian Carroll while the stars were still shining. We bicycled some distance to the hunt 'bus, one of the oldest buses in Delhi. As we chugged along, picking people up as we went, the day broke cold and grey. At the Meet, all the horses would be waiting with their grooms, and very soon we were off and the grooms (or syces) departed in the bus.

Of course, it wasn't quite like an English hunt, but both British and Americans greatly enjoyed it. There were no fences, but plenty of dips and ditches to be jumped. One run of seven miles I remember, and that season three or four riders fell, including a keen lady rider, who fell on her eye. She lay unconscious, her usual pink cheeks turned an ashen grey. Her daughter, aged ten, also in the field, was terribly upset and howled. Afterwards I soon caught up, having a fast horse and we narrowly missed a kill. There were only two kills but most of us couldn't care less.

Another day I was right behind the pack as one of them caught up with the jackal. The hound killed him so quickly I hardly saw what happened – death was instantaneous. The season lasted only three months, for by February the sun was warm and there was very little scent. We would return too late for breakfast but were more than ready for a good lunch. Unfortunately, due to my groom's neglect of his duties I wasn't able to hunt a full second season.

The Delhi Hunt staged an annual race meeting and Adrian and I entered a gentleman-riders' event. Rembrandt was pretty fit and rather to my surprise I nearly won, the winner passing me just before the post. The prize-money enabled me to go to a good tailor and be measured for an overcoat of good Yorkshire tweed, for one needed a coat to wear to the Meets.

New Delhi in wartime was a city of strict discipline. The Viceroy, the senior Civil servants and Service officers all worked extremely hard and set a fine example. The whole community was engaged in the war effort, though there were some slackers. One needed recreation but the opportunities were limited: not many could play tennis but most could swim. There was little time for cricket. The two cinemas were inadequate and one had to book in advance. The American Army had a welfare department which tried to provide recreation for their G.I.'s but the British and Indian Armies did not rise to such luxury.

New Delhi did not have a proper theatre but in the spring of 1945 a play was staged in the open air outside an old walled garden: A Midsummer Night's Dream. There was plenty of talent for all the parts and an experienced producer, while the R.E.M.E. provided superb lighting effects. The evenings were warm, but not too warm, the air was clear and to the audiences, starved of good entertainment, it was one of the most beautiful sights we had ever seen.

D-Day June 6th 1944

Those who are too young to remember the war can hardly imagine our yearning for the final invasion of Europe. We had been expecting it for over a year and a year of war is a long time.

When the news reached me I was, of all places, in one of the large lavatories in the Secretariat. Several others were there, we discussed it eagerly and all shook hands. I told one of my colleagues in the office, who immediately telephoned several of his friends - one of them knew already, but hadn't passed it on, for secrecy can become a habit! The end of the war in Europe, we felt, could not be long delayed, but the defeat of the Japanese was expected to take another two years.

I badly needed home leave and almost lived for Sundays. A young cousin of mine, Guy de Moubray, used to come and share my Sunday bottle of beer. He had fought in the Burma campaign and survived without a wound; also an old friend of ours Reg Payne, whose job was Deputy Provost-Marshal, R.A.F. Police and a charming friend of his – Captain de la Mare, a nephew of the poet: he was an attractive man, but not a soldier and I could see that he was longing for the war to end.

Another of my cousins, an older man – was P.E. de Chazal, of Perth, S. Australia. As he had served in the Great War, in the second war his job was a desk one: at All-India Radio. He was lonely without his wife and son and glad of my company. When I entered his room for the first time he had two bottles of spirits. "How on earth did you get these?" I asked. He had called at Phipson's, the local wine merchant and asked, "May I have a drink ration? I'm an old customer." "Are you, Sir?" replied the assistant.

"Yes, when I was stationed near Bombay in the last war with the King's African Rifles." So they checked with their Bombay office, found his account in their ledgers and promptly allowed him their full quota of a bottle of Scotch and one of London gin per month.

Christmas 1944 in Lahore

Christmas in the East has its own flavour. Far less fuss is made and there was a tradition that it was the best time of year for sport and dinner parties with dancing.

C.H. (Chris) Everett, the Bureau's officer in Lahore and Mrs Everett, had very kindly invited me to stay. For about ten days beforehand I ate and drank sparingly, then on Christmas Eve I caught the evening train. Early next morning in the Punjab the frost lay thick in the fields and puddles were frozen over. Chris' driver met me but the Everett's had already gone to the Cathedral – I wish I had gone, late.

Afterwards, we were invited by the Regional Food Commissioner, Sir Colin Garbett, I.C.S., who was six feet five tall inches tall. His wife was quite small and received us with genuine pleasure. I was especially pleased to see among the guests a number of British soldiers, both Privates and N.C.O.'s. We sat or stood on the lawn enjoying excellent Murree beer and Christmas cake. Later, I learnt that Sir Colin was a close relation of Dr. Cyril Garbett, Archbishop of York.

On Christmas afternoon the Everett's gave a children's party. Next day we took a picnic tea to the spacious Shalimar Gardens, laid out by the Moguls. It was divided into courts, each of which covered ten or twelve acres, in one of which stood a fine old mausoleum.

In the evening there was a club dance. Chris and I watched a Boxing Day golf match between the I.C.S. and the Police which was won by the latter; there was, I noticed, quite a rivalry between these two Services in the Punjab.

Vernon Bailey of the Punjab Police kindly asked me to lunch and my last evening we went to the Races, at which I won the modest sum of seven rupees, about ten and sixpence.

Lahore was the least Hindu of the big Indian cities and the Punjabis – Hindu, Muslim, Sikh and Europeans had a superiority complex over the rest of India. For the Punjab was the granary of India and was it not the chief recruiting ground for the Army? Also the glories of the Moghul Empire and Sikh Kingdom of the Punjab seemed to outshine the deeds and achievements of the Hindus. Punjabis didn't take much interest in the rest of India, but were being obliged to, owing to the rapidly-growing power of the Muslim League, who wanted the Punjab as their stronghold.

I thoroughly enjoyed my Christmas with the Everett's and did not forget to say goodbye to their English Nanny. She was a robust, middle-aged woman who wore grey uniform, one of the sort who believed in plenty of bread and butter, boiled beef, rice pudding, prayers and discipline. The children were devoted to her. In fact she was one of the last of a famous breed that could be found in every capital and nearly every country of the world.

In the following February, 1945, the Rajah Sahib of Khetri invited Adrian Carroll, his former tutor and me for a short stay. The young Rajah was a well-educated young nobleman with beautiful manners. I certainly think that the manners of a Rajput nobleman take a great deal of beating. He was wealthy and surrounded by old servants and retainers, yet he was a Socialist; he had read quite a lot about its doctrines and his socialism was sincere. But soon I could understand it: he had imbibed Liberal ideas through his education at the Princes' College; he was sensitive and this sensitivity reacted with the feudalism of his State, its court and elite, its wide inequalities between rich and poor.

The high-light of my stay was a panther shoot. Sitting up for the occasional village panther is a chancy business, those panthers are extremely wary. This was a much more organised affair: the Rajah Sahib gave orders to village headmen to be on the lookout. Their vigilance bore fruit and a kill was soon reported. His *shikari* or hunter went ahead to collect beaters and three of us – Adrian, myself and another man – spread out in an open space at intervals of about thirty yards while the jungle opposite us was beaten from behind. Sure enough the panther was driven out and ran up a slope to our right. Three shots rang out, the animal was hit and disappeared; so we walked up to the spot, our loaded rifles at the ready. There was blood on the ground and drops of blood every few yards till we came near to a thicket. Cautiously, we advanced in line; the panther saw us and charged. We were perhaps twenty yards away and I could hear his deep bass growls as he charged. In a split second we fired our three rifles; the panther fell and didn't move. I threw a stone at him and thought he was dead. But Adrian, to make sure, put a bullet into his head. He was a fine big male of more than seven feet; the first shot had hit him in the thigh.

I was noticing that Yelliah, my servant, was having difficulty bending down and lifting things. He said he had been to the local Government Hospital and that a doctor had told him he needed an operation. He added: "Please may I have three weeks' leave and I go to American Mission hospital for operation?" I replied "Can't they do it here?" But he lacked confidence in the local hospital. So I gave him three weeks' leave and his fares and he went, I think, to the

American Mission hospital at Miraj, in the South. Three weeks later he had had the operation, visited his wife near Cocanada, and reported back – cured.

I mention this to show how ordinary, low-paid Indians had great faith in Mission hospitals, where they received the same attention as fee-paying patients.

★ ★ ★ ★ ★

Meanwhile, the 14th Army. ably led by General Bill Slim, was fighting hard in Burma. The terrain with high mountains, forest and rivers was extremely difficult so that rations, medical, and other supplies had to be dropped from the air.

U.S. Army General Stilwell, who commanded the Chinese contingent, had his own methods, one of which was, like Alexander the Great, to drop supplies one day's march ahead of the men.

As, for operational reasons tight security was observed, only a few could follow the campaign; but it was soon clear that the Japanese were no longer the better army, our men, trained in jungle camps in central and southern India, were driving the enemy back to Rangoon. One thing, however, was certain – Japanese soldiers were among the bravest in the world and did not surrender. The Japanese Army only surrendered when ordered to by the Emperor.

44

Weddings – British and Indian

"Heard melodies are sweet but those unheard
are sweeter, therefore ye soft pipes, play on"

ONE WINTRY evening my colleague, W.F.M. Davies, gave a dinner party and
dance at the club for a friend of his wife, Winifred Brook, a Queen Alexandra
Military Nursing Sister on leave from Assam. She was clearly tired and I did
not react to her but during the week we became friends. She was educated,
articulate and a lover of poetry. Then for months we exchanged long letters. In
one letter she described the visit of Lady Mountbatten to the military hospital
where she worked. She arrived by air simply dressed in cotton khaki uniform.
She was very knowledgable and inspected all parts of the hospital, Winifred
showing her round the operating theatre. She met the staff and shook their
hands. Afterwards Winifred's Indian orderly kept on looking at his right hand:
he could hardly believe that the Lady Sahib had actually held it in her own.

That summer, Winifred and I decided to take our leave together, which took
some doing, nor was it easy for me to find accomodation in a hill station as they
were nearly all booked up. Eventually, I found rooms at a guest house near
Darjeeling, 6,000 feet up in the Himalayas. One reason for it being less heavily
booked was because it had no bar.

I was on good terms with our office staff, but was not expecting a send
off.Rikki Kesh, a Head Clerk had obtained a berth for me in a four-berth
compartment and as he saw me off, handed over two bottles of beer, which
was a very generous gift with beer in such short supply. In the compartment
was a young Captain, formerly a detective-sergeant in the Shanghai Police,
also two Indians of the money-lender's caste, who asked me all manner of
personal questions, though no doubt they didn't mean to give offence.

The train arrived late at Howrah station, Calcutta; Kenneth Tolson had me
for the day while an Old Cliftonian, Colonel K.M. Bourne, took me to tea at
the Bengal Club. His regiment had been the South Lancs. from which he
joined the Shanghai Police, finishing up as Commissioner.

It was a magnificent club but its situation was not as attractive as the Madras
Club. Though the Conservancy did their best they never managed to remove
all the refuse of the huge population, swollen by refugees. From 1943, the
famine year, the air of Calcutta was never fresh. I was glad to have seen the city
years before when it was a dignified, clean and orderly capital.

For the journey to Darjeeling one takes the broad-gauge train to Sealdah then changes to the metre-gauge line. Finally, one takes the charming little mountain railway of two-foot gauge and on it I was delighted to find an acquaintance I made on S.S. Viceroy of India, the ship that took us to Bombay. He was A.K. Chanda, a big, stout, pipe-smoking Bengali in the I.C.S. He hadn't altered and was as humorous as ever. As the little train chugged up the mountain side, now and again a man with a shovel threw sand on the rails in front.

I had hoped Winifred would have arrived, but she came about two hours later, khaki-clad and very tired. After tea with Scotch bannocks we went for a walk and as luck would have it, the second highest mountain, Kinchinjunga, revealed himself in all his glory: the mists and clouds cleared, the sun was beginning to set when, some sixty miles away, the huge massif, 28,000 feet high, appeared in deep golden sunshine. It was a great moment in my life.

Apart from being the Bengal Government's summer refuge from the steamy heat of Calcutta, Darjeeling's fame rests, of course, on its tea. The surrounding hills grow what is, in the opinion of many, the finest Indian tea. The industry is not old: it began in 1841 when Dr. Campbell of the Indian Medical Service planted seeds of China tea. They grew so well that tea-planting spread rapidly to the South and before long both British and Indians became habitual tea drinkers.

All the hill stations have a common factor – they are Victorian – but Darjeeling differs from those further west in that the local people are mostly Mongoloid in appearance and the religious influence is Buddhist. We visited the Buddhist monastery at Ghoom; it is a well-proportioned building bearing no resemblance either to a temple or mosque. The prior was dressed in a woollen robe with a light woollen blanket round his shoulders. His and the monks' heads were shaved.

The bazaar was a busy one as it not only served the residents; the managers, clerks, coolies and pickers on the surrounding tea gardens and the Church of Scotland Mission, but also traders from nearby Tibet. Tibetan merchants and traders were well dressed in robes and hats but the porters, who carried the merchandise on their backs, looked poor and scruffy yet cheerful, for the Tibetans are a hardy and cheerful people.

One morning in the main street, we heard unmistakably, the skirl of bagpipes. Then a band came into view; it consisted of about a dozen bagpipes played by Gurkhas, short stocky men; a bass drum and tenor drums. They were dressed in kilts, tartan plaids, white spats and wore pill-box caps. It was the Darjeeling Police Band. I marvelled how well Indians and Gurkhas adapt themselves to our martial music and wind instruments.

After about ten days of courting I plucked up courage and proposed. She hadn't put the slightest pressure on me, but when it came, she accepted.

It had been a big decision for me and I was going to rest on my oars and just be engaged. But she pointed out that she wouldn't get leave again for a year and that she was likely to be posted to Ceylon as the Burma campaign would soon be over. So I took the hint – we called on the Chaplain at Darjeeling (we had been to church twice); he was most helpful and wrote for a licence to the Bishop of Calcutta.

We had a small wedding at St. Andrew's church but it was beautifully arranged by Rev. H.P. King and by Mrs. Betty Le Brocq, wife of Henry Le Brocq, the local Superintendent of Police. I borrowed one of his uniforms and he was my best man; Winifred carried gladioli; had a short white dress, the Deputy Inspector-General gave her away and the hotel organised the reception. We had a week together, then both had to go our respective ways.

We travelled together down the mountain in the little train; young American Servicemen shared the compartment and we gathered that their Welfare Department had provided them with unlimited beefsteak and icecream.

At Parbatipur[36] we parted and she caught the train back to Assam. The Commercial Attache of the Special Branch met me at Calcutta and after a bath, breakfast and lunch at his flat, drove me to the main station. The journey-time to Delhi was thirty-two hours, about the same as Bombay-Madras.

In the restaurant car were three British soldiers, the two privates were miserable – one was suffering badly from the skin irritation known as prickly heat. The third was a sergeant; he had made the best of the situation: he had made friends with Anglo-Indian families in the Railway. He had learnt to drink whiskey – which the two soldiers wouldn't touch. He had adapted himself and was quite content with his lot.

Next morning when the 'Statesman' newspaper arrived I was astonished to learn of my elder brother's engagement to Miss Mary Duncan, a Senior Commander in the A.T.S. Then I reported back to the office, to a stack of files and to the congratulations of my colleagues – 'A dark horse' they said, but Bill Davies merely smiled knowingly. In fact, it was difficult to realize I was a married man.

The Bureau wedding present was usually an inscribed salver, but as Mappin and Webb had none left we chose silver-plated dishes instead.

For two months I felt rather lonely; but my brother's wedding made a welcome break. Molly Duncan, his fiancee, arrived a few days before and Louis only the night before. I don't know how they made all the arrangements for the service, which took place at the Roman Catholic Cathedral on a particularly hot day – July 10th, 1945. My brother, who had just been demobilized, borrowed a thick and well-lined morning coat, with striped trousers and a waistcoat. I wore woollen gaberdine service dress, with collar, tie and Sam Browne. We both stewed, but such were the stupid things we British did.

Before the bride and groom departed from the reception I retired, my servant pulled off the clothes which were stuck to my skin and slid into a cold bath. They had barely five days' honeymoon at Simla, when my brother was re-called.

The next wedding was a Hindu one. During my first year, while at Vellore,

(36) The goddess Parbati is the consort of Shiva, the Destroyer.

I received an invitation from the Brahmin Judge to his daughter's wedding. The time stated was 2.30 a.m. I looked again, yes – 2.30 a.m. But as I had to be on parade four hours later, I declined. We heard the music faintly for the next two days and I learnt that the times of such weddings are fixed not by the family but by their astrologer.

While in Delhi, a clerk in my section, one Iqbal Behari Lal[37] was married and invited me to the wedding feast. In accordance with Eastern custom the ceremony took place after dark and the groom, who was dressed in silks like a nobleman, arrived on a horse, escorted by his groomsmen.

The wedding feast was good, but being war-time was not elaborate. We sat on carpets in two rooms, excellent vegetarian and non-vegetarian dishes being provided, followed by sweets and coffee. I much appreciated the honour, for it was quite unusual to receive an invitation to what is regarded as a family occasion.

★ ★ ★ ★ ★

After our wonderful victory in Burma, the next campaign was to be the assault and capture of Malaya, for which preparations had been going on for years. So we were all astounded at the news that two atomic bombs (August 6th and 9th) had been dropped on Japan, which then surrendered unconditionally.

So ended the second World War, a war fought on more fronts even than the first. Much has been made of all the harm done to many Japanese from the effects of atomic radiation. Against this it should be said that no one provoked the Japanese in the Far East. They were unquestionably the aggressors. Secondly, that the civilians killed or affected by radiation should be balanced against the far greater number of military, naval and air force personnel and civilians, Allied and Japanese, who would have been killed or wounded, had the Malayan and Pacific campaigns been fought out to the bitter end.

We had often talked about the 'end' and many said they were saving up a bottle of liquor for the celebration. But, as far as Delhi, the biggest Eastern Command, was concerned – there was no celebration and no bottles appeared. Though wearing white slacks and shirt I strapped on my heavy service revolver, intending to fire six rounds of feu de joie. Everyone at the club was relieved but too tired, weighed down by heat and fatigue; they just sat and smiled and my revolver remained in its holster.

One morning in October I was in pain and said I could not go to the office. My wife insisted I should see our doctor, who was Major Hassett, I.M.S. He recognized symptoms, which earlier examinations had missed and within three days I found myself in hospital being treated for chronic amoebic

[37] Iqbal, a distinguished poet.

dysentry. The treatment was almost successful and I was most grateful for Major Hassett's skill and to the Matron, a tall, London-trained Anglo-Indian. In fact I must pay a tribute to the Willingdon Hospital, New Delhi – the nursing, food and attention were of a very high standard. On my discharge, my Director granted me a week's leave plus a Sunday. My friend and colleague, Sydney Plew, generously agreed to put us up, so we had our first stay in a district of the United Provinces.

Bulandshahr wasn't far by the branch line and Sydney came to meet us himself – alone, as his wife was on the way out from England. We bounced along an appalling road to his house, which was in a peaceful situation outside the town.

It was late October-early November 1945 and the great heat was over. The nights were quite cool and after breakfast we would sit in a little summer house, drinking cups of tea. Every now and then Sydney would leave his office in the house and come and talk to us, for Bulandshahr was not a "heavy" district, though I suspect some of his callers postponed their business on account of his having guests, such is Indian politeness.

A nearby zamindar, or landowner, was extremely hospitable and invited us to a shoot on his land. After breakfast, an ancient bus arrived and several zamindars, shikaris, orderlies, servants and dogs got out. After introductions and shaking of hands, my wife sat by the driver, the rest behind, together with guns, boxes of cartridges, hampers, gun dogs and coats. The shikaris dragged undergrowth for partridge and hare; a rope was pulled across coverts of sugar-cane and we walked to reservoirs in search of duck, but the game was not there.

At lunch-time we chose a big tree and spread ourselves in its shade, eating generous helpings of cold palau and a sweet, followed by fruit.

At tea-time we were offered a selection of cakes and Indian savouries. As we drove back at dusk we held our guns and watched for partridge and the men dragged a couple more fields. The bag was very small and one man said all the shooting round Delhi had scared the birds away; but we thoroughly enjoyed ourselves. There was however something in what he said for the U.S. Army Welfare Department issued cheap guns and cartridges to the G.I.'s (or privates), who blazed away at every jackdaw and cocksparrow.

On our last morning, I borrowed Sydney's horse and rode to the Armed Police Lines, checked the armoury and magazine guards, visiting the barracks and cookhouses together with the Reserve Inspector, a smart Anglo-Indian and the Subedar, his Indian counterpart.

By then the time had come to say farewell. It had been a most pleasant stay and we were full of gratitude. We travelled back to New Delhi on the bus.

In December there was again a race for gentlemen riders in which I entered against my better judgement, for neither Rembrandt nor I was fit. On the day I felt very nervous and so was Rembrandt, who got himself into a lather. Wearing Adrian's colours I started second, gained the lead, then heard hooves thundering behind and was overtaken. We were unplaced. It was good fun but I was sorry to have disappointed some of the office staff who had backed me.

45

Christmas in Rajputana; Indian Titles

"O shoreless Deep, where no wind blows!
And thou O land, which no one knows!
That God is all, His shadow shows."

THE GYMKHANA Club was a very busy place during Christmas week and no
doubt hundreds of people were glad of all the the dances and parties; but we
were glad to escape, for we were privileged to have another invitation to
Khetri.

Adrian left before us. After picking up a friend of Adrian's, Miss Bunty
Humphries, we boarded a metre-gauge train and had a small compartment to
ourselves. It was a short night journey.

Next morning, before the sun was up we got out and warmed ourselves
with tea and breakfast. After an hour or two we caught a well- appointed train
of the Jodhpur State Railways and at a modest rate steamed across Rajputana.

The countryside was extremely dry; we saw extensive salt pans and semi-
desert sustaining only grasses and a few thorny shrubs. We saw villages
composed of grass huts, for the inhabitants, on account of drought, were
largely nomadic.

Adrian met us at the station, he even had a light van to follow behind with
the luggage. We arrived at Khetri, some miles away and were shown a suite of
rooms in a guest-house: a large double room with two dressing and two
bathrooms. That evening I had two whiskies and sodas, double our Club
ration. Sumptous meals were provided for the four of us and I feared for
Adrian who was a duodenal sufferer.

Christmas dawned grey and cool and I wore an English suit for Holy
Communion which was taken by a visiting chaplain, for the resident
congregation was quite small. Before lunch we had callers, Rajput gentlemen,
who brought various weapons and trophies for us to see. I was much taken by
a small steel bow and amused myself shooting arrows at a target. I managed to
shoot them sixty yards, but without any accuracy.

On Boxing Day we drove through the countryside to a reservoir formed by
a dam with some ornamental masonry and were followed by another car with
two servants (and a picnic lunch) who were happy to come with us.

On the way back we drove through a game reserve and I never saw so much
game from a car – we saw several wild boar in thickets, rather skinny ones. I
then spied a small herd of sambhar, the big deer and in the failing light

managed to crawl to within some thirty yards of them. Afterwards Adrian took us to the club, a very quiet one and the few people there were pleased to see new faces.

The second day after Christmas was a memorable one: we drove to the old Fort – Palace of Jodhpur and were shown round by an elderly gentleman, the Maharajah's uncle.

The Fort and Old Palace are strategically sited on a long, low hill, but following the establishment of Pax Britannica, the Maharajah built an enormous stone palace near the city. The Rajah Sahib showed us the Old Palace: banqueting halls with galleries, a large arsenal of swords, lances, muskets, rifles and pistols. We looked at the old bronze cannon on the ramparts, also a most interesting old gun – it had twelve barrels in two rows which could be touched off by one long powder train; this surely was a forerunner of the machine-gun. The biggest cannon were two heavy Mogul guns, captured in battle at Ahmedabad. How many bullocks were needed to bring back such huge trophies? Hundreds.

As guests of the Rajah of Khetri we were permitted to see the Jodhpur State Jewels. Their value was so great that all five of the joint custodians were needed merely to open the treasury, but I am the wrong man to describe them. I can only remember big diamonds, some cut, some uncut; great rubies; pearls as large as pigeon's eggs and all manner of personal jewelry. To me, they represented enormous wealth lying idle, but I knew that the Rajputs would have been shocked had I expressed this view, for they are romantics.

As a man I was more interested in the Palace gunroom which contained magnificent jewelled Rajput swords as well as sporting weapons. An Indian Army Colonel was also viewing them and was particularly interested in a new automatic hand gun which weighed only 4.5 pounds.

Visit to the former Jodhpur capital of Mandore.

This occupied an afternoon and whoever chose its situation had a keen eye for beauty. The old town was built in a quiet valley near a dam, which formed an artificial lake. The dam itself was a work of art for it was of Oriental design. The sides of the valley were of grey stone without much vegetation as little rain falls in Rajputana. I found a small rowing-boat, which I rowed for our little party, while Adrian trailed a line. Overlooking the lake was a small rest-house in which our servants prepared fresh tea and toast with cakes. Indian servants love picnics and would have been hurt if we had gone alone.

I was sad to leave this dream-spot and longed to return, but it couldn't be arranged.

On our last day I was taken shooting. An Indian gentleman drove me out for about forty miles and, stopping at a village, we picked up a game warden who was a dignified old Rajput with a grey cavalry moustache. He took us out into the scrub, mostly low bush and thorny trees; within an hour we found a small herd of blackbuck which I stalked. My borrowed rifle was a Mauser, a heavy weapon, which I could hold steadier than a light one and before long, I stalked and shot a fine stag. We then walked on, found another herd, or possibly the same one; I stalked it and managed another stag shot at somewhat longer range, about eighty yards.

We returned, driving the open car cross-country and scraping over low bushes in search of bustard, but didn't see one. Then we saw more buck and my companion, Mohan Singh, got a pretty good one from a standing load of eighty or ninety yards.

I was very pleased with the bigger of my two, the horns being well spread and measuring 21.5 inches. With true Indian courtesy I was invited to shoot first, then Mohan Singh had his turn.

Outside Jodhpur we saw the renowned polo player, Colonel Rao Raja Hanut Singh, (usually called Hanut Singh) trotting at the head of a string of seven or eight polo ponics. He was a slim, fair and very handsome man in his late thirties. Adrian told us he would hardly let a day go by without practising with stick and ball and exercising his horses.

So we left Khetri sadly, but full of memories. Adrian drove us the seventy odd miles to the metre-guage line, where we arrived covered with fine white dust. So ended our last Christmas of the war and the best I ever had.

Among many outstanding examplars of Rajput chivalry, dignity and courage, Maharajah Sir Pratap Singh of Jodhpur, will long be remembered. Primarily he was a cavalry commander and fought with distinction in the Palestine campaign of the Great War.

His innate chivalry led him to form a close friendship with his sovereign, Queen Victoria, whom he addressed as 'Mother' and who addressed him as 'My Son.'

When the old Queen died, he immediately left for London to attend the funeral and an incident occurred which I heard in Jodhpur State but have not seen recorded:-

H.H. Sir Pratap Singh was dissatisfied with the place he had been allotted in the cortège, he wished to be mounted and near the hearse. His request was granted and he rode alongside. But during the procession, a carriage moved too close and he was pushed against the hearse.

When it was over, everyone got out or moved away, but H.H. Sir Pratap remained seated on his horse. When it was suggested that he should dismount, he replied; "I am sorry but I cannot." One of his legs had been crushed.

Indian Titles

As I reach the end of our stay in New Delhi and the approaching end of Imperial Rule, I mention a subject which was of considerable importance to us and to many of the educated and ruling Indian classes.

We British like titles, as the saying goes 'Everyone loves a Lord' and we soon discovered that Indian titles were well established. So, titles such as G.C.S.I. and K.C.S.I were awarded to the Ruling Princes, who also had gun salutes: nine for lesser rulers and up to twenty-one guns for the greatest, with none for the small rulers. Some Princes with martial traditions liked being made Honorary Colonels, Brigadiers or Air Vice Marshals and there were two or three Honorary Major-Generals.

The title of Knight Bachelor was awarded to Princes, to leading officials both Indian and British and to some businessmen, especially Parsis.

But there were many more deserving people such as the thousands of private citizens and also Indians who served the Government faithfully and loyally. For these the Government adapted existing Indian titles to form a three-tier system, i.e. Rao (or Khan) Sahib; Rao (or Khan) Bahadur and Dewan Bahadur (Khan for Muslim title holders).

That there was jockeying for titles by both Europeans and Indians is undeniable and a number must have been awarded to well-to-do Indians who had contributed liberally to Governor's War Funds.

The Indian Army had their part in this system and were proud of their Royal titles. The most famous Regiment, the Corps of Guides, were Queen Victoria's Own. Probyns Horse, Skinners Horse, Hodson's Horse, Sam Browne's Cavalry and Gardner's Horse (2nd Lancers) had distinctive names and traditions and were pioneers in that they relied on Indian officers and had very few British; but others were Royal, e.g. the 2nd Royal Lancers, the Royal Deccan Horse, Prince Albert Victor's Own Cavalry (usually called P.A.V.O.), the Poona Horse (17th Queen Victoria's Own Cavalry), and the 7th Rajputs – Queen Victoria's Own Light Infantry. Both the Bengal and Bombay Sappers and Miners were 'Royal'.

Colonel of the 2nd King Edward's Own Gurkha Rifles is H.R.H. the Prince of Wales, while the oldest corps, the Madras Sappers and Miners, were Queen Victoria's Own, of which title the sepoys were immensely proud.

During the war, both the Indian Artillery and the Indian Army Service Corps were dubbed 'Royal' in recognition of their achievements. But the Congress Party disliked the 'Royals' and were pledged to drop them, which pledge they carried out promptly on Independence Day in August 1947.

A certain firm in the Punjab used to supply Regimental and Service Christmas cards and very good they were too. These were still available for the Christmas of 1947, the first Christmas after Independence and many Indian officers bought them, saying that the Government had abolished Royal titles, but they couldn't stop them sending out the old Christmas cards.

After Independence, any jockeying for personal titles was more than offset by the keen desire for positions of influence in the Government, the Congress Party and Local Authorities. Later in 1978, a distinguished officer wrote: "…. patronage, nepotism and chicanery, that all too many politicians developed into a way of life during long years in power". (Eric Stracey, retired Inspector-General of Police in 'Odd Man In' page 33).

The Russians have many orders and decorations and it will be interesting to see if the Government of India extend to civilians the medals which are awarded to Servicemen. The Republic of India struck medals for the armed services and police, but have not to my knowledge re-introduced civilian decorations; perhaps in time they will.

Tailpiece:

Epitaph from a tombstone at Peshawar

'Here lies Captain Ernest Bloomfield
Accidentally shot by his orderly
March 2nd 1879
Well done, good and faithful servant.'

The Mess, Vellore.
My servant on verandah.

Mahomed Kasim, faithful Mess Butler.

Probationers: R. R. B. Truscott, self,
      A. E. Spitteler and a Deputy
      Superintendent.

The Vellore Club.

Vellore Fort ramparts.

Fishing boat at Madras, the timbers are sewn together.

Group – Vellore club.
about February 1942 before it was disbanded. Top row: Ball-boys (3), the old waiter, the
Club Writer. Middle row: J. R. de C., T. M. S. Mani, Major P. L. O'Neill, G. F. Harrison, Indian Police
I.C.S.   I.M.S. Front row: S. Ahmed Ali, Mrs Mani, Mrs Harrison, Begum Ahmed Ali, O'Neill's sister,
Rosemary Coltham and Lt. Col. G. S. Gill, I.M.S. Children: Miss Harrison, Miss Ahmed Ali, Miss
Major O'Neill's nephew.

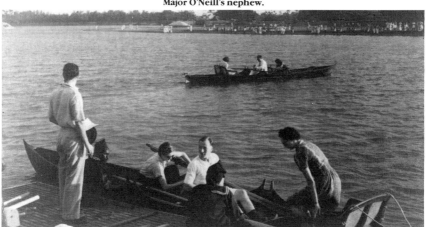

The Adyar River, Joy Westerdale at bow.

Madras Boat Club. At the table: Louis de C., Margaret Fyffe, Pamela, Major Waters,
I. M. S. My servant, Yelliah behind Pam.

Louis de C. garlanded.

F. J. McLintic, Punjab Province.

Rembrandt with his syce.

Royal elephant stables.

Orderly Hirelal with a hare.

Temple car at Vijayanagar.

Palace dancers, Vijayanagar Empire.

With Entwhistle on the
Tungabhadra River.

My terrier feels the heat.

Festival site at Pandhapur before the
pilgrims arrive – a million are expected.

Joint responsibility for keeping the peace:
Police officers and the District Magistrate
(E. W. Perry) in white coat. P. M. Stewart
in centre, G. C. Ryan on right.

Another of my year: J. M. Dean & friend
fishing in the River Jhelum.

Sans souci.

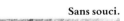

Srinagar.

Houseboats on the Dhal Lake,
near Srinagar.

Hillside at Gulmarg.

In the Sindh valley.

Trekking with Charles Filmer in the Sindh valley.

Kashmiri nomads.

Fort St George in late 18th century, St Thomas' Mount in background; Madras town is hidden.

Part of the Red Fort, Delhi. It is 1000 yards long by 600 yards wide.

Wireless elephant on Festival duty at Hardwar on the Ganges.

Wedding of John and Muriel Dean in New Delhi.

Three old friends foregather for a drink.

Wireless Constable, United Provinces.

In the Simla bazaar.

Buddhist monk with acolyte
near Darjeeling.

In the Simla Hills.

Prime Minister Pandit Nehru
in March 1947
visits riot-torn city of Multan
in the Punjab.

F. J. McLintic garlanded, leaving his district for a rest at Quetta before his next posting.

The Training College at Mount Abu,
West Rajputana. Probationers are shown
by an N.C.O. how to tie puttees.

Probationers in the Riding School. Sikh
Riding Master on right,
Principal, P. L. Mehta in background.

46

Farewell to Delhi

I said to the man who stood at the gate of the year:
"Give me a light that I may tread safely into the unknown"
And he replied "Go out into the darkness and put your hand
into the hand of God."   Minnie Louise Haskins, 1839.
Quoted by King George VI.

BEFORE LEAVING for Rajputana I gave my groom strict instructions to exercise Rembrandt daily, but when we returned a week later Rembrandt had been fed but not exercised and, fretting, he took a bite out of his chest. The Vet. tried very hard, but the poor horse couldn't bear the itching and wouldn't allow it to heal up. So Rembrandt had to be led away and put down and I, after seven years, lost one of the best friends I ever had, who before marriage, was almost a wife to me. I had one of his shoes silver-plated.

Work at the office became monotonous and I decided to study a treatise on philosophy. Jenkin, my superior, thought I wasn't doing enough work; that my job was the security of foreign personnel and that the war was over, didn't seem to matter to him – he was a man who could always find plenty to do; he worried me for several weeks. We couldn't agree because he was an office man, I was a district officer and felt that secretariat jobs should be kept down as much as possible. I duly applied for, and was granted, long leave.

We lost our horse but were soon to gain a baby. Our first child arrived safely – the father worrying much more than the mother. But as babies were not permitted in Club quarters, we spent our last few weeks in Delhi in one of the married hostels.

This made for a lot of extra packing and the hostel quarters were filthy and needed a good clean. The food was much inferior to the Club, but there were other families there with children, who were all very friendly and understanding.

Before long my wife, a nursing mother, had bacillary dysentery and I went down with a fever. The officer-in-charge of the hostel was very annoyed over the dysentery and gave the contractor notice. Part of the trouble, no doubt, was lack of refrigeration and a shortage of electric fans. Two of our visitors were Sydney Plew (of Bulandshahr) and his bride, Molly.

Our sailing date was announced – May 11th – and we worked hard at our packing but as I had good friends among the clerical staff, we had skilled help.

I had arrived in New Delhi with two dogs, a mother and son, but the son was aggressive and had to be put down. Now, with our packing done, I had the task of taking Dinah to the Vet. to be put down. She had been my companion for five years and had travelled with me for tens of thousands of miles. She was gentle and affectionate being half spaniel. My servant Yelliah, was also very fond of her, so it was with a heavy heart that I returned from the Vet.

Our break with Delhi was almost complete. Families and bachelors were leaving every day. Messrs. Thomas Cook and Grindlays must have been exceptionally busy, but it was not like peace-time farewells – with parties. We were tired, the weather was very hot and supplies of food and drink were short. So the farewells were not emotional. I sold various effects, gave others away and had our heavy luggage carefully labelled by a signwriter.

I said goodbye to the Office clerks and staff who had been so loyal, especially my secretary, Syed Ahmed Shah. The trunks were sent ahead to Bombay in charge of Yelliah. Finally, the office Cashier told me not to order a taxi – he came for us himself, drove us to the station and saw us safely into the compartment – no one can be kinder and more thoughtful than an Indian.

The journey to Bombay was so hot that we nearly roasted, but were saved by getting extra blocks of ice and placing cold, wet napkins on the windows with the fans blowing the hot air on them. After all my exertions I felt light-hearted for the first time in weeks.

Although the train was late, waiting at the Bombay terminus was my colleague and friend, W.G. Lang, one of my year, also our servant Yelliah. Bill Lang drove us to his flat on Cumballa Hill by the deep blue sea; we were cooled by sea breezes and it was heavenly compared with the airless hostel we had so recently left.

We had four days waiting for the ship, but went out little: once to order a fridge for delivery on our return to India, once to take Winifred, my wife and Bill Lang to tea at the Taj Mahal Hotel.

As the Taj Mahal is the most magnificent among the many splendid buildings of India, so the Taj Mahal Hotel is the most famous of India's hotels. It is always a pleasure to go there but my wife fretted a little, as it was the first time she had left her Baby in charge of a stranger. But she need not have worried – almost any Indian servant is a safe and trustworthy baby-minder.

At last the day arrived for the sailing. The great Customs shed was like an oven and Baby was sick; the long, slow-moving queues were over and we climbed the gangway. Our ship was an old luxury liner converted into a troopship for over 3,000 Servicemen, together with 800 parents and children.

It was so crowded, there was hardly room to sit down, there was no peace or quiet but no one minded. The ship was off, deep-laden and steaming rather slowly, but we were going - HOME! And every turn of the screws brought us nearer, and the thud, thud, thud of the mighty engines was like music in our ears.

The Red Sea lived up to its fearsome reputation for heat, but once we docked at Suez, the tropics were left behind. Our trunks were of course in the hold and we were allowed to go down to pack our cottons and extract our woollens. To reach the hold one descended to 'G' deck - six decks down - I saw the dormitories of the Servicemen, where sleeping was done in shifts and as I reached the lowest decks below the water-line I could smell Bombay: the odour of hot vegetable frying oil. Poor chaps, they were much worse off than the officers. Their part of the ship was worse than a prison but they didn't complain – they were on their way to Blighty.

So we steamed slowly through the Canal and reached the Mediterranean. Nine and a half years before, most of the sixteen Police Probationers had sailed through in October. And there was a difference, sailing through in May for the sea was violet rather than blue and I loved to stand in the bows and feel the cool moist air, soothing as balm.

There was little to do in the evenings, but "housey-housey" parties were held in the saloon, with three hundred or more taking part. I was new to this game, which was soon to become almost a craze – Bingo.

The last few days passed slowly by. Progress against the strong current in the Straits of Gibraltar was slow, then into the Atlantic, the last stage of our journey.

"In the dimmest North-east distance dawned Gibraltar grand and gray
"Here and here did England help me: How can I help England? – say"

A storm in the Irish Sea, followed by fog, slowed us right down. I saw the Captain, a grizzled Merchant Navy officer and thought he would be glad when he finally discharged his 4,000 passengers.

Yet another wait at the mouth of the Mersey, this time for the tide; it was grey and overcast but soon we were to see the famous Liver birds, the symbol seen by so many thousands of gallant seamen as they returned from the Battle of the Atlantic.

An English crowd was looking up at us; a puff of wind blew off the hat of one of the passengers and we all laughed as it rolled along the quay. A tall police constable looked so calm and so British. Our passports were checked rapidly in the saloons, but all the heavy luggage was mixed up and it took a long time, even with a helpful porter, to find all of ours. Then, we were put on a 'bus and reached Lime Street Station before the streets had begun to fill with people and traffic.

The steam train started up. We couldn't take our eyes off the countryside – neat fields and hedges, fat cattle, strong working horses and the woodlands. We drank up the English scene, it was like water to a man parched with thirst.

At one station I bought a glass of beer, but it was so weak compared with ten years before and in my ignorance I tried to buy chocolate, not knowing about food coupons.

At Bristol Temple Meads we needed two taxis to take all our luggage and ourselves. The appearance of Bristol, hammered and pounded by Nazis bombs, was a great shock to me, but at the end of the journey was my mother's welcome and I cannot say how deeply I felt as I hugged her. It was home, the same home I had left nearly ten years before. We were very weary and so very happy!

47

Last journey to South India

IT IS not relevant to these memoirs to describe our long leave of 1946. My wife and I were both run-down; we took my mother for a holiday in Cornwall, then Winifred and I spent a week in my family's favourite holiday village, Chagford in Devon. By then we were well on the mend. My leave was for six months, but I had to attend a 'Medical' by an India Office Consultant.

This showed that I was not yet clear of dysentry and I was given a course of treatment and two months' extension of leave. Those of us from India who had more than six months' leave in the United Kingdom had then to go somewhere else, otherwise we were liable to a full year's British Tax in addition to Indian Income Tax. So we decided to go to Jersey, C.I., for the end of our leave.

★ ★ ★ ★ ★

Early in January 1947 we were all ready to go; we were booked on S.S. Strathmore and were to board her at Southampton. It was cold and foggy. The Strathmore was sailing from London Docks, but due to the fog was several hours late. We had a long, cold wait in the Customs shed but at last the white-painted liner appeared and soon we were on board and in comfort, for though the Strathmore was not yet back to peace-time standards, she was far more comfortable than a troopship. The five hours' wait in the Customs shed gave me a heavy cold which lasted for weeks, but we escaped the great freeze of January to March 1947.

We made friends on the voyage with a missionary and his wife, Rev. Walter and Peggy George, our friendship lasted and Walter became Godfather to our second daughter. And now, as we steam towards Bombay I give, mainly for those interested in radio, an account of the development of radio communication over a whole sub-continent.

Radio Telegraphy

The system of Finger Print classification was developed in Bengal and the method of police radio communication began in Malabar. But first, it should be understood that internal communications in India were very slow. The Railways had telegraph offices at every station, but the wires could be broken in a storm or cut by saboteurs. The canals also had their telephones, but the canals were in certain areas only. By the 1920's, not all the District towns were connected by telegraph, which left vast areas of market towns and villages without modern communications. If for example, a district officer was fifty miles from headquarters an urgent message might take six hours to reach him, the messenger travelling by country bus and bicycle and conversely.

The Moplah Rebellion of 1921-22 was a traumatic experience and no one wanted to see another. Following the Rebellion, five police posts in remote parts of Malabar were equipped with radio-telephone sets. These did not require skilled operators, nor had wires that could be cut. They were supplied, installed and maintained by the Marconi Company.

The sets were installed for a particular purpose but no Police authority followed suit 'till 1930, when an enlightened Commissioner of Police, W.R.G. Smith, made use of the expertise of radio enthusiasts in the Bombay City Police, viz. S. Ferguson, ex-Indian Army Signals, Reggie Fox, a former operator at the British Mission, Lhasa, Tibet; Beck, an ex-R.A.F. operator; J. Adams and C. Greig, who was ex-Army, with experience in the South China Command Signals.

A Police Radio workshop was set up but progress was slow: expert telegraphists were not available, there was opposition, as always, in high places and little money to spend.

The next development area was the North West Frontier Province where the Inspector-General, Mr. A.F. Perrott, acquired portable V.H.F. sets, later called walkie talkies. But he had no workshop, so he went to Bombay where he obtained the necessary help from the Police and Railway Workshops. He planned to set up a radio network in his Province but the war disasters of 1941 brought progress to a halt.

Meanwhile, the Bombay City Police acquired twenty broadcast receivers, modified and installed them in selected police stations. Various difficulties were encountered but the network was completed shortly before the outbreak of war. By 1941 police vehicles were being equipped with radio.

We now turn to the United Provinces. In 1925 there arrived from England a Police Probationer, E.W. Hunt, who happened to be a radio enthusiast. He built a set capable of receiving the world news service, transmitted from Rugby in Morse. Thus the Police Mess in his Province had world news (and football results) 36 hours before the "Pioneer" newspaper arrived from Lucknow on Tuesday morning. There were at the time no other receivers in that part of Upper India capable of picking up foreign news.

Hunt steadily increased his knowledge of receiving and transmitting; he obtained a G.P.O. licence and so became a radio "ham". He visited the Police wireless establishments at Scotland Yard and in Nottingham, but neither system would meet Indian requirements.

Returning to India, Hunt obtained an Indian Amateur Licence and built a set powered by scores of dry batteries as his headquarters had no electricity. From there he had his first opportunity of using wireless for crowd control.

Everyone knows of Benares (Varanasi) but few foreigners have heard of Hardwar, a beautifully situated town on the Ganges as it flows down the Himalayan foothills. The festival known as Kumbh Mela is celebrated there once in twelve years, as fixed by astrology. Huge crowds of a million or more arrive by special trains, buses, bullock carts or on foot in order to bathe in the sacred pool and at the propitious hour. The festival continues for two months but the magistrates, the hundreds of police, health and sanitary officials required begin preparations a month in advance. Those who lead the ceremonies will be high on *bhang* , something like cannabis and, as usual at festivals, numbers of thieves and pickpockets mingle with the crowds.

Previously, the police tried to control the various processions by flag signalling, but this had its limitations and usually several persons were crushed to death. In 1937, the last festival before Independence, portable sets were borrowed from Indian Army Signals. One was installed in the control room, one in a patrol van, a third was placed on the back of a well-trained elephant lent by the Temple authorities. Complications arose in the timing of processions, but control was maintained, there was no rioting and no accidental death. The Wireless Elephant with his excellent view was a success! fact all went smoothly till there was a serious out-break of cholera, which caused the crowds to escape as though before an invading army. The Mela is also held at Allahabad, confluence of two sacred rivers, but without a sacred pool there is much less congestion.

Hunt continued to use borrowed Army sets but the Inspector-General of Police, Mr. Hugh Inglis, had been watching his work and appointed him Police Wireless Officer with the task of setting up a Wireless Section. So at the beginning of 1941, Hunt and twenty-five constables were sent to the Signals Depot, Eastern Command, Bareilly, for training. At first, the men were slow but then they picked up quickly and duly became proficient enough to reach the high standard required for Morse operators.

After practical experience in Bengal, the first Provincial Wireless Station was set up at Sitapur, which was the headquarters of the Armed Police battalions. From the electrical point of view it was an unhappy choice as the local supply was often overloaded, the voltage dropping to 160/180 volts. But Sitapur was by no means the only district town during the war with an inadequate power station.

Space does not allow the description of the many difficulties and hurdles which were met, mostly on the material side, not the human. By the time the Japanese war broke out the supply of equipment was far short of demand and police workshops were obliged laboriously to make their own.

In the political disturbances of August 1942 telephone and telegraph lines were cut on a big scale, but the United Provinces had portable wireless sets working. Bengal and Bihar followed their lead and sent their men to Sitapur to be trained. Later, in 1944, old aircraft were being broken up and provided materials required by the Wireless Sections.

With the end of the war in 1945, vast quantities of equipment became available. Assisted by C. Greig of the Bombay City Police – Hunt was examining equipment both in India and England and so the Wireless Grid was rapidly established across British India and in rich States such as Hyderabad.

In my province, Madras, an ex-Signals officer, Captain D.R. Clamp, was appointed Wireless Officer in 1946 and before the year was out he had ten sub-inspectors, eight sergeants and eighty constables trained or under training. They took to wireless with keenness and intelligence and when I arrived at Tanjore from leave in January 1947, I found the police wireless grid in smooth and efficient operation, with a Chief Wireless Officer in Delhi.

Towards the end of 1947 E.W. Hunt went on leave preparatory to retirement. Unlike most I.C.S. and Police lfficers retiring prematurely, he had more than one job offered him and accepted the post of Chief Signals Officer, Malayan Police.

After Independence and the creation of more States (formerly Provinces) the Wireless Grid was extended and made permanent, a tribute to the skill, patience and labour of the pioneers.

48

Tanjore District

I HAD been posted to a district called Madura South and was pleased as my parents had lived in Madura.

But on reaching Madras I was told that the posting had been changed to Tanjore. All our furniture had been carefully packed in a goods wagon and needed to be unloaded and re-loaded on a different Railway altogether, the metre-gauge. This the Railway staff did with very good grace, but it took several months of pushing before I received a refund of the booking charges.

I called at the C.I.D. office and was given a resume of Communist-led agrarian disaffection in the district.

It was an overnight journey to Tanjore. We were duly met at 5.20 a.m. and stayed in the Railway Retiring Rooms, which were comfortable, well-furnished with rosewood furniture and we fed in the Refreshment Room. We were weary after three weeks of travelling, but the Deputy Inspector-General, E.H. Colebrook, wanted me to take charge of the district from him straightaway so that he could return to Madura. So, bleary-eyed, I took charge and began work from the Railway Rooms.

Meanwhile, we went to see what was to become our first home. Our official bungalow was a two-storied one set in four or five acres, with verandahs on both floors, the upstairs verandah being suitable for sleeping out in the hot weather. The walls inside and out had been newly whitewashed and the contractor called and said: 'What colour would Madam like the woodwork?' He showed us a chart and she chose a mid-green. Within a week several men clad only in loin-cloths had completed the painting and made a good job of it, so we moved in.

A city with a long history, Tanjore was as far south as the Moghul and Maratha powers ever reached. Earlier, it was part of the Vijayanagar Empire. It is situated on a plain and its most conspicuous feature is the magnificent Temple, built by a Chola King in the 11th century with a high tower or gopuram on which is perched a huge, rounded boulder.[38] I could see little sign of Muslim influence in the town but some Maratha influence remained. It was Shivaji himself, who appointed his half-brother as king of Tanjore. The last of the Maharatta Kings of Tanjore was Serfoji, an enlightened prince who ruled in the latter part of the 18th century. Serfoji made friends with the Rev. C.F. Schwarz, the famous Danish missionary who laboured at Tranquebar,

[38] Estimated to weigh over 80 tons.

the Danish settlement on the coast and later at Tanjore, as Serfoji wanted Schwarz to be his Adviser.

I duly called at the Palace and found the Prince of Tanjore, as his official title then was. He was a rather frail elderly man, dignified, fair of skin and dressed from head to foot in the traditional Marathi fashion: a long, coloured tunic with a sash, upturned slippers on his feet and the very distinctive headgear worn by the Maratha nobility. It is a hat, rather than a turban, with a low crown and rising up to a point on the right side, which gives the wearer a dashing, jaunty look.

There was a large Roman Catholic Mission and the headmaster, Father Pinto, was most friendly. Several pieces of furniture that we needed were made to our order in their workshops. Also an Anglican church and missionary, the Rev. G.H. Lamb of the Society for the Propagation of the Gospel, a successor of the Rev. C.F. Schwarz.

Also at Tanjore is the famous library of manuscripts on palmyra leaf, a kind of palm the Indian equivalent of papyrus. I much regret that I was so busy during our stay of less than a year that I did not visit the library. The visitor to Tanjore should not fail to see it.

The year 1936, the year of my arrival in the country, had been a year of comparative calm while 1947, the year of our return from long leave, was a year of upheaval.

The District Magistrate, a Muslim, had upset the Revenue Minister in Madras and was under orders of transfer. In his place, J.R. Bett, a senior British I.C.S. officer, had been posted from the West Coast. He was annoyed because he was due to retire to Australia in a matter of weeks; but he was both very able and firm and with a little help from me did much in those few weeks to pacify and control disaffected kisans or cultivators. After his retirement, he was succeded by a tall and well-covered Anglo-Indian, a Mr McLaughlin – a Provincial Service officer. He had married an American missionary, who I think, was looking forward to their retirement in the United States.

Henry McLaughlin and I understood each other from the start. He was an experienced administrator and with us working closely together, magistrates and police worked together throughout the district. No trouble-maker could play one off against the other.

For the first two weeks we stayed put, arranging the house, starting a garden and receiving callers. We then set out on tour. As I did not have a car we all got into a police lorry: wife, baby, three servants, my Brahmin Camp Clerk and two orderlies; luggage in the back of the lorry and on the roof.

First I wanted to inspect an area which had been disturbed. The result was apparent in that many fields had not been cultivated, numerous small trees had been cut down and large numbers of coco-nuts had been stolen.

From there, we visited a small town, Muthupet, containing a number of Muslim traders. Most were honest, a few probably not, for one of the local occupations was smuggling from Ceylon. We boarded a smuggler's craft which had been captured by the Customs patrol and were shown creeks used by opium smugglers, protected from view by a thick growth of rushes and reeds. Finally, we reached a lagoon which was the winter abode of hundreds of law-abiding wild duck.

On our way to our next camp, we stopped at a Hindu monastery. The Inspector had warned the Mahant (or prior) and he received us in all his finery – a gold and pearl headdress, ropes of pearls on his bare chest, gold and jewelled earrings, diamond rings and gold pattens for his feet. We were garlanded with rose garlands, exchanged compliments and partook of light refreshments. On learning that Helen, our baby, was one year old that day he sent for a tray of silver ornaments, she chose a lion, which pleased him, so he told her to choose another gift which she was pleased to do.

After our departure, the Inspector informed us that this Mahant did not practise austerity and lived very well. From his portly figure and genial manner I was of the same opinion.

So we arrived at Negapatam, a minor port, formerly occupied by the Dutch. We had an invitation to the Indian Club and were made very welcome. Among the guests was a Mr. Bell of the Malayan Civil Service who was learning Tamil, his attractive wife and the Port Officer. We were served excellent cakes, so good that they were probably from a French patisserie in Karaikal.

It rained so heavily that night that our lorry would not start. It finally started after being pushed by a staff car from the Port Authority. The mud on the road was like thin porridge and we made very slow progress to our next camp, a place called Kumbakonam which is noted for intrigue. My wife received such a bumping on the way that she had a miscarriage.

We were to stay at the Municipal rest house; but it was so dirty we refused to move in till it had been washed and cleaned, a contrast to the P.W.D. i.e. Government bungalows which are always clean.

It wasn't long before I heard persistent complaints against one of my four Deputy Superintendents. He was a light-skinned Muslim of good family, Ghulam Mahomed Sayeed. He was very intelligent and capable and spoke three languages equally well – Urdu, English and Tamil. He gave me a great deal of trouble and worry but after much hard work I managed to frame a charge against him. But Sayeed managed, after Independence, to prejudice against me my new superior, one of his own religion. It was not till many years later that I learnt that he also prejudiced the Government against me through his elder brother who was a Judge of the Madras High Court; at the time I knew nothing of this.

Regretfully, I have to say that after Independence it was both difficult and risky to punish subordinates who had good connections or 'godfathers' in high places.

The Tanjore Club by then was an Indian club. We joined and attended now and again but were not expected regularly – they did not have club nights.

We attended the English service at St. Peter's church, which had been built by Rev. C.F. Schwarz. The missionary was elderly and tired and like an old country parson. We had him round to dinner now and again and he invited us to the Mission bungalow. To our surprise he had a fine old dinner service of Royal Worcester. When I admired it he said "It belongs to the Mission. It was ordered by Schwarz in the 18th century and we use it occasionally. It has 200 pieces – I have tried to sell it for the Mission, but so far without success."

One of the interesting places along the coast was Tranquebar. Formerly a Danish Trading Station older than Madras, it was a walled and fortified village. Over the main gate was a stone bust of King Christian IV. Though a small settlement it contained no fewer than four churches, including a very old one in a state of decay.

We stayed in the small fort, the Danesborg, built in 1623. It was just off the beach and a cool breeze blew through it from the sea. It felt heavenly after the hot, steamy camps close to the paddy fields and I had a long swim. Next day we motored to the French enclave of Karaikal where I met the Police 'Commissioner'. He turned out to be a handsome and very friendly young Frenchman who had served with the Free French Forces and had been attached to a British Regiment.

On our way back, we stopped at the best garage in the whole district. It was of the latest design and equipment and the creation of a man who started as a car cleaner. He gave us a good tea on new china with a rich cake, doubtless sent from Karaikal.

A short way out of Tanjore on a flat stretch of land which supported only a few bushes, a large airfield had been constructed. It was intended for the long-range bombing of Malaya, but with the sudden ending of the Japanese war, this and other airfields such as Arkonam were not required and Malaya was consequently spared devastation by Flying Fortresses and Halifax heavy bombers. It was guarded by only one policeman and I would sometimes check his alertness and then drive along the runways at full speed, which was almost as refreshing as a bathe.

My workload was heavy. I was doing the job which formerly only senior officers were entrusted with. But then occurred what was typical of British consideration: E.H. Colebrook, my superior officer, thought we needed a break, asked us to stay at Madura and we accepted gratefully.

There we watched the Police sports, followed by a conference lasting a morning. Naturally, we did some sightseeing as Madura is an ancient city known at its best period partly for its magnificence, partly for its trade. It remains the heart of the Tamil country and its literature. The two most imposing buildings are the huge four-towered temple of Meenakshi – the fish-eyed goddess, each tower elaborately carved and rising to a height of 150 feet. Another is the Hall of 1000 Pillars; the stone pillars are so richly carved and with so much variety that the visitor could profitably spend days studying them. For some time Madura was part of the Vijayanagar Empire, then after its fall it became independent under the Naiks. Tirumal Naik reigned for 36 years of the 16th – 17th centuries.

Tirumal Naik restored the palace, till in size and dignity it was the finest example of palace architecture in southern India. It is quadrangular and supported by hundreds of carved, stone pillars, great in height and girth. The Durbar Hall was where the King sat in state to receive the homage of his feudal vassals, visiting princes and rajahs, who with their retinues, body-guards, elephants, horses and musical instruments provided scenes beloved of the people.

The Temple is a very rich one and its treasures have to be carefully guarded. It was also reported to have a highly erotic carving depicting a rajah with several concubines, but I only met one European who said he had seen it.

There were two big cotton mills in Madura, both owned by the Harvey family and one evening we were invited to the Harvey mansion. Built on a hill it received all the breeze there was and was sumptuously furnished, with panelled walls. Mr. Harvey was a teetotaller, so the drinking was discreet and I couldn't help noticing British engineers of the mills and their wives, who had imbibed liberally the evening before at the Club, but were now sitting very straight and correct in their Burra Sahib's[39] presence.

A new factor in this interlude was that I did not have to worry about the situation in my district: the Police Wireless system kept me in constant touch.

Soon after our return it was time to organise the annual Police sports. I thought certain of the events at the Madura sports were too relaxed, so I took care that the programme was carefully prepared and rehearsed and that there were no delays. It was a very warm afternoon and the attendance at first was rather poor, but shortly before tea was served, many more spectators arrived. The fancy dress or disguise competition, beloved of Madras policemen, got under way and everyone began to enjoy himself, with the grand old man of the town presenting the prizes. My wife received one, having won the egg and spoon race.

Afterwards, we gave a dinner party with the Vellore Police Band playing in the compound. I supplied two bottles of arrack[40] for the bandsmen who were nearly all Christians and they played magnificently!

As the heat increased week by week, my wife and child began to wilt. It was too late to rent a small bungalow in the hills, so I sent them to the Carlton Hotel, Kodaikanal, in the Madura District, a family hotel at which my parents had stayed.

Soon afterwards our first new car arrived in Madras: a Standard 14 saloon; I was fortunate, as in 1947, new cars were not easy to come by. I sent a Head Constable driver to Madras to collect it and he drove back with great care, travelling at only 25 m.p.h..

With all my cares, I needed to go to some refreshing place and chose a camp

[39] Or chief.   [40] Distilled liquor.

near the sea where the Sub-Inspector arranged for me to stay in a small house owned by a friendly landowner. Every evening I motored to the beach – a magnificent one with 70–100 yards' width of firm sand. I enjoyed long walks in the cool wind and every evening had freshly-caught fish for dinner. There was nobody on the beach except the fishermen and I got on with my work without interference.

But this state of affairs did not last. Evidently, reports or tales about me had reached Madras. The Revenue Minister, who was not my Minister, said he wanted to see me next day at a certain town in the south of the district. I reached Tanjore about 8 p.m. and set off again early next morning, but had to wait several hours before he sent for me. He was charming and pleasant but said he was not prepared to take a strong line over the agrarian unrest in the district. It was an example of the difference between British administration and Swaraj: the fact that I came under the Home Department did not seem to worry him at all.

After a couple of days' hard work at Tanjore, I set off for Kodaikanal in our new car. Though it was not yet run-in, we covered the 160 miles in about five hours' driving time, including the 7,000 foot climb up the mountain.

Here the contrast was unbelievable: the cool, green hilltop, planted with trees and gardens seemed a paradise. My little girl hardly knew me after a month's separation and even seeing my wife seemed a little strange.

E.H. Colebrook was also staying for a couple of weeks and he took us for a lovely drive and picnic with a walk through sweet-smelling pinewoods.

On the Sunday evening we attended Evensong and though the European residents were beginning to leave for good, there was a pretty good congregation. When after ten days, the time came to leave, we filled every space in the car with fresh vegetables and fruit and so returned to our first home. Hot though the interior of the district was, we were always glad to return to a spacious house with lofty ceilings, quiet fans and a fridge.

I had offered to stay on after Independence and my offer was accepted. All over the country preparations were afoot for the old regime to be wound up and Home Rule (or Swaraj) to begin. My superior officer, E.H. Colebrook, who had been so kind and considerate, was packed and ready to leave. He asked us to Madura for his farewell party and arranged for us to stay in a fine new house belonging to one of the Harvey family, complete with an English nanny, who took complete charge of their baby and ours.

The farewell party was at the house of one of the Police Superintendents, a domiciled European, W.E. Middleton. As he didn't hit it off too well with the Congress Party he had not been offered a contract, so he too was leaving. The party was attended by numerous police officers, officials and their wives. Drinks were plentiful, but it was a sad occasion for me: I did not know what the future would bring.

Independence Day August 14th, 1947 at Tanjore

A dull day with intervals of drizzle. Osbourne-Jones, the Railway Superintendent, attended a flag-hoisting ceremony at dawn. One of the local Congress officials sent me a National pennant of silk for my car, which was duly fixed.

In the afternoon, a Police parade: McLaughlin, the Collector, arrived resplendent and imposing in black morning dress, grey cravat and a white topi. I wore slacks, tunic, forage cap and sword. We inspected the Reserve Police Companies and the parade was smart; we watched the Union Jack being lowered and the National Flag raised. The Roman Catholic nuns were impressed by the parade and they too were a little fearful for their future.

We then proceeded to the Durbar Hall of the Palace. Hundreds had already arrived and many more were coming in, including hundreds of schoolchildren. No request for Police bandobast (or control) had been received. The noise echoed through the massive stone hall and, without microphones, the accoustics were very poor. Both McLaughlin and I made speeches. During mine I dropped a page of my notes and concluded from memory but it made no difference: the speeches were almost inaudible.

Independence Day 1947 could have been unpleasant for us expatriates: McLaughlin and I could have been told: "Now you won't be able to lord it over us any longer!" or, "Wait and see, soon we shall be ruled by our own people!" But no such remarks were made, everyone was perfectly polite. There was not one taunt, nor any sign of hostility and I think they knew that we were doing our best for the people.

So we left the Durbar Hall, drove home, bathed and changed into cool white clothes. Osbourne-Jones had asked us to his bungalow where we drank to the occasion with tankards of beer, but our feelings were a mixture of relief, sadness and some apprehension.

You are going?
But you will visit again?
Any time, any day,
I am not believing in ceremony.
Always I am enjoying your company.

Nissim Ezekiel Babu.

49

Swaraj

"The tumult and the shouting dies-
The captains and the kings depart-
Still stands Thine ancient sacrifice,
An humble and a contrite heart.
Lord God of Hosts, be with us yet,
Lest we forget, lest we forget."

THE HANDING over of the reins of government affected us very soon. Within a couple of weeks the newly-appointed Deputy Inspector-General, a Muslim, Mr. Hussain, came to Tanjore, his first inspection. Had he been instructed to do so by a Minister? I think not. He was quite affable, we dined with him and he had tea with us; but later he strongly criticised my crime figures in his review to the C.I.D. in Madras.

After all my efforts to control crime, which had met with no little success, I was much put out. I replied at length with chapter and verse, so proving his criticisms to be unfounded. I don't think he liked it and the C.I.D. supported me.

Following this contretemps we left for what must be one of the finest camps in a large and varied Province: Point Calimere, a mere 40 miles from Ceylon.

As the road did not go all the way, a little old-fashioned steam train with wooden carriages takes one through mile upon mile of bright green paddy fields, then several miles of thin jungle to the terminus. We arrived in the dark, the air was cool and fresh and we enjoyed a good night's sleep.

Next morning, we saw the sea about a quarter of a mile away; all day long the air was fresh and there was no need of a punkah. Erected closeby was a tall R.A.F. watch tower about 200 feet high and built of tarred timbers. I decided to climb up the ladder which went to the top with a hand-rail. I reached a height of about 130 feet but could go no further; I looked for the Ceylon coastline, but it wasn't visible.

Next day, I decided to inspect the coast to which there was regular smuggling from Ceylon. There was no horse to be had, so I took a bicycle and pedalled merrily with a following wind. At dusk, I turned round but the wind had freshened, the sandy track was moist and my progress got slower and slower till I had to walk. Fortunately, an orderly with a lantern found me and took charge of the bicycle for I was near exhaustion.

Another day, the Inspector and I visited a smuggler's village, which entailed a short train journey. I entered a first class compartment and after a few minutes the guard came and asked: "May the train now start, sir?" I was thrilled and knew it was the first and last time my permission would be sought in this manner. From the train, we took an old Ford tourer, drove a few miles along sandy roads and reached the leading smuggler's village. He lived in a fine big house and was a large man; of course he affected to know nothing whatever about smuggling! He was master in the village and if the police visited it, they had to be armed. Some months earlier his right-hand man had been murdered close by. The police were not concerned with smuggling as such; but the keeping of the peace needed continual vigilance.

Another village we went to was an isolated one, for the track was impassable even with a Ford tourer, so we walked the five miles each way. Whether the Government is a foreign one or an Indian one makes no appreciable difference in such a remote village.

Our stay at Point Calimere would have been idyllic but for the hostile and critical letters coming from Mr. Hussain and I felt in my bones that my service was drawing to its close.

A pleasant duty awaited us after our return – the opening of a small Police Club mainly for off-duty armed policemen and District constables from outlying parts on case, Court or escort duties.

A keen Indian Sergeant had conceived it and supervised the building which was done by a departmental contractor at cost price. After a speech by the Sergeant my wife performed the opening ceremony with a silver key which is still in out possesion. Furnished with tables and benches it provided cooked meals, tea, coffee, coloured drinks and cheap cigarettes.

The Grand Anaicut across the Cauvery river

British people are apt to assume that the great works of irrigation in India were all initiated and carried out by the Public Works Department. In fact, previous Rulers were by no means unaware of the possibility of distributing river water over the land instead of letting it flow into the sea and Egypt and Babylon were masters of irrigation.

I mentioned the dam near Hospet, constructed by the King of Vijayanagar. Another example is the Periyar Project in the Western Ghats: the Prime Minister of Ramnad in 1798 dammed the Periyar river. Over a hundred years later the British turned the river round by blasting a huge tunnel in the mountainside, so that the water, instead of running westwards into the Arabian Sea, flowed eastwards into canals for the irrigation of paddy fields on a vast scale. I happen to be very proud of this as my father was one of the engineers on the Project under Colonel Pennycuick.

The Periyar lake, behind the dam, is surrounded by a game reserve containing wild elephant, wild buffalo – considered the most dangerous animal in the forest – panther, boar etc. and I am told it is well worth a visit.

In Trichy district the great Cauvery River divides into two arms, at the Trichy end a huge weir was built across the river, called Upper Anaicut.

Sixteen miles below was an even bigger engineering work: the Grand Anaicut. It was built originally by a Tamil King in the 2nd century A.D., improved by the Royal Engineers in the 1850's and rebuilt by their successors, the Public Works Department. Its aim was to control and distribute the waters of the two arms where they unite to form the Coleroon river. The work is in modern concrete with steel shutters and control screws.

The P.W.D. Inspection Bungalow stood at the water's edge near the top of the dam; far below, great spouts of water shot out through the regulators making a roar that could be heard a mile off. One lived in a delightful light spray. It was a refreshing spot, but the well at that season was too full and the water did not agree with us.

Madura and Trichy are the chief cities of Tamil Nad. We had never been to Trichy and as it is quite close to Grand Anaicut we decided to pay it a visit. The city is dominated by a colossal rock painted in red and white stripes, on top a fort and below it the Temple. At one time Trichy was the capital of the Madura kingdom and it has always had a strategic importance.

We had an excellent tea in the well-appointed Railway restaurant and then visited the bazaar. This was a very busy one with a number of streets teeming with people. For 1947, the shops were very well stocked and, guided by a Railway Officer's personal clerk, we made a number of purchases, including stores and liquor. We did not however have time to see the Fort, the Palace, the Railway Workshops or the renowned cigar and cheroot factory and headed back in the twilight to our riverside lodging.

So we returned to Tanjore to meet the Home Minister, who was coming to inaugurate Prohibition – that plank of Gandhi's philosophy. He arrived on the 5.20 a.m. train but neither McLaughlin, nor I were there to meet him and he called for our explanations. Later, he accepted my verbal apology, for we were very busy people.

Part of the tamasha[41] was a procession, headed by an elephant. We were not on him, but walked behind. He misbehaved and I wished I had a large bucket to take the result to our vegetable garden.

Later, the Minister sent for me at a nearby town. It was May and very hot; I left at four, the earliest I could drive in the heat and arrived at 5.30 p.m. to find that the Minister had already left. But he had not given me a time. However, he was pleased with all the Police arrangements and wrote me a nice letter of thanks.

At my next inspection near Negapatam, the Sub-Inspector turned out to have been a contemporary of mine at the Police Training College. We greeted each other like brothers, for we had drilled in the ranks and played hockey together.

Not far away was a Durga or shrine, where a Muslim saint lay buried. Small, fair-skinned men in white 'fez' caps met us and said they were descended from the original imam[42] who had come from the United Provinces in northern India. The tomb lay in a chamber adorned with many mirrors. The saint's

[41] Or ceremony.

[42] A religious leader.

sanctity was acknowledged by all, so one had the rare sight of Hindus and Muslims praying together.

Before we left there was a sudden change in the weather; heavy clouds gathered and it grew dark, an easterly wind sprang up, followed by very heavy rain, the temperature dropping rapidly: it was the Monsoon. We returned to Tanjore through the rain, liquid mud and puddles and it took my driver two days to clean the car inside and out, our little girl helping with a sponge.

The Government of India were then wrestling with the Pakistan Government over the accession of Kashmir and feelings between India and Pakistan were very tense. At this juncture I was surprised to receive a summons from the Prime Minister's secretary in Madras. So I left hastily by the night train, drove to the Madras Club, bathed and breakfasted. A taxi took me to the Premier's residence. There were many callers, but after less than an hour's wait I was ushered in. I had met Shri C. Rajagopalachari once years before, but he looked the same - aquiline nose, clear eyes, white teeth. He talked about the cases, which were Customs cases, pending against our smuggler prince and about smuggling in general. He had nothing specific to say. Evidently he wanted to form his own opinion of me.

I returned that night after paying calls and stocking up at the shops, but not for long, as certain police officers had received orders to attend an anti-smuggling conference in Colombo and I was one.

It was a long drive, I stayed the night with English missionaries at Ramnad, the Rev. W. and Mrs. George, then motored to the terminal at Dhanushkodi.

Sea Trip to Ceylon, now Sri Lanka

Security was tight and the Emigration Department took an hour to check pasengers but did not bother us officers. During the war there was a Naval establishment in the vicinity, but the Navy had departed, leaving empty buildings.

A smart, well-built young Ceylonese Police officer received me on board. He wore gold braid on his shoulder straps and I took him to be an Assistant Superintendent because he was so confident and at ease. I introduced him to my superior officer, Hussain and invited him to have tea with us and the young man turned out to be a Sub-Inspector. I fully endorsed the policy of letting junior officers look after their seniors.

After tea, the small ferry steamer sailed. I chatted to a British Army Major who said that officers were leaving in large numbers - he was going to Canada, where he'd applied for release.

Disembarking at Talaimannar, North Ceylon, a few hours later, we boarded a waiting train. To my surprise it was broad gauge i.e. five foot - the story went that, last century, the then Governor of Ceylon said he didn't like metre-gauge, which decision cost the Ceylon Government dear, as the broad-gauge railways ran at a loss.

Next morning early, I looked out on a countryside which was very noticeably more fertile and prosperous than most of India.

Three Superintendents met us at Colombo - one of them was my host, P.I.M. Irwin, who had chosen me as we had been contemporaries at school.

After a bath and breakfast we drove to the office of the Inspector- General. Nine or ten Superintendents and two senior officers were waiting. When the Inspector-General arrived we saw a well-set-up, dark-skinned and keen-eyed man of about fifty: Richard Aluwahare, later Sir Richard. He was a western-educated Sinhalese of the old school and a perfect gentleman. The conference was opened by the Home Minister, Sir Oliver Goonatillike, a large, plump, very fair-skinned man with a round, bald head. Neither of these gentlemen was acceptable to later, left-wing governments and Sir Oliver died in England.

The afternoon sessions included Customs officers from both countries; Civil Aviation and Security Officers together with the Prime Minister's secretary. Our main concern was the movement and control of illicit opium to India, which is light and easy to conceal; we were not bothered about luxury goods.

In the evening, we were invited to the Police Mess for drinks. It was a fine building and the Band were playing at one end of the lawn. I spoke to a handsome young Ceylonese who told me the bandmaster had been trained at the Royal Military School of Music, Kneller Hall; so also, the Fingerprint Bureau was in charge of a man trained at Scotland Yard: both signs of a prosperous Island, more prosperous than India.

Talking to Peter Irwin after dinner I said: "After three months of Independence I am not happy. I work hard. I chase corrupt subordinates and one at least of them carries tales behind my back to Ministers. I don't think I will stay much longer. What do you think about my becoming a tea-planter on your Island?" But he was not enthusiastic, he foresaw a strongly left-wing government coming to power in a few years' time.

On the Saturday afternoon, however, he drove me to Kandy in the heart of the Island.

It was not like driving up into the Indian hills. Kandy was only 1,100 ft. up; but it is a beautiful place and Lord Louis Mountbatten must have been comfortable there as South-East Asia Commander. Kandy and its lake, temple and shops were fascinating but I wanted to see a tea garden. So Irwin drove me up to one at about 2,000 ft. If Kandy was charming, the tea estate looked idyllic, but, he repeated, the future of British tea planters looked uncertain and he was proved right.

After a shopping expedition with Mrs. Irwin in Colombo's excellent shops, Irwin drove me to the station. I took their small boy up to the big engine, with its fire-box roaring and steam pipes hissing, but it was too much for him, he was frightened.

The Customs did not want to see the various presents I had bought, but the civilians' luggage was thoroughly examined and with justification, as there were many goodies available in Colombo.

On the ferry I asked the Tamil helmsman if I could steer; he showed me the course and allowed me to steer for a few sea-miles, which gave me a thrill.

It was a long, hot drive back and bumpy in places, my driver and I sharing the driving. Once again I stayed with our missionary friends, the Rev. Walter and Mrs. George at Ramnad, which seemed a pretty god-forsaken place. The well-water was brackish, so that tea tasted of it and the garden did not flourish.

Pudukottah State

The route lay through this small but attractive State ruled by a Rajah and a British Administrator, who then was Sir Alexander Tottenham, I.C.S., a most able and charming man. The State was not democratic but was governed by benevolent autocracy. Though the State was smaller than a District, Pudukottah town was much more impressive than most District towns. It was beautifully planned with a broad main street, a fine secretariat and other buildings.

I arrived back late and weary. Looking on my office table I saw a wireless message to the effect that I was to be transferred. I was too tired to take it in, but next morning felt indignant. What was the point of sending me to Ceylon in order to review security precautions between that Island and the mainland? I had not yet spent a year in Tanjore. My wife was expecting a baby in a month. Under British rule the Inspector-General sent postings to the Chief Secretary for approval. At the same time he wrote a personal letter to say 'you are likely to be transferred to such and such a post'. Clearly the Inspector-General had not recommended the transfer, which was therefore a political one. I said I would have to appeal against it.

But my wife was concerned for my health which was deteriorating. She asked me what the new district – Chittoor – was like. I said it was uplands – a much better climate with quiet, law-abiding people. 'Right', she said 'then we'll go!' So we cancelled the arrangements we had made at Tanjore Hospital for the baby and asked Osborne-Jones, the Railway officer, for a goods wagon. I sent for a squad of reserve policemen to help with the packing which was done under my wife's supervision, while I shut myself up in my office, working through a week's backlog, writing up all the personal files and preparing handing-over-charge notes.

A number of constables arrived with petitions. A big Inspector who had been a loyal friend came to my office and cried; I was very fond of him. One of the two chief landowners in the district gave an excellent lunch party for us at the club. The Special Branch staff gave a small tea party in our garden and the District Police gave a large tea party, with garlands for my wife, myself and the child.

I duly handed over to a young Deputy Superintendent of unblemished character, but he was reluctant. For our last two days we were guests of the McLaughlins, while Osborne-Jones personally supervised the loading and despatch of our heavy luggage.

It was the biggest send-off I have ever had and the best reward for my labours. I had only been there ten months – I had taken ten days' leave, otherwise it was work six and a half days a week, with very little recreation, shooting or other sport. When we walked over to the McLaughlin's house it was as though a heavy load had been taken off my back.

I drove off with an overloaded car. We covered only 150 miles that day and stopped for the night at a Mission bungalow. When, only twenty odd miles from our destination and some hundreds of feet lower down, the petrol gauge showed almost zero, I stopped at a petrol pump and handed the attendant my book of coupons. His reply was 'All books now have to be re-stamped.' 'To hell', I said and drove off; I was very careful and we arrived at Chittoor with perhaps a cupful of petrol to spare. Our bearer, luggage and luncheon were waiting and our turkeys gave us a welcome.

50

Chittoor. A delightful District

THIS IS a very different one from Tanjore. Most of it is hilly, rising to 4,000 feet. The land is poor, with little irrigation. The people are mostly poor and law-abiding. Politics were subdued and the Special Branch staff minimal.

Though an Indian Officer came to call I rested and refused to see anyone for two days. I then took charge but not in the same way as before: I could no longer give the Provincial Government of my best: after the casual and off-hand treatment I had received I no longer felt proud to serve them.

Our first task was to call at the Hospital. There we met the Medical Officer and his Lady Asst. Surgeon and we arranged for the baby to be born in our official bungalow. We then went to see it: it was a large one, set in a compound of some 30 acres of very poor, sloping land. One drove up through an avenue of mango trees and past a small paddy field of about half an acre, next to a well.

My predecessor, an Indian officer of the Provincial Service, had left under a cloud and discipline was very lax. Towards the end of his stay he was being harrassed and he shut himself up in semi-darkness. We found the bungalow in a filthy state, over-run by thousands of insects, the walls and ceilings festooned with cobwebs.

So we stayed in the Rest House while the bungalow was cleaned and the rooms whitewashed, one by one.

Shortly after our arrival, a new Collector and District Magistrate arrived – J.C. Griffiths I.C.S. We were both of an age and soon started up a close friendship. My relations with him were as happy officially as they were socially.

The first event was the beginning of a Provincial strike by the many thousands of Government clerks, dispirited after several years of inflation. It was non-political. Offices were kept running with skeleton staffs; the strikers were very well behaved and clearly had only come out as a last resort. After a number of the leaders were arrested and detained, the strike collapsed within a week. One man only in Chittoor was detained.

Stevenson Shield Competition

My first engagement was an invitation to Vellore, only some twenty miles away, to act as judge of a competition for that part of the Armed Police known as the Presidency General Reserve. This Reserve was for duty, when required, outside their Districts and generally they did not have much to do. Years before, a Deputy Inspector- General called Stevenson had given a shield for competition by all these reserves. It was basically a ten-mile march, followed, after some minutes' rest, by group firing. It was a rapid march – the ten miles being covered in just over two hours.

I stayed the night before with E.S. Treasure and found him in a very awkward situation: a bachelor, he had fallen head over heels in love with a young married woman in Madras, whose husband was more interested in the bar and billiard room than in her.

We got up next morning in the dark, drove to the starting point and then to the finish. I knew many of the men, having been stationed at Vellore and enjoyed marching seven of the miles back to the Reserve Lines.

I also met two Indian Probationers both of whom had served in the Royal Indian Navy. Next day the performance was repeated in my district, J.C. Griffiths being one of the judges. The marching was disgraceful and the firing poor: they were the worst Armed Police I had seen but the fault was not mine. Afterwards, the judges came back for a hearty English breakfast.

On December 21st my wife's labour began: the Lady Doctor came over and a smart young midwife, a Christian, stayed the night. By the next day a fine baby girl of 9.5 lbs. was safely delivered.

On Christmas Eve I attended Holy Communion at the little church which was homely, with a round chancel arch and lit by oil lamps. It was very beautiful. The celebrant was an Indian priest, who read a sermon which had originally been preached in Westminster Abbey – he was, I think, wise to read a good sermon; some two dozen people attended.

'Bill' Treasure spent Christmas with us and I was able to give my wife and little girl the presents I had bought in Colombo.

On Christmas morning the Griffiths called, my wife got up and we sat in the garden over bottles of Bangalore beer. When the Griffiths left, my wife, Bill and I sat down to a well-roasted turkey, followed by home-made Christmas pudding.

After tea Bill and I walked up a nearby hill for exercise. In the evening, the three of us went over to the Griffiths' and he had a new bottle of Scotch saved up. Though there were only five of us we thoroughly enjoyed ourselves, which shows that Christmas can be a happy occasion so far away from home; the gift of a baby girl was the best Christmas present I ever had.

Later that week I was invited to an Indian dinner, but my insides were not designed for rich Indian curries and I suffered from it for two days.

New Year's Day 1948

First thing in the morning we had a grand welcome: a column of Reserve Policemen in mufti attended by N.C.O.'s in uniform and their band came and garlanded us profusely - they gave fruit and English biscuits for the children and a photographer took a group photo.

Later, we left for a duck-shoot at a tank or *jheel* a few miles out. It was a great expanse of water with the artificial dam at the end. There might have been 1000 duck resting on the water. Bill had not brought a gun so John Griffiths and I took up positions as best we could – I fired into the middle, whereupon the whole lot rose up in formation, then wheeled this way and that. Some came within range but we only managed to bring down three brace and one brace could not be retrieved – the guns were too few and our reflexes were undoubtedly affected by Christmas and New Year's Eve celebrations! But we really enjoyed ouselves and foregathered at the Griffiths' for beer and more roast turkey.

The beginning of January 1948 saw me get down to office work in earnest: though I had only been in charge for a few weeks, reviews and reports had to be prepared for the previous year.

The Anglo-Indian nanny we had brought from Tanjore did not settle, so we sent her back and engaged an Indian ayah, a Roman Catholic about 40 years of age. She was a wonderful nurse, devoted to her charges and we never had the slightest trouble: we had complete trust in her.

With a baby in the house it was better that I should tour alone. My first camp was a distant one, well inland. The air was very dry, the days were cool and at night one needed a blanket, quite a change from the damp air or sea-breezes of Tanjore district.

We expected to stay in Chittoor for a couple of years and so made ourselves comfortable. Near the entrance to the thirty-acre compound was a well and Chadwick, my predecessor but one, who should have been a farmer, decided to mitigate the war-time food shortage by ploughing up half an acre and planting it with paddy. My Indian predecessor, was very foolish and in less than a year, was reverted to Deputy Superintendent, so though he kept the field irrigated daily by a squad of Reserve policemen, he did not harvest the crop. When we arrived the paddy was full-grown and within a month or two it yielded some eight bags of rice.

I kept two bags for our servants and orderlies and gave the balance to the Reserve, about two hundred and fifty men. But I did not approve of a lorry and eight men being used for the purpose and did not attempt a second crop.

The monsoon of 1947 was a very poor one, so milk was getting short. To ensure a good supply for our girls I hired a cross-bred cow with her calf and fed her on cotton-seed cake, (the residue after the seed is crushed for its oil). Both cow and calf flourished and we had plenty of rich milk, clotted cream in place of butter and our nine servants and orderlies had good milk for their tea and curds. When the cow began to go dry we exchanged her for a similar cow with a young calf.

Chadwick had also left two beehives. I knew nothing about them but got an agricultural assistant to watch them and in due course he extracted two or three pounds of honey. My wife could eat it but though it was tasty and sweet enough, for some reason it gave me heart-burn.

In front of the house stood some rather ancient lantana bushes, with tiny flowers and fragrant leaves. Sometimes, when sitting in darkness, we were treated to the sight of fireflies. They were apparently attracted by the bushes and actually produce a bright glow in their tiny bodies, which they turn on and off as they fly; being harmless they are a delight to watch.

The lower part of our drive was lined with mango trees which in the Spring of 1948 were loaded with fruit. The mangoes were of different varieties; we and our servants eat them two or three times a day. Big farmers also had a glut and thoughtfully sent us large baskets of ripe fruit, so either our servants gave them away or sold them for a song.

It wasn't long before our orderlies noticed that common ailments in our household were treated not by the local doctor but by my wife. Of course, word travelled to the Police Lines where the constables, who are low-paid, live and soon, beyond Chittoor, constables were asking her to look at their wives or children suffering from sores, infections, fever or anaemia.

Some District Officers took a box of medicines round with them for this purpose, but though my wife was a fully qualified Sister, she only did dressings. In other cases, following medical etiquette, she sent the patients to the surgery or village dispensary with a note, which carried weight, as they came to know she was London-trained and qualified. For this service the men and women never failed to show their gratitude.

Then the whole of India received a shock like an earthquake: Mahatma Gandhi was assassinated by revolver shots. The identity of the assassin was not immediately announced and at once a rumour spread that he was a Muslim. The atmosphere in Chittoor town was very tense, but there was no violence. The fanatic turned out to be a Hindu, a Maharatta, from the extreme right-wing party.

The assassination – of a peace-loving old man of eighty – was not only a dastardly crime but that the Apostle of Non-Violence should die a violent death was a tragic and bitter irony.

The Governor-General and Lady Mountbatten attended the cremation ceremony near Delhi and the ashes were despatched in caskets to all parts of India to be scattered into the Ganges, the Kistna, other sacred rivers and lakes. One leader said at the time:

"The light has gone out of our eyes."

For the whole country was plunged into mourning comparable, but of course more profound, with that following the death of their beloved Queen Victoria which my father had described to me.

But for the Home Departments of which we were a part, it was a period of intense activity: right-wing volunteer corps were disbanded and the extreme right-wing Hindu party was dissolved, but secret instructions from the Government of India somehow managed to find their way into the papers. This was a new embarrassement, for leakages which, later, everywhere became quite common, were virtually unknown hitherto.

On February 11th I went to meet the Revenue Minister who was on tour; but as February 12th approached, the day fixed for the scattering of Gandhi's ashes, excitement mounted. The drums beat all night in the town and men and boys shouted "Gandhi-ji ki jai, Gandhiji ki-jai"[43] till they were hoarse.

[43] 'Gandhi to victory.'

By the end of February, the temperature at Chittoor rose well up in the nineties which was well above the average, due to the serious lack of rain during the previous monsoon season.

I decided to camp at Palamaner, which was near the Mysore plateau at an altitude of over 2,000 feet. We went en famille and enjoyed ten cool days while I inspected police stations. Only for a couple of hours in the afternoon was it too warm, for there were no electric fans or punkahs.

Joyce Griffiths had recently given birth to a baby so they moved to another cool station, Madanapalle. We followed them, for there was plenty of accommodation in the Rest House. I think my inspection at Madanapalle, which took 5 days, was the most thorough I ever did.

I had arranged to have our baby christened Margaret Claire at Madanapalle Tuberculosis Sanatorium. The service took place in the small shady sanatorium chapel, Joyce Griffiths being godmother.

Afterwards, a lady doctor entertained the christening party, together with some Danish missionaries. The Griffiths gave a lunch party ending up with christening cake, while the subject of the celebrations was fast asleep in one of the bedrooms.

The hot weather that year of 1948 was a severe one. I left my family at Madanapalle and went down the hill into the heat. For several days I did double duty in my small bungalow office, clearing heaps of files and attending the main Office and Reserve parades. It was clearly too hot for young mothers and children but fortunately, the Griffiths had a friend who offered the use of his house at Coonoor in the Nilgiri hills, so it was arranged that the Griffiths and de Chazal families should share it.

Elaborate preparations were needed to pack all the furniture for four children with pots and pans for six and we saw them off at the nearest broad-gauge station, John Griffiths and I returning to Chittoor.

I planned to spend most of the hot weather in camp. My first one was again Madanapalle to attend the visit to the Tuberculosis Sanatorium of Lady Nye, wife of the Governor, Lieut.-General Sir Archibald Nye. A lunch-party was sine qua non and this was given by the senior doctor at the Sanatorium, Dr. Benjamin, an Indian.

After another spell in headquarters I drove back to Madanapalle, this time to attend Countess Mountbatten. She was perfectly charming and it was a pleasure to accompany her on her detailed tour of the great Sanatorium. Lunch at Dr. Benjamin's was a lighter meal than the last one, better suited to the weather and I had a very pleasant conversation with Lady Mountbatten who asked intelligent questions about my work and was interested in my negotiations with the Mysore State Police regarding her escort to and from the Kolar Gold Fields.

Though Lord Mountbatten had only fifteen crowded months as Viceroy and Governor-General he managed to find time to visit Madras and his reception was remarkable. Addressing a crowd of some 60,000 in the open air he began his speech with a greeting in Tamil (a very difficult language). Never before had a Governor or Viceroy done this and they roared with delight.

It has been said that Prime Minister Attlee chose Lord Mountbatten at Pandit Nehru's request. I have not seen this confirmed but Mr. Attlee's choice was certainly an ideal one and his elevation to an Earldom before he flew out made not the slightest difference in Indian eyes.

I would like at this juncture to record my gratitude to my Deputy Inspr.-General, S. Parthasarathy Iyengar. He was a cultured Brahmin with a great sense of humour, most kind and considerate. Certain senior officers were a privilege to serve under and among them I count S. Ramanuja Iyengar, J.S. Wilkes, L.A. Bishop, E.H. Colebrook and Parthasarathy Iyengar – each was as good as the other. He gave me ten days leave to join my family at Coonoor, even though Griffiths would be absent at the same time. He said he would keep an eye on the situation and would try and not re-call me. In the event, he didn't.

It was quite a long journey and we travelled together in John Griffiths' car. Stopping in Bangalore, we had tea with B.A. Harvey, I.P. who was on leave from Malabar.

We then drove the sixty odd miles along the fast road to Mysore city. The main roads in Madras Province were metalled but not asphalted, they were therefore dusty and often worn. By contrast, the main roads in Mysore were all asphalted and free from dust, a boon to travellers.

Heavy rain fell in the night and we made a cool and early start on the last lap of our journey, 115 miles. The Mysore jungles are magnificent: we drove through teak forest of huge, broad-leafed trees for some 25 miles; we saw no game, being broad daylight, but had to avoid a pile of fresh elephant droppings in the road.

The whole of the hill road was asphalted and we soon reached 7,000 feet and needed to put on coats. Passing through Ootacamund, we reached our destination which was attractively situated in a tea garden and received a great welcome from our wives and children who were dressed in woollies and looked pink and healthy.

For some ten days we did things we could not do at Chittoor: such as going to the club, the cinema at Wellington and the golf club: a green course set among the darker green of a thickly wooded valley, a superb situation and we even enjoyed the luxury of Danish beer..... On the Saturday, Joyce Griffiths' birthday, we were invited to a dance at the Wellington Club. John Griffiths wisely had brought his dinner jacket. I had not brought mine so I borrowed his blue suit, which was too large, but gradually I lost my shyness.

One evening we were invited by a couple belonging to the Planters' Company, that is tea and coffee planters. They had no children and she was extremely houseproud. The house was English - not Anglo- Indian in style - with modern fittings which gleamed like a sergeant- major's buttons. We thought it cold and unwelcoming. It is not wise to be so out of tune with one's surroundings.

All too soon it was time to say goodbye. At Bangalore we met a certain Jagirdar or landowner whom we knew, a western-educated Indian. He let it be known that he would be glad of sterling currency in exchange for Rupees, but I hesitated to oblige him.

On my return I found one of the Reserve Police sergeants measuring a crowd of recruits: the Government wanted extra battalions of Reserve Police to strengthen its pressure on Hyderabad State, as the Nizam[44] did not wish to accede to the Republic of India. In the event, the Nizam's Forces proved no match for the Indian Army and the Malabar Special Police, both hardened by active service.

Not surprisingly Chittoor seemed very hot. After the usual spell doing office work, auditing accounts and attending Reserve parades, I decided to camp on one of the sacred hills of India: Tirumalai.

On top of the 3,000 foot hill stood a famous temple and place of pilgrimage. Non-Hindus and Untouchables were prohibited entry – only the District Magistrate and Superintendent of Police were allowed, ex officio. Typical of Indian hospitality, I was not just tolerated, but officially welcomed and garlanded by the chief priest.

I did my work leisurely and inspected the small police station, but there was nothing else for a non-Hindu to do. Discarding my shoes, I was taken round the Temple, a mutt (or monastery) and part of the Mahant's[45] palace. The climax was permission to view from a short distance, Venkateswara, the life-sized god made of pure silver, to the accompaniment of musical instruments and incense.

After three or four days we motored down the mountain road into oven-like heat in order to meet a Minister, the Hon'ble the Food Minister of the Government of India. Petrol was very scarce and strictly rationed, but the Hon'ble Minister's cortege numbered ten cars and jeeps. I spoke to his Private Secretary, but did not take much notice of the Madras Food Minister who followed in the great man's wake, which perhaps was naughty, but I felt strongly that my Minister was the Home Minister.

Once again I drove up to Madanapalle as the heat at headquarters was almost unbearable (Vellore, lower down, would be worse). From a local Brahmin I learnt that the philosopher, Jiddu Krishna Murthi, formerly a disciple of Dr. Annie Besant, was a native of the town, he rejected Theosophy and settled in California (where he died at a great age).

One afternoon the sky became gray and lowering. Fans and punkahs not being installed, it was too hot to work at my desk and, looking at the thermometer, it showed 97 degrees F, at 2,500 feet! Suddenly, there was a mighty clap of thunder like a great cannon, torrential rain fell and in less than half an hour the ground was under water. Looking at the thermometer again I found the air had cooled by about 20 degrees F. The feature of this storm was the single, tremendous thunder-clap.

Working indoors in temperatures in the nineties is, for most Englishmen, exhausting. After more duty at headquarters I decided on a rest and planned a stay at Horsleykonda (or Horsley Hill). A bus conveyed us to the foot, where the village Headman was delighted to exercise his authority. He pressed young men into service to carry all the luggage up the hill. It was a four-mile walk up

[44] The hereditary Ruler.　　　　　　　　　　　　　　　[45] Mahant or abbot.

a broad path and a 2,000 foot climb, for the rest-house was at 4,000 feet.

When at last the house came into view it looked strange – because of the rising chimney stacks. I was weary but after a bottle of beer and a bath, dinner on the cool verandah was marvellous and later, the sheer luxury of sleeping under a blanket.

I imagined a Christmas house-party there in years gone by: the crisp morning air, walks, good food; after tea, carols and games before a log fire and blankets at night. The servants would need long woollen coats and every morning men from the village would carry up fresh food for a dozen or more people.

During my first evening walk two jungle fowl appeared within range but I did not expect them so close to the summit and had no gun. After that I carried a loaded gun but saw no game though I did see clear scratch marks of a bear.

Those days it was necessary always to keep in touch with headquarters. We did not bring a wireless set so I gave the Reserve Police practice with their heliograph and all important telegrams were transmitted, a distance of 60-70 miles. Transmission was quite satisfactory, except when thunderclouds obscured the sun.

It was a lonely spot, with no one to talk to, so I signalled for the Indian Probationer, Mr. Shenoi, whom I was training and examined him on his progress. He was a charming young man; I had placed him at Madanapalle, out of the great heat, trusted him to behave himself and never had the slightest cause for complaint.

After six days at Horsleykonda I was quite glad to leave; for after several weeks alone I craved for company.

My wife and two little girls had left Coonoor and were, by kind invitation, staying with the Supdt. of Police at Ootacamund, J.L. and Mrs. Ronson. I asked for short leave and it was granted.

Coonoor was 300 miles away. Again I spent the night in a Mysore hotel. Next day we made good time, my Hillman 14 was well run-in and climbed the steep part of the ascent in third gear.

I did not attempt anything strenuous for it takes a few days to adjust at 7,500 feet - but couldn't resist an invitation to a shoot, where some miles out, a tiger had killed a big buffalo. We got up before dawn and drove to the spot, the beaters beat round in a half circle, but did not disturb any well-fed tiger. One of the beaters, however, said he saw a panther, pushing his way through long grass 300 yards from him. I got lost but eventually found the others; so we returned with good appetites to a late breakfast.

A cousin of mine, Edmond de Chazal, was staying at Ooty for a conference of ECAFE, one of the United Nations' Divisions. I attended one of the sessions held at the Arranmore Palace but the proceedings seemed formal and not very useful. There was plenty of time for refreshments but prices in the restaurant were very high.

One afternoon, we went to an exhibition of Malabar dancing at the Ooty Assembly Rooms. As was explained to the audience this was normally performed in the open air. The costumes were magnificent, with headdresses

3-4 feet across; the accompaniment consisted of drums and brass percussion and the noise, indoors, was deafening. Most of the audience left at the interval, but the poor Governor, Sir Archibald Nye, whose seat was of course was in the front row, had to stay.

During the southwest Monsoon, mushrooms grow profusely in and around Ooty and we enjoyed platefuls morning and evening. But the days passed quickly and after enjoying the winds and rain for a week, it was time to return. On the way down we saw piles of wild elephant droppings, left by more than one elephant, which made me think of our garden.

At Mysore we stayed at our usual hotel and were given a large double room with three beds and two bathrooms. Next day we arrived at Palmaner in Chittoor district and enjoyed having tea with Miss Youngewaard, an American of Dutch descent, who was in charge of the Mission station. It is one of the pleasures of the East to drop in to people in lonely places and receive a warm welcome. Miss Youngewaard's hospitality was so good, however, that she was not often lonely.

Though our Chittoor bungalow was a large one with plenty of ground we never felt the same pleasure as when returning to our first married home – at Tanjore.

Conference at Bangalore

During the monsoon of 1948 a conference was convened by the Inspector-General of Police, Mysore, for all the superior officers of the Mysore State Police; two Deputy Insprs.-Genl. and some six Supdts. of Police of Madras and the Commissioner of Police, Coorg – a small, hilly territory on the west of Mysore.

The Inspr.-Genl. took the chair but he sat at the end of a very long table and those at the other end had difficulty in hearing him. The agenda was lengthy and there was not enough time for discussion – I was told afterwards that the senior officers wished to have their own conferences afterwards.

It was at the conference table that I made the acquaintance of an elderly officer, a Mr. Lindsay from the Kolar Gold Fields, who invited me to stay. In the evening British officers, including O.L. Burrell, J.L. Ronson, Bernard Harvey and I met privately in the bar of the West End Hotel.

Less than five years before Bernard Harvey had fallen in love with a girl beautiful both in countenance and character. We thought him very lucky but those whom the gods love...; she died not long afterwards and I tried to comfort him. Then his Alsatian hound went mad and clawed his master badly about the face: I was amazed that a man's friend could turn and become so dangerous and overpower a strong man. Gradually the scars disappeared.

In between inspection of police stations I camped in a little Forest bungalow set on a hill five miles inside the jungle - which stretched without a break as far as the eye could see. I did have some inspection to do of a registered criminal tribe, but my main object, I confess, was shooting. It was not the right season and our luck was out; however we saw a large deer (a sambhar) as he dived into cover. We came across a rock on which a panther had just recently urinated, it was still steaming. On a night shoot we heard a sambhar belling close at hand and the green eyes of a panther suddenly appeared quite close for a second or two, but my fool of a shikari was not well trained and did not shine the electric torch along the sights, so I missed a certain trophy. One afternoon, while sitting on the verandah drinking tea, I saw a fine fallow deer stag, broadside on. I ran for my rifle, but he was startled and dissappeared. Later, at another camp I sat up in a tree while beaters beat for wild boar but, to everyone's surprise, they had moved away and not one appeared.

I made two attempts to shoot a female panther, which was raiding villages. We found her faeces and set up a machan, [46] tied up a kid, which bleated piteously for half an hour then never made a sound. The next night I sat up again with a different goat but 'Spots' did not show herself. Thanks to the latest repellant I was not tortured by mosquitoes as one always used to be.

By this time our friends, the Griffiths', had left for good – he had been offered a job by Jacob's Biscuits in Dublin. It was not a very attractive offer but good jobs were so few that he felt he could not refuse. We had not had any indication as to how long the Government would be needing British officials, but we felt in our bones that the end was drawing near. Thereafter we had very little social life, E.S. Treasure had departed for Nigeria. John Griffiths' successor, an Acting District Magistrate, was a colourless individual and did not entertain.

So to Kuppam, a large zamindari or estate. As the accomodation there was good and as the town was situated at more than 2,500 feet we went en famille, with all our camp staff and paraphenalia. This meant Camp Clerk, cook, bearer, driver, ayah and orderlies. We travelled in a Dodge police van, which, when I took charge was derelict, but the transport section of the Reserve Police had worked hard to re- condition her - even the floorboards needed replacing.

Our accommodation was the second floor of the Kuppam Palace, which was unoccupied. Thanks to regular falls of rain our stay was enjoyable. I made a thorough inspection of the large police station. I also received unfortunate Muslim Sub-Inspectors who had been removed from the districts bordering Hyderabad State, for it was the Government of India's policy to move all Muslim officials away from the State borders. There were some good fellows among them but I think that they understood that a British officer could no longer do anything for them and that they were now the underdogs.

Not long afterwards, at the beginning of October 1948, a personal telegram arrived offering me the job of Asst. Commandant of a new Central Police College to be opened at Mount Abu in Rajputana. This took me by surprise, for I was considering applying for the job of Security Officer, Kolar Gold Fields, the position then held by Lindsay. So I decided to consult him; after sending a telegram to the Gold Fields we arrived next day in the evening, before the telegram.

I asked Lindsay about the job he was giving up, then showed him the telegram from the Home Department. He read it, paused and said 'Take it.' He was considerably older, I respected his opinion and took his advice.

[46] A hide in a tree.

I was then shown over the Gold Mines down to a depth of 7,500 feet. The deepest working was 10,000 feet down, where the rock temperature was 132 degrees F and where picked men worked a two-hour shift. Only Indians or Italians could stand this heat.

So again, after only a year, we began to pack; but the Indian Government's operation against Hyberabad State was being stepped up: for the Nizam was refusing to accede to the Indian Republic. The Indian Army closed in from four sides and advanced rapidly. The Hyderabad Forces however were no match for them: within a few days their resistance collapsed and the great State, ruled for over 200 years by the descendants of the Moghul Viceroy of the Deccan was forced to submit to the Indian Government.

While waiting for the end of the Hyderabad compaign, we stayed at Palmaner as guests of our dear friend, Miss Youngewaard. From a selfish point of view we left at a good time, for the monsoon was late and had not yet broken. Subsequently, we heard from a missionary friend that it was a failure and in a few months the district was declared a Famine Area. No crops could be grown and the water-table sank so low that the wells went dry, trees died, food grains, drinking water and fodder for the cattle had to be sent by rail.

The transition to Home Rule had not made much difference to us in Tanjore, except that in place of a kind and considerate superior, E.H. Colebrook, I had to put up with his Muslim successor who was prejudiced against me from the start.

In the North and around Delhi, however, it was a very different story. The situation was so grave that almost the first step the Indian Government had to take was to impose a tight censorship on the news. So we were kept in ignorance: we knew less than readers of the London papers; I learnt the facts years later.

The formation of Pakistan led at once to a migration on an unprecedented scale of Hindus and Sikhs one way, Muslims the other. They travelled by train, bus, cars, bullock cart, horse-drawn carriages and on foot, taking such possessions as they could. Law and order broke down, millions were murdered and no one was charged with murder, rape, looting or arson. In Amritsar, for example, all the Muslims, including half the police force, were murdered.

Much of the Punjab became a charnel house and the stink of rotting corpses and animals could be smelt from over-flying light aircraft.

Surely the British Government could have prevented the holocaust? Delhi and the Punjab knew there would be civil war; but Lord Wavell's warnings were heeded neither by the Secretary of State, the ageing Lord Pethwick-Lawrence, nor by the Congress High Command. If the latter had taken the danger seriously surely they would have retained, on short contracts, the services of a substantial number of British officers? In the event, they kept on very few and mostly in the South which was peaceful. The great majority of British magistrates and police officers either resigned or were made to resign by Independence Day. Thus Independent India and Pakistan got off to a bad start.

51

The Central Police College and Farewell

"My friends, do they now and then send
A wish or a thought after me?
O tell me I yet have a friend,
Though a friend I am never to see"

IN LATER years, long overland journeys between one posting and the next were avoided and one flew with light baggage between airports. Such means of travel are fast, but one then has to wait, perhaps weeks, for the heavy luggage to catch up and one also misses a great deal of interest.

Our journey from Chittoor to Mount Abu began in late October 1948 following a telegram from Madras telling me to proceed. So we started the same afternoon after making reservations along the route by telegram. We motored to the junction called Renigunta, where my faithful Deputy, Subba Rao, and a police party were waiting. I paid out what seemed a large sum, hundreds of rupees, for the tickets. The Inspector had wired for sleeping-berths, but when the train arrived from Madras about 10 p.m. all the berths were occupied. He arranged for the first-class passengers' tickets to be checked and, sure enough, two men, sleeping on upper berths, could only produce second-class tickets. So we moved into the compartment and were able to sleep.

In the morning we were on the cool Deccan plateau and a merchant, finding who I was, quietly and without any word from me, betook himself either out of shyness or politeness, to the second-class.

At one station in Hyderabad State there was a good-humoured demonstration by Hindu youths cheering the accession of the State to the Republic of India. It reminded me of August 1947 when Independence was celebrated all over the country.

We saw considerable numbers of State troops and police at some stations but there was no fight left in them. It was a great triumph for the Government of India and on the strength of it they promptly floated a loan of 50 crores of rupees, (about £46 million) which was a lot of money in those days.

The following morning, a Sunday, we steamed into Bombay. I went up to the Thos. Cook representative but they had not received my telegram to book a Retiring Room. A couple of smart young Anglo-Indian Railway officials in spotless white suits walked up and we chatted; but when I asked about a retiring room, they replied briefly that they were all booked.

So we went to the Refreshment Room for breakfast. There I noticed a police officer, an Indian, breakfasting alone. He looked a very good type and turned out to be a Railway Police Inspector. He was most sympathetic, went off smiling and after a couple of hours showed us into clean, vacant retiring rooms where we could have a shower, a rest and a change of clothes.

Our little girls behaved very well and were over-awed by the bustling Railway Terminus. Meanwhile, our Inspector friend reserved berths on the Sind Mail and taxis for us, two orderlies and our ayah.

We thanked the Inspector profusely and crossed three busy miles of Bombay in the taxis. We had a small first-class compartment to ourselves and next morning glided into the great city of Ahmedabad, the second cotton city of India, not far from which was Gandhi's ashram. [47] There we had to change to a metre-gauge train.

I reported at the Railway Police station on the platform where the old Head-Constable in charge was delighted to serve us. He was a dear and supervised the transhipment of trunks and baggage. Finally, I thanked and shook hands with the luggage clerk; the Head Constable saw us to our compartment and soon the train steamed slowly out.

We passed a big tented camp for Hindu refugees from the North-West Frontier Province; then a great mansion, built originally for the Mogul Governor and on to a neat, well-laid-out suburb, where officials and millowners lived in peace and comfort. Little did I guess that before long I would be staying there for a short holiday.

After a second meal on the train we arrived at Abu Road station near the foot of a mountain of grey rocks and green jungle. The Head-Constable had been warned; he met us and assisted with the unloading. I chartered a small bus and we left, seven of us plus a couple of people with a lot of luggage who were going up to Mount Abu.

The winding ghat [48] road was well maintained. About half way up we saw a long, wide valley, clothed with thick green forest, greener and thicker than in the plains. Down the middle was a rocky water-course. Evidently the monsoon was over, for it only held pools of water. Panther and sambhar, I reflected, must have roamed safely in those miles of thick forest.

It had been a long journey but not a single item of luggage was missing or tampered with. To my great surprise and pleasure, one of the former Law Instructors at Vellore Police Training College was there to greet us – Inspector Bhaskhara Rao. He led the way to a furnished bungalow where Mr. Pratt, the Head Drill Instructor supervised the unloading, giving our men orders in pure, flowing Urdu, for he was a well-educated Anglo-Indian from Allahabad.

After a while, the Commandant, a plump, fair-skinned man arrived. He had blue gorgettes and was wearing a soft forage cap and smoking a pipe, Mr. Mehta, a Hindu from the Punjab. He greeted us and asked us over to tea. We were very travel-weary and would have loved to settle in, but had no choice.

So, after a change of clothes, we walked over to the Commandant's residence which was imposing surrounded by lawns and a well-kept garden.

[47] A kind of hostel.   [48] Or mountain.

Mount Abu, an extinct volcano, was lower than I expected: the cantonment was situated at about 3.5 thousand feet, well below the summit. I had put on an English suit, but in October it proved much too warm. Mr. and Mrs. Mehta were both friendly and welcoming, so we returned for the first night in our last station in India.

The College

The Indian Police possessed an excellent esprit de corps and I never hesitated, when travelling, to ask officers I didn't know for hospitality. But we were trained at some nine provincial training colleges. After Independence, the Government of India decided to recruit a new officer-cadre to replace the hundreds of British officers; they also decided, I believe wisely, to train them at a central college even though this would involve them in considerable expense. But it wasn't necessary to erect buildings: there were a number of cantonments vacant after the war and they carefully chose one in a fairly central position where the climate was favourable for both study and exercise. It wasn't oppressive in summer, nor was it cold in winter.The cantonment they chose was a centre of the Jain sect, a summer resort and a former leave station for British troops.

The ground was uneven so the buildings did not form a regular pattern like civil and military stations in the plains. Besides the Club, there was a Lawrence School, in memory of Sir Henry Lawrence of Lucknow and run by expatriates; a small Irish Mission and an Anglican church; the chaplain had his house at Abu but spent most of his time in the plains.

Among the graves in the cemetery is one of Lady Honoria Lawrence, the beloved wife of Sir Henry Lawrence; she died of debility in 1854 at Abu. Another burial, shortly before our arrival, was that of a young English woman who was tragically drowned while walking along a stream. After a cloudburst, a wall of water poured down and she was engulfed.

There was plenty of room for sixty or more Probationers; a medical officer, instructors, constables, a small office staff; horses and a riding master. Nothing was yet organised, but policemen are used to sorting out, so we gradually became a college. The constables were very hard-up and one of my first tasks was to work out proposals for increases of pay and allowances for N.C.O.'s and men.

But, before long my wife suffered an infected mosquito bite followed by malaria, then I too went down with malaria. As I lay recovering, I heard the cheerful clop-clop of horses' hooves: our first draft of ten horses had arrived from Jodhpur. Soon I got up and decided to have three of them in our stables, for they had to be quartered in various stables.

With the Commandant away in Delhi, though weak after the fever, I began to sort out the problems which inevitably arose.

By December, the air was cool and dry and we all went into khaki jerseys. The routine was similar to a provincial training school but different in that by far the largest group were the Probationers from all Provinces, a number of whom were fine young men. The Chief Law Instructor was a Bengali Deputy Superintendent. There were other instructors in Law and Medical Jurisprudence, all of Inspector's rank, also a Wireless Instructor and one for Scientific Aids. He was from Bihar and impressed me as very keen and knowledgeable.

Mr. Pratt, the Head Drill Instructor, a Deputy Supdt. in rank, had a good presence. He was in his late twenties. He knew his job but was not like a sergeant-major at Sandhurst: for being an Anglo-Indian he was deferential towards the many high-caste young officers in his charge. He could not for example say: "You bloody little fool, Sir."

The Medical Officer was an experienced Government doctor from the North West Frontier Province, a refugee who had lost everything, so also the Quartermaster, Harbans Singh, a big Sikh, who was most helpful with our domestic problems. The Riding Master was a Sikh, ex-Indian Cavalry, he too was polite towards high-caste young officers, but was perhaps less deferential than Mr. Pratt.

A platoon of constables and head-constables, who were without their families, provided guards, officers' orderlies and office orderlies, who sometimes travelled to Delhi. One of the functions of this platoon was to help the Probationers to learn their drill and practice their words of command. There was one vacancy on the staff: a map-reading instructor from the Army. As I had learnt to use Ordnance maps while in O.T.C.'s, [49] Junior and Senior, I took this on and did it as best I could.

The daily routine consisted of morning parade, on foot or mounted; breakfast, followed by instruction till lunch-time. In the afternoon – games: hockey, cricket, football or tennis; but there was no local team whatever for the college to compete with. One could also ride in the afternoon and I liked to go out with three or four Probationers; they were very keen and alert and picked my brains. One well-built officer, S.C. Gupta, wanted to learn boxing and I took him on as a private pupil.

The Probationers each had their own room and bathroom. There were several Christians, including a very fine young man who had been an Inspector in the Bombay City Police. There was no Muslim and no problem about feeding together in the Mess, but they were inclined to grumble at the standard of cooking and it was part of my job to supervise the food, which was supplied and cooked by a contractor. The orderly officer for the day, a Probationer, had to inspect all the buildings and make a written report to me which was a valuable experience for him. In the evenings they did private study and one evening a week was free.

We had a formal Mess Dinner once a week with the two ladies, followed usually by games or entertainment.

Some four fifths of the Probationers were young men with 1st or 2nd Class Honours straight from College. The rest were somewhat older and had been recruited from various Government Departments. Out of the total I was sure

[49] Officers Training Corps.

that three or four would never make good policemen and I would have liked to have sent them away. If however, I had made such a recommendation, the Commandant would have suspected me of bias: he was not a trusting man.

Our stay at Mount Abu was not a very happy one, but I look back with pleasure on my warm relationship with the young officers. Apart from riding and games, my wife used to ask four of them at a time to play Monopoly at our house, followed by tea. They picked it up very quickly and I feel sure some of them bought Mononpoly sets subsequently. They also pressed me to play cricket or at least umpire, though I was a poor cricketer and did not score more than five runs.

The Lawrence Memorial School

This was an excellent school, run on British lines and many of the places were taken up by wealthy Indians who appreciated the discipline. A new Headmaster had been appointed, he was M.A. Young, a New Zealander and a bachelor who stayed with us for a month while his house was re-decorated. He didn't have an easy time, for the Congress Party was very suspicious of British schools and I don't think the school lasted much longer.

There were formerly two Residencies: for the Resident for Rajputana and for the Western India States. Maharajahs and a number of Rajahs had small summer palaces where they stayed during the great heat. So Abu was noted for its social life. But in the cool season, social life was at a low ebb.

We made friends with the two Irish teaching Brothers at the Mission School. I had no touring to do so my petrol ration was a small one and I would not say to an orderly, 'Here are ten rupees, take the car to the petrol pump, ask for four gallons and say he can keep the five rupees change." So we had to be very careful and one day when we had taken the Irish Brothers out on a picnic, the petrol gave out on an incline and we all had to push the car to the top.

The family who were the most hospitable and never changed their attitude was a Parsi[50] family called Mervanji. The youngest was a charming young man and my best friend in Abu. He did not work as they had plenty of money and his chief interest was western classical music.

As Christmas approached, we had a children's birthday party for Claire, our younger girl, born on 22nd December. Inspector Bhaskara Rao was a clever conjurer and the children were enthralled; the party finished with fireworks.

We asked an Indian Police widow, a Mrs. Rivers Wright, to Christmas dinner, but she declined, she had become a recluse.

All morning, policemen came over to present their respects and the grooms, sweepers and watchmen came for baksheesh. But it was a drab Christmas for us. I had a sort of Xmas tree (there are no evergreens in Abu) with presents for our household; but one of the orderlies was in a bad mood and refused to accept his present. Such rudeness was very rare and we were shocked.

While the Commandant was very affable to start with, his true nature

[50] A prosperous community centred in Bombay and originating from Persia (Pars).

gradually showed itself, he was not a bit politically inclined, so we had no differences of that kind: his vanity and self-esteem were the key to his character.

All the Probationers called on him on Boxing Day, except me. I had never been required so to call, before Independence. I needed a day off so we arranged to take a picnic. Next day he asked me why I hadn't called – he had clearly taken offence. A further grievance he nursed was the fact that the young officers and I got on very well indeed.

On that Boxing Day we thought our ayah would be glad of a day off to spend some of her Christmas present. But she stayed at home and was sad, because she didn't know what to do with herself without the two little girls! This was typical of good servants, they chat happily to each other on the back verandah but have no desire for free time. When they ask for leave, it is always for some family reason or to see a doctor.

For some reason best known to himself, the Commandant tried to turn me against the (Indian) District Magistrate, who, he alleged, was corrupt. I was surprised, made some enquiries and decided there was no basis for the accusation. But Abu was such a small place that it reached the ears of Club members who accused me of making enquiries about one of their number. After that we were cold-shouldered, but the Magistrate was a good man and we made it up.

Two of the visitors to Abu were an English couple, Mr. and Mrs. Morrey, whom we liked very much. They kindly invited us to stay with them in Ahmedabad, but at the very last hour my wife was unable to go as Helen, the older girl developed mumps, so I went alone.

As soon as I boarded the train I felt a marvellous sense of freedom, for staying in a small place, with no petrol to spare and no touring didn't suit my roving spirit. I really enjoyed my four days with the Morreys, but it was clearly an unhealthy city, sanitation was poor and the air was never fresh. I picked up a virus which became active soon after my return.

I found my wife sad and subdued for, during my absence, she heard of her mother's death. Shortly afterwards, I told her of my decision: she never interfered with my big decisions and when I told her I had decided to resign she agreed. She was used to India, her father having been seconded to the Indian Army, but was not happy with our situation and, for her, there was no place like England.

We lived close to the cinema and twice a week were kept awake by the loud music and voices, so I asked for a change. The Commandant had no objection and asked the Quartermaster, Harbans Singh, who proposed an altogether better house: it had been the summer residence of the Inspector-General of Police, Ajmer and its last occupants were Gilbert Waddell, C.I.E. and Mrs. Waddell, who had gone home a year and a half earlier.

The faithful Harbans Singh hired a lorry at so much a load; he supervised the loading and got so much on at each load, that it only needed two trips. Anyone else would have needed three trips!

Next morning I watched Dhana, our ayah, go off on her morning walk, Helen, the bigger girl walking, Claire the small one in her pushchair, with our black-and-tan dachshund as escort. Dhana always went into the little Catholic church for a prayer, together with her three charges.

My wife lost no time in starting a flower garden, for after eighteen months of neglect there was nothing left. She had three beds well stocked with flowers when, one day, a cow entered the garden and ate them all up, which naturally upset her.

During the warm weather I slept on the verandah in a cot with mosquito curtains. One clear, still moonlit night I was awakened by our dog barking from the verandah. He stopped and stiffened, looking at some bushes fifteen or twenty yards away. I couldn't see anything, but could hear a rustling sound. Next morning in the dusty ground, were clear pug marks (or footprints) of a panther, which are like those of a large dog, but bigger: four to five inches across. We were relieved, for if our dachshund had ventured out, as a puppy might have, he would have been snapped up.

The Dilwara Temples

Close to Abu is a temple complex of the Jain religion, a fairly austere religion which did not make many converts. As at Chitor, the extensive carvings, dating from the eleventh century are of pure white marble. The artists who executed the carvings must be among India's finest, for they are fantastic. Many of the figures are of beautiful and seductive women, the marble surfaces polished and clean. To the European they may seem erotic and to the Muslim – shocking, but Hindus, especially of the south, are accustomed to these art-forms and Jain carvings certainly do not go beyond the bounds of decency. [51]

The Holi Festival

As this is not commonly observed in the south and as Imperial New Delhi, in a sense, was extra-territorial, I saw Holi for the first time at Mount Abu.

The festival is in honour of the Lord Krishna, images of whom are carried in processions. It is a joyful occasion with music and song dedicated to Krishna and much humour, some ribald. It is the one occasion in the year when servants may play practical jokes on their masters and mistresses, when inferiors may fool their superiors, surely an excellent safety-valve?

Each reveller carries a supply of crimson powder which he throws over his friends and superiors. Others squirt coloured water, so that the crowds present a strange sight, their clothes all coloured and stained. There was much drinking and noise, so that very respectable people stayed indoors. I had powder thrown over me once or twice.

At the end of ten days the College grooms reported to me: they looked thin and drawn and were flat broke!

[51] c.p. temple carvings which portray explicitly a range of sexual acts, a number of which carvings have been destroyed by offended Muslims.

So the winter receded, the days grew steadily warmer, shrubs were covered with blossom and the first visitors arrived, complete with their servants and luggage. By May, there was a number of Rajahs from Western India.

Though our social life was restricted, we were able to meet some of the young nobility from Western India and parts of Rajputana. These healthy and relaxed young men and women, educated at expensive schools, would have mixed well in British society had these not gone home two years before.

They enjoyed a freedom denied to their social inferiors: they played tennis, went on picnics, attended lunch and evening parties and even danced sometimes though there was no band.

With the departure of the British, the golf club closed, there was no swimming by the lake and no flat ground for a race-course. So sport was limited.

They spoke English as easily as Hindi and were interested in films in both languages, but after the ciné palaces of Bombay, the local cinema was too primitive for them. Some were probably married and may have had a baby, but with plenty of servants, a baby is no problem.

I noticed that earning money, which the middle classes are so preoccupied with, was not a subject of their conversation: 'Why bother with money when Father has plenty?'

As long as some social activity was arranged they were happy, but they dreaded boredom and being young and energetic, sitting round a table and talking, they left to those increasing in years and embonpoint.

The Rajahs knew that with the end of British protection, the good life they enjoyed was coming to an end. Despite this I neither noticed nor heard of any scandal at Mount Abu during the years 1948-49.

It was a popular view that most of the Princes were pleasure-loving, eccentric or effete. That if they spent less on themselves their subjects would be better-off. But from what I have learnt since a reduction in the privy purse might benefit the officials rather than the people.

I had been told we would have plenty of social life, but only one of the Rajahs, the Rajkumar of Limbdi, had us on his guest list and invited us three times. I was puzzled by this but think I discovered the reasons: it was largely because the Commandant did not pass on my name to them and partly it was political. After the Great War, the Princes and Rajahs were all rewarded for their loyalty by means of increased gun-salutes, honours, decorations and military ranks. During the Second War they were just as loyal to the Crown and gave even more help, but they received no thanks or recognition. Mr. Churchill had been defeated and the Labour Government abandoned them to their fate. Can one wonder, therefore, that they were bitter?

I spent a full year at the College during which we did not have one visit or inspection by a senior official. Nor did we have a visiting lecturer. No Rajah was ever invited and when H.H. the Maharajah of Jaipur arrived for a short stay, the Commandant took him on a picnic but did not invite him to the College. I thought this a serious lapse as His Highness was Governor of Rajputana and a visit by him would have raised our morale. Nor was an invitation sent to the Maharajah of Jodhpur who also stayed a week or two.

His Highness of Jaipur, a very handsome and attractive man in his thirties, gave an At Home, which my wife and I attended and he spoke kindly to us. He told us how he went to London every year to discharge his duties as an officer of the Household Cavalry and also to play polo. As a waiter brought glasses of sparkling champagne he said: "I don't care for spirits. My drink is champagne, but if it isn't available I don't mind taking liqueur brandy!" Years later, he died in England after playing polo; which for him would surely be the perfect exit from this life on earth.

So we spent the season very quietly. I sent in my resignation and date for retirement and when this was accepted, we had plenty of time to make our arrangements. I knew that if I stayed on till February 1950 my compensation would be appreciably more, but I was getting very frustrated and felt that health and peace of mind were more important than money.

The rain-fall that year was below average but some sixty inches fell between July and September. We had missed the north-east monsoon in South India and when we arrived at Abu in the previous October the south-west monsoon was all but spent. So we experienced hardly any rain for eighteen months and more. I used to dream of rain and when it came, it was sheer delight; the rain was quite warm so the brown hillsides soon turned to a fresh green; savoury mushrooms appeared on all the grassy slopes and we ate them two or three times a day. The moss on the small jungle trees revived, also little ferns. Beautiful orchids came into bloom and were picked to adorn our tables. For three days only was the rain heavy – ten inches fell; all parades and games stopped and we hardly went out for it was difficult to dry clothes and shoes.

As soon as the downpour ceased on the fourth day, we went for a walk and found the streams pouring down into the river below. But the monsoon was not prolonged: in a few weeks the skies cleared, the sun shone all day and the streams and torrents dwindled to a mere trickle.

The Commandant did not help our departure, nor did he bother us in any way. We said goodbye to all, but there was no farewell party or send-off. I thought he would have informed the Railway Police, which was the least he could do, but he did not. So we left by 'bus, travelled to Bombay by train and there was a lot for me to attend to. In Bombay I dropped one of my documents and had urgently to obtain a temporary one for a permit was still needed to leave the country. My wife and children were ahead and I was the last man on board the fine ship, M.V. Caledonia of Glasgow.

Within half an hour we sailed. It was five o'clock in the afternoon and we all stood at the rails, gazing at the city and port of Bombay, then, as we made way, we saw Malabar Hill gradually sink below the horizon.

We left in a blaze of glory – the glory of a superb sunset.

> "I strove with none, for none was worth my strife,
> Nature I loved and, next to nature, art:
> I warmed both hands before the fire of life;
> It sinks, and I am ready to depart." (Landor)

Epilogue

Many of the men who sailed away in 1947 and afterwards were still in their prime, their careers cut short. My own feelings were further saddened – because of just one man's injured pride and jealousy we had no send-off, no garland. The customary farewell ceremonies accorded by a warm-hearted people were totally lacking.

But before long, an enlightened Commandant was appointed, the College was opened out to distinguished visitors and lecturers, just as I had wished and my former colleague and successor, Eric Stracey, who was domiciled in the country, was able to build up the library.

To many of us officials it seemed that our life-work was destroyed in a few months. But we had departed with honour and, thanks to the lead of men of the calibre of Lord Mountbatten and his compassionate wife; Pandit Nehru and Raja-gopalachari, India stayed in the British Commonwealth and, as many travellers later noticed, the two countries came to enjoy mutual respect and regard,

For example, numbers of retired British Officers have been invited back by their former Regiments and received a very warm welcome. Likewise civilians; I was invited some years ago to Police Week in Lucknow and was very disappointed at being unable to accept.

Not long after Independence, a certain Minister proposed to remove the portraits of British Governors hanging in Government House, Ootacamund. But Rajagopala-chari disagreed. "Leave them alone," he said, "for you can't alter history by removing a few oil paintings."

When Lord Mountbatten, the last British Governor-General, was foully assassinated, the Indian Government was deeply moved and ordered a week's official mourning with all flags flown at half-mast. Could any gesture be more eloquent?

One of the most imperial of Viceroys, Lord Curzon, reigned as long ago as 1899-1905, but his daughter, Lady Alexandra Metcalfe, still visits India and the Times of India invariably announces her landing at Bombay under the heading:

'Viceroy's daughter returns.'

For thirty years the views of Winston Churchill and Pandit Nehru were diametrically opposed, but in old age the two Harrovians met at Chartwell – the old warrior and imperial statesmen and the eminent statesman-philosopher. 'They greeted each other, talked easily and parted – friends.'

I quote this from the autobiography of Mrs Vijaya-Lakshmi Pandit, Nehru's sister, as the symbol of post-Independence goodwill.

Appendix
The Vellore Mutiny

In 1806, the fiftieth year after the beginning of the British-Indian Empire, a young Governor, Lord William Bentinck, only thirty-two years of age, presided in Madras and was joined by a newly-arrived Commander-in-Chief, Sir John Cradock.

General Cradock, reviewing regiments of the Madras Army, was irritated by their lack of uniformity, especially their turbans and facial adornments. Some even, wore earrings. He therefore ordered new regulations to be drafted and these introduced a plain and standard turban, more like a hat, prohibiting caste-marks and regulating the cut of beards and length of moustaches.

He did not realise that to an Indian these things are important, (as are hair styles to the modern teenager) and the regulations, approved by the Governor, caused deep offence to both Hindus and Muslims, who suspected them of being a preliminary to their forcible conversion to Christianity, having in mind earlier and quite recent forcible conversions to Islam.

The regulations were tested first on a veteran grenadier company of Native Infantry, stationed at Vellore, who rejected them with perfect discipline and respect. The C.-in-C. was annoyed, transferred the regiment and sentenced all those who refused to obey the regulations to 500 lashes. This severe sentence only confirmed the worst fears of the sepoy army. A very experienced colonel warned the C.-in-C. of the dangers but the Governor refused to give way.

The seeds of revolt duly germinated and one of the princes, the sons of Tipu Sultan confined in Vellore Fort, was drawn into the conspiracy.

In June, Colonel Forbes, commanding the Vellore garrison, was warned first by a local sepoy, then by a British soldier's widow, that serious unrest was developing. But as his Indian officers failed to confirm these reports he disbelieved them, never guessing that they were personally involved.

The garrison consisted of approaching 400 men in all of the 69th Regiment of Foot – later to become the Welch Regiment and two regiments of Indian Infantry totalling nearly 2,000 men.

By modern standards discipline was not strict. Owing to congestion in the Fort many of the sepoys lived outside in a camp or 'pettah'; the Indian Regiments did not parade every morning but before a morning parade all were assembled in the Fort the night before.

One clear night in July, the British captain on duty, a Company, not Royal officer, was too lazy to do the rounds and deputed a subedar to take his place, who was a leader of the plot. About 2 a.m. the moon rose and shone brightly and the order to massacre the white men was given. Sleeping men and hospital patients were butchered. Numbers of the 69th fought back but they only had six rounds apiece. Cheered by their success, the senior Prince was declared Sultan of Mysore and the Tiger flag was hoisted to the flagstaff.

Fortunately, an officer living in the town was woken by the firing and despatched a messenger who galloped to nearby Arcot, which was a Cavalry station. En route he met the Commanding Officer, Colonel (later Sir Rollo) Gillespie of the 19th Light Dragoons, who was taking his early morning ride.

Quickly assembling the stand-by squadron of his Dragoons and a troop of Native Cavalry, Gillespie led the way to Vellore, covering the sixteen miles in an hour, the rest of the Horse and the galloper-guns following some way behind.

He arrived not a moment too soon and found the remnants of the 69th crouching by the main gate without any ammunition. Unable to force open the gates, he managed to lead a party up the ramparts and capture the battery while waiting for the galloper-guns. On their arrival, they quickly blew open the main gate, the Cavalry stormed in and cut down, bayoneted or shot mutineers in large numbers.

According to Thornton (History of the British Empire in India) there were survivors among the mutineers, but they must have successfully hidden from the Dragoons, who were fighting men and their blood was up, for soldiers do not feel merciful in such conditions.

Gillespie put the palace buildings under a strong guard, but the subsequent enquiry confirmed that the prime cause of the mutiny was the new and offensive dress and beard regulations.

Meanwhile in Hyderabad, a similar situation had developed, the 10,000 strong garrison took grave exception to the above regulations, but the Commanding Officer was experienced and, supported by the Resident, he cancelled the regulations and calm was restored.

If Colonel Gillespie had not acted so promptly and decisively the mutiny would have succeeded and very likely have spread to the other stations. Understandably, it had a very unsettling effect on civilians and on the officers of the Madras Army.

The Government in Calcutta reacted firmly – as a result both Lord Bentinck and Sir John Cradock were recalled, the sons of Tipu Sultan were moved to Calcutta, while Colonel Gillespie was rewarded by a grant of money and duly promoted to Inspector-General of Cavalry. The Madras Army recovered and there were no further acts of indiscipline, but to the British Regiment of Foot which had no part in the dispute, no compensation was made, except that the brave sergeant was promoted.

Lord Wm. Bentinck grew in wisdom and stature: from 1833 as Governor-General, he went for the thugs and abolished not only *sati* but also the flogging of Indian soldiers, so anticipating by over thirty years its abolition in the British Army.

The Vellore Mutiny

He thundered back to Arcot gate
He thundered up through Arcot town
Before he thought a second thought
In the barrack yard he lighted down.

"Trumpeter, sound for the Light Dragoons
Sound to saddle and spur," he said
"He that is ready may ride with me
He that can – may ride ahead."
They ride, as ride the Light Dragoons
And never a man could ride with him....

"Sergeant, Sergeant, over the gate
Where are your officers all?" he said.
Heavily came the Sergeant's voice,
"There are two living and forty dead."

From 'Gillespie' by Sir Henry Newbolt.

Acknowledgements

MY SINCERE thanks are due to George Millar Esq., for good advice, to O. L. Burrell, OBE., for material, to E. W. Hunt, OBE., for much help with the section on wireless and for photographs; to Mrs J. C. Cartwright of Sydling for material on the Vellore Mutiny. For permission to quote from the Oxford Book of English Verse I wish to thank the Oxford University Press, while Messrs. Weidenfeld & Nicolson kindly allowed me to quote from Scope of Happiness by Mrs Vijaya-lakshmi Pandit. I am indebted to Mark Bence-Jones, who having lived in the Punjab as a boy, writes with understanding and sensitivity, especially in 'Clive', the Viceroys of India and Palaces of the Raj. For the loan of or permission to reproduce photographs I thank J. M. Dean Esq., the late G. C. Ryan, MBE., F. J. McLintic, MBE.; also the India Library and Indian Police (UK) Association to whose Benevolent Fund for Widows I hope from sales of this book to be able to make a donation. Last but not least I wish to thank Mrs Nicky Willis, Mrs Jo Towner and Mrs M. Duke for their willing and accurate secretarial help.